Writing a Wider War

Writing a Wider War

Rethinking Gender, Race, and Identity in the South African War, 1899–1902

EDITED BY

GREG CUTHBERTSON, ALBERT GRUNDLINGH, AND
MARY-LYNN SUTTIE

Ohio University Press
Athens

David Philip Publishers
Cape Town

Ohio University Press, Athens, Ohio 45701
© 2002 by Ohio University Press
Printed in the United States of America
All rights reserved

Ohio University Press books are printed on acid-free paper ⊗ ™

10 09 08 07 06 05 04 03 02   5 4 3 2 1

Published in South Africa in 2002 by David Philip Publishers,
an imprint of New Africa Books (Pty) Ltd., PO Box 23408, Claremont 7735,
Republic of South Africa

ISBN 0-86486-607-0 (David Philip paper)

Library of Congress Cataloging-in-Publication Data

Writing a wider war : rethinking gender, race, and identity in the South African War,
1899–1902 /edited by Greg Cuthbertson, Albert Grundlingh, and Mary-Lynn Suttie.
    p. cm.
Includes bibliographical references and index.
ISBN 0-8214-1462-3 (alk. paper)—ISBN 0-8214-1463-1 (pbk. : alk. paper)
    1. South African War, 1899–1902—Historiography. 2. South African War,
1899–1902—Social aspects. I. Cuthbertson, Gregor. II. Grundlingh, A. M.,
1948– III. Suttie, Mary-Lynn.

DT1896 .W74 2002
968.04'8—dc21

                                                    2002030740

Contents

Preface

Centenaries are seductive—especially for historians. Intellectually they probably realize that there is little new to add to a historical event that has been given as much attention as the South African War of 1899–1902, but public interest is enticing enough for them to spruce up old insights and repackage them with attractive wrapping and a commemorative bow. The editors and contributors to this anthology do not claim that they have been more original. Indeed, it is doubtful whether the book would have seen the light of day if it had not been for the centenary of the war. But we have tried to go beyond standard conceptualizations of the conflict by placing it in a wider context and taking particular note of scholarly trends—especially concerning gender, race, and identity—over the past decade or more.

Like other academic enterprises it has been expensive in terms of time and energy. We would therefore like to thank Patrick Furlong and Rodney Davenport for their extremely comprehensive critical comments on the manuscript. Gill Berchowitz at Ohio University Press saw the possibility of producing this book before we did and has very patiently brought the project to fruition. Nancy Basmajian steered us through the long technical process of turning the manuscript into a book, Evan Young painstakingly copyedited it to the highest professional standard, and Dawie Malan took on the thankless job of compiling the index. We are also grateful to all those who played an important role in the "Rethinking the South African War" conference at the University of South Africa on the eve of the centenary of the war, especially Karen Harris, HlezIphi Napaai, Gwenda Thomas, John Willemse, Marie Coetzee, Ammi Ryke, Annette le Roux, and Herma van Niekerk. Most of all, we thank the participants who sparked a series of debates that have worn well during the three years of the centenary and whose writing is collected in this anthology.

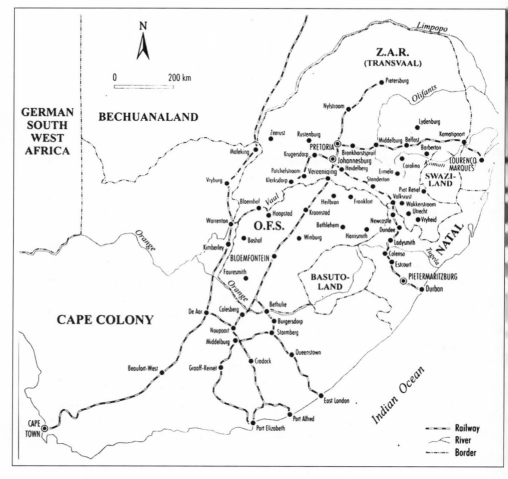

South Africa, 1899.

SOURCE: L. Changuion, *Silence of the Guns: The History of the Long Toms of the Anglo-Boer War* (Pretoria: Protea Book House, 2001), 2

Introduction

More has been written on the South African War of 1899–1902 than on any other aspect of South African history, so the "Writing a Wider War" in our title means showcasing sustained new, wide-ranging research rather than claiming a paradigm shift. The collection, based on revised versions of papers given at the "Rethinking the South African War 1899–1902" conference organized by the University of South Africa (Unisa) Library in August 1998, avoids exaggerated reinterpretations but pushes the limits of a vibrant social and cultural historiography that has developed since the 1980s. It is receptive to new historiographical impulses and reflects broader trends in South African historical writing. The chapters challenge, qualify, and extend our understanding of the war, its origins and effects, and how it has been used to construct different national identities since the beginning of the twentieth century.

This anthology also "rethinks" the South African War by de-emphasizing political economy and exploring other equally important new research in the areas of commemoration, gender, health, nationalisms, identities, ethics, and morality. The influential British historian David Cannadine has criticized the economistic explanations of the South African War as "excessively mono-causal, ... [giving] inadequate weight to other explanations of empire—not just political-diplomatic-strategic, but also religious, humanitarian, ideological and cultural." He argues that the approach of writers such as P. J. Cain and A. G. Hopkins, for example, "is too much concerned with the imperial metropolis" and is unconvincing in its dismissal of interpretations "which stress the autonomous impulses emanating from the periphery." In Cannadine's view, which informs some of the chapters in this volume, "Empire was always an imaginative construct, existing as much (or more) inside the minds of men and women as it existed on the ground and on the map."[1]

There is no doubt that the Anglo-Boer War was a framing event both for the British Empire and for white South Africa. It was the last of the colonial and the first of the modern wars. It was an intimation of the decline of British power and it put colonial economic, social, and political institutions under severe strain. Once opened, these fault lines left spaces for previously marginalized and subordinated groups to assert themselves. Such groups attained few enduring benefits, however. The effect of the Milnerian Reconstruction that followed the end of hostilities in 1902 greatly consolidated and enlarged the exercise of white power throughout the region.[2] That process ironically paved the way for white South African politicians effectively to exclude imperial Britain from any involvement in the country's domestic affairs and its race policies by the time of Union in 1910. Little wonder then that a war attended by such momentous consequences has attracted so much historiographical attention.[3] South African and imperial historians have contested just about everything to do with this war: who fought in it; why they fought; why the war went on for so long; who if anyone won it; and what enduring consequences it had.[4]

This book is the product of a conference. The Unisa Library decided to hold its conference a year before the war's official centennial commemoration in October 1999. Historians were asked to rethink the South African War ahead of its entry into the public domain. The chapters therefore reflect this intention and were all written before the official commemoration. Bill Nasson's opening chapter looks at the history-making techniques of centenary committees and their attempts to reinvent the South African War as everyone's war: "In such therapeutic reordering and reconstruction, the ugly phenomenon of imperial concentration camps becomes a levelling time for Afrikaner and African war trauma, as exclusivist Boer martyrdom becomes shared suffering across the colour divide."

The ANC government naturally sees an opportunity to use the commemorations for reconciliation. Its project entails promoting popular interest in the war to achieve the political purpose of interracial harmony and national reconstruction. One way to further this objective is to emphasize the shared suffering of Afrikaners and Africans in the war. Another is to focus on the Boers as defenders of liberty and to portray that dimension of their history as something in which all South Africans can take pride. Albie Sachs took that approach in the heady days that followed the unbanning of the ANC and the return of the exiles in 1990:

There is so much in Afrikaans history in which we can all take pride. I take pride in the history of the heroic struggle of the Boer fighters, in the history of the world and in our history. You cannot talk about human rights, unless you take into account the fate of the women and children in the concentration camps. So much of Afrikaans History is part of the struggle for freedom. "Vryheid" (freedom) has real resonance and meaning, although it has been hi-jacked by a narrow form of ethnic exclusivism.[5]

While some authors shy away from such a reading of the war's history[6]—notwithstanding Sachs's magnanimity and strategic nation-building discourse—their view is unlikely to prevail among those in search of the roots of an inclusive nationalism for a new, democratic South Africa. Something of the experience of Africans in refugee camps was captured in the books by Peter Warwick and Bill Nasson in the 1980s and early 1990s.[7] However, these works were focused more on the impact of British imperialism and Boer republicanism on African participants as a prelude to the creation of a racial state in South Africa. By unearthing more evidence about the numbers of Africans involved, the extent of mismanagement in the camps, and the appalling loss of life, researchers bring new charges against Kitchener, an interpretation made no less questionable by its possible utility in promoting interracial harmony in the post-apartheid era.[8]

Through an emphasis on shared suffering, the South African War becomes a crucible for a common identity. This new myth may replace the earlier, and equally problematic, suggestion in English South African historiography that Boer-British unity was an achievement of white South African leaders in the aftermath of the war and was crowned by the unification of the country in 1910.[9] This new reading of the shared sacrifice in the concentration camps has been used to make the Anglo-Boer South African War Centenary a national project. It is predictable that a "democracy of suffering and loss" should be asserted to broaden the myths of Afrikaner identity and Anglo-Afrikaner unity and to make them available for all South Africans. Yesterday's white man's conflict is thus transformed, however improbably, into a founding democratic myth for the new millennium.

It is tempting to speculate about the differences between the War of 1899–1902 and recent apartheid wars, contrasting the morally unfinished settlement of Vereeniging with the peacemaking processes of the Truth and Reconciliation Commission (TRC). This comparison alerts us to the fact that Afrikaners now have to cope with a present in which they are confronted with what they regard as a threatening new political environment. Unsettling revelations by the Truth and Reconciliation Commission have added to a general sense of unease and disillusionment. Under these circumstances, the centenary of the war in 1999 has been viewed in some circles as an opportunity to present a heroic period in Afrikaner history, one for which they do not have to apologize. They can now be the accusers and not the accused. It is not, however, mere unthinking nostalgia and escapism. There is an acute awareness that blind acceptance of past versions of their history led them dangerously astray and that they now live in a country ruled by a predominantly black government. Accordingly, there is an insistence that the role of black people in the war and also that of the Boer "joiners" who defected to the British side during the latter stages of the conflict should be recognized and accorded their rightful place.[10] There may, of course, be a degree of opportunism involved, in that this new place in history for those who were previously excluded provides a useful cover for commemorating the war in a traditionally ethnic way, only paying lip service to inclusivity.

The South African War certainly calls up vivid personal memories among Afrikaners whose national identity remains moored in their struggle against Britain. The public memory of the war is often informed by such personal recollections that feed into an Afrikaner consciousness now faced with the challenge of repositioning itself in relation to a triumphal African nationalism. It remains unthinkable, therefore, to imagine the war without Afrikaners at its core. As much as we have tried in this collection to recover African participation in the war—indeed, tried to make it a *South African* war—it nevertheless remains a preeminently Afrikaner struggle against British imperialism.

The "Boer War" in many ways still hinges on the Afrikaner women and children in the concentration camps. While the establishment of the camps has not been the subject of reinterpretation, the changing nature of their memory enshrined in the national women's monument in Bloemfontein is analyzed by Albert Grundlingh in chapter 2. The war, he argues, put Afrikaner women on center stage, where they held public attention long enough to erect a monument to women quite different from the usual warrior male hero kind of memorial. At the same time, various countervailing contemporary political forces saw to it that the women's monument was not unveiled as essentially a part of the broader Afrikaner nationalist project. The potential for such mobilization always existed, however, and with the rejuvenation of Afrikanerdom in the 1930s and 1940s, the monument became more and more a nationalist shrine. Grundlingh points out that Emily Hobhouse's universalist message of womanhood, which originally inspired the monument, was gradually played down as the louder clamor of the Afrikaner *volk* drowned out an English woman's voice and therefore, ironically, also the voices of Afrikaner women.

The role of Afrikaner women in the making of nationalism is presented in chapter 3, Helen Bradford's historiographical "rethink" about gender and the war. Her argument, which made front-page headlines in a leading Afrikaans newspaper during the Unisa conference, calls for a thoroughly gendered rewrite of the war on the grounds that "Boer women took the lead in opposing British aggression, threatening to take up arms if men were too timid." Her essay marks a break with a war history that has tended to be dominated by "great men," either military or political. The "different" experiences and consciousness of women are needed to dispel the notion that mainstream historical accounts are representative. Understanding gender dynamics actually changes our understanding of the trajectory of the war, forces us to rethink the peace settlement, demonstrates the need for a new interpretation of Afrikaner nationalism in the twentieth century, and demands a reassessment of the literature on the *volksmoeder*. Bradford gives decisive agency to Afrikaner women, which also opens up space for a reconsideration of how war shapes the contours of masculinity. Her concentration on Boer women provides a useful contrast to a growing body of knowledge about imperial women, especially recent work on gender and race in public discourse during the South African War.[11]

Juxtaposed with Bradford's chapter, Fransjohan Pretorius's discussion in chapter 4 provides an interpretation of nascent Afrikaner nationalism based on his extensive research of Boer commandos and their struggle against British imperialism during the guerrilla phase of the war. He shows how Boer men in the field made the war into an ardently "Republican war."

A string of chapters on African experiences helps to steer this volume toward a more inclusive interpretation of the war. In chapter 5 Bernard Mbenga draws our attention to the role of the Bakgatla in the Pilanesberg district. His research clearly shows how Africans suffered under Boer rule and reinforces the view that fear of a widespread African jacquerie after the war led Boers to the negotiating table in 1902. In chapter 6 John Lambert looks in detail at the experiences of "loyal" Africans in Natal. He describes the disastrous impact of war on African farmers, records Zulu participation in the war, analyzes the support of chiefs for the British cause, and discusses the inducements offered to those who assisted the British army. He suggests that the failure of both the imperial and the colonial state to recognize or reward African loyalty during the South African War ultimately led to the Bambatha Rebellion of 1906 and alienated the *Kholwa*, who felt they had been taken for granted as a Christianized African elite. And in chapter 7 Manelisi Genge carefully assesses the significance of the Boer War in the making of Swazi identity and shows how Africans tried to exploit the conflict for their own economic and political gain. These focused case studies on Africans help us to rethink the South African War in small, incremental ways, as evidence is gathered and the bigger picture is gradually filled out. They provide a more textured history of Africans torn by competing national ambitions.

It is still important to note, however, that in contrast to the way the war is embedded in Afrikaner memory, relatively little is known about the conflict's long-term impact on African historical consciousness.[12] Nasson's pioneering work on the martyrdom of Abraham Esau and the Coloured community of Calvinia has yet to find a counterpart that deals with African memories of the war.[13] Some recollections might have been part of African oral tradition, but these will be difficult to recover because of the intervening century.[14] Luli Callinicos, who is currently involved as an adviser to the government on the public commemorations of the war, has recently admitted that owing to a lack of evidence it is a daunting task to provide a rounded view of African involvement in the war.[15] It may, on the other hand, be argued—from an Africanist perspective—that in the long run the South African War is a Eurocentric time capsule, artificially introduced into the African context. From this point of view, the war can be seen as a squabble between rival colonial overlords that constituted only a single episode in a much longer history of subjugation. Such considerations will probably have to come into play in research that attempts to determine whether the war indeed lived on in African memory.

The changing nature of nursing that the war initiated and the medical history of the Boer concentration camps are also foregrounded in this collection of historical essays. In chapter 8, Shula Marks's gendered perspective on British nursing and the struggle for professional status introduces a different angle to the importance of the war. It proved—more than the Crimean War—to be a turning point in the organization of imperial nursing. British nurses were also keen to come to South Africa as more and more women clamored to share the adventures of volunteers. Marks also salvages the record of British women to add their voices to those of Boer women in this anthology. Elaborating the medical history of the war, Elizabeth van Heyningen looks in chapter 9 at mortality rates in the camps in terms of a clash between Western and Boer medical cultures. She deftly discussed the scientific advances in Western medicine by 1900, which were not implemented in the camps mainly because of the unflattering representation of Boer women as "the domestic face of the enemy, the epitome of sluttishness, ignorance and unmotherliness." Her pathbreaking research brings gender, health, and concentration camps together in a striking way, using a wide range of sources and rich statistical data.

Lord Herbert Kitchener too comes in for a major rethink, in chapter 10. According to Keith Surridge, Kitchener was very aware of the complexity of Anglo-Boer relations and realized that some form of accommodation would have to be made with the Boers. Kitchener therefore came into conflict with Lord Alfred Milner, the British High Commissioner, who rejected such a settlement. Surridge's portrayal of Kitchener as a careful military tactician debunks the conventional view of him as a villainous British commanding officer responsible for scorched-earth policies and concentration camps.[16]

In chapter 11, another reconsideration of individual influence, Alan Jeeves reassesses J. A. Hobson's pronouncements on the origins of the South African War. His verdict is that "Hobson in his polemical attack on the Rand-lords made claims far beyond his evidence," but this should not "detract from his suggestive assessment of the modernity of the South African racial system, its essentially industrial character and the impact of the war on its probable course of future development." Jeeves's return to Hobson rethinks the origins of the war by examining again the strong demand by mine magnates for the transformation of the state in the Transvaal, thus challenging Patrick Harries's recent revisionism on the issue of African mine labor.[17]

Concentrating on "religious imperialism," Richard Mendelsohn reflects in chapter 12 on Anglo-Jewry and the war. He examines Jewish links with the imperial forces and provides an alternative version of the South African War as a "Jewish War," not in J. A. Hobson's negative sense of a capitalist-Jewish conspiracy, but in the positive sense of full participation in Britain's struggle. He explains that Jewish military service was seen to be Anglo-Jewry's main response to anti-Semitic charges of culpability in the war and of a lack of patriotism. And in a rethink of liberal critiques of the war in Britain, David Nash in chapter 13 considers the role of the Secular Movement in opposing British imperialism. Freethinkers and atheists have often been overlooked in assessments of the "pro-Boer" lobby, which makes Nash's contribution extremely important. The ethical and religious aspects of the war have generally been under-researched until recently, with the possible exception of Quaker pacifism.[18]

Among the twenty-three speakers from abroad—including the United States, Britain, Canada, Australia, and various southern African countries—who attended the Unisa conference, many focused on the imperial dimensions of the war. The final chapters in this collection reflect this important research. In chapter 14 Andrew Porter provocatively asserts that the South African War was economically and politically much less important to Britain at the turn of the twentieth century than the historiography would have us believe.[19] This view is questioned by Andrew Thompson in chapter 15, on propaganda in Britain during the war. Thompson shows that the conflict was not only a turning point for the British Empire in South Africa, but was also of enormous metropolitan concern. Both these chapters take us back to some of the "big questions" about the war, its economic and political significance and its place in world history.[20] Recently, Bill Nasson has characterized the South African War as "well up the evolutionary scale" toward total war, and the military historian Ian Beckett regards it as "a precursor of the greater conflict to come between 1914 and 1918." In Beckett's view, the war "was much more than a colonial war writ large"; it was arguably "the most significant conflict since the American Civil War."[21]

Recent histories of the American Civil War suggest that it can serve as a useful counterpoint to the South African experience, different though the two conflicts were in many ways.[22] Both were modern wars in terms of their duration, intensity, and all-encompassing nature. The South African War too had some of the characteristics of a civil war.[23] In both struggles there were strong appeals to universal principles and rights that were thought to have relevance far beyond the sites of struggle.[24] The Confederacy fought to protect the rights of the states and a particular way of life. The Boers fought to preserve the independence of their republics. On the Union side, the issue was slavery and the achievement of a "new birth of freedom." Imperial Britain went to war in 1899 ostensibly to defend the rights of British subjects in dependent territories.

The aftermath of war on both continents was remarkably similar. The reborn political prospects in the former Confederacy in the eight months after the South's surrender resembled those in southern Africa after Milner's resignation in 1905 and the Liberal Party victory in Britain in 1906. The Confederates faced a president who was no longer their wartime adversary, but a politician receptive to their arguments. Former secessionists accepted the need for cautious, conciliatory southern leadership to restore the economy. The Afrikaner-English rapprochement of 1907–10, however fragile and superficial it turned out to be, resulted in the making of a white nation. Louis Botha personified a white South Africanism that succeeded in managing the enmities of the Boer War. It was reconciled to the empire, but on a basis that excluded future imperial interference in South African affairs and entrenched white hegemony. This brand of "colonial nationalism" was a crucial ingredient in the process of cultural and political accommodation among the whites that, despite ongoing tensions between English and Afrikaner and the early reassertion of Afrikaner cultural exclusivity, secured the basis of white supremacy in South Africa and helped to redefine its role in the empire and among the white dominions.[25]

Writing a Wider War: Rethinking the South African War is a historian's book of the South African War. It moves from reporting, representing, and commemorating to the "actual history" of the war, which uncovers the themes of war and identity, war and nationalism, and war and internationalism. It draws inspiration from a stimulating conference, which itself drew on some of the themes in the book Peter Warwick edited on the South African War, published in 1980.[26] The latter was written when the imperatives of social history held sway. Although no longer in the ascendancy twenty years later, this tradition still has influence in South Africa. This volume cannot claim to have made a paradigmatic shift away from the discourses of social history or to have reconceptualized the war in dramatic new ways. It does, however, rethink and extend many of the important themes tentatively explored in the Warwick collection. We have also added new themes that reflect wider historiographical advances, especially in gender history, medical and health history, and the history of remembrance.

GREG CUTHBERTSON
ALBERT GRUNDLINGH
MARY-LYNN SUTTIE

Notes

1. D. Cannadine, *History in Our Time* (New Haven and London, 1998), 154. Cannadine made these remarks in a review of P. J. Cain and A. G. Hopkins, *British Imperialism.* Vol. 1: *Innovation and Expansion, 1688–1914;* Vol. 2: *Crisis and Deconstruction, 1914–1990* (London, 1993).

2. See M. Legassick, "British Hegemony and the Origins of Segregation in South Africa, 1901–14," in W. Beinart and S. Dubow (eds.), *Segregation and Apartheid in Twentieth-Century South Africa* (London and New York, 1995), 43–59; and S. Dubow, "Colonial Nationalism, The Milner Kindergarten and the Rise of 'South Africanism,' 1902–10," *History Workshop Journal* 43 (1997): 53–85.

3. S. B. Spies (ed.), *A Soldier in South Africa* (Boston, 1989), 17; C. Saunders, "Some Reflections on the Significance of the South African War," paper presented at the "Rethinking the South African War, 1899–1902" conference; D. Lowry (ed.), *The South African War Reappraised* (Manchester and New York, 2000); G. Cuthbertson and A. Jeeves (eds.), "Special Issue: South African War 1899–1902: Centennial Perspectives," *South African Historical Journal* 41 (November 1999).

4. For example, see I. R. Smith, *The Origins of the South African War, 1899–1902* (London, 1995); W. R. Nasson, *The South African War, 1899–1902* (London, 1999); I. R. Smith, "Reading History: The Boer War," *History Today* 34 (1984); S. Marks and S. Trapido, "Milner and the South African State Revisited," in M. Twaddle (ed.), *Imperialism, the State and War* (London, 1992), 80–94; A. N. Porter, "The South African War (1899–1902): Context and Motive Reconsidered," *Journal of African History* 31 (1990): 43–57.

5. *Leadership,* 9 March 1990, quoted in A. Grundlingh, "Die Wisselende Betekenis van die ABO in Afrikanerkringe, 1930–1998," in *Afrikanerperspektiewe op die Anglo-Boereoorlog, 1899–1902* (Bloemfontein, 1999), 56–57.

6. Especially, K. Surridge, *Managing the South African War, 1899–1902: Politicians v. Generals* (London, 1998).

7. P. Warwick (ed.), *The South African War: The Anglo-Boer War, 1899–1902* (Harlow, 1980); P. Warwick, *Black People and the South African War, 1899–1902* (Cambridge, 1983); W. R. Nasson, *Abraham Esau's War: A Black South African War in the Cape, 1899–1902* (Cambridge, 1991).

8. See G. Cuthbertson and A. Jeeves, "The Many-Sided Struggle for Southern Africa, 1899-1902," *South African Historical Journal* 41 (1999); and P. Hawthorne, "A War's Hidden Victims," *Time,* 25 October 1999.

9. Cf. K. Surridge, "The Politics of War: Lord Kitchener and the Settlement of the South African War, 1901–1902," chapter 10 in this collection.

10. Grundlingh, "The Bitter Legacy of the Boer War," *History Today* 49, no. 1 (1999): 25.

11. P. Krebs, *Gender, Race, and the Writing of Empire: Public Discourse and the Boer War* (Cambridge, 1999).

12. L. Vergnani, "Scholars Unearth Evidence of the Boer War's Black Victims," *Chronicle of Higher Education (Research and Publishing),* 7 January 2000, 17.

13. Nasson, *Abraham Esau's War.*

14. Cuthbertson and Jeeves, "Many-Sided Struggle for Southern Africa."

15. G. Dominy and L. Callinicos, "'Is There Anything to Celebrate?' Paradoxes of Policy: An Examination of the State's Approach to Commemorating South Africa's Most Ambiguous Struggle," *South African Historical Journal* 41 (1999).

16. See also Surridge, *Managing the South African War.*

17. P. Harries, *Work, Culture and Identity: Migrant Labourers in Mozambique and South Africa, c. 1860–1910* (Johannesburg, 1994).

18. See, for example, H. H. Hewison, *Hedge of Wild Almonds: South Africa, the "Pro-Boers" and the Quaker Conscience* (London, 1989); G. Cuthbertson, "Pricking the 'Nonconformist Conscience': Religion against the South African War," in Lowry (ed.), *South African War Reappraised,* 169–87; and L. Chrisman, *Rereading the Imperial Romance: British Imperialism and South African Resistance in Haggard, Schreiner and Plaatje* (Oxford, 2000), 150–62.

19. For a recent assessment of Boer War historiography, see A. Porter, "The South African War and the Historians," *African Affairs* 99 (2000): 633–48.

20. See D. Lowry, "When the World Loved the Boers," *History Today* 49, no. 5 (1999): 43–49; and D. Lowry, "'The Play of Forces World-Wide in Their Scope and Revolutionary in Their Operation [J. A. Hobson]': The South African War as an International Event," *South African Historical Journal* 41 (1999): 83–105.

21. Nasson, *The South African War,* 8; and I.F.W. Beckett, "Britain's Imperial War: A Question of Totality?" paper presented at "The Anglo-Boer War: A Reappraisal" conference, University of the Free State, Bloemfontein, 12–15 October 1999.

22. On the public history of the American Civil War, see Tony Horwitz, *Confederates in the Attic: Despatches from the Unfinished Civil War* (New York, 1998).

Another instructive American comparison, between the impact of the South African War on Britain and that of the Vietnam War on domestic American politics, is found in A. S. Thompson, "The Language of Imperialism and the Meanings of Empire: Imperial Discourse in British Politics, 1895–1914," *Journal of British Studies* 36, no. 2 (1997): 150–51. See also D. Hickey, "Legends of the Fall: Cultural Consequences and Mythic Reconstructions of the Boer War and the American Experience in Vietnam," paper presented at "The Anglo-Boer War: A Reappraisal" conference, University of the Free State, Bloemfontein, 12–15 October 1999.

23. I. R. Smith, "Was the South African War (1899–1902) a Civil War?" paper presented at the Africa Studies Forum, University of South Africa, 19 March 1993.

24. D. Lowry, "When the World Loved the Boers."

25. Dubow, "Colonial Nationalism."

26. Warwick, *South African War.*

Writing a Wider War

CHAPTER 1

The War
One Hundred Years On

BILL NASSON

IN DEMOGRAPHIC DEPTH and human cost, let alone in geographical scale, the South African War may well be topped by the disruptive precolonial *Mfecane* wars that raged across a swath of the southern African subcontinent in the early decades of the nineteenth century, pulverizing old African worlds and providing the hammer for building new societies from the rubble. Yet, while the climactic *Mfecane* ("the crushing") conflict is remembered principally in invented rural oral tradition, in popular mythologies about Shaka and the Zulu kingdom, and in scholarly debate in South African and African historiography, there can be little question that in modern South African historical consciousness it is the South African War that today still counts in national memory, however historically narrow the context of that construction has been.

In any wide view, it counts with fairly good reason. The war has left many memories of the more enduring residues of early-twentieth-century colonial war. Generating hundreds of books, including even Anglo-Boer spy thrillers like the 1907 production *The Secret of the Scarlet Letter,* the war's varied literary epitaph remains unrivaled locally, and this cultural deposit may make it the modest South African equivalent of an American Civil War, a British Great War, or even a Spanish Civil War. In part, that reflects the extent to which both colonial and imperial observers were drawn to the obvious contrast between the quick, dashing war that was envisaged or imagined and the rather more lengthy and arduous war that was actually fought. Given the sobering experiences of the Crimean War and the American Civil War, any major contest of modern arms and prepared opposition was almost bound to be a protracted and bitter enterprise. In part, too, the weight of the war is an illustration of the degree to which, even—or especially—after 1902, its meaning continued to be contested between South African empire loyalists

3

and defeated but unreconciled Afrikaner republicans. As in post-1939 Spain, a war of arms was to continue as a war of words for those for whom the Anglo-Boer War became the massive building block of a nationalist "Afrikaner" history, "a myth of national origin."[1]

The war of words was certainly of some importance to the balance of white political forces in South Africa even into the early post–World War II years, when the survival of cultivated memories of concentration camp cruelties and brutal conquest remained closely connected with the appearance and eventual ascendancy of a republican nationalist Afrikanerdom. The emotive expression of a subordinate yet combative nationality, tilting at the political and economic citadels of South Africa's languid English establishment, Afrikaner War commemoration provided a moral legacy of heroic manly struggle and female fortitude and sacrifice. That reflection began in the 1900s, through pilgrimages to grave sites, the disinterring and ritual reburial of the remains of fallen combatants, the later creation of war memorials, such as the 1913 Women's Monument or *Vrouemonument* as a male-inspired shrine to female martyrdom (some organized Afrikaner women had favored a memorial of more utilitarian social benefit), the issuing of commemorative medals to veterans or *oudstryders* in the 1920s, and other resurrectionary modes of expression.

The fatal clash between Briton and Boer was not to be just another miserable vestige of the outrages inflicted by imperial conquest. As leading nationalistic war poets like Jan Celliers, Eugene Marais, and Totius asserted after 1902, cathartic memories of blood sacrifice could kindle consciousness of national identity and help to renew dignity and purpose.[2] It is not stretching things too much to see the war enshrined as the Verdun of Afrikaner society, or even as its 1905. In this, Afrikaner nationalist writers and historians worked as hard as anyone to keep the war a live and burning issue within the crucial social networks of religion, politics, family, and friendship. In the aftermath of conflict it was obviously necessary to construct a view of the republican struggle that countered the ludicrous and frequently offensive portrayal of warring Boer society peddled by various imperialist writers. In the crudest of these depictions, the "Boer" was a degraded rural specimen, an untidy premodern with no proper place in capitalist modernity, and a warrior who displayed shifty fighting qualities in waging a criminal war against progress.[3] These stereotypes became refashioned: the bearded toad on Lord Roberts's mess table would turn out to be handsome and dashing Albert Viljoen, a commando lion easily outwitting plodding British Tommies.

But there was always more to these representations than mere counter-history. For popular historians such as Gustav Preller, a former war correspondent on the Boer side, accounts of republican doings all came to serve an overriding purpose—to awaken the Afrikaners to the truth about their war of freedom and their national mission. As Albert Grundlingh has underlined, the message was to make the inheritance of war the powerful core of an imminent Afrikaner "nationalist spirit," with popular histories reminding readers of the Christian Boer crusade "against the mighty British Empire, and the suffering of women and children." The experience of war "had to serve as a constant reminder of the Afrikaners' bitter fight for freedom. Although they had lost ... they were exhorted not to sacrifice a common identity as Afrikaners.... History had to be used in such a way that it enhanced patriotism and national consciousness.... Contemporary Afrikaners had to complete the historic mission of the Boer die-hards—they had to continue the fight for Afrikaner independence in the present."[4]

The splintering impact of the war upon the fabric of Boer society did not make it easy going for a bookish, middle-class, nationalist intelligentsia; it took time to stitch together a meaningful sense of war and an awakened ethnic nationhood. Ideological industry was further hampered by the incoherence and fragility of the Afrikaans literary culture. But once the assertion of a standard Afrikaans language became buttressed by official recognition in the 1920s, magic could be worked with war writings. Much of this alchemy was pursued in popular magazines such as *Die Brandwag* (The Sentinel) and *Die Huisgenoot* (The Home Companion). By soliciting personal war testimony for publication, they plumbed a rich seam of earthy folk memory of suffering that appealed to republican patriots, particularly rural women, as well as to veterans and their families. In this genre, the war largely ceased to be a disputed and internally divided struggle against imperial domination; instead, it was resurrected as an imprint of the unity of the Boer nation at war, a tribal defense of hearth and home by a small and virtuous Christian people.

While few Afrikaans books on the war appeared between the 1900s and the end of the 1920s, the ensuing two decades witnessed a surge of popular works, ranging from tendentious histories like Sara Raal's *Met die Boere in die Veld* (With the Boers in the Field) to spirited historical fiction like Mikro's *Die Ruiter in die Nag* (The Rider in the Night). Populist writings of this kind helped to harden a consolidating collective mentality and memory by creating an exalted sense of national character: wiry, valiant, and persevering. While it was important to harp on memories of bitterness, anguish, and redemptive Christian fortitude, it was no less necessary to commemorate superhuman republican bravado, exemplified by the gritty epic of *bittereinder* resistance, and the seemingly clairvoyant genius of younger Boer generalship. In this mostly masculine legacy, "the courage and determination of the die-hard Boer fighters revealed those character traits supposedly typical of the Afrikaner and deemed worthy to emulate."[5]

As in post–Civil War Francoist historiography in Spain, the overlap between popular and scholarly representations of the South African War that turned history into nationalist propaganda was quite marked. Through the 1940s and even for some time beyond, much academic writing presented the war as mainly a militant and emotive moral covenant of Afrikaner nationalist mobilization. Such classic studies of the later 1940s as J. H. Breytenbach's *Die Betekenis van die Tweede Vryheidsoorlog* (The Meaning of the Second War of Freedom) portrayed a war between the godless and meretricious British and the upright guardians of a freeborn Boer people, men of the elect who listened to the prophets and women who would continue to carry the seed of a republican freedom whose time would come. Integral to the professional promotion of an Afrikaner people's history or *volksgeskiedenis,* this gloss on the war became its historical truth, part of an "objective-scientific" truthfulness about the past furnished by nationalist historians.[6] An accepted truth was the pervading resonance of a *Vryheidsoorlog,* or War of Freedom, first coined in the 1880s after the defeat of the British at the Battle of Majuba. Retrospectively, the 1880–1881 Transvaal War was represented as the *Eerste Vryheidsoorlog,* or First War of Freedom, an epic tribe-of-Israel struggle for justice and independence in the promised land. As a living parable, this imagery went on to season the spiritual palate of the second conflict. The confection of a *Tweede Vryheidsoorlog,* or Second War of Freedom, served to affirm the spiritual heights occupied by the war in the long upward march of a republicanist Afrikanerdom.

At the same time, we must remember that this is not the whole picture. More modern Afrikaans scholarly writing on the war, emerging essentially between the end of the 1960s and the later 1980s, has been less crusading in purpose, reflected not least in the use of a more prosaic *Boereoorlog* (Boer War) and *Anglo-Boereoorlog* (Anglo-Boer War), and in a shift toward a less partisan historical assessment. In this, the liberal significance of victory or defeat has generally mattered less, as has the search for "meaning" in the war; it was comprehensible as tragedy, a fateful fissure between English and Afrikaner with profoundly regrettable consequences. There is, in some of this, an echo of those British officers who were concerned that the bitterness of the war would completely alienate the two white "races," when what the country needed was an alliance of their common European kinship.

There were good reasons for exaggerated nationalist reminders of the moral lessons and animosities of the war to weaken appreciably through the decades after the Second World War. In part, this was because many Afrikaners found themselves enjoying unprecedented prosperity under National Party rule after 1948. In these circumstances, brooding over the privations and losses of the English War inevitably became a less important element of *volk* propaganda. Whatever the English had done in the past could now be undone by means of the rising soufflé of Afrikaner nationalism. There were also other factors that explained the declining interest in the war. One was the long-awaited satisfaction at the achievement of a national South African Republic and its withdrawal from the British Commonwealth at the beginning of the 1960s: at least in spirit, the old Boer Republics could waltz again. Another was the need to glide English South Africans into a more companionable and inclusive white supremacist nationalism. This also produced a judicious thaw in war sentiment, with a commensurate decrease in staunch Afrikaners' tendency to associate English speakers with the sins and brutishness of old imperial conquest.

By the early 1970s, memory of the South African War as an ideological totem had largely migrated to the khaki shirt, nationalist ultra-Right. Remaining combative, its gaze fixed firmly on the past, this mostly lower-middle-class and working-class cluster began to keep incriminating war memories active on the margins, with a festering bitterness about the fate of Afrikaners in the war a crucial part of an anti-English *curriculum vitae*. Naturally enough, the currency of remembrance was of facing up to war from the front. It entailed submerging and forgetting the very large number of those who had had enough of male sacrifice in war: men who hid, surrendered, or became turncoats by enlisting in the British army. What mattered was making remembrance of the trauma of war inextricably part of a continued demonizing of the old imperial enemy.

Britain's camps and their atrocious conditions of internment continued to be a symbol of the atrocity of conquest, as the Boer women and children of August 1901 became the equivalent of the Belgians of August 1914. The violation and capture of the domestic space of the "home front" continued to help in knitting together a focused will to remember. And, as a focal point of memory, what the resettlement camps of the occupied Boer states continued to bequeath is victimhood and martyrdom. They have also long been a site of historical mythology. Thus, within contemporary South Africa, it is fair to assume that most people still see the use of concentration camps as a uniquely cruel strategy invented by the British and pioneered by a devilish Kitchener to do in the Boers. Britain's "methods of barbarism" lit the way to Nazi concentration camps forty years later. In fact, as a standard tactic to stop a dispersed rural guerrilla war becoming an indefinite war, policies of forced resettlement and internment had earlier been put into service by Spain in the Cuban War, and by the republican Mexican army in the 1870s. Detention was how regular armies came to wrap up the challenge of squirming irregular warfare. No less tangibly, invocation of memory of the camps has long been the special path of an Afrikaner War trauma; only now is there a dawning, wider recognition that living and dying in internment sites was something shared by African refugees.

In defining memory of the South African War, it is, in the end, always the England of the past that asserts itself. The creation of a unified English-Afrikaner Union Defence Force in 1912 saw Boer veterans and others filled with righteous indignation about an Anglicization of military methods and the imposition of a common khaki—a fairly insufferable color, given recent history.[7] Another obvious thing is how the crisis has remained related to the position and claims of the British monarchy in South Africa. Take the 1920s tour of the Prince of Wales when, among some Afrikaner representatives, reconciliatory welcome and lingering war resentment mingled uneasily. Or take the 1947 royal visit to South Africa that had as its Churchillian sub-text Britain's desire to acknowledge Prime Minister Jan Smuts for having been the War Office's finest Boer general of 1940. Appropriately enough, on a Transvaal leg of their tour, the royal family was escorted by a folksy commando, complete with serge suits, slouch hats, republican medals, and vintage Mausers, to a garden tea party where they met a scraping band of 1899–1902 *oudstryders*. Radical nationalists, now within a year of electoral office, were unimpressed by so ignominious a ceremonial.[8]

Equally noteworthy were the pricks felt during the first visit of the Windsors since the 1940s, the 1995 tour of Elizabeth II in the wake of South Africa's transition to majority rule and its reentry to the Commonwealth in 1994. In some quarters, old war words and images were rapidly revived. An incensed Afrikaner *Boerestaat* (Boer State) Party declared the Queen unwelcome in the "Boerestaat of Transvaal and the Free State." From "a dynasty of conquerors," she was "the great grand-daughter of a cruel queen" whose invading armies had not only "destroyed our Boers' freedom," but had also committed "the infamous holocaust in which a sixth of our people were murdered in concentration camps."[9] Other Afrikaner responses were less apoplectic, if still chastening. The blustery African National Congress (ANC) parliamentarian Carl Niehaus called upon the Queen to observe a more inclusive act of South African War remembrance by commemorating the Boer dead. "If she is going to lay wreaths at World War II and World War I graves," he declared, "she ought also to lay wreaths on graves of the tens of thousands of women and children who died in the camps."[10]

At the heart of that particular attitude lay South Africa's post-1994 political settlement and the project of national integration for the post-apartheid ruling political elite. South Africa's World War experience and its experience of its modern colonial war were to be pulled closer together through enlarged, common commemorative rites, with Afrikaner losses in the South African War becoming more universally acknowledged as the *nation's* war dead. It was in this sense that Elizabeth II was urged to make a redemptive Boer War gesture in the image of a new South African nation, or in the "imagined community" of that nation. Far from continuing as a divisive historical legacy, the legacy of the war could become part of the fabric of a newly reconciled and healed country, affirming shared understanding between Afrikaner and English, and also between black and white. Indeed, for some more wide-eyed observers of the royal visit, the presence of the Queen signified both a final transcendence of Anglo-Boer War bitterness and the ratification of the "equal footing" of the three symbolic strands of South African society, "Bantu, Boer and Briton."[11]

Perhaps nothing exemplifies this gradual recomposition of the South African War better than the way its commando and internment camps' past can now be detached from conservative nationalist Afrikaner history and imbued with new national patriotic meanings; the purpose of a war imagination is to structure consensus. In 1996, on the fortieth anniversary of a famous African women's march against the apartheid pass laws, the ANC Women's League urged the wives of some prominent Afrikaner politicians to stretch "across the divides" and to join in a commemorative walk to "cement the unity of South African women." According to the League's president, what sealed such female solidarity was a shared history of imperial and colonial brutality. Just as African women had been victims of merciless racist decrees, so "we recognise that Afrikaner women suffered and died under the British."[12] In an even more grandiose gesture, an ANC judge of the Constitutional Court reclaimed idealism and the universal story of freedom as the meaning of the war. Linking the language of the present with that of the past, he asserted his personal "pride in the heroic struggle of the Boer fighters in the history of the world and in our history." Any history of a liberal human rights culture had to "take into account the fate of the women and children in the concentration camps. So much of Afrikaans history is part of the struggle for freedom. *Vryheid* (freedom) has real resonance and meaning."[13] If there is any irony here, it clearly comes at the historical expense of the black majority.

Assimilation of the history of the war into a broader new South Africanism is a model illustration of how a populist public agenda may seek to recreate or reinvent the place of armed conflict in modern national identity. Thus, according to one provincial government cultural department in 1996, the purpose of any centenary anniversary would not be to commemorate an Anglo-Boer War; it would be to recognize a South African War, or rather a series of South African wars, in which "virtually all ethnic groups" played a role, thereby forging "the common historic destiny of all South Africans."[14] This version of everyone's war around some military maypole has the cozy ring of a shared bonding, even though adversarial responsibility for the war and its operations did not exactly rest with all of South Africa's inhabitants. In such therapeutic reordering and reconstruction, the ugly phenomenon of the concentration camps acts as a leveler for Afrikaners and Africans. In this way, the trauma of war, previously an exclusively Boer martyrdom, becomes shared suffering across the color divide.

At the same time, this is not all that needs to be said. Within the lower levels of the ruling party itself, the war is not up for grabs as a war of South African "people," rather than an Anglo-Boer War. In 1996, for instance, Cape Town ANC councilors denounced war centenary initiatives as "celebration of a colonial war" that produced "a new period of oppression and exploitation of our people." Having "just got back our dignity," there was no appetite for remembering an insular war "which has nothing that unites our people."[15] By 1997, in some places this feeling had gone further. For one government official, the protracted misery endured by black people throughout most of the twentieth century had been the direct product of the Anglo-Boer War; for him, there could be no question of official public commemoration. For another, as the cause of the war was no more than a British-Boer squabble over African land, it was neither appropriate nor politic for a majority-rule government to mark the centenary of an episode of colonial expropriation.[16]

Elsewhere, the ground so well watered by radical Afrikaner nationalism in earlier decades began to bear its own distinctive fruit. Although by the 1980s well past its zenith as a mobilizing cult of war remembrance, the embers of 1902 were stoked by the terminal crisis of apartheid. In a striking 1993 observation, the quixotic Afrikaner historian Floris van Jaarsveld concluded that "Afrikanerdom has suffered two great defeats in its history: the first at the beginning of the twentieth century in the war with Britain, which inflicted a military defeat on it, and the second at the end of the century—a political defeat at the hands of Africa."[17]

Elements of a *bittereinder* aesthetic took shape around this view, as British domination became African domination, with ANC President Nelson Mandela its odious High Commissioner; for its far right, Afrikanerdom once again faced the prospect of complete deracination in a unitary mongrel state. "Again," intoned Ferdi Hartzenberg of the Conservative Party, "dark days have come to our people."[18] In turn, to his right, there was a rekindled yearning for a Transvaal and Orange Free State *Boerestaat* or *Volkstaat* (People's State) to secure the bloodlines of ethnic self-determination. In a burst of unvarnished Anglophobia, Robert van Tonder of the *Boerestaat* Party called for "Boers" to consecrate a pure "Boerestaat" as a posthumous revenge upon Queen Victoria, who had seen to it that "our Boer republics were crushed in 1902 and 14 other 'peoples' were forced to live with us in one state." This had amounted to breaking the rules of warfare to foment civil war, but then, as now, civil war could not defeat Afrikaners; "after all, it was the Afrikaners who invented it."[19]

In the 1990s, this descending Boer War flank engaged on a number of fronts, not just against the old enemy of rampant Englishness, but against a dawning age of racial equality and majority rule, and against a now despised National Party leadership for capitulating to racial and cultural cosmopolitanism. At one tragicomic pole there was the seizure of Pretoria's Fort Schanskop and military museum, a place in thrall to a virile Boer commando heritage. Under the billowing *Vierkleur* flag of nineteenth-century Transvaal, a knot of armed vigilantes protested against multiracial political negotiations whose sole purpose was seen as selling off the assets of Afrikaner sovereignty. After their arrest and conviction for illegal armed occupation, the group's leader, Willem Ratte, wrote from jail to contest his newspaper depiction as "right-wing." All that informed his thinking was a First Anglo-Boer War antecedent. In a torrential yet powerful manifesto, Ratte declared:

> Were the Boers of 1880 called right-wingers for resisting the imperialist British occupation? Then, as now, you had an alien regime lording it in Pretoria over our people, whose gutless president had betrayed and handed over his sovereign state. Then, as now, the new (neo)colonialist administration pretended to be God's gift to the supposedly "dirty and dumb Dutchmen" and tried its best to smear the pro-independence party as only a few backward "Don Quixote tilting at windmills." Our struggle has nothing to do with right or left ... this being incidental, like religion in the Irish-British conflict, but everything to do with a nation having an inherent right to be free, to be able to choose its own representatives and leaders democratically.[20]

At another eccentric pole, a Kruger Day commemoration in October 1992 saw a sliver of rough-hewn Englishness regain its luster in right-wing

nationalist Afrikaner life. In a cameo of bonding between Afrikaner and English ultra-right interest, indefatigable ex-Rhodesians and English-speaking
adherents of the Afrikaans Conservative Party lumbered into the Vaal River
to retrieve rocks from a camp memorial reputedly torn down by departing
British soldiers in 1903. Under the solemn gaze of a crowd of several thousand, the rock was piled up close to the official Paardekraal camp monument, thereby symbolically atoning for past desecration. Calling the act "the
greatest conciliatory gesture by English-speaking countrymen since before
the Boer Wars," Conservative Party leader Andries Treurnicht announced
that "the time has certainly come for all English-speaking patriots to let
bygones be bygones, and to join hands with the Boer to resist the common
enemy of black domination."[21] This was a fairly droll gesture from a man
who had spent a good part of his political career railing against English influence in South African life.

In April 1998, there was appreciation of news from Ireland of stiff opposition in Listowel to the raising of a plaque to commemorate Kitchener's
birthplace, because of his inhumane prosecution of the Anglo-Boer War.
One correspondent noted that it would be received "with great satisfaction
by Afrikaners in general, but particularly by descendants of the Boers who
fought against Kitchener's barbarism." Several others invoked the obvious
popular analogy, arguing that Kitchener's concentration camp policy had
been the genocidal work of a "Hitler" in South Africa or the creation of an
unrecognized British Vietnam. J. A. Marais, "son of a Boer father" exiled and
imprisoned on St. Helena and "a mother who was interned in the Klerksdorp
concentration camp," urged the idea of an Irish-Afrikaner "war crimes tri-
bunal for Kitchener" in 1999, to mark "commemoration of the centenary
of the outbreak of the Boer War."[22] It was all caught neatly by a call for the
British Prime Minister, Tony Blair, to apologize for Britain's "appalling concentration camp record," in the light of blushing contrition before the Irish
for the potato famine and Indians for the Amritsar massacre. Yet readers
were advised not to expect too much sentiment, for while there were "many
Irish and Indian voters in the UK," "there is no Afrikaner vote."[23]

Such flickerings, and Fort Schanskop and Paardekraal, must surely be
seen as being among the last prickly episodes of an antique Afrikaner past,
dredging up for a self-conscious and ailing "Boer" minority the nostalgias
and resentments of a world with dwindling points of reference. For those
still attached to a *volkisch* war memory, it might not be too much to say that
in the 1990s they were being undone by history. Indeed, there was a quite
knowing sense of this. Likening African political demands to those of the
Uitlanders who had been so unwelcome a blot upon Kruger's republic,

Afrikanerweerstandsbeweging (AWB) (Afrikaner Resistance Movement) leader Eugene Terreblanche growled that not to grant Afrikaner "freedom" in a people's state would be to "play with fire," as British statesmen had discovered in the 1890s. Skeptics were referred to Thomas Pakenham's *The Boer War*, a work that in his view gave the Boers their due and more. Terreblanche called the book as admirable as Shakespeare, therefore "not part of any English conspiracy."[24]

Within the AWB, the coming of black majority rule represented "a second invasion," requiring the invocation of a national Boer state defense and heightening the inclination to ride about on horseback in an assertive display of Boer commando lineage. Because of the danger to Afrikaners from untrustworthy news editors, slippery politicians, and meddling imperialists (now American, not British), the call was for a "return" of "the generals," as nationalist Afrikaners had looked historically to their tough military men and spirited irreconcilables, the De la Reys and De Wets, for salvation. Just how much things turned on emotive memory of the ashes of 1899–1902 could be glimpsed in puffy Conservative Party talk of an imminent *Derde Vryheidsoorlog* (Third War of Freedom), in the use by the AWB and Boerestaat Party of the old Transvaal flag and its theme, *Ken u die Volk* (Do You Know the People), in sniping gunshots at the British Embassy in Pretoria in 1990, and in a bomb attack on Melrose House, where Boer leadership had signed its pained surrender in May 1902. Back where it all started, rabid ideologues of national purity demanded the reclamation and renewal of the old Boer Republics. This was not something to be created, for historically they had already been in full, legitimate existence, based on a Boer occupation that had "enjoyed internationally recognised independence until 1902."[25]

In a further poignant echo from the early 1900s, there was denunciation of reformist National Party leadership as traitors or *verraaiers* for having submitted to the ANC. Politicians to their right went for the government as "a lot of traitors" guilty of "treachery" and "acts of treason against its own people."[26] The base appeal of the idea of treachery was to a form of atavism, a replay of the closing stages of the South African War and its full-blown *hendsopper* ("hands-upper") and *bittereinder* ("bitter-ender") split between folding for peace and rigidly holding out under arms. In other words, here again were the more flabby of Boer generals turning traitor through capitulation or spineless surrender. The principal modern embodiment of this behavior was, of course, President F. W. de Klerk, who in 1997 tellingly let slip in London that he had bowed to the inevitable need to "surrender the right to national sovereignty."[27] In terms of the conventional content and discourse of nationalist Afrikaner history, the very word "surrender" has long continued to be particularly pregnant in meaning. Equally, this may have been the final historical moment when the partisan fires of traditional Afrikaner nationalist bitterness and self-righteousness can still be fanned by consciousness of the moral relevance of the Anglo-Boer War.

As the centenary of the war is commemorated, it is increasingly clear that a shifting historical context will affect the established ways in which the war has been remembered. In what for want of a better term one might call "popular society," the legacy of the war remains a sectional business. Outside of elite cultural and academic missionary circles, the Anglo-Boer conflict is not *felt* to be a shared South African history, let alone a shared tragedy. By and large, the impulse of the black majority is to dissociate; for white Afrikaners and English speakers, it is to associate, however reticently in many instances. In this, 1999 was not entirely unlike 1949. Yet, following the decline of Afrikaner power, there are other obvious differences. In a new society being directed by the liberation aristocracy of African nationalism, busily creating its own national myths, what will happen to the historical Anglo-Boer War?

One likelihood is that it will come to be seen as a more and more remote episode from a vanished European imperial age. As the Johannesburg *Sunday Independent* put it on the centenary of the 1895 Jameson Raid, that mad moment of imperialist buccaneering Churchill later considered to be the real start of the Anglo-Boer conflict, "with this tumultuous century drawing to a close hindsight puts the do-or-die battle between Afrikaners and English-speakers into its proper, smaller context. White men were never going to win indefinite control of this African continent."[28] The notion of the war having a narrow context certainly contains a truth, given the social basis provided by the war for a unified South Africa, and the form of a twentieth-century South African nationalism. Its direction was made abundantly clear by many local veterans of the war, not least Smuts. When, in the 1930s, he invoked a "philosophy of non-racial, inclusive South Africanism,"[29] it meant closing the book on Anglo-Boer War divisions, and nothing Whiggish in intention toward the rightless black majority. Toward the end of the twentieth century, some members of that majority, in power at last, seem still to be laying the blame for this on the 1899–1902 War. This is probably misconceived. It is true that it put things straight for a unified national colonial state that tied up a white supremacist order. But that had long been on the way, in one form or another.

Almost a century ago, Kipling despaired of the Boer War as a bad business, plainly "No end of a Lesson." In Britain, it was a lesson rued across a wide spectrum of opinion, from professional military staff to fastidious liberals. For South Africa, something of that became embedded in old republican Afrikaner imagery, while the backward gaze of others has gradually become infused by newer experiences or by the need to recast the war's legacy, by reflecting long unacknowledged black sacrifice or loss. Already ambiguous in its significance, in some ways the future of the Anglo-Boer War in popular South African historical memory looks quite uncertain. It is even conceivable that with the disappearance of a distinctive Afrikaner "political nation," the war will come to have little core meaning at all, and will live on in the refined cultural climate of heritage. Consider the fate of the old Orange Free State, central to freehold Boer trekker identity since the mid-nineteenth century, and the location of some of the war's stiffest republicanism and most destructive fruition. Moving with African nationalist times, the Orange Free State lost its distinctively Dutch "Orange" stamp in 1994, to become simply the Free State; in 1997, its ANC provincial government decided to swap Afrikaans for English as its sole official language. Less than a century after the war, African nationalism has in some ways begun to realize Milner's failed post-1902 Anglicization policy. And as with Orange, so with Vaal. The Transvaal, too, has been dismembered, retitled and demarcated as new territorial entities with chunky, noncolonial African names like Gauteng and Mpumalanga. Post-Boer and politically odorless, on a history map reading they may appear to have become the provinces of nowhere.

And yet, in our time, let alone in the longer run to come, the erosion of the South African War's political inheritance, sentimentalized or institutionalized, is unlikely to mean the end of an Anglo-Boer imperial war remembrance. This has little to do with the politics of identity, or with war as a legitimizing myth; in its imaginative temperament, the Anglo-Boer War is first, and the South African War still quite some way second. At the time of writing, able-bodied devotees of the renowned guerrilla commandant Christiaan de Wet can take guided hikes along his legendary flying escape route in the western Transvaal. As war tourism, this may be the South African version of tripping along the Ho Chi Minh Trail. In the Cape Karoo region, addicts can scrabble up to remote rock faces on which resting or hiding Boer commandos scratched poignant personal messages or etched images of fellow burghers. Visitors to a minor 1900 battlefield outside Bloemfontein can have, as it were, a bite of the cherry by firing a restored Boer Martini-Henry rifle at a British infantryman dummy target, or by guessing the standard provisions and equipment carried by a commando. Boer War enthusiasts from Britain and the white Commonwealth, swollen in number by the pull of the South African War's centenary, tramp the battlefields of Modder River or Paardeberg, ponder at the still exposed Boer trench lines at Magersfontein, amble through the Ladysmith siege museum, or chart the whereabouts of some of the eight thousand blockhouses erected over large parts of South Africa by British forces.

The remnants of the *soldiering* war clearly remain as powerful an attraction as ever, the sites of decisive battle or marks of guerrilla attrition a source through which to imagine the concrete realities of a European colonial war. From the perspective of the late 1990s, it is the significance of political memories of the war that looks set to decline. Something of that ideological mood may remain; it will merely touch ever fewer people. Indeed, it is hard to see how it could naturally be otherwise in a country of such limited commonalities. South Africa's modern war is not, and has never been, an American Civil War in the sense of a "never-to-be-forgotten moment" in "the collective consciousness that makes Americans American."[30] To conjure up "We are marching to Pretoria" is not to summon up the shared image of a universally transforming war, of the kind endowed by "Marching through Georgia" or "Dixie." Unlike the Blue and the Gray, Boer and departing British war veterans were slow in scrambling toward campfire brotherly reconciliation. Equally, this was not merely a big war in the modern life of an evolving nation state. It was also the most violent expression of the prolonged engagement between South Africa and the British Empire. In this, it is high time to summon A.J.P. Taylor, who decades ago concluded memorably that in the long term, "the eclipse of Boer independence was of less importance than the deflation of British imperialism."[31]

Notes

1. Isabel Hofmeyr, "Building a Nation from Words: Afrikaans Language, Literature and Ethnic Identity, 1902–1924," in S. Marks and S. Trapido (eds.), *The Politics of Race, Class and Nationalism in Twentieth-Century South Africa* (London, 1987), 109.

2. T. Dunbar Moodie, *The Rise of Afrikanerdom: Power, Apartheid and the Afrikaner Civil Religion* (Los Angeles, 1975), 17.

3. W. R. Nasson, "Race and Civilisation in the Anglo-Boer War of 1899–1902" (M.A. thesis, University of York, 1977), 44–50.

4. A. Grundlingh, "War, Wordsmiths and the 'Volk': Afrikaans Historical Writing on the Anglo-Boer War of 1899–1902 and the War in Afrikaner Historical Consciousness, 1902–1990," in E. Lehmann and E. Reckwitz (eds.), *Mfecane to Boer War* (Essen, 1992), 52.

5. Grundlingh, "War, Wordsmiths," 45–46; also, Isabel Hofmeyr, "Popularizing History: The Case of Gustav Preller," in S. Clingman (ed.), *Regions and Repertoires: Topics in South African Politics and Culture* (Johannesburg, 1991), 67.

6. Grundlingh, "War, Wordsmiths," 48; Grundlingh, "Politics, Principles and Problems of a Profession: Afrikaner Historians and Their Discipline, c. 1920–c. 1965," *Perspectives in Education* 12, no. 1 (1990/91): 6–14.

7. S. S. Swart, "The Rebels of 1914: Masculinity, Republicanism and the Social Forces That Shaped the Boer Rebellion" (M.A. thesis, University of Natal, 1997), 55.

8. *Cape Argus,* 26 March 1947.

9. *Die Burger,* 21 March 1995.

10. *Cape Times,* 21 March 1995.

11. Ibid., 18 March 1995.

12. *Cape Argus,* 8 March 1995.

13. Judge Albie Sachs, cited in Grundlingh, "War, Wordsmiths," 54.

14. *Cape Argus,* 1 October 1996.

15. *Cape Times,* 26 September 1996.

16. Ibid., 8 December 1997.

17. *Beeld,* 12 February 1993.

18. *Die Burger,* 17 December 1993; *Rapport,* 20 December 1993.

19. *Beeld,* 18 January 1993; *Aida Parker Newsletter* 163 (1993): 2.

20. *Sunday Independent,* 31 December 1995.

21. *Weekly Mail,* 16–22 October 1992.

22. *Sunday Times,* 5 and 19 April 1998; *Rapport,* 12 April 1996.

23. *Sunday Times,* 26 April 1998.

24. *Sunday Independent,* 31 December 1995.

25. Johann van Rooyen, *Hard Right: The New White Power in South Africa* (London, 1995), 43; *South African Foundation Review,* September 1992, 8.

26. *Patriot,* 5 April and 7 June 1991; *House of Assembly Debates,* col. 106, 6 February 1990.

27. *Cape Times,* 19 February 1997.

28. *Sunday Independent,* 31 December 1995.

29. Quoted in T.R.H. Davenport, *South Africa: A Modern History* (London, 1987), 177.

30. N. A. Trudeau, *Out of the Storm: The End of the Civil War, April–June 1865* (Baton Rouge, 1995), 422.

31. A.J.P. Taylor, *From the Boer War to the Cold War: Essays on Twentieth-Century Europe* (Harmondsworth, U.K., 1996), 38.

CHAPTER 2

The National Women's Monument

The Making and Mutation of Meaning in
Afrikaner Memory of the South African War

ALBERT GRUNDLINGH

THIS CHAPTER HOPES TO add to our understanding of the discourses revolving around historical memory, war, and identity. It focuses specifically on the Women's Monument in Bloemfontein and the way the monument reflected Afrikaner remembrance of the South African War in terms of gender and nationalism. "Commemorative history" presents its own set of analytical problems, as Peter Carrier has alerted us:

> Commemorations whether occurring "naturally" after a predictable lapse of time, or else organized in order to diffuse and implant a specific interpretation of the past, pose an essential interpretative problem for the historian, for their meaning derives from elements of both the original event and the new context within which the commemorative "event" takes place. By definition, a commemoration both calls an event of the past to memory and preserves this memory in a ceremony, monument or cultural artifacts.[1]

Such a layered analysis is required to "discover" the "message" of the Women's Monument.

Building a Women's Monument for Patriarchal Purposes?

Of all the aspects of the South African War, few have been more controversial than the British removal of Boer women and children from their farms to an incarceration in concentration camps. It was a strategy employed by the British high command in an effort to curtail the activities of Boer guerrilla fighters who lived off the land and used farmsteads as bases. The administration of the camps left much to be desired, and 27,927 Boers died of disease, mainly through neglect and incompetence on the part of the British. This amounted to approximately 10 percent of a relatively small Boer population in the two Republics. Moreover, in terms of deaths, it was undoubtedly a white women's war—fatalities in the concentration camps were more than double the number of men killed in action on both sides.[2]

The enormity of this catastrophe left a legacy of bitter memories and mutual recriminations that dominated much academic and popular writing on women and the war. Understandable as this might have been, the focus on the concentration camps and the patent suffering of the inmates had the effect of seeing women almost exclusively as victims of the war.[3] What is lost in such a view is the way gender relations were affected by wartime developments. It has been observed that in Europe, the First World War gave women "considerable independence and public experience, often leaving them with a greater familiarity with confronting local bureaucracy than their husbands had when they returned from the front, the experience brought with it ... a pride and social identity."[4] During the South African War, some women managed to rise above the situation despite the depressing conditions of the concentration camps. Having had their homes destroyed, being grief-stricken by the loss of a child or children, and without the usual family support, they had only their inner resources to rely on. Many of them did this stoically, publicly undaunted by the folly of the male invaders who were responsible for the deplorable state of affairs: "The women maintained extraordinary composure and seldom lost mental control under this ordeal; a striking feature was their profound consciousness of the want of common-sense in those who initiated this movement against them."[5]

While wartime developments opened up spaces and presented challenges to Boer women (albeit not of their own making), with the coming of peace such gains as there might have been were likely to recede with the return to the relative "normality" of prewar society. "As soon as life returns to 'normal,'" one writer has argued, "the women's sphere becomes re-defined and maintained by the prevailing patriarchal structures, regardless of the events of the ... immediate past."[6]

In many respects this might have been true of the way Boer women had to adapt to everyday life in the postwar period. But in terms of memory, the concentration camps could not simply be consigned to oblivion. The war propelled Boer women onto center stage, and their experiences demanded public recognition. So powerful and pervasive was the impact of the concentration camp experience that ultimately the dominant Boer symbolic representation of the South African War assumed the form of a women's, and not a men's, memorial. The fact that the principal frame of remembrance of the war was that of a memorial for women is unusual; most war memorials conform to the masculine stereotype of the warrior/hero.[7] By the same token, it is significant that the concern about what had happened to women in the war gripped the public mind sufficiently for a memorial to be erected within a relatively short period. The women's memorial in Bloemfontein was completed less than eleven years after the war; in contrast, the Voortrekker Monument in Pretoria had a much more protracted history.[8]

The organizational initiative for a memorial came from the former president of the Orange Free State, M. T. Steyn, and his wife, Tibbie. President Steyn received medical treatment in Europe after the South African War; while there he reflected on ways to commemorate Boer deaths in the concentration camps. Whether Europe's rich heritage of monuments acted as a spur is impossible to tell in the absence of reliable evidence. What is clearer is that although M. T. Steyn took the organizational lead on account of his former political office, his wife did not act as an adjunct. She showed a personal interest in the project because she had lost a number of relatives and friends in the camps. Mrs. Steyn also had a close relationship with Emily Hobhouse, who had risen to prominence through her reports on British maladministration of the camps and her attempt to relieve the plight of Boer women and children.[9]

Upon his return to South Africa, President Steyn began preparations for a suitable memorial. It was not a foregone conclusion that a monument was the appropriate way to commemorate Boer deaths in the camps. Some members of the working committee argued in favor of a school or a hospital as a more practical alternative. Steyn objected on the grounds of the high costs of maintenance, which could easily rob the enterprise of its inspirational value. He wanted a monument that paid homage to the women without the intrusion of any utilitarian motive.[10] Steyn won the day, and after further consultation with various Afrikaner organizations it was decided to erect a monument "in glorious memory of the mothers, women and children who died during the recent war."[11]

A large-scale fund-raising campaign followed, and M. T. Steyn did much to keep the issue in the public eye. A concerted attempt was made to reach the target of £10,000 by means of collection lists and appeals to churches and to cultural and women's organizations. Contributions came from all classes of Afrikaners and each contribution was personally acknowledged by Steyn. The required amount was collected over a four-year period and in 1911 an architect and sculptor were approached to begin work on the project.[12]

The monument was erected approximately three kilometers south of

Bloemfontein. It consists of a 35-meter obelisk; close to it is a statue of a woman holding a dying child, supported by another woman gazing resolutely into the distance. On either side, two bas-relief panels depict women being herded into a concentration camp, clutching their few paltry possessions, and an emaciated child dying while a woman kneels at the bedside. The whole monument stands in a circular enclosure. Situated between some small hills against the background of a vast open veld, the monument blends in with the natural surroundings; the landscape itself becomes part of the monument, reinforcing the idea of the Boer people as a rural nation. Those sympathetic to the project could claim lyrically "that the obelisk overlooks the surrounding kopjes and distant plains, proclaiming its message to the nation with persuasive eloquence."[13]

But what was the message? Given the prominence of the obelisk, it is not surprising that some modern critics regard it as a "phallic symbol" and a "transcendental signifier of a phallocentric volks-metaphysic."[14] In this reading the aesthetic ideology of the Women's Monument primarily revolves around its "maleness." Without wanting to deny the unintended and unconscious meanings that monuments can convey, it is debatable whether such interpretations bring us closer to an understanding of what the Women's Monument represented in genderized terms at the time. Writing on monuments in general, Nathan Glazer has made the salutary point that

> today, in the wake of Marxism, deconstruction, postmodernism and other contemporary critical movements, it is all too easy to detect … the symbols of … Western cultural hegemony, male chauvinism, homophobia, and on and on—so many meanings multiplied by contemporary theory that these monuments are sitting ducks before modern critics.[15]

Equally problematical are interpretations that regard, in a timeless and ahistorical fashion, the depiction of women as the martyrs of the South African War as a form of male entrapment, confining women to the role of passive sufferers. One such argument suggests that

> Afrikaans women were maltreated during the war by the British to achieve their war ideals; after the war their own men misused them to accomplish nationalist ideals. Martyrdom did not introduce Afrikaans women into the male dominant culture. On the contrary, because of the nationally honoured martyrdom, suffering became an inseparable part of the nature of these women.

It is further averred that the building of the Women's Monument was a "male effort to win international sympathy for the nation."[16] It has been pointed out that excessive emphasis on the suffering of women during the war can draw attention away from other dimensions of women's experiences. While this is true, interpreting the theme of suffering as a male way of subordinating women is simplistic and misleading, and the claim that men used the monument to gain "international sympathy for the nation" lacks evidence. Significantly, the depiction of suffering as represented by the central statue close to the base of the obelisk did not originate from male deliberations; it was the idea of a woman, Emily Hobhouse. She drew inspiration from a particular incident she had witnessed during the war at the Springfontein camp when she had been asked to visit a sick baby. Later she recalled:

The *Vrouemonument* in Bloemfontein, erected in 1913

"NIET VERLATEN"

"VOOR VR

AAN ONZE
HELDINNEN
EN LIEVE KINDEREN

"UW WIL GESCHIEDE"

DIT NATIONAAL MONUMENT
IS OPGERICHT
TER NAGEDACHTENIS AAN DE

26370 VROUWEN EN KINDEREN
DIE IN DE CONCENTRATIEKAMPEN
ZYN OMGEKOMEN
EN AAN DE ANDERE
VROUWEN EN KINDEREN
DIE ELDERS TENGEVOLGE
VAN DEN OORLOG 1899-1902
ZYN BEZWEKEN

ONTHULD 16 DECEMBER 1913

A. VAN WOUW.   FRANS SOFF
                               ARCHITECT

The mother sat on her little trunk with the child across the knee. She had nothing to give it and the child was sinking fast.... There was nothing to be done and we watched the child draw its last breath in reverent silence. The mother neither moved nor wept. It was her only child. Dry-eyed but deathly white, she sat motionless looking at the child ... far away into the depth of grief beyond all tears. A friend stood behind her who called upon Heaven to witness this tragedy.[17]

When the sculptor, Anton van Wouw, went to Rome to work on the monument, Hobhouse related the scene to him "as the center and core of the tragedy: broken hearted womanhood, perishing childhood."[18] Hobhouse, who did not have a high regard for van Wouw as a sculptor, thought that the end product failed to do justice to the pitiful event. She commented that the child "only appears to me to be a sleeping child and neither sick nor dead." She felt that the child should have borne more directly the "aspect of emaciation and death."[19] It was, therefore, not only a woman who chose the specific theme of the Monument, but one who viewed its portrayal as inadequate in capturing the suffering of Boer women and children.

It cannot be denied that Afrikaner women during the 1900s were locked into an overarching patriarchal system, but it was a system that also imposed certain obligations on the men. "Protection" of the "weaker sex" was one social and moral imperative. During the South African War men were confronted with news of the horrors of the camps experienced by their wives and daughters, horrors they were largely unable to alleviate. This invoked a strong sense of guilt. President Steyn, acutely aware of the trials and tribulations of Boer women and their effects on the men on commando, regarded a deeply felt sense of indebtedness as the main incentive for building the Monument. In the light of this he asked rhetorically: "Is it therefore surprising that the men felt a need to build a memorial for the heroines and their children who had passed away?"[20] This interpretation is given further weight by a modern study that identifies the motivation for the Women's Monument "as an opportunity for the survivors to 'pay their debts' to the perished generation."[21] To some leading women of the time, the issue was beyond doubt and they regarded the Monument as paying homage first and foremost to women *per se*. Mrs. Steyn saw the project as an attempt to place "women on a high pedestal,"[22] while Hobhouse made it very clear that it was essentially a *women's* monument of which all the "world's women should be proud."[23]

These declarations make it difficult to accept the contemporary meaning assigned to the Monument as one of female subservience. They do not, however, rule out subsequent mutations of the initial symbolism that introduced new meanings on the basis of a changing social and political context. Even at the time, although it did not necessarily have the effect of distorting the original symbolism of the monument, the preponderance of men in the organizing committees did lead to some other gender-blind oversights. Hobhouse felt that more women could have been invited to the unveiling ceremony. She wrote to Mrs. Steyn, mentioning the women's organizations in Cape Town that had supported the Boer cause. These women, she argued, had "worked themselves to the bone for the camps and naturally feel they should be specifically invited ... you know committees of *men* often forget these little but important amenities."[24]

A Monument Unveiled in the Name of Afrikaner Nationalism?

Moving from gender matters to other discourses relating to the monument, one has to probe the validity of the easily accepted assumption that the monument has been a political expression of Afrikaner nationalism since its inception.[25] In evaluating the contemporary lineages between the Women's Monument and the promotion of ethnic nationalism, countervailing political constraints should be considered.

In 1913, the year in which the Monument was inaugurated, fissures rather than a sense of unity characterized Afrikaner politics. Intra-Afrikaner tensions about South Africa's relationship with Great Britain were reflected in the opposing views of Prime Minister Louis Botha and General J.B.M. Hertzog, of whom the latter was regarded as the main protagonist of Afrikaner rights. Matters came to a head when Botha left Hertzog out of his cabinet in 1912. In addition, an uneasy relationship existed between Afrikaans and English speakers in wider white politics; this was often described as "racial animosity" in the parlance of the time.[26] These developments had a marked impact on the politics that surrounded the building and unveiling the Monument.

Botha was a central figure in what was described as a policy of reconciliation that addressed the various divisions after the South African War. Although a redoubtable commander of the Boer forces in the Transvaal during the hostilities, in the postwar period he emerged as a pragmatic politician who became premier of the Transvaal Colony in 1907 and of South Africa in 1910.[27] Botha was concerned about the potentially damaging effects of concentration camp commemorations on reconciliation politics. In 1907 he opposed the idea that political meetings in the Transvaal be used to promote the campaign for the Women's Monument.[28] He also tried in vain to derail Steyn's proposal for an Anglo-Boer War monument by suggesting a national monument for the Voortrekkers instead.[29] This suggestion would have pushed back the historical frame and shifted the focus away from a near contemporary and highly emotional war to a more remote and heroic representation of nation-building during the Great Trek.

In Bloemfontein the predominantly English-speaking city council had reservations about the advisability of erecting a monument that might reflect negatively on Great Britain, and also, by implication, on those in the Free State capital who had supported the British war effort. It was only after considerable debate that permission was granted for the Monument to be built.[30]

The tensions between Botha and Hertzog supporters and the apprehensions of white English-speaking South Africans threatened to undermine what was supposed to be a national, as opposed to a regional, monument. In November 1913, C. Brits, a former Boer general in the eastern Transvaal who planned to travel to Bloemfontein with his erstwhile comrades-in-arms, recommended to Steyn that the unveiling of the monument be delayed:

> Father is against son, brother against brother, etc. Internal wrangling makes co-operation on a national level impossible.... It is a most inappropriate time to unveil the monument. Would it not be better to postpone proceedings until such time that peace and co-operation have been restored? What I fear is that during the occasion political discussions and speeches may lead to internecine strife and bitterness which would detract from the solemnity of the event.[31]

Emily Hobhouse was also perturbed by the political undercurrents in Afrikanerdom and wrote to General J. C. Smuts, Botha's lieutenant: "I am very sorry to read of all the political unrest in South Africa ... I can only beg of you to kiss and be friends for my visit to Bloemfontein and bury the hatchet beneath the Vrouwen-Monument!"[32]

The unveiling of the Monument took place on December 16, 1913. The date was not without significance—it was the Day of the Vow ("Dingaan's Day," as it was also known) upon which the Voortrekker victory over the Zulu at Blood River (Ncombe) was celebrated, and these commemorations often carried a directly ethnic political message. It was not a date to allay the fears of those who had their reservations about the Monument. In the English-language press regret was expressed that "Dingaan's Day was chosen for the performance of a ceremony that might with no diminution of the solemnity of the event itself, have been fixed for another date."[33]

When the day arrived, a crowd of approximately 20,000 people from all corners of the country gathered at the Women's Monument. A newspaper reporter graphically described the sight:

> Wherever the eye roamed there was nothing but slowly moving or station-ary humanity! The hillside seemed as if alive. There was a continually changing pattern in the movement before one's eyes, occasioned by con-stant streams of newcomers. Denser and denser became the crowd, cover-ing the barrenness of the rocky ground until there was not a bare spot to be seen on either side of the kopjes.... The general colour tone was black and white, but here and there bright splashes provided by the sunshades were in evidence.... The ladies who had seats inside the monument were nearly all attired in deep mourning and the men wore the conventional frock coat and top hat.[34]

The atmosphere was solemn and devotional. The tone was set in Presi-dent Steyn's preamble to the proceedings, printed in the official program:

> Our hearts will be filled by sadness and a sense of loss. We are after all standing at the grave of thousands of women and children.... Let us exer-cise the well-known restraint and dignity of the Afrikaner. We are here to mourn the dead, not to honour the living. Let us therefore avoid all applause and rowdiness.[35]

The proceedings were choreographed to suit Steyn's call for calm and pious reflection, devoid of demonstrations that might cause offense. A com-mando of burghers on horseback led the procession; they were followed by the Kimberley Volunteer Regiment, representing the former foe, with the regiment's band playing Chopin's funeral march. The participation of erst-while enemies in the commemoration was symbolically significant because it emphasized the extent to which the organizers sought to be inclusive. As a climax to the procession, large numbers of women dressed in white arrived; a hush descended on the crowd as they made their way to the Monu-ment and, in sympathetic silence, laid wreaths at the base of the obelisk.[36] This act of homage was meant to convey a strongly spiritual message, not a political one.

The speeches that followed the wreath-laying ceremony complemented the dignified tone and conciliatory aim of the procession. Steyn's address was read to the crowd by one of his adjutants, since he was too ill to do it himself. Steyn emphasized that "the memorial has not been erected here in order to cause pain to any one, or to be an eternal reproach; but it is placed here out of simple piety."[37] John X. Merriman, the prominent Cape politician, later congratulated Steyn on an "admirable speech" and was impressed with the way "the whole proceedings seem to have gone off with the utmost dignity and good taste and the entire absence of anything which could have jarred."[38]

Botha, who predictably was expected to adopt a conciliatory stance, was careful not to give the impression that he was promoting a political position. His message was cast in religious terms to fit the general tenor of the proceedings: "God has not willed that we should exterminate one another. After all the misery and shedding of blood of the past, both races are still here. May we not, must we not, believe that it is His will that we should attempt to take a different path, the path of love and peace?"[39] Hobhouse's speech, read in her absence because of ill health, also invoked a religious dimension: "Alongside of the honour we pay the Sainted Dead, forgiveness must find a place. I have read that when Christ said, 'Forgive your enemies,' it is not only for the sake of the enemy He says so, but for one's own sake, 'because love is more beautiful than hate.'"[40]

Other Afrikaner leaders, such as D. F. Malan and Rev. J. D. Kestell, made speeches in a similar vein. Christiaan de Wet, the renowned bitterender general, was a significant exception, however. De Wet spoke "from the heart," and he had "the hearts as well as the ears of his audience." As a "rugged defiant figure," it was reported, "he stood out among the rest of the ... notable persons in the whole assembly." He recalled the historical travails of the Afrikaner and questioned whether the "progress" that had been made since the South African War was "progress in the right direction." His words were enthusiastically received, and Steyn had to ask the crowd to stop cheering in keeping with the solemnity of the occasion.[41]

De Wet's popular appeal serves as a reminder that underneath the surface of calm and dignity, the crowd yearned for a more robust political message that would assuage their sense of injustice. It was a sentiment shared by another prominent bitterender general, C. F. Beyers. Beyers was unable to attend the unveiling ceremony, but in October 1913 he interpreted the Women's Monument as a "source of memories," informing the future and signposting the way ahead for a "free nation (vrij volk)."[42] Given these firm convictions, it is not coincidental that a year later both De Wet and Beyers were involved in the ill-conceived Afrikaner rebellion of 1914.

From a review of the initial meanings assigned to the Women's Monument it is clear that on the whole, explicit programmatic political messages of nationalist intent did not dominate the proceedings. Deliberate attempts were made to elevate the occasion to a spiritual level and not to turn it into an Afrikaner political rally promoting ethnic exclusivity. Afrikaner political

life and religion were, however, often intertwined, and the memories associated with the Monument provided a vast reservoir of unexpressed emotions
that could be channeled along nationalistic lines of common suffering,
humiliation, and a need for retribution. The reaction to De Wet's speech was
a clear indication of this, yet these forces still had to be harnessed effectively.
And that lay in the future.

The Turn to Nationalism

The process of fostering an overarching Afrikaner national consciousness
involved hard ideological labor on several fronts over a number of years.
One of the key areas that had to be developed was an Afrikaner literary
culture with the capacity and status to serve as an effective vehicle to convey
the wishes and aspirations of the "volk" in its own language. It was with
the vigorous promotion of Afrikaans as a standard, respected, and written
language, distinct from Dutch, and its official recognition in 1925, that the
potential for cultural and political mobilization increased greatly.[43]

During the 1930s and 1940s especially, cultural entrepreneurs and politicians attempted to unite a rather disparate constituency of Afrikaans speakers, divided along class and regional lines, under the banner of nationalist
Afrikanerdom. These developments, which took place within the wider socioeconomic context of increased industrialization, urbanization, and the erosion of what were considered "traditional values," spawned the need for a
"usable" past.[44]

This growing vitality of the Afrikaans language and the political demands
of the time led to the publication of a spate of popular books on the South
African War. Almost without exception these glorified the Boer generals and
bitterenders and railed against the injustices of the concentration camps.
The hope was expressed that the "past will contribute to the promotion of
and love for the fatherland amongst the younger generation, and that it will
help to forge stronger links amongst Afrikaners."[45]

The ethnic mobilization of Afrikaans speakers subsequent to the unveiling of the Women's Monument was bound to affect the symbolism and
meaning assigned to it. What was muted in 1913 became more shrill and strident in the 1930s and 1940s. In September 1939, students at Potchefstroom
University who were strongly opposed to South Africa's participation in
World War II gave a clear indication of this shift:

And even if England today talks sweet, even if she appears as a champion
of small nations, we know better. The *vroue monument* continually cries

out for vengeance! That injustice perpetrated against our nation, that brutality which cries out to heaven. The mark is too deeply branded in our
heart; it is too close to our heart ever to forget.[46]

The physical terrain of the Women's Monument became more and more
often the site of nationalist political rallies. In 1940, a huge gathering of
70,000 Afrikaners congregated at the monument to voice their demand for
a republican form of government in South Africa. Featuring appearances by
National Party leaders such as Jim Fouché, N. J. van der Merwe, and C. R.
Swart, exhorting the crowd to understand and support the historical basis of
the call for a republic, the occasion bore all the hallmarks of nationalist
mobilization. Yet, the original intention that the Monument should not be
an overt political symbol remained strong enough for the commission in
charge of it to prohibit ceremonies conducted at the foot of the obelisk. As
a compromise it allowed the proceedings to go ahead a short distance from
the statues.[47] The concession did not, however, detract from the fact that
symbolically the Women's Monument became enveloped in the swirl of
Afrikaner nationalism.

Cultural entrepreneurs, including ministers of religion and teachers, regularly used the Monument as a symbol to drive home nationalistic messages.
The author Marq de Villiers, who went to school in Bloemfontein during
this period, recalls:

> When I was a boy in Bloemfontein we would be taken by bus once a year
> to the small rise outside town on which stood a simple stone obelisk; there
> we would be subjected to a memorial service of suffocating boredom and
> a sermon of interminable length; we were all affected by a desire to disap-
> pear *oor die bult.* But on the other hand we all understood why we were
> there.... We understood viscerally as children that the monument was not
> merely a stone expression of the evil that outsiders do; it is a symbol of how
> the *volkseie* is fundamental to a people's identity: outsiders, people outside
> the *burgerstand*, foreign to the fundamental thought patterns of the people,
> will always try to do you harm. The only solution is tight solidarity.[48]

Although the Women's Monument became a focal symbol of ethnic alle-
giance, it did not attain the same status as the Voortrekker Monument in
Pretoria. The cornerstone of the Voortrekker Monument was laid on
December 16, 1938, at the height of the centenary celebrations of the Great
Trek, which evoked a huge emotional response among Afrikaners.[49] Eleven
years later, on December 16, 1949, after the historic victory of the National

Party in 1948, the Voortrekker Monument was inaugurated with great fanfare. It was conceived and constructed during an intensively nationalistic period that made the meaning attributed to it unambiguous. In contrast, the Women's Monument did not bear the mark of nationalism and had to "grow" into the movement; its meaning had to be reassigned. Moreover, the Great Trek represented a preeminently successful period in Afrikaner history with the establishment of independent Boer Republics in the interior, while the South African War, despite the endurance of the bitterenders and the sacrifices of the women, ultimately represented defeat; it constituted a period of suffering that would serve as a constant reminder of past grievances and therefore did not lend itself to celebration.[50]

The refiguring of the meaning associated with the Women's Monument points to the instability of collective memory and its vulnerability, as well as the silences, denials, and sublimations traumas produce.[51] This process can take place over several years and the passing of time does not significantly erode memories of social upheaval. Through oral transmissions and literature, memories of the South African War and the deprivations of inmates in the concentration camps were kept alive.[52]

While memories of the camps were often a salient feature of Afrikaner historical consciousness at least until the 1950s, of particular interest is the way different generations dealt with and remade the meaning of what they perceived the Women's Monument to represent. Collective memory has to operate in an ever-changing present and its dynamics are determined by the political and social boundaries of the day. Somewhat ironically, the generation that experienced social trauma firsthand may be less inclined to react vigorously, and it is left to the next generation to redress the wrongs of the past. In a general survey of war memories and their impact, it has been found that "youthful experience of a particular event or change often focuses memories on the direct personal implications of the experience, whereas the attribution of some larger political meaning to the event is more likely to be made by those who did not experience it during their adolescence or early childhood."[53]

As far as memories of the Women's Monument are concerned, it is significant that the generation that bore the brunt of the South African War, even though it harbored many bitter feelings, generally did not publicly object to the muted political meanings initially attributed to the Monument. This generation was still in the process of recovery after the war and, as the ill-fated rebellion of 1914 orchestrated by certain elements of Afrikanerdom proved, it lacked the capacity to change the new order. It was left to a younger generation to interpret the meaning of the Monument anew, and in

a much more robust fashion, during the resurgence of Afrikaner nationalism in the 1930s and 1940s. Following a constitutional route, as opposed to
the armed resistance of the rebels in 1914, it was also this generation that in
1948 successfully managed to reclaim what they had lost in 1902.

The different political context also brought a changed emphasis on the
Women's Monument as a monument for women. Whereas the position of
women was the focus of concern during the unveiling of the monument in
1913, subsequent brochures and other material interpreting the symbolism of the statues increasingly depicted the role of women as singularly in
the service of male nationalism. It was often no longer a case of honoring
women *per se,* but one of yoking them to another project in which they were
represented as silent victims who sacrificed their lives on the altar of freedom and love of the fatherland.[54] Although one should guard against a
timeless notion of the *volksmoeder* in Afrikaner circles, there is considerable
merit in the argument that during the era of rampant nationalism women
became a muted group, often unwittingly, as they were entrapped by the
rhetoric of a "greater cause," which had the effect of locking them "into a
confinement that suited Afrikaner patriarchy."[55]

The aesthetic, genderized ideology of the Women's Monument also
changed over time. Initially no men featured in the representation and the
surrounding precinct. In 1916, however, Steyn, as the last president of the
Orange Free State, was buried at the base of the obelisk. In 1922, it also
became the last resting place of the war hero, Christiaan de Wet, and of J. D.
Kestell, "the man of God," in 1941. These additions meant that the Monument had become, partially at least, a more inclusive South African War
memorial. After the burials of President Steyn, General De Wet, and Rev.
Kestell, Mrs. Steyn was particularly concerned that the area surrounding the
Monument not be turned into a cemetery for Afrikaner luminaries, as it
would detract from the focal point—the women and children who had died
in the camps. In 1926, however, it was acceptable to inter Emily Hobhouse's
ashes at the foot of the monument. Mrs. Steyn did not want to be buried
there, but her wish was ignored and she was laid to rest next to her husband
in 1955. Dr. D. F. Malan, the National Party prime minister until 1954, argued
that Mrs. Steyn was the last link with the Boer Republics and that the "volk"
wanted to see the symbolism complete by burying her among the prominent
Afrikaner leaders of a bygone era.[56] Ultimately, the male nationalism of the
time prevailed even in death.

As Afrikaner nationalism and apartheid developed in the post-1948 period,
messages and meanings that could contradict the creed had to be expunged
from the historical record. This brought a diminution of the role of people

like Emily Hobhouse. In the 1960s, Hobhouse's universalist message of womanhood, which she delivered at the unveiling of the Women's Monument, was played down. "In the hands of Afrikaner nationalist ideologues," Elsabe Brink has argued, "Hobhouse's material, which she had placed in the context of a broad and non-sectarian vision of womanhood, was taken from its general framework and applied parochially to the role of women in Afrikaner society."[57] Moreover, in brochures on the monument that reproduced Hobhouse's speech of 1913, her reference to black concentration camps was omitted.[58] The legacy and memories of the camps were deemed to be a whites-only preserve.

From the 1960s onward the cultural terrain of the Women's Monument gradually changed as it became a more general site commemorating the South African War. Cultural organizations used their resources to shore up the "absent male" statue space. Such "transgressions" on the terrain originally dedicated to women and children—"the sainted Dead"—occurred with the erection of statues calling into remembrance burghers going on commando, bitterenders, and prisoners of war.[59] One can argue that these additions complemented the Women's Monument, but that in itself would be an admission that the focal point has shifted.

While the process of assigning meaning to and remaking Afrikaner memory of the South African War as embodied in the Women's Monument took place under white governments and patronage for the greater part of the twentieth century, at the centenary of the war cultural brokerage has to be conducted in a political context that has changed significantly under the predominantly black government that has ruled South Africa since 1994. Such an eventuality was unforeseen by the majority of whites, and certainly by the Afrikaner cultural entrepreneurs and custodians of the memory of the war. Since 1994, black claims and perspectives long officially neglected in public life have had to be grafted onto and integrated into a less than receptive, congealed body of historical and cultural understanding. Pertinent in this respect is the question of how to commemorate the more than 14,000 black people who died in separate concentration camps during the South African War. The long history of selective commemoration is now under threat, but as yet it is too early to tell how the new cultural and commemorative map of the South African War will be constructed.

Notes

1. P. Carrier, "Historical Traces of the Present: The Uses of Commemoration," *Historical Reflections* 22, no. 2 (1996): 435.

2. S. B. Spies, *Methods of Barbarism? Roberts and Kitchener and Civilians in the Boer Republics, January 1900–May 1902* (Cape Town, 1977), 265.

3. See E. van Heyningen, "The Diary as Historical Source: A Response," *Historia* 38, no. 1 (1993): 24.

4. J. Fentress and C. Wickham, *Social Memory: New Perspectives on the Past* (London, 1992), 141.

5. E. Hobhouse, *War without Glamour: Women's War Experiences Written by Themselves, 1899–1902* (London, 1924), ii.

6. E. L. Cloete, "Frontierswomen as Volksmoeders: Textual Invocations in Two Centuries of Writing" (M.A. thesis, University of South Africa, 1994), 109.

7. J. Damousi and M. Lake (eds.), *Gender and War: Australians at War in the Twentieth Century* (Cambridge, 1995), 306.

8. P.J.J. Prinsloo, "Die Oorsprong Van die Ideaal om 'n Monument ter ere Van die Voortrekkers op te Rig," *Historia* 4, no. 1 (1996): 62–73; E. Delmont, "The Voortrekker Monument: Monolith to Myth," *South African Historical Journal* 29 (1993): 70–102.

9. E.J.J. Truter, "Rachel Isabella Steyn, 1905–1955" (Doctoral dissertation, University of South Africa, 1994), 59. A revised and expanded version of this thesis has been published as *Tibbie Rachel Isabella Steyn, 1865–1955: Haar Lewe Was Haar Boodskap* (Cape Town, 1997).

10. M.C.E. van Schoor, *Die Nasionale Vrouemonument* (Bloemfontein, 1993), 6; N. J. van der Merwe, *The National Women's Monument* (Bloemfontein, n.d.; first edition probably published between 1926 and 1941), 17.

11. Van der Merwe, *National Women's Monument*, 14.

12. N. J. van der Merwe, *Marthinus Theunis Steyn*, vol. 2 (Bloemfontein, 1921), 165; Truter, *Steyn*, 59–60; Van Schoor, *Vrouemonument*, 6; *De Volkstem*, 20 December 1908.

13. Van der Merwe, *National Women's Monument*, 17.

14. E. Cloete, "Afrikaner Identity: Culture, Tradition and Gender," *Agenda* 13 (1992): 15.

15. N. Glazer, "Monuments in an Age without Heroes," *The Public Interest* 123 (1996): 25.

16. C. Landman, *The Piety of Afrikaner Women: Diaries of Guilt* (Pretoria, 1994), 4, 19.

17. R. van Reenen (ed.), *Emily Hobhouse: Boer War Letters* (Cape Town, 1984), 112.

18. Ibid.

19. Letter from Emily Hobhouse to Mrs. Steyn, 5 April 1912, in van Reenen, *Hobhouse*, 513–14.

20. Van der Merwe, *Steyn*, vol. 2, 131 (my translation).

21. J. Snyman, "Suffering and the Politics of Memory," in C. W. du Toit (ed.), *New Modes of Thinking on the Eve of a New Century: South African Perspectives* (Pretoria, 1995), 131.

22. N. Kruger, *Rachel Isabella Steyn: Presidentsvrou* (Cape Town, 1949), 93 (my translation).

23. *The Friend*, 17 December 1913.

24. Letter from Hobhouse to Mrs. Steyn, 30 October 1913, in van Reenen, *Hobhouse*, 395–96.

25. For example, I. Hexham, *The Ivory of Apartheid: The Struggle for National Independence of Afrikaner Calvinism against British Imperialism* (New York, 1981), 23–24; J. J. Oberholster, *Die Nasionale Vrouemonument, Bloemfontein* (Bloemfontein, 1961), 20.

26. On this see, for example, G. D. Scholtz, *Die Ontwikkeling van die Politieke Denke van die Afrikaner, Vol. 6: 1910–1924* (Johannesburg, 1979), 12–122.

27. N. G. Garson, "'Het Volk': The Botha-Smuts Party in the Transvaal, 1904–1911," *Historical Journal* 9, no. 1 (1966): 101–32; N. G. Garson, "Louis Botha or John X Merriman: The Choice of South Africa's First Prime Minister," in *Commonwealth Papers*, vol. 12, University of London, 1969, 1–47.

28. Letter from A. Louw to M. T. Steyn, 3 July 1907, in Free State Archives, M. T. Steyn Collection, A156/11/5.

29. Van der Merwe, *Steyn*, vol. 2, 165–68.

30. Kruger, *Steyn*, 94–95.

31. Letter from C. Brits to M. T. Steyn, 3 November 1913, in Free State Archives, M. T. Steyn Collection, A156/1/1/8.

32. Letter from Hobhouse to Smuts, 20 August 1913, in van Reenen, *Hobhouse*, 394.

33. *The Transvaal Leader*, 18 December 1913.

34. *The Friend*, 17 December 1913.

35. *De Kerkbode*, 18 December 1913 (my translation).

36. *The Friend*, 18 December 1913.

37. Ibid., 17 December 1913.

38. Letter from Merriman to M. T. Steyn, 17 December 1913, in Free State Archives, M. T. Steyn Collection, A156/1/1/8.

39. *The Friend*, 17 December 1913.

40. Ibid.

41. Ibid.

42. Letter from C. F. Beyers to M. T. Steyn, 3 October 1913, in Free State Archives, M. T. Steyn Collection, A156/1/1/8.

43. I. Hofmeyr, "Building a Nation from Words: Afrikaans Language, Literature and Ethnic Identity, 1902–1924," in S. Marks and S. Trapido (eds.), *The Politics of Race, Class and Nationalism in Twentieth-Century South Africa* (London, 1987), 109.

44. The standard works on Afrikaner nationalism are D. Moodie, *The Rise of Afrikanerdom: Power, Apartheid and the Afrikaner Civil Religion* (Berkeley, 1975); H. Adam and H. Giliomee, *The Rise of Afrikaner Power* (Cape Town, 1979); D. O'Meara, *Volkskapitalisme: Class, Capital and Ideology in the Development of Afrikaner Nationalism, 1934–1948* (Johannesburg, 1983). For a contemporary perspective on urbanization and its social effects, see J. R. Albertyn, P. du Toit, and H. S. Theron, *Kerk en Stad* (Stellenbosch, 1948).

45. S. Raal, *Met die Boere in die Veld* (Cape Town, 1937), preface. The Afrikaner literature on the war in the 1930s and 1940s is discussed more fully in A. Grundlingh, "War, Wordsmiths and the 'Volk': Afrikaans Historical Writing on the Anglo-Boer

War of 1899–1902 and the War in Afrikaner Nationalist Consciousness, 1902–1990," in E. Lehmann and E. Reckwitz (eds.), *Mfecane to Boer War: Versions of South African History* (Essen, 1992), 45–47.

46. Quoted in Moodie, *Afrikanerdom,* 192–93.

47. Van Schoor, *Die Nasionale Vrouemonument,* 27.

48. M. de Villiers, *White Tribe Dreaming: Apartheid's Bitter Roots as Witnessed by Eight Generations of an Afrikaner Family* (Toronto, 1989), 237.

49. Compare A. Grundlingh and H. Sapire, "From Feverish Festival to Repetitive Ritual? The Changing Fortunes of Great Trek Mythology in an Industrialising South Africa, 1938–1988," *South African Historical Journal* 21 (1989): 19–37.

50. Grundlingh, "War, Wordsmiths," 48.

51. On the fluidity of collective memory, see S. Robins, "Silence in My Father's House: Memory, Nationalism, and Narratives of the Body," in S. Nuttall and C. Coetzee (eds.), *Negotiating the Past: The Making of Memory in South Africa* (Cape Town, 1998), 125.

52. Snyman, "Politics of Memory," 131.

53. M. Kammen, "Frames of Remembrance," *History and Theory* 34, no. 3 (1995): 255.

54. Compare Cloete, "Frontierswomen as Volksmoeders," 111. For one such brochure, see Van der Merwe, *National Women's Monument,* passim.

55. Cloete, "Frontierswomen as Volksmoeders," 111–12.

56. Van Schoor, *Die Nasionale Vrouemonument,* 17.

57. E. Brink, "Man-Made Women: Gender, Class and Ideology of the *Volksmoeder,*" in C. Walker (ed.), *Women and Gender in Southern Africa to 1945* (Cape Town, 1990), 279.

58. Snyman, "Politics of Memory," 137–38.

59. Cloete, "Frontierswomen as Volksmoeders," 119.

CHAPTER 3

Gentlemen and Boers

Afrikaner Nationalism, Gender, and Colonial Warfare in the South African War

HELEN BRADFORD

AT THE CENTENARY of the South African War, scholars have demonstrated some frustration with its historiography. Called to revisit "the really seminal questions of the 1899–1902 years," they have placed three issues on the agenda: using more Dutch and Afrikaans sources to re-examine Afrikaner attitudes; exploring British imperialism in broader Africa; and—rarely seen as a "seminal" question—addressing the neglect of women.[1]

The issue of sources arises in the context of anglophone texts that rely heavily, often entirely, on records in English. This has attractions: "the records on the British side are so much richer and more extensive, and in English."[2] Yet heavy reliance on sources with an inherent gender and imperial bias has deeply scarred many texts—and listening more carefully to the conquered, in their non-English languages, is indeed critical.

What of the call to revisit Afrikaner views and nationalism? This, too, seems crucial—and can be extended to exploring Boer views, almost unknown terrain in a historiography that has tended to assume "Boers" and "Afrikaners" were synonyms. Yet the long historical trek through which "Boers" (farmers) became "Afrikaners" was not over in 1899. In 1900 in the Transvaal, a foreigner was told how to tell Boers from Afrikaners: Boers lived on farms; Afrikaners lived in cities, and were mainly educated at the (aptly named) Victoria College in the Cape.[3] The missionaries of Afrikaner nationalism, like their African counterparts, tended to be multilingual, urbanized, middle-class men, trying to convert rural communities. During a war in which farms—the material base of Boer identity—were devastated, this mission achieved startling success. But if historians are to analyze *why* this war "did more than anything else to fire the furnace of Afrikaner nationalism," it is important to move beyond the elite into a world where "Boers" and "Afrikaners" were not synonyms.[4]

Men and humanity, too, have been regarded as one and the same. This well-known problem in Western history has, however, a distinctive twist in war stories: the absence of women relates to "how war gets defined (where *is* the front?)."[5] "War," in South African and other war historiography, has typically revolved around actual or potential clashes between armed men. "[G]eneric war stories are masculine," concludes an Australian scholar. "In these gender-biased narratives, men's war occurs in a space in which women ... are a rarity, and the drama is the emotional and technological adventures of soldiering."[6]

These insights can be extended. In most South African war tales, activities, spaces, and identities with markers of *valorized* adult masculinity have been highlighted; those with the sign of aberrant masculinity have been neglected. The privileged perspective is that of the "real *man*" connected to armed combat.[7] It is not that of "weaklings."[8] It is not that of husbands. It is not that of Tommy Atkins or African men enthusiastically descending on feminized spaces to loot cattle, blind sheep, hang cats, hack slices off pigs, fire houses and load black and Boer civilians into carts destined for concentration camps. This was "the occupation of most British troops" for most of the South African War, the "principal activity of the British Army." For rank and file participants, it was a way of affirming masculinity; for Boers, it was a "War Against Women."[9] Nonetheless, in almost all texts, a veil has been drawn over these activities, a veil urged by Victorian gentlemen, for whom these practices were either odious to "chivalrous Englishmen" ("things which later on we had better hide in decent oblivion"), or not "real war" (because they were police work, or because "methods of barbarism" meant, as the famous indictment ran, that war conducted on these lines was "not a war"[10]). Following Victorian gentlemen's definitions of "real war"—not those of feminists positing injuring and terrorizing as defining features of any war—historians have overwhelmingly shied away from a definition of war highlighting what the imperial army did most of the time: terrorize unarmed people, in feminized spaces.[11]

Yet this was how the imperial army waged wars of colonial conquest in Africa. Firing homes, looting stock, and destroying crops was the standard way of suppressing resistance. Similar patterns were evident in Asia. Moreover, victory achieved by these means allowed Victorian men to become soldier heroes, quintessential representatives of imperial masculinity and the nation.[12]

Frederick Roberts's first command from 1878 to 1880, for example, involved invading and occupying Afghanistan. The invasion badly damaged Indian agriculture due to mass requisitioning of stock; rebellious Afghan villages were razed *en route*. The occupation involved hanging rebels, expropriating grain, and conducting an epic march to Kandahar that "might have been likened to Sherman's march through Georgia."[13] It also turned "Butcher Roberts" into a national hero. His horse received the Afghan War Medal. He was lauded as "*a man*" by the Oxford Vice Chancellor, who awarded him an honorary degree.[14] He became Commander-in-Chief in India. In 1900, he became Commander-in-Chief in South Africa. He was allegedly "the greatest British soldier of the century between Waterloo and the world wars."[15]

A wider geographical and a longer historical perspective than the standard "1899–1902 years" is thus crucial in analyzing imperialism and the masculinities implicated in it. "Butcher Roberts" was injected into this conquest of two African states as Lord Roberts of Kandahar, carrying his Kandahar sword, surrounded by staff and generals from Kabul days, talking to regiments about their glorious Afghanistan past.[16] On the imperial (and the Boer) side, the South African War was awash with men who moved from one colonial war to the next. In the immediate 1896–99 pasts of many soldiers of the empire were experiences in crushing the revolt in Rhodesia (through scorched earth aimed at starving Africans into submission); in conquering the Sudan (when Lord Kitchener looted, sanctioned looting, and favored starvation as a weapon of war); in crushing the uprising on India's northwestern frontier (by razing the countryside, leaving a trail of people who starved or died from exposure). The Boers "get into the hills much like the Afridis," remarked a corporal in 1899, referring to this last revolt: an ominous remark, since burning Afridi villages was legitimated because "assailants retire to the hills. . . . Only one remedy remains—their property must be destroyed."[17] Deploying fire, starvation, and expropriation as weapons of war was how many gentlemen mastered tribesmen. They used this arsenal whether natives fought pitched battles, guerrilla wars, or, as the Xhosa had cause to know, when natives were not fighting at all. Racialized otherness facilitated this—and the South African War, too, was seen as "a race war" against "savages," "a kind of nigger."[18] Alternatively, Boers were animals. The media led him to expect a creature, noted an Australian who thought he would find in Africa a cave man with "the principles of a gorilla.'"[19] Seeing Boers "reminds me irresistibly of a visit to the Zoological Gardens," stated an aristocrat.[20] That the text acclaimed as the single best account of the South African War represents Boers as beasts is no accident: this reproduces "knowledge" constructed under imperialism.[21]

In all, what follows seeks to engage with "seminal" issues already partly on the agenda: extending a national frame of reference to the broader imperial

world; transcending a gender-biased analytical framework at odds with
masculine practice; examining how Afrikaner nationalism became a popular force. It does so by examining the 1900 invasion and occupation of the
two Boer republics by troops commanded by "Butcher Roberts."

"A Sort of Sherman's March"

Homesteads were a target from the first day—February 11, 1900—the vanguard of the imperial army invaded the Orange Free State. At the first halt,
a farmhouse and African quarters were gutted. The men responsible scrawled
their nickname, "Tigers," over the farm door and rode on.[22]

In February, men on commando in the Free State saw other farmhouses
visited by what they called *vernielzucht* (lust of destruction). The Kimberley
and Paardeberg victories perhaps intensified this "lust." Wherever the English went, they destroyed, cried a Transvaal commandant near Kimberley.
Troops on the Paardeberg-Bloemfontein route were pillaging farms "in a
most barbaric manner," noted a Russian military attaché. "Everything was
stolen, spoilt or destroyed."[23] The devastation, claimed the *Manchester Guardian* correspondent of both the Kimberley and Paardeberg routes to Bloemfontein, was not mere looting. There was "wanton and savage" destruction,
"domestic outrages" on "the foundations of civilised life."[24]

According to South African War historiography, almost none of this
happened. The "gentleman's war," or "conventional warfare," lasting until at
least mid-1900,[25] is construed as very different from the "distasteful," "most
unpleasant" phase of guerrilla war.[26] In the gentlemanly period, little or no
destruction occurred. Instead, Roberts urged burghers to surrender with
lenient measures, with a "kid-glove policy," assuring them their property
and persons would be safe if they swore an oath of neutrality and laid down
their arms.[27] Very many Boer men "voluntarily surrendered ... in response"
to this "velvet-glove policy," becoming *hendsoppers* (hands-uppers).[28] "Lured
by British promises of peace and protection, large numbers of burghers laid
down their weapons."[29]

Up to May 31, 1900, Roberts's proclamations did promise security of
property and person to most civilians and *hendsoppers*. Yet his promises—
more accurately, those of Sir Alfred Milner, the High Commissioner for
South Africa, who was responsible for the "leniency"—were largely nullified
in practice.

First, after Boer invasion and looting in the Cape and Natal in 1899, after
Boer victories, support for *implementing* leniency was minimal. The "black
week" defeats fractured the assumed link between imperial masculinity,

military superiority, and British supremacy—and, as Winston Churchill mourned, vindictiveness ruled. Immediately after these defeats, the Colonial Secretary asked if a force could be sent through the Free State on "a sort of Sherman's march through Georgia."[30] Retribution through devastation was being considered long before guerrilla war. It would be suicidal to apply international law for "*Civilised* nations" to Boers, scoffed the Commander-in-Chief at the War Office; as a race, they were worse than "the Kaffir."[31] Three days after invading the Free State, Roberts declared that he intended to confiscate the property of all Boers absent from their farms. This proclamation was printed, then vetoed in London; but there was more than one way to skin a Boer cat. When Roberts occupied Bloemfontein, a local ruling stated that unless they surrendered, all men within a ten-mile radius risked loss of their property. Threatening the possessions—or persons—of primitive upstarts challenging British supremacy had considerable social support (and occurred in Natal *before* war was declared). The Russian military attaché noted that he had witnessed "the most disgusting scenes of plunder and did not on any one occasion see any officer intervening."[32] "*The whole Nation has its relatives in the field,* and gets sulky if the Generals sacrifice them … in misguided leniency," Milner was told. They "cry out for the firmest measures of repression."[33]

Second, confiscating burgher (and other) property was an economic as well as a political desideratum. It took about a ton of provisions daily to keep a hundred men on active service. Supplies from imperial sources had to cross an ocean, dribble through crammed ports, and come overland via a single-track railway and wagons. Moreover, just before invading the Free State cross-country, Kitchener and Roberts abolished the decentralized transport and supply system, instituting a centralized one. To this, "one of the great blunders of the war," a Boer raid provided the *coup de grâce*.[34] Four days after the invasion, 3,000 oxen, 30,000 forage rations, and 150,000 soldiers' rations were ambushed. The advance proceeded by reducing men to half-rations and horses to starvation rations, and by recouping losses from civilians. The Director of Supplies, with two oxen to feed tens of thousands of men, offered troops payment for stock; 2,000 sheep and 600 cattle were handed to him the next day. Plentiful meat supplies continued thereafter. Days later, Roberts—whose depredations in India and Afghanistan come forcibly to mind—told officers to use local resources "to the fullest extent," and to appropriate them if they were not for sale or seemed unowned.[35]

Long after this debacle, officers troubled by the "eternal supply question" found the answer in these local resources, for which an army this size— some 80,000 men, 38,000 oxen, and 25,000 mules ultimately advanced on

Pretoria—had a gargantuan appetite.[36] Seven thousand men seeking fire-wood and food could camp on a farm. All animals capable of being ridden had to be requisitioned, Roberts ordered in April: the invasion was taking a colossal toll of horses and transport animals on starvation rations. In May, one of Roberts's Afghanistan disciples, needing food for 11,000 men and 12,000 animals, appropriated crops; he also required, as one day's supplies alone, 30,000 pounds of mealies, 13,000 pounds of flour, 400 pounds of salt and 2,500 pounds of sugar. He found that farmhouses contained insufficient flour, although meat was readily obtainable; the general passing through this district in his wake also ordered farm-to-farm visits to root out resources for his 4,000 hungry men. He was followed by more troops. As Boer women saw it, they were being stripped of maize, wagons, trek gear, horses, and for-age; they spoke of "wholesale robbery," of the "utter ruining of the country."[37] With various officers told to "Take as much as you can," some localities were "cleared" of all supplies.[38] This generated problems for troops in the rear. Flanking columns marching from Bloemfontein to Pretoria fed themselves with great difficulty; troops plundering her farm seemed starving, noted a Transvaal woman. "We were half-starved all the time," recalled one soldier of the entire war.[39] In many ways, the "eternal supply question" is a better key to analyzing this war than *koppies* lost and won.

Third, troops embellished official policy. Routine destruction occurred, as soldiers marched over crops, hacked down fences, and lit fires. Food and fuel were essentials in these epic marches, when penalties for looting were effectively fictitious, and power to appropriate could derive from guns. Houses provided firewood. "Sometimes you got part of a door, or a window-sash, or a flooring-board. A baby's cradle, the leg of a piano...."[40] Troops, overwhelmingly young and unmarried, in an institution designed to turn boys into men, could prove their masculinity through scorn for domesticity—and through "a *physical* identification with the quintessentially masculine ethos of empire."[41] Hard-bitten marauders created warrior guilds, charging "down on the farm across the flat veldt with all the blood-curdling cries that forty men of varied nationality can invent."[42] Moreover, injuries, ranging from defeats to alleged atrocities, had been committed against military manhood, necessitating revenge. One division recruited from the invaded eastern Cape was notorious for vengeful pillage. Looting was one of the "perpetual joys" of the "slum-bred" Tommy, claimed a middle-class "Tiger":

Not merely looting for profit, though I have seen Tommies take possession of the most ridiculous things—perambulators and sewing machines ... but looting for the sheer fun of destruction; tearing down pictures to kick their boots through them; smashing furniture for the fun of smashing it, and maybe dressing up in women's clothes to finish with; and dancing among the ruins they have made. To pick up a good heavy stone and send it *wallop* right through the works of a piano is a great moment for Tommy.[43]

It had been a great moment for many burghers engaged in similar vandalism in Natal in 1899; some Transvalers continued these practices in the Free State. Pillage in a state supposedly their ally generated calls for stern punishment from leaders. Yet looting continued to be "fun" for many men, of various ethnic and class origins, on both sides. Vandalism in Natal was not for the goods but for "the joy of ransacking other people's property," claimed an elite Afrikaner.[44] Rough people liked destroying what the poor did not own, argued another. Seldom, if ever, did men introduce gender, the common denominator, into their analyses. Yet the "lust" displayed by men able to exert mastery over feminized spaces, acting as brigands without fear of punishment, cries out for such analysis. "It's the boyish way of feeling like a 'man' all over the world, it seems."[45]

Empty houses facilitated vandalism: the great majority of farms pillaged on the routes to Bloemfontein had been abandoned. Rumors of rape had burgeoned; women were often acutely aware of their vulnerability to sexual violence. Loss of cattle was typically economically ruinous—and the prospect of having shells crashing through homes was an added incentive for flight. Thousands of refugees herding stock fell back before the advancing troops. The price attached was that soldiers often assumed that absent men must be on commando and that looting was therefore legitimate. *Hendsoppers* risked destruction of their property if they were absent. A mother who fled was only hours away when "thousands of khakis . . . destroyed everything."[46]

Fourth, resources were destroyed for military reasons. From March, as their commissariat collapsed, men on commando were heavily dependent on local supplies. Boer women were deeply implicated in fighting this war; colonizers recognized this months before deciding men were guerrillas. Women were told why "every bit of forage, and food, and mealies" was being wrecked or confiscated: so they "had nothing to give Boers if they came."[47]

Finally, various offenses elicited punishment. Men were arrested for such crimes as trampling on the Queen's portrait. If Boers fought on a farm, the farm could be burned or stripped of all movable goods: a harsh punishment when many farms, thousands of acres in extent, doubled as battlefields. Starvation loomed among (white) women and children, warned a press correspondent alarmed by the number of burned homesteads; Roberts's military

secretary agreed. In the adjacent northern Cape, arson was the penalty for
rebellion against British rule. Punishment was taking "a wild form," stated
the *Guardian* correspondent, who was disconcerted by male exultation during the burning of six rebel farmhouses in an afternoon. He implicitly outlined the gendering occurring as men exercised mastery over women and
homes. Troops, yelling "cries of vengeance," were engaging in "an exhibition
of power"; a "kind of domestic murder" seemed involved as flames con-
sumed "the chairs and tables, the baby's cradle...."[48]

By May, very many farms had been wrecked, very many urban houses
pillaged. The prescient Cape politician J. X. Merriman condemned the "burning, plundering and turning helpless women and children adrift in this
winter weather, doing as Weyler did when he made the *reconcentrados* [con-
centration camps] in Cuba."[49] A note of panic entered Boer leaders' assessments: Transvalers were warned that everything in occupied areas was being
destroyed. "From end to end the Orange River Colony lies ruined and starving," stated a British newspaper on May 28, the day the republic was annexed
and immediately placed under martial law.[50] This was journalistic license,
but confiscation of property was so standard that the May 31 proclamation
encouraging surrenders in the Transvaal differed from its Free State counterparts. *Hendsoppers* were promised only that they would not be imprisoned.
The declaration that their property would not be seized had disappeared.

In all, conventional warfare in the Orange Free State was conventional
in a colonial sense as well. To take at face value proclamations protecting
property and persons, to excise the draconian punishments and wrecked
farms providing a proving ground for an anarchic masculinity, is to misrepresent this war of colonial conquest. The motives of officers and troops
alike were tightly tied to acquiring supplies and suppressing resistance—and
to their gendered desires for exhibitions of mastery or revenge. The savage
vernielzucht displayed by a parasitic, all-male imperial army shocked numerous observers—and was of profound significance to Boer men.

"An Intensely Domestic People": Boer Men, February to May 1900

"[I]t is a well-known fact," declared General Smuts during the war, "that the
Boers are an intensely domestic people," deeply attached to their families
and homes.[51] This is less well known today, due not least to a historiography
that assumes men, unlike women, can be analyzed in isolation from the
opposite sex. Nonetheless, Boer men's domesticity was proverbial; their dia-
lect term for "man" also meant "husband." These parochial loyalties profoundly affected the South African War; they were in sharp tension with a

broader nationalism. Persuading Boer patriarchs oriented to farm and family to identify with the cause of urban-based states, manned by professionals like the Cambridge graduate Smuts or the London-educated President Steyn of the Free State, was a battle.

This was exacerbated because Boer men were not "soldiers," as some scholars have conceptualized them.[52] They *volunteered* for any battle. Nor, despite efforts to explain British defeats by invoking Boers' other masculine attributes, were Free Staters, not mobilized for war for forty years, best seen as "crack-shots."[53] Burgher masculinity cannot be squeezed into these imperial images of "real frontier men": Boers called themselves and acted like farmers, republicans, or family men. Whatever military skills they possessed— and there were many Free Staters who expected Transvalers to teach them how to fight—domestic concerns often dominated. The Free State Commandant General refused to participate in an attack that coincided with a cattle sale he was attending. "Kruger is certainly the president, but the *volk* is king," declared a Transvaler, riding home because his wife was sick.[54] Boer men, their domestic needs often tended by black men—about one in four men on commando was black—and/or by wives, children, and wagons loaded with comforts, were often reluctant to leave their temporary homes. The great majority could refuse to fight. "The one was sick, the other one tired, but the real cause was, that most did not want to get up so early," explained a commandant arriving for battle with three men.[55]

The invasion of the Free State, and the almost simultaneous reversal of military fortunes throughout South Africa, greatly intensified the reluctance to fight. The Boers were being put to rout by a numerically vastly superior army. Moreover, men were positioned as protectors of their families from other men. One Boer man declared that he went home to defend his wife from soldiers and his "insolent Kaffirs," well aware that the invasion had fueled African hopes for defeat of their own oppressors.[56] White male nightmares about a black fifth column were compounded by gendered concerns about possessions. Husbands, not wives, legally controlled all familial property. Men, not women, were traditionally associated with cattle and crops. Numerous Free Staters went home in March because they feared confiscation of their property; Transvalers, "all hurrying to Transvaal to protect there," also wanted to gather in harvests, to locate winter grazing.[57]

Consequently, commandos melted away. One Free State field-cornet commanded two hundred men in early March; by mid-March he led eight, seven of whom were youths. The "great majority thought more of their farms, their families and their private affairs than of the fate of the Republics," noted Smuts.[58] Or as Milner saw it, the "Boer on the veld" cared intensely about his farm and his supremacy over *the Natives;* that he cared greatly about his *volk* or state "is a fiction of the political Afrikaners."[59]

As the fiction dissolved, an emergent younger generation of Afrikaner leaders floundered. The most innovative response of these urban professionals or landlord-Parliamentarians derived from Christiaan de Wet, the upwardly mobile backvelder, the new Free State Commandant General. As commandos collapsed, De Wet, notorious for his *machismo,* with all its Boer inflections, granted home leave to every man. He could not corner a hare with reluctant hounds, he told his shocked Transvaal counterpart.[60]

The politics of war was deeply entwined with gender politics (as it would be in Kenya: "Mau Mau issued many more statements about the nature and proper organization of marriage than it did about land or freedom"[61]). Typically, Afrikaner leaders, often located in patriarchal configurations that differed from those of the Boers, tried to force through what, historically, had never occurred outside their own elite circles: the demarcation of "home" as a feminine domain, the splitting-off of men from domestic concerns. By (again) banning women from laagers, they tried to pack them off to defend homes. "*Mannen, Broeders!*" on the other hand had to fight like men, to regard commandos as a family of *broeders,* to sacrifice property and families for Afrikanerdom. Men reluctant to fight were *bangbroeke:* "I wish the British would catch and castrate every one of them, so that they may be old women in reality," shouted De Wet.[62] Brute force underpinned the politics of masculinity: the *sjambok,* draconian threats.

Some responded, but most black men left commandos. So did two out of three white men. Some 40 percent of burghers mobilized at the start of the South African War surrendered between March and July 1900. It was almost impossible to hear a patriotic word, noted a Dutch volunteer; every man seemed only too glad to exchange war for home. Men were greatly affected by the rumor "that those farms which are left without a master, will be treated as war booty," reported a Russian military attaché.[63] "Rumours again did the rounds that the approaching enemy respected neither family members nor private property," reported a Transvaler as his commando retreated to its home district and disintegrated. "Now that the enemy was almost on the farms, patriotism faded away."[64] The class dimensions of this collapse have interested anglophone historians. The division between "*bittereinders*— the irreconcilables who had fought to the end of the War—and the *hendsoppers*—those burghers who had betrayed their country's cause … coincided by and large with that between landed and landless." [65] Yet contemporaries failed to see a pattern of landed men staying on commando. They, unlike historians, noticed confiscation of property and the prominence of notables among those who fled or surrendered. Many wealthy farmers, officers, and middle-class men were the first to abandon the cause, they commented. "The richer Boers in particular remain surreptitiously at home, because they after all have something to lose!'"[66] Poor people were refusing to fight, declared a small Transvaal farmer, because rich people "just stay at home and farm."[67]

Yet class wisdom should not be stood on its head. Landless Boers typically owned movable goods; men owning any property at all had motive to desert. Free Staters fled home to save cattle; men abandoned the cause for "just a few worldly possessions."[68] Generational differences, differences in relationships to women, were more significant than class. Patriarchs, "not daring to leave their wives and daughters at the mercy of soldiers," peeled away faster than youths.[69] *Penkoppe* (young bulls) lacked property or paternalist obligations, and, like black youths in Rhodesia, could exploit war to assert their virility.[70]

In all, the fraternity splintered on the rock of propertied patriarchs. The lure of a velvet glove was less significant than the fear of hostile men threatening jealously guarded domestic spheres: a core component of Boer manhood. Generals, tackling this much more substantive problem with alien gender ideologies, could do little to stem the hemorrhage. Transvaal forces were almost nonexistent in early June; Kruger teetered on the brink of surrender. "I have knocked the bottom out of 'the Great Afrikaander nation' forever and ever, Amen," rejoiced Milner.[71]

He had not. Historians have offered a Real Man Theory of History as explanation. De Wet, with his "hunter's eyes," singlehandedly changed the Anglo-Boer War.[72] Outstanding in his "tenacity," he attacked in his "ledgendary" (*sic*) style; under "the inspirational influence of pres. Steyn and genl. Christiaan de Wet many waverers ... acquired new courage"; in June, Steyn and De Wet "stood firm."[73] Military leadership had been assumed by "men of vision, boldness and determination"; the "soldiers" returned.[74] There is a less masculinist reading.

Bittereinde *Women, February to May 1900*

"Remember," urged a historian in March, this was not a European war. Eurocentric gender stereotypes were inapplicable: "the *women* are the fiercest advocates of war to the bitter end. For independence the Boer women will send husbands and son after son to fight to the last."[75]

A longer historical perspective is badly needed to explain what contemporaries saw: anti-imperialism had a gender gap. In the Transvaal, this long predated this war; in 1899, again, Boer women took the lead in opposing British aggression, threatening to take up arms if men were too timid.[76] Fierce anti-imperialism was also evident among Free State women: gendered incorporation into a capitalizing world is perhaps a partial explanation. The Boer man, noted a Bloemfontein observer, went to town, traded with the Englishman and learned to tolerate him; the Boer woman, isolated on her farm, nursed "intense hatred of the Englishman, which she looks upon as part of her religion."[77] But the reasons for this apparent gender gap have yet to be explored. They are not illuminated in the literature on pre–South African War Afrikaner nationalism or on the origins of the war, which typically neglects women, and not infrequently assumes all "people" were "men."[78]

If a gender gap preceded 1899, the war prised it open. First, imperial relegation of white women to subpolitical status gave them, ironically, political privileges. Women did not have to take oaths of neutrality or surrender their guns. Women were not being imprisoned for flaunting republican sympathies (the politically active found Eurocentric gender stereotypes very useful). Second, a war that emasculated many burghers—that stripped them of property, arms, ability to keep hostile men away from "their" women— spawned female heads of household, female trekkers, female wielders of revolvers against troops invading homes, female farmers feeding commandos. Admiring (or shocked) accounts of this gender inversion often noted that women farmed at least as well as men. This meant a husband could bluntly be told there was no need "for his presence on the farm and that he could remain where he was."[79] Third, while Boers were seen as the most Bible-reading people in the world, the sexes were positioned differently in relation to God. Many a woman, stripped of male protectors, shifted her hope to an Almighty masculine deliverer. He could literally replace men (one prayed to God who "promised to be a husband to me"[80]). If Boer women preferred the death of husbands and sons to surrender, this was partly because they had "an unconquerable faith" in a male Almighty.[81]

Due to their sex and their centrality in domestic economies, Boer women often felt quite concretely the dystopia of replacing one male-only colonial state with another. In the western Free State, many refugees returned to violated homesteads. In the east, it "was as if hell was let loose" as thousands of "civilised barbarians" pillaged and burned the harvest that had cost so much female labor.[82] "God would punish the damned English for their robbery and violence," cried the general manager of a farm to troops commandeering her horses. Her father remained silent as she redoubled her curses when an officer suggested burning the farm.[83] In the Transvaal, women panicked by Free State depredations mobilized "sisters" against looming conquest:

"Our country, our houses and also we and our daughters will be laid waste (*verwoes*)."[84] Male deaths at khaki hands also generated bitterness. She would dash her daughter's "brains against the door-post" rather than have her marry "one of your English," swore a bereaved mother.[85] There was a violent edge to female hostility toward imperial penetration of domestic domains; it contrasted starkly with the acquiescence of many patriarchs to British rule. Troops began expressing unease about the depth of female hatred, warning that the "Boer woman—strong, fierce, and uncompromising—is a force to be reckoned with."[86]

Colonial spaces were being changed into hostile zones by black as well as khaki men. Many settler women struggling to replace white men at the pinnacle of racial hierarchies found themselves challenged from above and below. Repressive apparatuses had been weakened by the outflow of armed men and the inflow of occupying forces supporting retaliation on a common enemy. "The (black) people were not as faithful and good as when the *baas* was there," mourned one, expressing a common grievance.[87] African men looted stock, cried a teacher, who vainly mounted guard with a gun, despite not knowing how to shoot. Unlike burghers, who fairly easily maintained the subordination of black men on commando, white women were disadvantaged by gender in trying to uphold older relations of racialized authority—especially when occupying forces were obliging them to carry a pass "just like a kaffir."[88] Consequently, and significantly, gender fueled their commitment to racist republican states, seemingly central in upholding white supremacy for non-English women. In the Transvaal, elite Afrikaner women singled out equality between black and white, and miscegenation, as the central meaning of conquest. "Sisters," cried one, "what will become of our whole race? We shall have to work for the English just as the Kaffirs work for us and ... shall hardly be treated as whites."[89]

Boer men, anxious about "Kaffirs" on their own farms, seemed far less concerned about overturn of the entire racial order. As they flooded home, many a Boer woman, with stern ideas about what it meant to be a white man, was deeply distressed. A minister's wife hostile to war noted that "so many women in the land are content (!) their men should be away" and were "so afraid any of theirs may come back!" A "red-hot" woman put her in her place: "there must be tooth & nail resistance."[90] If acceptable colonial hierarchies were to be recreated, then burghers had to fight.

Some women invoked disintegrating republican states to send "other" men back to war. For their "own" men, they resorted to gender politics: refusing to feed them, threatening to replace them on commando, taunting them for being less than men by being at home rather than fighting. Tales circulated about wives' injunctions. "Go and fight. I can get another husband, but not another Free State." "Remain and do your duty.... I can always find another husband, but not another Transvaal."[91] Men privileging their domestic identities, men placing family above nation-state, were being met by women opposed to exchanging their country for a patriarch at home. In demanding that the personal be subordinated to the political, Boer women had, however, the edge on generals: daily opportunities for gender politics, and the power to make what men had imagined as a refuge singularly unpleasant.

Thus De Wet, with his remarkably successful tactic legitimizing immersion in homes, was not solely or even largely responsible for male return to war. Women could construct gender; women could alter the balance of power between armed men. Many had already met retreating commandos with stony refusals to provide food or shelter, complaining they were being delivered into English hands by men failing to fire a single shot. It "was largely due to [women's] cooperating patriotism" that De Wet recruited some 1,500 men for his crucial Sannah's Post victory, claimed an observer; De Wet's influence was particularly great among women, due to his "triumphs over the enemies of their homes and country."[92] Men shamed by their womenfolk rejoined commandos, noted a nurse; women's tart remarks probably drove some Transvaal office workers into joining up in April, wrote one on commando; the "fanaticism of the women has done much to stiffen Boer aggression," warned a British officer; pressure from Boer women, the "*one* element ... that could deal with deserters in a much more effective manner than the government," was central in propelling men back into war, claims J. H. Breytenbach.[93]

Yet women were not massively successful in persuading men to return to the miseries of war. "Be quiet!" a Transvaal woman was told. "You have still seen nothing, and what we see, is dead and wounded, destruction and fleeing women."[94] In the Orange Free State, however, destruction was personalized: about a thousand men streamed back to fight from the southeast, where reprisals were particularly severe, after experiencing plunder of their farms or arbitrary arrests. Roberts, crowed De Wet, was the best man he had. In May, responding angrily to Kruger's urging that peace be made to prevent further devastation, Steyn grimly replied that too much property had already been destroyed.[95] Imperial troops waging war on homes, combined with women demanding compliance with racialized gender norms: *this* was the key dynamic underpinning Free State resurgence.

In the unoccupied Transvaal, the ironic alliance of "Butcher Roberts" and the Boer woman had yet to be forged. Here, in mass women-only meetings, in written appeals, elite urbanites called on women to drive back to war men who were skulking away and evading "the call of Manhood and Patriotism."[96] But many went beyond the politics of patriotic masculinity, inscribing feminist issues onto the nationalist agenda. Women should take up arms; an "Amazonian Corps of Afrikander Women" under a female general should be formed; women should take over male jobs to release combatants; if men still refused to fight, they should "doff male attire, and don that of the opposite sex."[97] Cowardly men could "look after the children at home." "One brave woman is worth more than a 100 cowardly men."[98] According to a man reporting secondhand—when women took over Pretoria's parliament, they excluded men to give women more freedom of speech—women wanted to go to the front to shoot men who retreated.[99]

Amazons, however, profoundly transgressed gender norms—and dominant ideas of Afrikaner national identity, which centered on masculine prowess against imperialist aggression. Members of both sexes recoiled from the image of women killing white men with Mausers. Many mothers declined to abandon their children for this "decidedly unwomanly" activity.[100] That men had Mausers and women did not was another defining feature of the gender order. Consequently, General Louis Botha told women simply to persuade the "weaker of our sex" to fight for the *volk's* independence.[101]

Most burghers declined to do this, settling for being seen as less than real men. Nonetheless, neither women nor domestic spaces can be omitted in satisfactorily accounting for why war did not end with invasion of the Transvaal. By the time the Transvaal generals and Kruger were urging peace on June 1, both Boer women and "Butcher Roberts" had made central contributions to creating *bittereinders* on whom Free State leaders could rely. Gender politics in homes and gendered warfare on homes were more important than generals with *machismo* for continuation of the war.

Creation of a Volk, *June to November 1900*

By September 1900, claimed a German fighting with Free Staters, the central event of the war had occurred: the birth of "a *volk* of *broeders.*"[102] By then, farm-burning had become standard practice. Arson and nationalism went hand in hand.

Since imperial supply problems continued, farm-burning occurred alongside ongoing pillage. In the western Transvaal, this alone—combined with African raids on farms—drove many Boers back to war.[103] But arson poses a problem of a different order. Why were so many people stripped of shelter as well as of resources useful to the imperial army or commandos?

In some analyses, this is not a problem: arson is positioned in a later period.[104] In others, the explanation for scorched earth and concentration camps centers on Boer military tactics. Arson was an "inevitable" response to guerrilla war.[105] The "success of the Boers' [guerrilla] tactics enforced draconian methods of reprisal" from September onward.[106] This was a "classic military strategy" in response to a "classic guerilla situation," a policy "probably as good as could be devised."[107] "With the onset of the guerilla phase in the War, Boer women and children—whom the commandos were unable to look after—were herded into camps."[108] Concentration camps were "a known, necessary—and hard—tactical expedient for a guerrilla war fought over hostile enemy territory."[109] This mainstream interpretation—like that concerning Maori lack of prowess in New Zealand wars—has acquired truth-status through repetition and through marginalization of contesting views: it has "*dominated* the exceptions."[110]

Yet the flaw in such arguments is evident from this same war. Guerrilla war was also waged in the Cape. This did not enforce arson and camps. Instead, the successful counterstrategy revolved around martial law and confiscating horses from civilians. Inability to acquire horses and a scrub-rather than grass-covered veld crippled Smuts's campaign. Arson was *not* inevitable—and deporting hundreds of thousands of civilians to concentration camps was an extraordinary measure; it did not occur in almost all preceding guerrilla wars, with the key exception of Cuba. Arson and internment, argue historians analyzing counter-guerrilla tactics, emerged as a standard response only after World War II. In the South African War, they were due to local specificities, not doctrine.[111]

An older history is less pious about the origins and intent of arson. "British officers who had served on the Indian frontier had been accustomed to the destruction of the towns and villages of the tribesmen as a normal act of war." Roberts, with forty-one years in the Indian Army, now used this as intimidation.[112] This had already occurred in the Free State and Cape; with the Free State a British colony, and both capitals occupied, its geographical range extended. This occurred *before* September, the usual dating of guerrilla war "proper."[113]

In the winter of 1900, the houses of men still fighting were targeted, especially in the Free State, where they were legally "rebels." "Many of the farmhouses are smoking ruins, the enemy, after annexation, being rebels."[114] Military leaders were targeted first; those who fed or sheltered fighters, failed to report Boer presence, or lived close to disrupted railways were also vulnerable. Moreover, firing farmhouses might simply seem a good idea: indiscriminate arson in the western Transvaal was probably due to a series of imperial defeats.[115]

Huis-aan-die-brand-steek (setting houses on fire) had great success. Many *bittereinders* and Boer women balked at being rendered homeless. The "spirit of unbelief walketh about like a roaring lion," cried Kruger.[116] Consciousness of unity as a *volk* was weak, preached a Free State minister; men should think of their *volk* instead of their self-interest. Again, many thought otherwise; thousands surrendered or fled. Commando leaders threatened deserters with death and intensified forcible recruitment. Roberts responded in kind. The death penalty was invoked for men breaking the oath of neutrality by returning to war. Burghers who did not take the oath became prisoners of war. So did all new *hendsoppers*. Numerous potential recruits—old men, young boys—were detained. New camps were established for the swelling numbers of men (and sometimes their families) seeking or obliged to accept internment.[117]

Simultaneously, a turning point, almost absent from the historiography, occurred in rural policies. With De Wet reduced to a paltry 2,500 fighters, with Steyn engaged in "the well-nigh hopeless cause of re-animating the demoralised burghers," with various branches of the imperial army preparing to leave, columns of occupation fanned out over the countryside.[118] They were mainly infantry; their prime task was not to fight. "The British walked where they pleased, and the Boers rode where they pleased, and, under such conditions, the campaign might have continued for ten years."[119] Conditions, however, could be altered. A stream of draconian metropolitan proposals, including *reconcentrados,* explored ways of finalizing conquest. But the imperial past provided enough examples of "pacification by police methods" without resorting to Spanish examples. In late August, just before a pitched battle reduced Botha to 2,500 men, every commander was told to ensure there were no means of subsistence for a commando infiltrating his zone.[120]

One officer objected: Africans and well-disposed whites would starve. Another, committed to "starvation as a lever to bring the recalcitrant fanatics to their senses," had starvation of Boer supporters alone in mind. All their stock, from poultry to oxen, together with all their inanimate goods, should be destroyed or removed; all their houses should be burnt; men should submit or "see their families starve."[121] Yet Roberts was losing metropolitan popularity as a result of his alleged leniency; he and other generals experienced in colonial warfare were becoming firmly committed to *wholesale* expropriation. "Clear the whole of supplies," ordered this aristocratic general in September, when the Transvaal became a colony. If "small, and in very many cases, insignificant bodies of men" chose to fight, "they and their families will be starved." He would "starve into submission" the remaining "banditti," he wrote; it was as if, notes Thomas Pakenham, "he were leading a punitive expedition on the Indian frontier."[122]

In less than a year, the currents of war thus carried the imperial army from fighting, to firing whites' houses, to laying waste two British colonies, all to starve a tiny settler minority. This overkill was fueled from below: activities "to starve the Boojers out" provided many a soldier with "the best day's sport we had had."[123] Licensed looting, butchery, invasion and inciner- ation of female spaces—what an alarmed administrator saw as "pillage and slaughter," and a woman described as arsonists shrieking with joy with "vio- lence, desire" in their faces—was certainly preferable to plodding after Boer men.[124] That clearing all supplies came to include burning all farmhouses was partly because symbolic rape of female surrogates was one way of being a man when militarily impotent.

Yet there was something odd about white female responses to mass arson and mass detention. In the Cape, women, not expected to speak in public, led nationalist protest. In the ex-republics, exile and house arrest elicited defiance. Isabella Steyn, house-arrested for refusing to ask her husband, the president, to surrender, declared women would continue the war to the end. Asked how long she thought this would be, she replied: "I expect and hope till our last cartridge is shot."[125] Threatening not house arrest but farm- burning, officers ordering Boer women to tell their menfolk to surrender found this threat, too, had lost its potency. A *hendsopper* and his family were now interned—and everyone knew what happened to deserted homesteads. Women dragged out of houses declared they preferred arson to male sur- render. Women watching houses burn made biting comments about the masculinity of men who fought women. "I scarcely know how to convey to you any idea of the spirit of determination," wrote an officer after burn- ing Free State farms for two months. He had never seen anything like this before. Without exception, women said the same thing: "we shall go on fighting"; "God sooner or later will see us through."[126]

Burned-out people had long been left to shift for themselves. But desti- tute blacks and whites were now streaming to towns already buckling under food shortages. One response centered on deporting the whites among them to commandos. This was not successful. Either commandos could not be found, or women urged men to fight on. The "women throughout were the more irreconcilable element," concluded the *Times History* of this experi- ment.[127] Then, with the new "starvation system" developing in towns, some officers sent burned-out people into them. Here whites with men on com- mando were often denied rations; storekeepers were forbidden to sell them food; they were explicitly intended to starve.[128] This, too, had limitations.

Women set up networks to obtain and share food; unlike men, who feared confiscation of their property, they rallied round, commented one. Imperialists began internalizing what many burghers knew: "Women were more bitter and irreconcilable than the men."[129]

Punitive practices were gendered and racialized. Since the oath of neutrality was open only to white men, only white men became prisoners of war for refusing to swear it; only white men were being detained to prevent their recruitment; men were imprisoned while women were exiled or placed under house arrest. In September 1900, this changed. Women were interned in the new camps; women were in the emergent Cape and Natal camps for "undesirables." Camps, not "choko," came to be seen as suitable for the more disaffected sex.[130] If white women were sent to supervised camps rather than towns, this bypassed female resistance networks, lessened local supply problems, and removed the problem of implementing the "starvation system" to someone else's terrain. From September, burned-out whites (as well as the wives of prisoners of war coming to town to shop) were being deported to a camp. Moreover, if arson were no longer an effective threat, what about camps? These were *punishment* camps, insisted a former inmate; there were "*numberless* cases where the wives were sent to the camps" for refusing to ask husbands to surrender.[131] Or as Kitchener declared immediately after replacing Roberts, women outstripped men in their bitterness and fueled the war; "the only solution that will bring them to their senses is to remove the worst class to … a camp."[132] The approximately ten camps for whites established under Roberts rapidly expanded into a concentration camp archipelago.

What of Boer men? There is a "wealth of evidence" that mass farmburning, far from being a "good" policy, lengthened the war.[133] Combined with mass imprisonment, it radically reduced male options. Burning farmhouses, exulted one as early as July, aided the Boer cause: the homeless could not flee home. A British colonel imprisoning civilian men was his best recruiter, rejoiced a Free State leader; his commando rose from 25 to some 1,000 over two months. Boers had no reason to surrender due to the appalling error of farm-burning, noted a member of Milner's staff. Many were ruined; they could outstrip columns; shooting men who had rendered them homeless and given them the choice of fighting or imprisonment was not an unappealing occupation.[134] In essence, the contradictions between self-interest and *volk*, patriarchy and patriotism, were being forcibly resolved. The enemy, noted Smuts, was grinding Boer men's "selfish hearts to powder." As columns fanned out, so men fleeing to evade capture also lost property, families, and homes. "The private and individual ties—so dear to the Boers' hearts—were loosened in order that they might cling with all the more dis-interested devotion to their national ideal."[135] Or as a "Tiger" disillusioned with arson expressed it, "we shall end by bringing about ... a Dutch South African conspiracy, but it will be one of our own making."[136]

In late 1900, there was still a long way to travel on this route. Total war had regional variations; many had yet to be wrenched loose from their homes; less enthusiasm for war in the Transvaal was attributed to less dev-astation. Nonetheless, by eroding the material basis of rural patriarchy, the imperial army was forging a *volk* of *broeders*. Between June and November, there was "deliberate, massive, widespread and ruthless devastation of Boer property in the two republics by British forces."[137] One estimate was that one in three republican farms had been burned by late November; S. B. Spies argues that a very large percentage of the 30,000 farmhouses ultimately gutted were destroyed between September and November; towns were being laid waste; the Free State was becoming a desert.[138] Simultaneously, the *mentalité* of men on commando was changing: toward greater nationalist consciousness, greater discipline, greater lust for revenge. By the end of the year, the number of white men on commando was close to the numbers mobilized at the start of the war. Attacks on communications increased fifteenfold between June and November; an invasion of the Cape began the same month ("the burghers would be less than men if they allowed the enemy to go unpunished after ill-treating their wives and destroying their homes"[139]). Boers were absolutely confident they would regain their inde-pendence, noted Merriman the same month. "They will fight as long as they have a cartridge, and then they will set to work to plot and struggle to throw off the yoke if it takes 25 years."[140] The time span seemed shorter to other observers. By November 1900, concludes the *Times History*, the British "had lost their grip of the war, and the initiative had passed into the hands of the roving partisans."[141]

According to mainstream historiographical wisdom, laying waste two countries and creating concentration camps were "enforced" by the "suc-cess" of Boer guerrilla tactics. So far as scorched earth is concerned, cause and effect have been confused. British imperialists, using tactics honed in Asian and African colonies, *created* mass guerrilla war—by attempting "pacification" when the few "rebels" that remained faced popular antago-nism and had yet to wage guerrilla war "proper." With regard to concentra-tion camps, "malestream" wisdom focuses on the wrong sex. Women were seen as more irreconcilable than men; the punitive dimensions of camps were transparent; this particular punishment was extraordinary; it arose in specific circumstances when others had failed. According causal centrality to Boer military tactics obscures what was more significant: the infusion of techniques of colonial warfare into the South African arena; their enthusiastic reception by militarily impotent men; their failure to break Boer women's resistance; and the emergent transformation of Boer men into *broeders*, not by waging war on battlefields, but by imposing "pacification" on homes.

~

In 1900, Lord Roberts of Kandahar interpreted his relations with Boers. "Not a farm was destroyed, not a pound of grain was taken without payment at the commencement of the war."[142] His proclamations had their desired effect in generating surrenders; steps were taken against any "rebel" causing "unrest."[143] From September onward, his public discourse changed. "War" had degenerated into "guerilla warfare"; he was "compelled" to use harsh means to end it; these were methods "which civilised nations have at all times found it obligatory to use."[144] The destitution of "helpless" Boer women and children was because their "natural protectors" declined to "fulfil their duty"; Roberts was therefore "obliged to deport them."[145] The war was effectively over, he declared on departing in December for Britain, where he received £100,000 and the highest military post in the empire.[146]

This interpretation has stood the test of time remarkably well. The modern malestream version diverges in only one feature of note. It admits into the fraternity Real Boer Men, who, with their successful guerrilla tactics, continued the war until 1902.

Yet the past can look different if gender-biased definitions of war, causation, and periodization are re-visioned. War need not be seen only as armed combat between men: those undergoing conquest claimed a "War Against Women" existed. Causation need not center on Real Men in the veld; there were other masculinities and a wider imperial context. Periodization need not revolve around white military masculinities infused with class and national conceptions of difference. A gentlemen's war associated with velvet gloves, leniency, male combat, conventionality, and Britishness (and, often, the great bulk of textual space) need not be contrasted to a guerrilla war linked with hunter's eyes, herded women, distastefulness, irregularity, Boers, and slipshod analysis. There is another way of telling the tale.

First, the "gentleman's war" went hand in hand with methods of barbarism. In this war as in Afghanistan, "Butcher Roberts" commanded a "sort of Sherman's march"; to excise this is to misrepresent a war of colonial conquest. Second, Eurocentric gender stereotypes are unhelpful. Many Boer men privileged patriarchal homes over political and military domains; they

mostly declined to display "Manhood and Patriotism" when core components of their class and gender identities were threatened. Boer women, on
the other hand, constituted the backbone of opposition to British imperialism; the Boer woman, challenged by "Khaki" men from above and "Kaffir"
men from below, was notorious for reckoning she could acquire another
husband but not another racist republican state. The ironic alliance of Boer
women and "Butcher Roberts" was central in driving some Boer patriarchs
back into war.

Third, the draconian reprisals that became much more common once
both capitals were conquered were not an "inevitable" response to successful guerrilla war. Arson and starvation were standard weapons of colonial
warfare; they were applied to intimidate all "rebels," whether they were fighting guerrilla war, pitched battles, or not at all. Moreover, the turn to "pacification" in August 1900 occurred as the "irregular" methods of imperialists,
not of Boers, demonstrated success. But "pacification" failed. It created mass
guerrilla war. It revived male identification with a nationalist cause. The
gender gap—fueling the emergence of practices unprecedented in British
colonial warfare—began to close. Military fortunes changed. "Ironically,"
notes a military historian who devotes one bracketed clause in a thirty-
seven-page article to destruction of crops and homes under Roberts, "a
widespread recrudescence of hostilities marked the close of Roberts's command."[147] It was not ironic. It was a predictable result of forcing ever more
Boer men into a world stripped of the underpinnings of rural patriarchy.
Like imperial troops, many now found new ways of being men; this change
has not been adequately recognized. Bill Nasson represents the republican "enemy" as "rampaging" brutes from the start to the end of war, even in
mid-1900. Yet the Boer atrocities he details were all committed in 1901–2.
Relegating ("Kitchener's") scorched-earth policies to one sentence, and concentration camps to three, whitewashes the contribution of British imperialism to the spiraling brutality of Boer men.[148]

In all, breaking with the gender-biased imperialist discourse structuring
many war stories does not merely enrich accounts; it alters interpretations.
Abandoning periodization centered on the gentleman/guerrilla dichotomy—
which carries with it an androcentric, national focus—also opens new
perspectives:

In the ordinary course a frontier campaign begins with a raid upon British
territory, is followed by the forward march of an avenging column, and
ends by the defeat of the tribesmen of the field, the destruction of their
towers and dwellings, and the submission of the foe.[149]

This refers to India. It might be a thumbnail sketch of the entire South African War—except that the tribeswomen did not submit: not in 1900, and not in 1902, when burghers again peeled away from war. The South African War was the single most important factor in creating not merely Afrikaner nationalism, but an Afrikaner nationalism shifting its center of gravity to the more irreconcilable sex. This was what "gentlemanly" imperialism bequeathed to South Africa and the world.

Notes

1. W. R. Nasson, "*Tot Siens* to All That? South Africa's Great War, 1899–1902," *South African Historical Journal (SAHJ)* 32 (1995): 205; see also A. Porter, "The Origins of the South African War," *SAHJ* 35 (1996): 158; E. van Heyningen, "Women and the Second Anglo-Boer War," paper presented at the "Women and Gender in Southern Africa" conference, University of Natal, 1991, 1; I. Phimister, "Unscrambling the Scramble for Southern Africa: The Jameson Raid and the South African War Revisited," *SAHJ* 28 (1993): 218.

2. I. Smith, *The Origins of the South African War, 1899–1902* (London, 1996), xi. In P. Warwick (ed.), *The South African War: The Anglo-Boer War, 1899–1902* (Harlow, 1980), only four of the seventeen chapters refer to sources in Afrikaans/Dutch. P. Warwick, *Black People and the South African War, 1899–1902* (Johannesburg, 1983), uses only the English columns of African papers and has three Afrikaans/Dutch sources in a nine-page bibliography.

3. "Dagboek van Oskar Hintrager," *Christiaan De Wet-Annale* 2 (1973): 28.

4. Smith, *Origins*, 404. See also H. Bradford, "Sisters and Brothers: Gendering Africander Nationalism, 1895–1902," paper presented at "Gendered Nations: International Comparisons" conference, Technical University of Berlin, 1998.

5. J. Elshtain, *Women and War* (New York, 1987), 213. Van Heyningen's critique, which centers on Anglophone work and is less applicable to leading Afrikaans texts, can be extended. Women occupy less than 1 percent of the space in Smith, *Origins* and Warwick, *Black People;* gender stereotypes include women being "encumbrances," an "impediment," "family baggage" of men: S. B. Spies, *Methods of Barbarism? Roberts and Kitchener and Civilians in the Boer Republics, January 1900–May 1902* (Cape Town, 1977), 142, 32; D. Cammack, *The Rand at War, 1899–1902* (London, 1990), 10.

6. K. Darian-Smith, "Remembering Romance: Memory, Gender and World War II," in J. Damousi and M. Lake (eds.), *Gender and War* (Cambridge, 1995), 122.

7. T. Pakenham, *The Boer War*, 10th ed. (London, 1995), 210.

8. J. Breytenbach, *Geskiedenis van die Tweede Vryheidsoorlog 1899–1902*, vol. 5 (Pretoria, 1983), 65.

9. H. Bailes, "Military Aspects of the War," in Warwick (ed.), *South African War*, 98; G. Le May, *British Supremacy in South Africa, 1899–1907* (Oxford, 1965), 106; C. de Wet, *Three Years' War* (Westminster, 1902), 241.

10. A. Methuen, *Peace or War in South Africa* (London, 1901), ix; G. Arthur, *Life of Lord Kitchener*, vol. 2 (London, 1920), 55; Le May, *British Supremacy*, 94.

11. Warwick, *Black People*, contains three sentences about black men participating in arson or deportations to the camps. W. R. Nasson, "Tommy Atkins in South Africa," in Warwick (ed.), *South African War*, refers to scorched earth and concentration camps in two phrases and represents all encounters between Tommies and women in terms of whether or not sex occurred. Spies's invaluable text is not an account of the "War against Women," but of military authorities' policy for civilians. There were only "isolated instances of women being caught up in hostilities," he claims: "hostilities" clearly means armed combat (*Barbarism*, 18.)

12. L. Gann and P. Duignan, *The Rulers of British Africa, 1870–1914* (London, 1978), 144; G. Dawson, *Soldier Heroes* (London, 1994), 1.

13. C. Miller, *Khyber* (London, 1977), 212.

14. Miller, *Khyber*, 202; D. James, *Lord Roberts* (London, 1954), 178.

15. L. S. Amery, "Foreword," in James, *Lord Roberts*, v.

16. James, *Lord Roberts*, 295, 303, 364.

17. F. Emery, *Marching over Africa* (London, 1986), 26; Gann and Duignan, *Rulers*, 143–44, citing Winston Churchill.

18. J. Macdonald, *What I Saw in South Africa, Sept. and Oct. 1902* (London, n.d. [c.1902]), 10, 12; Pakenham, *Boer War*, 500.

19. J. Abbott, *Tommy Cornstalk* (London, 1902), 237.

20. R. Price, *An Imperial War and the British Working Class* (London, 1972), 227.

21. Pakenham, *Boer War*, is framed as a hunt of Boer-animals ("View halloo!"); they emerge from lairs and range from foxes and tigers to sharks and worms.

22. Pakenham, *Boer War*, 311.

23. "The Despatches of Col. Stakhovitch of the Russian General Staff Attached to the British Military Forces in South Africa," *Christiaan De Wet-Annale* 3 (1975): 166; see also Breytenbach, *Geskiedenis*, 5.328; O. de Villiers, *Met De Wet en Steyn in Het Veld* (Amsterdam, 1903), 16; H. Ver Loren van Themaat, *Twee Jaren in den Boerenoorlog* (Haarlem, 1903), 24.

24. F. Young, *The Relief of Mafeking* (London, 1900), 98, 140–43. See also F. Unger, *With 'Bobs' and Kruger* (Cape Town, 1977), 182.

25. Pakenham, *Boer War*, 433; Le May, *British Supremacy*, 86; Price, *Imperial War*, 190, 193; Warwick, *Black People*, 3.

26. P. Warwick, "Introduction," in Warwick (ed.), *South African War*, 9; R. Morton, "Linchwe I and the Kgatla Campaign in the South African War, 1899–1902," *Journal of African History* 26 (1985): 183.

27. Pakenham, *Boer War*, 440; see also Spies, *Barbarism*, 29, 35. Spies argues that destruction of property occurred either before Roberts arrived, or after the occupation of Bloemfontein, when it was contrary to his orders, or, in limited cases, to punish treachery. Most other accounts excise even this.

28. A. Grundlingh, "Collaborators in Boer Society," in Warwick (ed.), *South African War*, 258–59; Pakenham, *Boer War*, 434.

29. F. Pretorius, *Kommandolewe Tydens die Anglo-Boereoorlog 1899–1902* (Cape Town, 1991), 14.

30. Spies, *Barbarism*, 31. See also W. Churchill, *My Early Life* (London, 1930), 345.

31. Spies, *Barbarism*, 13–14; Gann and Duignan, *Rulers*, 86.

32. "Despatches of Stakhovitch," 166. See also Spies, *Barbarism*, 29; S. Malan, "Die Britse Besetting van Bloemfontein, 13 Maart 1900," *Historia* 20 (1975): 42; Le May, *Supremacy*, 46–47.

33. C. Headlam (ed.), *The Milner Papers (South Africa) 1899–1905* (London, 1933), 96.

34. Pakenham, *Boer War*, 328; see also Arthur, *Kitchener*, 272–74; A. Page, "The Supply Services of the British Army in the South African War, 1899–1902" (DPhil thesis, Oxford University, 1976), 101.

35. Spies, *Barbarism*, 31. See also Page, "Supply," 155, 279; Pakenham, *Boer War*, 381.

36. H. Colvile, *The Work of the Ninth Division* (London, 1901), 149; see also Page, "Supply," 158.

37. L. Marquard (ed.), *Letters from a Boer Parsonage* (Cape Town, 1967), 76, 83. See also Colvile, *Ninth Division*, 66, 137; W. Churchill, *Ian Hamilton's March* (London, 1900), 191; Headlam, *Milner*, 80; R. Kruger, *Goodbye Dolly Gray* (London, 1996), 302.

38. Colvile, *Ninth Division*, 128, 146.

39. Pakenham, *Boer War*, 571. See also James, *Lord Roberts*, 325; Mev. Wijlen ds. H. Neethling, *Vergeten?* (Cape Town, 1917), 118.

40. Abbott, *Tommie Cornstalk*, 89.

41. J. Tosh, "What Should Historians Do with Masculinity? Reflections on Nineteenth-Century Britain," *History Workshop Journal* 38 (1994): 194.

42. R. Rankin, *A Subaltern's Letters to His Wife* (London, 1901), 220.

43. L. March Philipps, *With Rimington* (London, 1902), 130–32. See also Spies, *Barbarism*, 42.

44. D. Reitz, *Commando* (London, 1968), 32; see also Pretorius, *Kommandolewe*, 238.

45. K. Theweleit, "The Bomb's Womb and the Genders of War," in M. Cooke and A. Woollacott (eds.), *Gendering War Talk* (Princeton, N.J. 1993), 303. See also Pretorius, *Kommandolewe*, 236.

46. Neethling, *Vergeten*, 34. See also Breytenbach, *Geskiedenis*, 5.278.

47. J. Balme (comp.), *To Love One's Enemies* (Cobble Hill, British Columbia, 1994), 101.

48. Young, *Mafeking*, 224–26. See also Unger, *With 'Bobs,'* 251–54; Breytenbach, *Geskiedenis*, 5.144; Balme, *One's Enemies*, 298; Spies, *Barbarism*, 44; Headlam (ed.), *Milner*, 80; Rankin, *Letters*, 220–21.

49. P. Lewsen, *Selections from the Correspondence of John X. Merriman, 1899–1905* (Cape Town, 1966), 215. The first camp had been established by July, at Mafeking, by women themselves.

50. G. Beak, *The Aftermath of War* (London, 1906), 19. See also Spies, *Barbarism*, 38.

51. W. Hancock and J. van der Poel (eds.), *Selections from the Smuts Papers*, vol. 1 (Cambridge, 1966), 469.

52. D. Denoon, "Participation in the 'Boer War': People's War, People's Non-War or Non–People's War?" in B. Ogot (ed.), *War and Society in Africa* (London, 1972), 116, 120; J. Krikler, "Agrarian Class Struggle and the South African War," *Social History* 14,

no. 2 (1989): 171; J. Krikler, *Revolution from Above, Rebellion from Below* (Oxford, 1993), 13; Nasson, '*Tot Siens*,' 199.

53. C. Barnett, *Britain and Her Army 1509–1970* (Harmondsworth, U.K., 1974), 338.

54. Pretorius, *Kommandolewe*, 224; see also Reitz, *Commando*, 93.

55. F. Seiner, *Ervaringen en Herinneringen van Een Boerenstrijder op het Slagveld van Zuid-Afrika* (Rotterdam, 1902), 77. See also Pretorius, *Kommandolewe*, 317.

56. K. Schoeman, *Die Herinneringe van J. C. de Waal* (Cape Town, 1986), 74. See also Seiner, *Ervaringen*, 129.

57. Marquard (ed.), *Letters*, 63. See also Breytenbach, *Geskiedenis*, 5.141, 294; Ver Loren van Themaat, *Twee Jaren*, 37.

58. Hancock and Van der Poel (eds.), *Smuts Papers*, 1.565. See also I. Meyer, *Die Ervarings van 'n Veldkornet in die Engelse Oorlog 1899–1902* (n.p., 1952), 9–10. The same pattern occurred in the last war Free Staters had fought: when Basotho men, retaliating for the scorched-earth practices of the commandos, seized Boer stock and burned Boer homes, burghers fled *huis toe*—and war, perforce, ended.

59. Le May, *British Supremacy*, 78–79.

60. De Wet, *Three Years' War*, 78.

61. L. White, "Separating the Men from the Boys: Constructions of Gender, Sexuality, and Terrorism in Central Kenya, 1939–1959," *International Journal of African Historical Studies* 23, no. 1 (1990): 10.

62. P. Pienaar, *With Steyn and De Wet* (London, 1902), 103. See also Spies, *Barbarism*, 38; Pretorius, *Kommandolewe*, 251; Breytenbach, *Geskiedenis*, 5.159, 169. *Bangbroeke* (scaredy-pants) was a common form of gendered abuse.

63. "The Despatches of Lt-Col Gurko of the Russian General Staff Attached to the Boer Forces in South Africa," *Christiaan De Wet-Annale* 3 (1975): 192. See also De Wet, *Three Years' War*, 118; Ver Loren van Themaat, *Twee Jaren*, 86; A. Grundlingh, *Die Hendsoppers en Joiners* (Pretoria, 1978), 21, 23.

64. W. Mangold, *Vir Vaderland, Vryheid en Eer* (Pretoria, 1988), 180, 186.

65. T. Keegan, *Rural Transformations in Industrializing South Africa* (Johannesburg, 1986), 27. For other claims associating landless whites and *hendsoppers*, see Denoon, "Participation," 119; I. Hofmeyr, "Building a Nation from Words: Afrikaans Language, Literature and Ethnic Identity, 1902–1924," in S. Marks and S. Trapido (eds.), *The Politics of Race, Class and Nationalism in Twentieth Century South Africa* (London, 1987), 99; Smith, *Origins*, 7–8.

66. "Dagboek van Hintrager," 31, and see also 35; and Headlam (ed.), *Milner*, 528; Ver Loren van Themaat, *Twee Jaren*, 87; C. Badenhorst, *Uit den Boeren-Oorlog 1899–1902* (Amsterdam, 1903), 17–18; Mangold, *Vaderland*, 194, 204; Pretorius, *Kommandolewe*, 275.

67. Ver Loren van Themaat, *Twee Jaren*, 87.

68. A. Jackson (comp.), *Uit die Dagboek van 'n Wildeboer deur P. S. Lombard* (n.p., n.d.), 62–63. See also Badenhorst, *Boeren-Oorlog*, 14, 17–18; Mangold, *Vaderland*, 194. Grundlingh, in *Hendsoppers*, 24–25, notes both the alacrity with which many richer farmers surrendered and that they were not the only ones who did so.

69. D. van Warmelo, *On Commando* (London, 1902), 39–40. See also M. Davitt, *The Boer Fight for Freedom* (New York, 1902), 408; Pretorius, *Kommandolewe*, 256.

70. S. Izedinova, *A Few Months with the Boers* (Johannesburg, 1977), 180; T. Ranger, *Revolt in Southern Rhodesia, 1896–7* (London, 1967), 238, 247–48, 310; M. Kesby, "Arenas for Control, Terrains of Gender Contestation: Guerrilla Struggle and Counter-Insurgency Warfare in Zimbabwe, 1972–1980," *Journal of Southern African Studies* 22, no. 4 (1996): 577–78.

71. D. Denoon, *A Grand Illusion* (London, 1973), 59.

72. Pakenham, *Boer War*, 331, 383.

73. Bailes, "Military Aspects," 95; Grundlingh, *Hendsoppers*, 22; F. Pretorius, *The Anglo-Boer War, 1899–1902* (Cape Town, 1985), 26.

74. Warwick, "Introduction," in Warwick (ed.), *South African War*, 61; Denoon, "Participation," 120.

75. University of Cape Town (UCT), James Stewart Collection, South African Conciliation Committee (SACC) pamphlet, no. 29, "An Interview with Dr Theal," 5 (my emphasis). Thanks to Greg Cuthbertson for alerting me to this source.

76. E. Brink, "Man-Made Women: Gender, Class and the Ideology of the Volksmoeder," in C. Walker (ed.), *Women and Gender in Southern Africa to 1945* (Cape Town, 1990), 276; S. B. Spies, "Women and the War," in Warwick (ed.), *South African War*, 162; Davitt, *Boers Fight for Freedom*, 77; H. Hillegas, *With the Boer Forces* (London, 1900), 276.

77. Van Heyningen, "Women," 26–27.

78. There is a large literature almost blind to women in the prewar period: see for example H. Giliomee, "The Beginnings of Afrikaner Ethnic Consciousness, 1850–1915," in L. Vail (ed.), *The Creation of Tribalism in Southern Africa* (London, 1989); J. Marais, *The Fall of Kruger's Republic* (Oxford, 1961); S. Marks and S. Trapido, "Lord Milner and the South African State Reconsidered," in M. Twaddle (ed.), *Imperialism, the State and the Third World* (London, 1992); S. Malan, *Politieke Strominge onder die Afrikaners van die Vrystaatse Republiek* (Butterworth, 1982); A. Porter, "The South African War (1899–1902): Context and Motive Reconsidered," *Journal of African History* 31 (1990); Smith, *Origins*.

79. E. Hobhouse, *War without Glamour* (Bloemfontein, 1924), 49.

80. M. E. Rothmann (comp.), *Tant Alie van Transvaal* (Cape Town, 1939), 206.

81. UCT, Stewart Collection, SACC pamphlet no. 29, 5.

82. J. Rijksen-van-Helsdingen, *Vrouweleed*, 2d ed. (Cape Town, 1918), 51; Hobhouse, *War without Glamour*, 101; see also De Wet, *Three Years' War*, 112.

83. Rankin, *Letters*, 99.

84. JAD to "Myne Zusters in de ZAR, en OVS," *The Standard and Diggers' News* (*S&DN*), 5 May 1900.

85. Abbott, *Tommie Cornstalk*, 248.

86. Rankin, *Letters*, 99.

87. Transvaal Archives, Dr. D. Sleigh Collection, Mrs. N. Kruger's testimony. The marginalization of black women in accounts of black participation in the war makes discerning the gendered nature of challenges to settlers difficult, but men appear to have dominated.

88. Transvaal Archives, Dr. D. Sleigh Collection, Mrs. N. Kruger's testimony. See also Hobhouse, *War without Glamour*, 133.

89. Letter to the Editor from Anna du Plessis, *S&DN*, 23 May 1900. See also petition from Mev. H. Bosman and five hundred others to generals, *S&DN*, 21 May 1900.

90. Marquard (ed.), *Letters*, 48, 61, 83.

91. Rankin, *Letters*, 98; R. Schikkerling, *Commando Courageous* (Johannesburg, 1964), 311–12. See also Ver Loren van Themaat, *Twee Jaren*, 61; Breytenbach, *Geskiedenis*, 5.452; Hillegas, *Boer Forces*, 285–86.

92. Davitt, *Boer Fight for Freedom*, 409. See also Ver Loren van Themaat, *Twee Jaren*, 33–34; N. Hofmeyr, *Zes Maanden Bij de Commando's* (The Hague, 1903), 333.

93. Izedinova, *A Few Months*, 93; Mangold, *Vaderland*, 167; Rankin, *Letters*, 99; Breytenbach, *Geskiedenis*, 5.451.

94. Rothmann, *Alie*, 126.

95. Breytenbach, *Geskiedenis*, 5.278, 298–99; De Wet, *Three Years' War*, 106; N. van der Merwe, *Marthinus Theunis Steyn* (Cape Town, 1921), 2.59.

96. *S&DN*, 12 May 1900.

97. *S&DN*, 12 May 1900; Izedinova, *A Few Months*, 249.

98. Letter to the Editor from Maria Nel, and JAD to "Myne Zusters in de ZAR en OVS," *S&DN*, 5 May 1900.

99. "Dagboek van Hintrager," 20.

100. Letter to the Editor from "A Burgher's Wife," *S&DN*, 13 May 1900; see also *S&DN*, 12 May 1900.

101. *S&DN*, 22 May 1900.

102. "Dagboek van Hintrager," 142.

103. J. Meintjes, *De la Rey—Lion of the West* (Johannesburg, 1966), 170.

104. Scorched earth is linked to Kitchener, not Roberts, in W. R. Nasson, *Abraham Esau's War* (Cambridge, 1991), 179; Morton, "Linchwe I," 183; R. Sibbald, *The War Correspondents* (Johannesburg, 1993), 227. When arson is admitted into this period, it is often as an aside in discussing Kitchener: Pretorius, *Kommandolewe*, 14, 54, 60–61, 327, 357, 364–65.

105. Pakenham, *Boer War*, 473.

106. Warwick, *Black People*, 3.

107. Denoon, *Illusion*, 20.

108. Smith, *Origins*, 5.

109. Nasson, "*Tot Siens*," 196.

110. J. Belich, *The Victorian Interpretation of Racial Conflict* (Montreal, 1986), 311. The marginalized exceptions are the most detailed investigations: Spies, *Barbarism*; E. Hobhouse, *The Brunt of the War and Where It Fell* (London, 1902); J. Otto, *Die Konsentrasie-Kampe* (Cape Town, 1954).

111. I. Beckett and J. Pimlott, *Armed Forces and Modern Counter-Insurgency* (London, 1985), 3. See also Pakenham, *Boer War*, 497, 526; J. D. Kestell and D. E. van Velden, *The Peace Negotiations between the Governments of the SAR and the OFS, and the Representatives of the British Government* (London, 1912), 60.

112. L. Amery (ed.), *The Times History of the War in South Africa 1899–1902*, vol. 4 (London, 1906), 494.

113. Breytenbach, *Geskiedenis*, 5.179; Pretorius, *Kommandolewe*, 56; Pakenham, *Boer War*, 472–473; Warwick, *Black People*, 3.

114. E. Childers, *In the Ranks of the CIV* (London, 1900), 122; see also UCT, Stewart Collection, SACC pamphlet 59, "Farm Burning in South Africa"; Hobhouse, *Brunt,* 19.

115. I. Uys, *Heidelbergers of the Boer War* (Cape Town, 1981), 58; "Dagboek van Hintrager," 44, 55; Spies, *Barbarism,* 103, 124; Marquard (ed.), *Letters,* 93; Neethling, *Vergeten,* 87.

116. Kruger, *The Memoirs of Paul Kruger,* vol. 2 (London, 1902), 467. See also "Dagboek van Hintrager," 41, 57, 59, 98 ("setting houses alight"); Pienaar, *Steyn,* 119–20; A. Oberholster (ed.), *Oorlogsdagboek van Jan F. E. Celliers, 1899–1902* (Pretoria, 1978), 125.

117. "Dagboek van Hintrager," 46–47, 59, 121; Pakenham, *Boer War,* 444; Grundlingh, *Hendsoppers,* 44–45; M. van Schoor, S. Malan, and J. Oberholster (eds.), *Christiaan De Wet, 1854–1922* (Bloemfontein, 1954), 45; Meintjes, *De la Rey,* 180; Hobhouse, *War without Glamour,* 11; Hobhouse, *Brunt,* 51.

118. L. Amery (ed.), *The Times History of the War in South Africa,* vol. 5 (London, 1907), 2; see also Pakenham, *Boer War,* 450; Warwick, "Introduction," 60.

119. Amery (ed.), *History,* 5.5.

120. Ibid., 5.1, and see also 4.458; Pakenham, *Boer War,* 455, 463. Hobhouse, *Brunt,* 28.

121. Spies, *Barbarism,* 121–22.

122. Amery (ed.), *History,* 5.8; Le May, *Supremacy,* 87; Pakenham, *Boer War,* 458; see also Spies, *Barbarism,* 121–22, 171; H. Gaskell, *With Lord Methuen in South Africa* (London, 1906), 255.

123. Pakenham, *Boer War,* 438.

124. Otto, *Konsentrasie-kampe,* 22; Rijksen-van-Helsdingen, *Vrouweleed,* 76.

125. K. Schoeman, *In Liefde en Trou* (Cape Town, 1983), 40. See also K. Schoeman, *Only an Anguish to Live Here* (Cape Town, 1992), 98.

126. Philipps, *Rimington,* 203, 208. See also Hobhouse, *Brunt,* 56; L. Curtis, *With Milner in South Africa* (Oxford, 1951), 143. For a woman who persuaded her husband to surrender, and then found he was imprisoned and her house was burned down, see E. Neethling, *Should We Forget?* (Cape Town, n.d. [c.1902]), 94.

127. Amery (ed.), *History,* 4.393.

128. Hobhouse, *War without Glamour,* 21, and see also 11; Marquard (ed.), *Letters,* 110; Neethling, *Vergeten,* 142; Mangold, *Vaderland,* 219, 302; Spies, *Barbarism,* 122; Spies, "Women," 165.

129. Spies, *Barbarism,* 153. See also Hobhouse, *War Without Glamour,* 11; Neethling, *Vergeten,* 142.

130. Cammack, *Rand at War,* 153.

131. Neethling, *Forget,* 46. See also Marquard, *Letters,* 108; Hobhouse, *Brunt,* 57.

132. Spies, *Barbarism,* 184.

133. Pretorius, *Kommandolewe,* 357.

134. "Dagboek van Hintrager," 72; Badenhorst, *Boeren-Oorlog,* 77, 79, 80; Curtis, *Milner,* 185.

135. Hancock and Van der Poel (eds.), *Smuts Papers,* 565.

136. Philipps, *Rimington,* 214–15.

137. Spies, *Barbarism,* 116. See also Ver Loren van Themaat, *Twee Jaren,* 304.

138. Spies, *Barbarism,* 118; J. Fraser, *Episodes in My Life* (Cape Town, 1922), 282; UCT, Stewart Collection, SACC pamphlet no. 59.

139. Hobhouse, *Brunt,* 99. See also Spies, *Barbarism,* 114; Pretorius, *Komman-dolewe,* 354.

140. Lewsen (ed.), *Merriman,* 237.

141. Amery (ed.), *History,* 5.26.

142. Spies, *Barbarism,* 116.

143. Amery (ed.), *History,* 4.488; Pakenham, *Boer War,* 449; see also James, *Lord Roberts,* 305.

144. Headlam (ed.), *Milner,* 88; Le May, *British Supremacy,* 87; Otto, *Konsentrasie-Kampe,* 21.

145. Spies, *Barbarism,* 138–39.

146. Pakenham, *Boer War,* 456.

147. Bailes, "Military Aspects," 98.

148. Nasson, *Abraham Esau's War,* 10–11, 179, and see also 122.

149. Amery (ed.), *History,* 4.494.

CHAPTER 4

Afrikaner Nationalism and the Burgher on Commando

FRANSJOHAN PRETORIUS

THIS CHAPTER INVESTIGATES the manifestations of Afrikaner nationalism on commando during the South African War. Initially, the many expressions of Afrikaner national sentiment during the war were parochial, the product of self-interest, and generally limited to achieving the independence of the republics. Increasingly, however, Afrikaner nationalism was geared to the independence of both republics, as Transvalers and Free Staters found a common goal. From the outset, an Afrikaner nationalism existed that stretched farther than the borders of the two republics back to the earliest stirrings of settler nationalism, but this was mainly the preserve of some intellectuals. The main movement was a "republican nationalism" that aimed at nothing more than preserving the independence of the republics.

This process toward republican nationalism went through three distinct phases: the initial boldness between October 1899 and February 1900, when the Boers experienced military success; the vacillating phase, between March and September 1900, when military setbacks caused many of those who were lukewarm about Afrikaner nationalism to lay down their arms; and the emergence in the guerrilla phase, between September 1900 and the end of the war in May 1902, of a new Afrikaner elite—the *bittereinders.*

The initial boldness, when the Boers experienced military success, was not caused by a very deep-rooted nationalism. In the midst of bitterness against the enemy, nationalist feelings were inflamed. "Ons sal die Engelse in die see jaag!" [We will drive the British into the sea!] and "Ons gaan piesangs eet in Suid-Natal!" [We're going to eat bananas in southern Natal!] were spontaneous slogans heard on the way to the fronts. "Kaapstad of bars!" [Cape Town or burst!] was the motto on the hatbands of some burghers. Republican flags and pennants were waved and women's committees sent banners embroidered with "God bescherme het Recht" [May God Protect Justice].[1]

At the beginning of the war declarations of patriotism abounded. "Zij hadden hun land lief en geloofden ten volle, dat de oorlog noodzakelijk was voor het behoud hunner onafhankelijkheid en nationaliteit" [They loved their country and fully believed that the war was necessary to preserve their independence and nationality], Nico Hofmeyr reported on the spirit at the Natal front when war broke out.[2] In late November 1899, Roelof de Boer of the Lydenburg Commando wrote to his wife from Ladysmith that he was missing her, "maar als pligt mij roept zal ik gehoorzamen" [but when duty calls I shall obey].[3] From the same front, Joachim Potgieter of the Heilbron Commando informed his brother after the victory at Colenso in December 1899: "Nu kunnen wij zien dat de Afrikanders waarlijk wakker geworden zijn. Nu is het tijd dat wij onze onafhankelijkheid moeten en zullen krijgen" [Now we can see that the Afrikaners have truly been aroused. Now is the time that we must and will get our independence].[4] At the end of January 1900, J. P. Bredell wrote from Natal to his girlfriend that the Afrikaner's entire existence was at stake. Apprehensively he added: "En wee ons indien die Rooies de overhand krijgen" [And woe befall us if the Reds (British) get the upper hand].[5]

But after the euphoria of the first victories had died down it became apparent that not all burghers were dedicated Afrikaner nationalists. When the various fronts collapsed in March 1900 and the British swept everything before them in their advance on Pretoria, which they reached in June 1900, many burghers yielded to Lord Roberts's proclamations and laid down arms. An estimated twelve to fourteen thousand burghers surrendered between March and July 1900.[6]

Although this removed a significant percentage of burghers from the war scene—those to whom self-interest came first—not all the burghers who remained on commando in the guerrilla phase did so out of undying love for their country, as evidenced by the roughly six thousand who laid down arms between January 1901 and May 1902.[7] In the latter half of 1900, however, the collective mentality of the burghers underwent an important shift: the lack of self-sacrifice that had featured so prominently at the beginning of hostilities receded during the guerrilla phase, making way for a determination to continue the war whatever its cost. A sense of solidarity in the struggle emerged and, as a result, the vast majority of burghers still on commando braced themselves psychologically to remain loyal to the Boer cause to the end.[8] In a sense, Roland Schikkerling has argued, the reverses of the earlier period had been a purging and chastening process, leaving only the staunchest and most steadfast men. "Generally speaking, a fuller national [Afrikaner] consciousness was coming to us," he wrote in September 1900.[9]

In effect, the reasons for burghers staying on commando until peace was declared can be attributed to this sense of independence and nationalism. In January 1901, Dirk van Velden wrote to a friend from the Transvaal government laager in the Middelburg district that there was only one way: "Blijf bij je volk tot het einde toe" [Stay with your people to the end].[10] Early in June 1902, unaware that peace had been concluded a few days earlier, P. J. du Plessis admonished an older burgher near Cradock in the eastern Cape for speaking about pay for his commando service. "Nee, oom Tys, ons veg nie vir geld nie. Ons veg net vir die vryheid en behoud van die twee Republieke!... 'n Mens moet 'n oortuiging en ideaal hê, anders help al hierdie swaarkry niks nie" [No, Uncle Tys, we are not fighting for money. We are fighting only for the freedom and the preservation of the two Republics!... One must have a belief and an ideal, otherwise all this suffering is pointless].[11] To many burghers, therefore, the struggle became a sacred duty that kept them on commando. After the British seizure of the Delagoa Bay railway line, Philip Pienaar declared in the eastern Transvaal in October 1900 that the burghers would persevere, not because they were sure of success but because it was their duty.[12] They suffered voluntarily, Dietlof van Warmelo said in September 1900, but they were driven to it by a sense of honor and duty.[13] In September 1901 Jan Celliers, who after the war was to become a leader in the Second Language Movement that promoted Afrikaner nationalism, clarified the issue to himself on commando: "Ik *kan* niet terug van den ingeslagen weg, mijn plicht is duidelijk en ondubbelzinnig.... Ik mag en kan nergens anders zijn dan hier" [I *cannot* turn back on this course I have taken, my duty is clear and unambiguous.... I cannot and may not be anywhere but here]. He then reasoned that if it should ever enter his mind to surrender, he would either be sent away as a prisoner of war or be permitted to stay with his family. In the first case, he would still be far from home and in both cases he would suffer such mental anguish that the present tribulation would seem insignificant.[14]

During General de Wet's second abortive attempt to invade the Cape Colony in February 1901, D. W. Steyn of the Heilbron Commando refused to turn back on account of the hardships as some other burghers were doing: "Ik was getrouw aan myn roepen en wou niet ontrouw wees" [I was true to my call and did not want to be untrue].[15] The dreadful suffering on this expedition made R. D. McDonald admire the burghers' stamina, fortitude, and determination. As a preacher, he found it a joy to minister to men who so loved their country. Surely they, who were ready to give their all for freedom, would triumph in the end.[16] De Wet felt that the burghers who accompanied him were of the right stamp, offering everything for the freedom of the people. They realized that freedom was "a pearl of such value that no man since the world began had been able to set a price upon it."[17]

The response of many burghers to the abortive peace talks between General Botha and Lord Kitchener at Middelburg in February 1901 showed clearly that it was their desire for independence that kept them in the field. According to J. F. Naudé, who was to become an influential minister in the Dutch Reformed Church (and the father of Dr. Beyers Naudé) after the war, the burghers were highly indignant about Kitchener's proposals: "Hoe verlangend allen ook waren naar vrede, wilde niemand daarvan hooren als de onafhankelijkheid daarvoor zou moeten prijs gegeven worden" [However great their longing for peace, nobody wanted to hear about it if it was going to cost them their independence]. It was evident, Naudé continued, that the burghers were determined to continue and that their spirits were still filled with the republican fervor for which they had already sacrificed so much.[18]

That they had sacrificed too much to surrender now surfaced elsewhere. Writing to General de Wet from the Aberdeen district in the eastern Cape in July 1901, Commandant Gideon Scheepers said that the blood of too many brave burghers had been shed for them to give up the struggle. The thought of leaving the rising generation a legacy of servitude to Britain made them fight to the death.[19] Six months later, Scheepers was executed by a British firing squad. Others, too, felt that they had suffered and sacrificed too much to give up the fight.[20]

These burghers seem to have understood what freedom and independence were about. Less educated burghers might not have had the same insight. Nevertheless, McDonald explained: "A Boer may not exactly know all that independence includes; he may not be able to enumerate the benefits accruing from it, but instinctively he covets it as a jewel of great price."[21] Indeed, the *bittereinders* considered it important to be counted among the steadfast, as Marthinus Viljoen explained in the eastern Transvaal, late in April 1902.[22] And shortly after the war, H. Hilhorst wrote to his parents: "Dat ik tot het einde toe aan mijn Regeering getrouw was, daar ben ik trotsch op" [That I remained loyal to my government to the end is something I am proud of].[23]

The majority of burghers did not have a broad nationalism extending beyond the boundaries of their republics and encompassing the whole of South Africa. There were some, mostly intellectuals, who saw a united South Africa for Afrikaners and their friends as the ultimate goal. These included Jan Smuts, who broached the issue even before the South African War in the Transvaal propaganda brochure, *A Century of Wrong*.[24] J. F. Naudé, who dreamed about it in his diary on commando and in his published memoirs in 1903,[25] and J. J. Theron, who advocated a united South Africa in *De Volks-stem* of April 24, 1900. But many burghers' statements on commando, like those of Paul Kruger with his strongly Transvaal-centered approach, conceived of nationalism in far narrower terms. Their vision was confined to the independence of the republics, or even to their own republic. Their immediate goal was to drive the enemy out of the republics and restore their independence. Many of them did not look beyond this, even in the guerrilla phase of the conflict.

On commando, C. J. Asselbergs found that the Boers had a certain fortitude that enabled them, once they had started something, to persevere for a long time. Whereas it was difficult to get them to move, once they decided to follow their leader on a given course, they did not give up easily. They were phlegmatic and did not easily switch from one mental state to another. Asselbergs decided: "Ik ben dan ook bepaald van oordeel, dat hun volhouden van den strijd vooral te danken is aan eene actie, die zich niet uit in een krachtig handelen doch wel in een hoogen graad van taaiheid en volharding" [I am definitely of the opinion that their steadfastness in the struggle is attributable primarily to a disposition which manifests itself not in forceful action but in a high degree of toughness and perseverance].[26]

To the average Afrikaner, religion and nationalism were closely connected. Robert de Kersauson de Pennendreff, a French volunteer with Smuts in the northwestern Cape, mentioned this in his diary. He wrote that in April 1902 Jan Smuts had appealed to the burghers to fight for their freedom and independence with renewed vigor in a speech in the church at Concordia, whereupon the minister (probably Ds. A. P. Kriel) climbed into the pulpit and conducted the service. The Frenchman commented that it might strike a European as odd that a general should assemble his men in a church in order to address them and exhort them to fight, but from what he had seen in the Transvaal, the Free State, and the Cape Colony he could understand it. In fact, he had the impression that among the Boers, the Christian faith and the war effort were closely linked.[27]

Thus, the Afrikaners' religious outlook, in conjunction with their nationalism, kept many burghers in the field. The vocation that some of them felt, that God had called the Afrikaner to inhabit this land as a free inheritance, and the notion that God was on their side, greatly contributed to this. In addition, the view that they should trust in God, even through the most bitter affliction, because he would deliver them in his own time[28] made *bittereinders* of some burghers. The belief that they were fighting for a holy and a just cause also prevented some of them from laying down arms. In late September 1900, a year after the first burghers' departure for the front,

J. F. Naudé contemplated the situation. The future certainly looked gloomy and nobody knew how they would manage to hold out. He explained: "Wij gingen alleen voort, gesterkt door re rechtvaardigheid onzer zaak en met het oog des geloofs steeds op den Heer gericht" [We just carry on, strengthened by the justice of our cause and with our eyes fixed on the Lord in faith].[29] Van Warmelo recorded that by March 1901, they were resigned to their lot and endured it willingly by strengthening and encouraging one another, knowing that they were living and dying for the sacred right of an independent existence.[30] At the end of June 1901, General de la Rey reported to his burghers in the western Transvaal that, after consultations in the eastern Transvaal, the Boer leaders of the two republics had informed Lord Kitchener that they had no option but to fight to the bitter end. With reference to this, De la Rey observed in his memoirs that the burghers naturally found it dispiriting, after suffering and sacrificing all they held dear, that they still could not see the dawn. But, he said, even in such dark nights they responded: "God regeert en Hy heeft de oorlog doen beginnen en ook zal Hy het op zynen tyd beeindigen, want ... wy vechten niet om ons land te vergroten ... maar wy vechten slechts om ons heilig recht te behouden" [God is king, He caused the War to start and will end it in his own time, for ... we are not fighting to enlarge our country ... but merely to preserve our sacred right].[31]

The spiritual growth that many burghers experienced in the course of the struggle helped them to stay on commando.[32] In a letter to W. T. Stead, dated January 1902, the famous champion of the Boers in England, Jan Smuts, described this spiritual growth among the burghers and their desire to preserve Boer independence. He continued:

> This aspiration, purified and deepened a hundredfold by loss and suffering and sorrow during the course of the war, remains today the most vital and vitalizing force in the Boer mind, and must be carefully studied by all who wish to understand the true conditions of the continuance of the present war.... This view, which will seem strange and unintelligible to matter-of-fact politicians, is today held by the bulk of the Boers in the field and explains much which must otherwise forever remain inexplicable. To call them names—to call them pig-headed or obstinate or fanatical—explains nothing, and one must explore to a deeper level of their national consciousness in order to find the true cause of their unique persistence in the face of the most appalling sufferings and discouragements.[33]

In the eastern Cape, P. J. du Plessis acknowledged that it was God's supportive grace and the conscious ideal of independence that continually spurred on the Boer commandos. In the eastern Transvaal, Marthinus Viljoen roundly declared in his diary in January 1902: "Het is goddelijke steun die dit alles gaande houdt" [It is God's help that keeps it all going].[34]

Another factor that strengthened the nationalist sentiment of the burghers was the havoc the British scorched-earth policy caused around them. In 1977, S. B. Spies suggested that this policy, which Lords Roberts and Kitchener had hoped would bring the war to a speedy conclusion, had in fact had the opposite effect. He quoted Commandant L. E. Krause's comment to Lionel Curtis that the burghers were staying on commando because the razing of their farms meant that they no longer had homes to go to.[35] There is ample evidence to support Spies's argument. In July 1900, Oskar Hintrager, a German volunteer with the Free Staters, twice noted in his diary that the burnings were benefiting the Boer cause, since those who no longer had houses could no longer go home.[36] Similar statements were made by the Rev. J. D. Kestell of Harrismith and the Rev. J. P. Liebenberg of Bethal, General P. H. Kritzinger in the Cape Colony, Commandant J. Krige of the ZARP (South African Republic Police) in the eastern Transvaal, J. F. Naudé operating with General J.C.G. Kemp's commandos, J. F. van Wyk of the Wolmaransstad Commando, and Lieutenant Gerrit Boldingh, a Dutch artillery officer with the Free State forces.[37]

Apart from the practical reality that there were no homes or family to flee to, there was also an ideological consideration: the scorched-earth policy and the suffering of Boer women and children in the concentration camps made many burghers more determined to carry on the struggle against Britain. In January 1902, Smuts wrote to W. T. Stead that in adopting the scorched-earth policy, the British military leadership had made the mistake of believing that the Boers were cowards. "A weak man," he observed, "is broken by adversity; the sight of the ruin of his property and family is sufficient in most cases to utterly crush his spirit. On the other hand a brave and hardy spirit is braced up by adversity—he does not sink hopelessly under calamities and wrongs; if he is really brave these will only nerve him to greater efforts, to grapple with adverse fate until he wrings from it a noble crown of victorious achievement."[38]

Among the burghers, there was some soul-searching about whether or not the struggle had become too costly, but the terrible price in loss and suffering heightened the value of Afrikaner freedom and independence and inspired the Boers to fight on. In March 1901, Van Warmelo recorded that they often discussed whether or not they should abandon the struggle for the sake of the women and children in the concentration camps, who were living in the most horrendous conditions. Was the "fatherland" so exalted above the family that innocent blood had to be shed for it? "It cost us more than we can tell to remain firm and brave in our undertaking," he wrote.[39] In March 1902, J. J. Heijnecke of the Potchefstroom Commando wrote about the suffering of women and children in his diary: "Is det tog niet zwaar voor vleesch en bloed om het tecdraag [sic] en det voor ons eigen recht. Maar de volk van Aferka die draag al die smarte om een vry volk te weest. Die volk van Aferka zien beddende op tot God den Heer om hulp en redding" [Is this not hard for flesh and blood to bear and for our own rights at that. But the people of Africa are bearing all these sorrows in order to be a free people. The people of Africa prayerfully look to the Lord God for help and deliverance].[40] Six weeks before the peace he wrote: "Ons land die al zoo veel duurbaar levens en bloed en tranne gekost hebben kan wij tog niet op geven, want wij hebben niets op aart meer oor.... Zoo wellen wy maar stryden tot overwenning maar op geven nooit" [After all, we cannot give up our country that has already cost so many precious lives and blood and tears, for we have nothing else left on earth.... So we shall fight for victory, but give up? Never].[41] Late in 1901, J. H. Coetzer of the Marico Commando was shocked to see the ruins of his burned homestead and realize that his family had been carried off. It was enough to make him say vengefully, "Noit noit in ge nie liewers dood" [Never never give in, rather die].[42]

The role played by the Boer leaders also promoted steadfastness in the struggle. The British alleged that the Boer leaders kept the burghers on commando with lies and false propaganda.[43] Acting President S. W. Burger of the Transvaal hotly denied such an accusation by Kitchener in April 1902.[44] Naturally, De Brandwacht, mouthpiece of the Free State government, also rejected this charge in the final phase of the war. Even Jan Celliers repudiated it.[45]

Although the burghers on commando were individualists who often reacted to the war situation according to their own insight, the Boer leaders had a vital influence on the burghers' beliefs and often persuaded them to continue with the struggle in all sorts of ways. The officers' influence should not be underestimated—in fact, there was a clear correlation between the caliber of an officer and that of his commando.[46] J. A. Smith, a young rebel who fought under General Wynand Malan and Commandants Gideon Scheepers, Carel van Heerden, and Piet van der Merwe in the eastern Cape, rated the value of officers highly. In his view, they had a grave responsibility. Officers wielded great influence over the burghers in word and deed and were always a source of strength. Smith continued:

Wanneer ek soms op die punt staan om deur die gewaarwording van my eie swakheid of vrees oorval te word; wanneer ek begin huiwer of twyfel, het die gedagte aan hulle [die offisiere] meteens weer die nodige moed in my gewek en my laat volg.... In alles was hulle 'n voorbeeld en dit so deurdringend dat ek my steeds aangevuur gevoel het om selfs in oomblikke waar my moed of krag dreig om my te begewe, nie te verslap nie.

[Sometimes when I was on the verge of succumbing to a sense of my own frailty or fear; when I began to waver or doubt, the thought of them (the officers) suddenly rekindled the necessary courage in me and made me follow.... They set an example in everything, so convincingly that I was constantly inspired not to weaken, even in moments when my courage or strength threatened to fail me.][47]

Apart from setting an example, the Boer leaders had two main means of influencing the burghers: by making encouraging speeches and by disseminating war bulletins. Eloquent speakers among the Boer leaders exploited the general awe and esteem in which Afrikaner leaders were held to urge the burghers to continue fighting. Their success is evident in Schikkerling's comment at Pilgrim's Rest early in May 1902 after a former general, Lukas Meyer, had addressed them. In hunger and hardship people often became dispirited, Schikkerling wrote, but when a number of them were reminded of the glorious deeds of their forebears, they soon became brave and haughty, ready to fight to the death.[48] There was no doubt that the eloquence of many Boer leaders inspired their men. With simple yet powerful oratory, De Wet often exhorted his burghers to steadfastness. His statements combined religion with nationalism, as on one occasion in late July 1900:

Broeders, ons moet volhou! Die tyd sal kom, ek weet nie wanneer nie, maar ons moet veg, as God dit wil, tot ons kinders groot is. Ek is die laaste wat wens of glo dat dit só lank sal duur. Maar as God wil, moet ons so lank veg. Dit is ons heilige plig, want ons veg vir 'n heilige en regverdige saak. [Brothers, we must persevere! The time will come, I don't know when, but if God wills it, we have to fight until our children have grown up. I am the last person to wish or believe that it will last that long. But if God wills it, we have to fight that long. It is our sacred duty, for we are fighting for a sacred and just cause.][49]

In October 1900, President Steyn and Louis Botha delivered powerful addresses to a large gathering at Nylstroom in which they urged the burghers "to do their duty towards their country and towards themselves by remaining faithful to the Cause, as the very existence of our nation depended on it."[50]

Leaders also encouraged their men to remain committed by reading out official war bulletins. In one such bulletin, dated May 30, 1901, the Transvaal State Secretary, F. W. Reitz, after some heartening reports, concluded that the government had received many other favorable tidings from Steyn and the Free State officers "waaruit wij overtuigd zyn dat het misdadig zou zyn van ons om zelfs er aan te denken om dezen stryd op te geven. Daarom is de ernstige wensch en raad van de regeering dat alle burgers en officieren zullen blyven volharden" [which convince us that it would be criminal on our part even to think of abandoning this struggle. It is therefore the government's earnest wish and counsel that all burghers and officers should persevere].[51]

The war bulletins had great propaganda value, as they contained truths, half truths, and blatant lies. Sometimes, British defeats were exaggerated and Boer debacles were either understated or presented as victories. In February 1901, Schikkerling observed cynically that the war bulletins read out to them were parboiled by the government before being served up.[52] Apart from news about the various war zones, the war bulletins covered overseas events that could in the long run affect the outcome of the war. The progress of Abraham Fischer's deputation to Europe and the United States to promote the Boer cause and persuade those governments to intervene in the struggle was highlighted, as were Britain's problems in Europe and Asia. It was alleged that Britain was prepared to end the war in South Africa and it was implied that the independence of the republics would be retained in the process.[53]

Edgar Wallace, the journalist later turned famous novelist, maintained that the burghers were motivated to carry on fighting because a British victory posed a double threat: to the survival of their language and to their political status because blacks would be made their equals.[54] The only reference to this is in the commando tabloid, Die Spook, of September 26, 1900. Here, the editor, C.F.L. Rademeyer, commented:

> Verder vra ek nog my ou neef of jy ... op die selde bank in die kantoor neffens outa Johannes sal sit, en of jy sal uithou dat outa Joosop ver jou sal seh "jy en jou vervlakste boer jys nie nou baas nie." As jy verplig word jou kinners skool toe te stuur sal dit lekker wees om te sien hulle sit tussen Klein Kameel, Kaatjie en Kamboes? ... Dus slaap nie.
> [Furthermore I would ask you my old friend whether you ... would sit on the same bench in the office next to old Johannes, and whether you will be able to take it when old Joosop says to you, "you and your bloody Boer you're not the boss now." If you are forced to send your kids to school would you like to see them sit alongside Klein Kameel, Kaatjie and Kamboes? ... So do not be caught napping.][55]

The relationship between the Transvalers and the Free Staters needs to be investigated more closely. The Free Staters initially admired their brave compatriots north of the Vaal River, but unfortunate events such as the surrender of the Transvaal general Piet Cronjé, with four thousand Transvalers and Free Staters, at Paardeberg in February 1900, and the British occupation of Bloemfontein in March 1900 cooled relations considerably. After the British occupation of Pretoria in June 1900, however, relations improved dramatically. Whereas in February 1900 the Transvalers had not been fully prepared to accept the authority of the Free Stater De Wet, preferring instead to fight under their own officers,[56] during the guerrilla phase they became more amenable. In November 1900, a member of the Transvaal State Artillery, J. G. de Jager, referred to the Free State general deferentially as "onze geachte Genl de Wet" [our esteemed General de Wet].[57] In the final year of the war, Transvalers and Free Staters in the Cape Colony fought under the same officers and in the same commandos.

What caused this positive change in relations? First, it is clear that some mutual acceptance was effected through leaders such as Steyn, De Wet, De la Rey, Louis Botha, Jan Smuts, Wynand Malan, and others. Second, it appears that some Transvalers changed their supercilious attitude toward the Free Staters once the loss of their own capital impressed on them that they had all passed through the same mill. In addition, most burghers who were still armed during the guerrilla phase became *bittereinders* in a common struggle, and this awareness of a unified cause eclipsed geographical boundaries. It was only then that relations between the Transvaal and Free State burghers could be maintained on a healthy footing and they could work together for the independence of both republics.[58]

A new Afrikaner elite with new leaders emerged as a manifestation of nationalism in the guerrilla phase of the South African War. Although the Jameson Raid of 1895 and the impending war led to a closing of political ranks and ended any chance of the "progressives" toppling Kruger as president of the Zuid-Afrikaansche Republiek (South African Republic, ZAR), the Transvaal leadership changed significantly during the war.[59] And when Kruger went into exile in September 1900, the Afrikaner's political hierarchy was transformed and a new elite emerged. G.H.L. le May points out that Kruger's followers were replaced by able young men who had gained political influence because of their military talents and because their authority reflected the strict commando discipline of 1902, rather than because of the near anarchy of 1899.[60]

The year 1900 was a watershed for the Republican war leadership. In February, Piet Cronjé surrendered at Paardeberg. Piet Joubert died in March. Before and after the fall of Pretoria, J. P. Snyman, C. E. Fourie, H. J. Schoeman, F. A. Grobler, and D.J.E. Erasmus were relieved of their generalships. In April 1901, Schoeman went to live in Pretoria under British rule; Kruger went into exile in September 1900. After the fall of Bloemfontein, a number of Free State generals, such as Marthinus and Jacobus Prinsloo, C. J. and J. B. Wessels, and A. P. Cronjé, forfeited their ranks. The last two were appointed to the Executive Council of the Free State government and thus were removed from the battle front until their capture in July 1901. Marthinus Prinsloo was put in charge of the Free State commandos again in the Brandwater basin in July, only to surrender with 4,400 men. In May 1901, P. J. Blignaut, Secretary of State of the Free State, remained in Kroonstad under British rule. Several other government officials had done the same after the fall of Bloemfontein.[61]

Who took over the leadership in 1900? Donald Denoon indicates that they were landowners and professionals. The landowners had links with the new Afrikaner professional elite of Pretoria and the Witwatersrand. After the mineral revolution, this professional elite had begun investing in land and could afford to educate its children to give them an edge over the majority of Afrikaner youth.[62] Landowners included Schalk Burger, Acting President of the Transvaal from September 1900 (a token leader with little real influence), J. H. de la Rey, and Coen Brits. In the Free State, there were men like C. R. de Wet, C.C.J. Badenhorst, and C. A. van Niekerk. Professionals from Pretoria and the Witwatersrand included Louis Botha (also a landowner), J. C. Smuts, C. F. Beyers, J.C.G. Kemp, and C. H. Muller. Two important Free State intellectuals were J.B.M. Hertzog and A. Fischer.

Both Le May and Denoon substantiated their findings from a letter written by John X. Merriman, the Cape politician, on July 21, 1902 (barely two months after the end of the South African War) to the British politician and jurist James Bryce:

> The old Boer—the so-called "takhaar" of whom Paul Kruger was the idol and the most prominent representative—has practically disappeared as a factor. He it was who by his impracticable attitude, forced the Progressive section into the attitude that led up to the hostilities and brought on the suicidal ultimatum. When actual hostilities began he did not bear the brunt of the fighting. All, or nearly all, the prominent leaders were either progressive farmers like De la Rey, de Wet, Botha, Kemp or educated men from the towns like Steyn, Hertzog, Smuts and others. The soul of the fighting force consisted of young men and progressive farmers, many of them well-to-do, in some cases rich men.[63]

The findings of Le May and Denoon can be amplified. Participants in the South African War, including Ben Viljoen and the Austrian volunteer Franco Seiner, also mentioned the changed leadership and the creation of a new elite during, or shortly after, the war.[64] The keenest observations, however, were those of Jan Smuts, Lodi Krause, and Ben Bouwer. In his memoirs, Smuts called H. J. Schoeman the representative of "a whole vanished or vanishing order of things, both political and military"; and in his report to the Transvaal government on the position in the Cape Colony on December 16, 1901, Smuts stated that great names no longer mattered, only great deeds.[65]

In March 1901 Krause, Smuts's contemporary at Cambridge and an outspoken antagonist of Kruger, judged Kruger harshly:

> As soon as we sent Pres. Kruger out of the country, and his money-grabbing, traitorous hangers-on were out of the way, the whole tone and aspect of things were altered for the better, and to-day, March 1901, our men in the field are led by tried and able officers, and discipline is the rule and not the exception. The day of the Krugers, Erasmusses [sic], Cronjes, Schoemans, Groblers and men of that stamp are over, never to return, and men like Louis Botha, Christiaan Beyers, Koos de la Rey, and Christiaan de Wet, show the world what true and patriotic Afrikaners can do.[66]

In his memoirs, Ben Bouwer added an important dimension by pointing out that the new elite did not consist only of the leaders of the *bittereinders* but also of ordinary burghers who fought as *bittereinders* until the peace: "By this time the attrition of war had rubbed out every distinction but that of intrinsic quality," he observed significantly. Worldly possessions no longer counted, since there was no assurance that their owners would ever be able to use them again:

> Nobody was despised or socially sunken for accidental reasons. If a man was looked down upon it was because his actions called for contempt. I never have mixed, nor, I suppose, ever shall mix again in such a select company though here and there a man might have signed his name with difficulty.... I refer now to the company who endured to the end without hope of reward, but rather with the threat of banishment from their country hanging over them, purely for the sake of an ideal.[67]

At the outbreak of the South African War, the mainly rural elite came from the upper socioeconomic echelons and, in the Transvaal, from those who were favored by President Kruger. But the set-piece battle phase showed that they could not cope with the new challenges facing a narrower Afrikaner republicanism. A new elite consequently emerged during the guerrilla phase—*bittereinders* who, through their actions and stamina, empowered or supported the leadership and thus, in Bouwer's words, became a "select company." They took a less republican, though no less passionate, Afrikaner nationalism into the first decade of the twentieth century.

However, the rift in Afrikanerdom that was to appear after 1912 and culminate in the founding of the National Party in 1914 and the Afrikaner Rebellion of the same year can probably be traced back to the South African War. Some important Boer leaders, whose wavering and pessimism about the outcome of the war had induced them to favor peace on a number of occasions long before the final Peace of Vereeniging, with few exceptions turned out to be supporters of General Louis Botha's South African National Party, while men who had resisted these attempts to end the conflict before Vereeniging became notable supporters of General J.B.M. Hertzog's National Party.[68]

The first of these occasions was when Louis Botha lost faith in the Boer effort at the end of May 1900. He influenced President Kruger, and the two informed General de Wet and President Steyn of their sentiments on May 31, 1900. Steyn and De Wet condemned peace overtures without hesitation. This was the last time Kruger favored peace moves. Botha then held peace talks with Kitchener at Middelburg on February 28, 1901, but he was not prepared to sacrifice the independence of the Transvaal, so the negotiations ended. This was not the last time he failed to honor the earlier agreement between Kruger and Steyn that on no account would peace be discussed with the British without the knowledge of the allied government. On April 15, 1901, the Republican governments unanimously decided at the Klip River, in the eastern Transvaal, that the Boer war effort would continue. Steyn and De Wet's presence undoubtedly had a lot to do with the decision. However, in a spirit of pessimism, the Transvaal government, Louis Botha, and some of his staunch supporters decided on May 10, 1901, near Ermelo, that they would ask Kitchener to allow a delegation to visit Kruger in Holland to discuss peace. In the light of his later actions, for example at the signing of the peace agreement in Pretoria, State Secretary F. W. Reitz, who was to remain faithful to Hertzog's cause after 1914, was probably outvoted or silenced by Acting President Schalk Burger (a Botha supporter), Lukas Meyer (who died in August 1902), Louis Botha, Jan Smuts, Ben Viljoen (who later emigrated to Mexico), and Chris Botha (who died in October 1902). The absence of General de la Rey, a close ally of Steyn and De Wet, from the discussions is significant. Finally, the Republican governments, no doubt strengthened by the presence of Steyn, De Wet, Hertzog, and De la Rey, and by the recent Boer victories at Vlakfontein, Wilmansrust, and in the Gatsrand, decided on June 19 and 20, 1901, near Standerton, to continue the war. These are the strands that developed more than a decade later, with the Botha supporters on one hand and the Hertzog supporters on the other.

Notes

1. N. Hofmeyr, *Zes Maanden bij de Commando's* (The Hague, 1903), 325; D. Reitz, *Commando* (London, 1929), 21; H. J. May, *Music of the Guns* (London, 1970), 16; D. S. van Warmelo, *On Commando* (Johannesburg, 1977), 18; M. Maritz, *My Lewe en Strewe* (Johannesburg, 1939), 10; A. G. Oberholster, *Oorlogsdagboek* van Jan F. E. Celliers (Pretoria, 1978), 28 November 1899, 36 and 2 December 1899, 39; Transvaal Archives Depot (T.A.D.), Kommandant-Generaal (K.G.), 818, Ladies under Mrs M. E. Coetsee of Belfast to P. J. Joubert, 16 December 1899, 57; H. C. Hillegas, *With the Boer Forces* (London, 1900), 79–80; C. H. Muller, *Oorlogsherinneringe* (Cape Town, 1936), 23; F. Pretorius, "Life on Commando," in P. Warwick (ed.), *The South African War: The Anglo-Boer War, 1899–1902* (Harlow, 1980), 107.

2. Hofmeyr, *Zes Maanden*, 29, and see also 16, 18, 19.

3. T.A.D., A246, R. de Boer Accession, R. de Boer to Wife, 26 November 1899.

4. War Museum, Bloemfontein (O.M.), Correspondence, File 6, J. Potgieter to Brother, 20 December 1899. Cf. T.A.D., A878, J. S. Smit Collection, 35, D.J.C. Pieterse to L. Williams, 24 January 1900; A. G. Oberholster, 11 November 1899, 24 and 13 November 1899, 25; Private Collection, F. H. Beyers, Correspondence of C. F. Beyers, Colesberg, 9 December 1899, 3; J. H. Meyer, *Kommando-jare* (Cape Town, 1971), 9–11; C. Plokhooy, *Met den Mauser* (Gorinchem, 1903), 6; H.J.C. Pieterse, *My Tweede Vryheidstryd* (Cape Town, 1945), 4–7; J. F. Naudé, *Vechten en Vluchten van Beyers en Kemp "Bôkant" de Wet* (Rotterdam, 1903), 24, 25–26, 67.

5. T.A.D., A1361, Dinah Badenhorst Accession, C.J.P. Bredell–D. Badenhorst, 24 January 1900.

6. A.M. Grundlingh, *Die 'Hendsoppers' en 'Joiners'* (Pretoria, 1979), 23, 133.

7. Grundlingh, *Die 'Hendsoppers,'* 133.

8. F. Pretorius, *Kommandolewe tydens die Anglo-Boereoorlog 1899–1902* (Cape Town, 1991), 227–34; Naudé, *Vechten en Vluchten*, 235–36, 263.

9. R. W. Schikkerling, *Commando Courageous* (Johannesburg, 1964), 66.

10. T.A.D., A464, P. J. Louw Accession, D. van Velden to One Hendrik, 29 January 1901.

11. P. J. du Plessis, *Oomblikke van Spanninng* (Cape Town, 1938), 173–74.

12. P. Pienaar, *With Steyn and de Wet* (London, 1902), 173.

13. Van Warmelo, *On Commando*, 54.

14. A. G. Oberholster, 26 and 29 September 1901, 294 and 295.

15. O. M., Reminiscences, 5774/1, Reminiscences of D. W. Steyn, 1.

16. P. H. Kritzinger and R. D. McDonald, *In the Shadow of Death* (London, 1904), 66, 69.

17. C. R. de Wet, *Three Years' War* (London, 1902), 263.

18. Naudé, *Vechten en Vluchten*, 235.

19. T.A.D., A239, Maj. A. L. la C. Bartrop Accession, G. J. Scheepers to C. R. de Wet, 3 July 1901.

20. Naudé, *Vechten en Vluchten*, 235–36. Cf. J.C.G. Kemp, *Vir Vryheid en Vir Reg* (Cape Town, 1941), 377–78; Warmelo, *On Commando*, 115; R. W. Schikkerling, 22 March 1901, 163–64.

21. Kritzinger and McDonald, *Shadow of Death*, 124.

22. T.A.D., W81, Viljoen Accession, 3, M. J. Viljoen, Diary No. 10, 29 April 1902.

23. T.A.D., A283, H. Hilhorst Accession, 1902, H. Hilhorst to Parents in the Netherlands, 12 July 1902.

24. F. W. Reitz, *A Century of Wrong* (London, 1900), 98. The name of State Secretary F. W. Reitz appears on the pamphlet as the author, but it is well known that the authors were Smuts and Jimmy Roos, with Smuts writing the major share.

25. T.A.D., A119, Renier Collection, No. 420, Diary of J. F. Naudé, 14 November 1899; Naudé, *Vechten en Vluchten*, 52–53, 55.

26. A1149, Anglo-Boer War Accession, Speech by J. C. Asselbergs before the Rotarians in the Netherlands, n.d., 6.

27. R. de Kersauson de Pennendreff, *Ek and die Vierkleur* (Johannesburg, 1960), 26 April 1902, 120–21.

28. Pretorius, *Kommandolewe*, 191–97.

29. Ibid.; Naudé, *Vechten en Vluchten*, 175.

30. Van Warmelo, *On Commando*, 112.

31. T.A.D., A313, Gen. J. H. de la Rey Collection, 17, Reminiscences of de la Rey, 38.

32. Pretorius, *Kommandolewe*, 191–97.

33. W. K. Hancock and J. van der Poel, *Selections from the Smuts Papers*, vol. 1 (Cambridge, 1966), 477, 479.

34. Du Plessis, *Oomblikke*, 71–72; T.A.D., W81, Viljoen Accession, 3, M. J. Viljoen, Diary No. 10, 10 January 1902.

35. S. B. Spies, *Methods of Barbarism? Roberts and Kitchener and Civilians in the Boer Republics, January 1900–May 1902* (Cape Town, 1977), 285, 293.

36. J. J. Oberholster, *Dagboek van Oskar Hintrager—Saam met Christiaan de Wet, Mei tot September 1900* (Bloemfontein, 1973), 13 and 27 July 1900, 72 and 92.

37. J. D. Kestell, *Through Shot and Flame* (London, 1903), 171–72; W. H. Ackermann, *Opsaal: Herinneringe aan die Tweede Vryheidsoorlog* (Johannesburg, 1969), 289; T.A.D., A239, Maj. A. L. la C. Bartrop Accession, Notice, P. H. Kritzinger, 6 January 1901; T.A.D., Preller Collection, 68, clipping from *The Detroit Free Press*, 2 December 1901, 436; J. D. Kestell and D. E. van Velden, *The Peace Negotiations between Boer and Briton in South Africa* (London, 1912), 172; J. F. van Wyk, *Die Mauser Knal* (Johannesburg, 1971), 111; G. Boldingh, *Een Hollandsch Officier in Zuid-Afrika* (Rotterdam, 1903), 48–49, 187.

38. Hancock and Van der Poel, *Smuts Papers*, 1.469.

39. Van Warmelo, *On Commando*, 93–94, 115.

40. T.A.D., A1242, Dr. A. J. van Rooy Accession, Diary of J. J. Heijnecke, 16 March 1902.

41. Diary of Heijnecke, 17 April 1902.

42. T.A.D., A1594, Family Röscher Accession, Reminiscences of H. J. Coetzer, 148. Cf. T.A.D., Preller Collection, 35, P. R. Viljoen to Unknown, n.d. [1901]; T.A.D., Preller Collection, 73, Reminiscences of P. E. van Wyk, 185; T.A.D., Preller Collection, 73, Reminiscences of D. L. Hattingh, 133–34; T.A.D., Preller Collection, 80, Reminiscences of L. E. Krause, 676; C.C.J. Badenhorst, *Uit den Boeren-Oorlog* (Amsterdam, 1903), 135; Reitz, *Century of Wrong*, 148–49, 150; Naudé, *Vechten en Vluchten*, 263; Kestell, *Through Shot and Flame*, 136, 189–90; T.A.D., W81, Viljoen Accession, 3, M. J. Viljoen, Diary No. 4, 10 January 1902; Kemp, *Vir Vryheid*, 435–36; T.A.D., A140, F. V. Engelenburg Collection, 22, 425; Kritzinger and McDonald, *Shadow of Death*, 124; T.A.D., A1321, J. H. Breytenbach Accession, 1, *Die Spook*, 11 November 1900; Pieterse, *Tweede Vryheidstryd*, 228; Hancock and van der Poel, *Smuts Papers*, 1.460.

43. Cf., e.g., T.A.D., A1643, Lord Roberts Papers: 48, T. Kelly-Kenny to F. Roberts, 17 September 1900, 157; 49, E. H. Dalgety to F. Roberts, 26 September 1900, 79–80; H. de B. de Lisle to F. Roberts, 26 September 1900, 83; J. French to F. Roberts, 1 September 1900, 132; 50, Barter to F. Roberts, 19 September 1900, 15; Barter to F. Roberts, 26 September 1900, 19; E. Wallace, *Unofficial Despatches of the Anglo-Boer War* (London, 1901), 237–38.

44. T.A.D., A117, Col. D. Reitz Accession, S. W. Burger to H. H. Kitchener, 5 September 1901.

45. Private Collection, Mrs. M. van Bergen, *De Brandwacht*, 25 April 1901; A. G. Oberholster, 28 April 1902, 373.

46. Pretorius, *Kommandolewe*, 206–11; T.A.D., A356, Dr. H. D. van Broekhuizen Collection, 9, Si Omong, "Met Genl. de Wet in den Vrystaat," 14; T.A.D., Preller Collection, 225, 157–58; Preller Collection, 226, 17–18; A. P. Smit and L. Maré, *Die Beleg van Mafeking* (Pretoria, 1985), 5 December 1899, 134–36; H. Verloren van Themaat, *Twee Jaren in den Boerenoorlog* (Haarlem, 1903), 334, 336; van Warmelo, *On Commando*, 22; Reitz, *Century of Wrong*, 107.

47. J. A. Smith, *Ek Rebelleer*, 3d ed. (Cape Town, 1946), 133–34.

48. R. W. Schikkerling, 3 May 1902, 382–83.

49. J. J. Oberholster, 28 July 1900, 92–93. Cf. Badenhorst, *Uit den Boeren-Oorlog*, 29.

50. B. J. Viljoen, *My Reminiscences of the Anglo-Boer War* (London, 1902), 149. Cf. T.A.D., Preller Collection, 61, Diary of Gustav Preller, 16 July 1901, 38–42, and Reitz, *Century of Wrong*, 138 for more examples.

51. T.A.D., Preller Collection, 21, War Report, F. W. Reitz, Ermelo, 30 May 1901, 106.

52. R. W. Schikkerling, 25 February 1901, 157.

53. Cf., e.g., Hancock and Van der Poel, *Smuts Papers*, 1.398, 401–2; Van Warmelo, *On Commando*, 51; T.A.D., A1048, J. G. de Jager Accession, 1 and 3 July 1900, 88–89; J. J. Oberholster, 30 July 1900, 96; T.A.D., Preller Collection, 60, Diary of Gustav Preller, 15 November 1900, 141–42; T.A.D., A239, Maj. A. L. la C. Bartrop Accession, M. T. Steyn, Senekal, 14 April 1901.

54. Wallace, *Unofficial Despatches*, 214.

55. T.A.D., A1231, Dr. J. H. Breytenbach Accession, 1, *Die Spook*, 26 September 1900, 61, 62–63.

56. F. D. Conradie, *Met Cronjé aan die Wesfront (1899–1900)* (Cape Town, 1943), 93, 101.

57. T.A.D., A1048, J. G. de Jager Accession, Diary of De Jager, 1, 22 November 1900, 175.

58. Pretorius, *Kommandolewe,* 262.

59. H. Giliomee, "The Beginnings of Afrikaner Nationalism, 1870–1915," *South African Historical Journal* 19 (1987): 129.

60. G.H.L. le May, *British Supremacy in South Africa, 1899–1907* (Oxford, 1965), 213–14.

61. Gens. P. D. de Wet of the Orange Free State and A. P. Cronjé of the ZAR, who laid down their arms and in 1902 became commanders in British military service, were not part of the old guard of incompetent officers referred to here.

62. D. Denoon, "Participation in the 'Boer War': People's War, People's Non-War, or Non-People's War?," in B. A. Ogot (ed.), *War and Society in Africa* (London, 1972), 117–19.

63. Le May, *British Supremacy,* 214; Denoon, "Participation," 117. See Lewsen, *Selections from the Correspondence of John X. Merriman, 1899–1905* (Cape Town, 1966), 352. Denoon's argument (which he borrowed from Merriman) that the *bywoners* took up arms on the British side during the guerrilla phase is not developed here as this chapter is concerned with the burghers on commando.

64. Viljoen, *Reminiscences,* 310; F. Seiner, *Ervaringen en Herinneringen van een Boerenstrijder op het Slagveld van Zuid-Afrika* (Doesburg, 1902), 3.

65. Hancock and Van der Poel, *Smuts Papers,* 1.575, 440.

66. T.A.D., Preller Collection, 80, Reminiscences of L. E. Krause, 611.

67. O.J.O. Ferreira, *Memoirs of General Ben Bouwer* (Pretoria, 1980), 94–95.

68. For details of these events see W. L. v. R. Scholtz, "Die Betrekkinge tussen die Zuid-Afrikaansche Republiek en die Oranje-Vrijstaat, 1899–1902" (M.A. thesis, Rand Afrikaans University, 1972), 124–32, 162–83.

CHAPTER 5

The Role of the Bakgatla of the Pilanesberg in the South African War

BERNARD MBENGA

THIS CHAPTER EXPLORES and analyzes the place of the South African War in the experience of the Bakgatla-ba-Kgafela of the Pilanesberg district in the Western Transvaal. As Bill Nasson shows in his study of the black and coloured experiences of the South African War in parts of the Cape Colony, locality is an important factor in the way it was perceived and fought by black people in South Africa. He poses and answers fundamentally important questions about the war: what were the content of and divisions among the leading adversaries in the conflict, and what were the ultimate terms of settlement and compensation? The answers depend on *whose* war one is discussing and where it took place—the burden of the war effort differed sharply in terms of how it pressed upon different regions.[1]

It is no longer necessary to repeat the generally acknowledged fact that black people were very active participants in a wide range of roles in the war, including armed combat, on both the British and the Boer sides.[2] Historians have shown that blacks were "active shaping agents as well as victims" in the war.[3] R. F. Morton and I have written extensively about Bakgatla participation in the war.[4] Morton, however, has tended to emphasize the Bechuanaland (i.e., Mochudi) side of Bakgatla participation. This chapter adds new information and perspectives on the Bakgatla's participation in the war, which it filters through the works of Morton, Peter Warwick, and Jeremy Krikler, and shows how the Bakgatla were both shaping agents and victims in the conflict, from the vantage point of the Pilanesberg. While it is not clear whether the Bakgatla appreciated the reasons why the British and the Boers went to war, they understood why they had taken up arms against the Boers. A further objective of this chapter, therefore, is to demonstrate that although the British used the Bakgatla to fight the war for them in the Pilanesberg, the Bakgatla had their own agenda and used the war to achieve

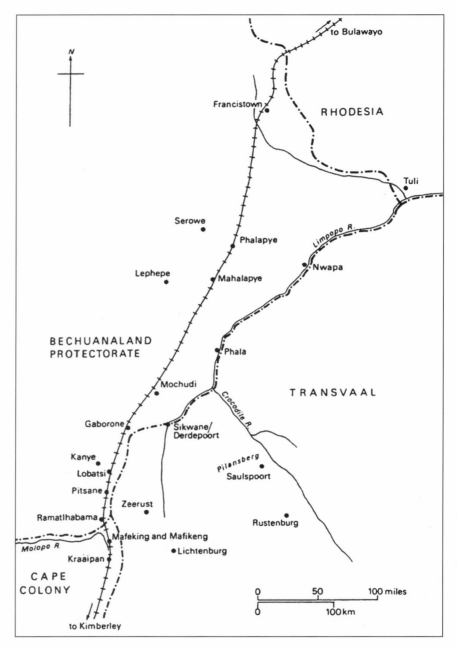

The Bechuanaland Protectorate and Western Transvaal.

SOURCE: P. Warwick, *Black People and the South African War, 1899–1902*
(Cambridge: Cambridge University Press, 1983), 29. Reprinted with the
permission of Cambridge University Press.

their own aims. The immediate physical and psychological impact of the Bakgatla's military role on the Pilanesberg is also emphasized.

A number of detailed explanations have been advanced for the outbreak of the South African War. Such explanations, however, can be read elsewhere.[5] While they apply to the major combatants at the national level, in the various regions where Africans became involved in the war, they did so for their own reasons. The Bakgatla harbored specific historical grudges against the Boers, including the Boers' incessant demands for Bakgatla labor over several decades. This finally culminated in their chief, Kgamanyane, being publicly flogged by Commandant (later President of the South African Republic) Paul Kruger in April 1870, an incident that led to half the Bakgatla emigrating to Mochudi, in today's Botswana. This resulted in the Bakgatla being permanently split into two sections.[6] In both the Pilanesberg and Mochudi, this episode was remembered with bitterness by older Bakgatla men and women, who gave graphic accounts of the flogging and the subsequent split. It was not surprising that the Bakgatla saw the war as an opportunity for revenge against the Boers.[7] To use a contemporary traveler's words, the Bakgatla were "eager to wipe out old scores,"[8] a reason that was also rooted in the very harsh nature of Boer rule over the Bakgatla, especially with regard to forced labor.[9] In addition to settling old scores, the Bakgatla wanted to regain their land in the Pilanesberg, which they had lost to the Boers, and to reunite their divided people.[10] The immediate reasons for the Pilanesberg Bakgatla's involvement in the war, however, lay in Mochudi. Since April 1870, the overall chiefly authority of this group had always emanated from outside the Transvaal, in Mochudi.[11] Thus, they entered the war by force of "outside" circumstances—their paramount chief Linchwe in Mochudi had made the decision.

British Policy Regarding African Participation in the War

As war became imminent, whites in South Africa generally feared that the fighting between Boers and the British might be used by disaffected African groups to advance their own interests and even to attempt to overthrow white rule. This explains the elaborate preparations by both sides to counter any possible African insurrection.[12] As late as June 1899, it was still official British policy not to use blacks in armed combat against the Boers. There were two reasons for this. First, the British were uncertain about black loyalty in the Transvaal. The official thinking was that since the British defeat by the Boers in 1881, Africans in South Africa had lost faith in Britain's military power and were, therefore, likely to keep on good terms with the

Boers.[13] Second, the British considered it distasteful, morally reprehensible, and outrageous to use blacks in a "white man's war" because of "the profound indignation that would be aroused by such a policy, not only in the Dutch Republics, but in the minds of English and Dutch settlers alike throughout the whole of South Africa."[14] The British doubted the loyalty of Linchwe and his Bakgatla in the Bechuanaland Protectorate shortly before the war. Half his people, after all, lived under Boer rule in the Transvaal. If Linchwe took sides, it could mean exposing his people to danger. Indeed, the contemporary writer L. S. Amery expressed Linchwe's predicament when he wrote that "his [Linchwe's] interests, even in peace time ... pulled him two ways."[15] As war approached, this doubt about Bakgatla loyalty must have worried the British, especially since the railway line that was essential for the transportation of the (British) Rhodesian troops to the south passed through the center of Bakgatla territory.

Linchwe's vacillation, however, was meant to buy time. Before openly declaring his intentions, Linchwe gave the Boers in the Derdepoort laager the false impression that he was on their side by sending them gifts of livestock. The Boers came to have a misplaced confidence in Linchwe. An Afrikaner scholar of the 1940s erroneously believed that "Although not trusted by some people, Linchwe was in fact a friend of the Boers" and for this reason President Paul Kruger had even considered seeking Linchwe's support in the conflict between the Boers and the Bangwato chief, Khama.[16] Following the Transvaal government's declaration of war on October 11, 1899, Boer commandos in the Transvaal and the Orange Free State embarked upon a preemptive campaign against the comparatively few British troops in South Africa, hoping for an early Republican victory. As part of this campaign, the Boers besieged the town of Mafeking. To prevent the (southern) Rhodesian troops from relieving Mafeking, the Boer commandos, numbering some three hundred, moved into the Protectorate to destroy the railway line and cause havoc, especially in the area between Gaborone and Mafeking, which was closest to the Zuid-Afrikaansche Republiek (South African Republic, ZAR).[17] These events must have had a bearing upon the Bakgatla's decision to join in the war.

The more immediate factors that confirmed Linchwe's decision to join the war, however, were Boer acts of aggression in, or close to, Bakgatla territory in the Protectorate. During the last two weeks of October 1899, the Boer forces under Commandants P. D. Swart and J. P. Snyman captured Lobatse, occupied Gaborone, engaged the British at the Pools on the Transvaal-Bechuanaland border, and wrecked a railway culvert north of Mochudi. Commandant P. Kruger at Derdepoort "occupied his men with ... the looting of Linchwe's cattle."[18] At the same time, Bakgatla cattle in the Pilanesberg were seized by the Boers. Such incidents were reported in Mochudi, and calls went up for Linchwe to "prepare for war because the Boers are coming to do the same thing there."[19] Linchwe remained cautious and refused to support either side.

The incident that finally decided him, however, was the "insult" that, as Bakgatla traditions widely assert, was publicly hurled at Linchwe by the Boer Commandant P. J. Hans Riekert. Riekert was riding through Mochudi at the head of a commando *en route* to destroy the railway line when the chief asked them not to disturb the women and children of the town. Riekert then "answered scornfully, picking up a stone from the *kgotla* [and said]: 'Your chieftainship is no more than a piece of dust.'"[20] Although this incident must have swung his sympathies in favor of the British, Linchwe was still too weak militarily to retaliate against the Boers. Until the British troop reinforcements arrived from Rhodesia, the Bakgatla remained vulnerable to Boer attacks. As *The Times History* put it: "Until Plumer [the Rhodesian troop commander] came up the British were not strong enough do much more than patrol the railway with armoured trains."[21]

Entry of the Bakgatla into the War

With the arrival of the Rhodesian troops at Mahalapye early in November 1899 and the news that Chief Khama of the Bangwato had repulsed a Boer attack at Selika Kop, Linchwe told W. H. Surmon, the Assistant Commissioner for the Southern District based at Gaborone, that he was ready to fight the Boers and asked for arms. In response, the commander of the British troops at Mochudi railway station, Lieutenant-Colonel G. L. Holdsworth, told Linchwe and Segale (Linchwe's half-brother) that the Bakgatla regiments would be part of, and led by, the British forces. In mid-November 1899, the Bakgatla began to prepare for war.[22]

Three Bakgatla regiments joined the British troops to attack the Boer laager at nearby Derdepoort. Before their departure, Holdsworth "impressed on them [i.e., the Bakgatla] the necessity of their remaining on their own side of the border and that they were not to fire unless ordered."[23] He had also been told by the British High Command that he was to use the Bakgatla as guides and carriers. Assistant Commissioner Surmon also made it clear to Holdsworth that he was "unable to consent to the employment of his [i.e., Linchwe's] men in military operations in the Transvaal, as it might lead to deplorable consequences."[24] A further stipulation was that if the Boers invaded any of the British Bechuanaland Reserves, it was the inhabitants' duty "as loyal subjects of Her Majesty the Queen, to assist in repelling the invasion."[25]

It is significant, however, that the Bakgatla's role as guides and transport assistants only was omitted from the telegraphic instructions sent to Holdsworth on November 22, 1899, by his superior, Colonel J. S. Nicholson, Commandant-General of Police in Bulawayo, Southern Rhodesia. The omission meant that Holdsworth could "make his own arrangements."[26] This left Holdsworth free to use his discretion about whether or not to commit the Bakgatla troops to armed combat. He exploited this loophole, with serious consequences for both the Boers and the Bakgatla. Moreover, the condition that the Bakgatla were not to fire unless ordered to do so presupposed that, if circumstances demanded, they could be armed.

As a result of the Boer authorities' ignorance of the military plans of the combined British/Bakgatla troops, the attack on Derdepoort caught its white residents by surprise, with disastrous results. The Boer miscalculation and lack of preparation needs some explanation. Early in November 1899, most of the Boer commandos in the western Transvaal, some seven thousand strong, were based at Ottoshoop, east of Mafeking, under the command of Generals P. A. Cronjé, J. H. de la Rey, and J. P. Snyman. Their objective was to capture Mafeking and Kimberley, while a part of the Rustenburg commando, camped near Lobatse, was to destroy the railway. Derdepoort had only a "small force"[27] of about one hundred men in the laager, under Commandant J. F. Kirsten, and another eighty-five policemen under police Commandant H. Riekert.[28] The defense of Derdepoort in the event of a British attack was clearly not a priority for the Boers.

About 500 Rustenburgers were sent, not to Derdepoort, but to the southern front on the Modder River. This was carried out on the advice of General P. A. Cronjé, who, like the rest of the Boer military hierarchy, was ignorant of Derdepoort's vulnerable security. Indeed, Cronje gave "constant and misleading reports" to President Kruger "that Derdepoort was a comparatively safe place," which suggested that Boer military attention should be directed elsewhere.[29] There were two reasons for the Boers' misjudgment. First, Linchwe's acts of "friendship" toward the Boers misled them. His real intention was, as an old Mokgatla man told Schapera in 1932, "to blind the Dutch."[30] Second, the British-Bakgatla military plans and preparations for the Derdepoort assault were made in great secrecy.

The Derdepoort Attack, November 25, 1899

The combined British-Bakgatla force of about 120 men left Mochudi for the Derdepoort laager on the evening of November 24, 1899. Holdsworth ordered a Bakgatla regiment, instead of the British troops, to secure the ground leading up to the Boer laager across the Madikwe River. He effectively told them to enter the ZAR, contrary to "strict" official instructions.[31] Ellenberger recorded that Holdsworth "feared that our men's heavy ammunition boots would betray us when climbing up to the laager and he decided that the bare-footed natives should do the climbing, Segale guiding us to a place from which we could see the laager and open fire on it."[32] The rest of the Bakgatla were in the Protectorate, while Holdsworth and his men were inside the Transvaal border, strategically placed with a maxim gun on a ridge on the western bank of the Madikwe, overlooking the Boer laager. All the troops went into action when they saw smoke. Shooting began immediately north of Holdsworth's position. Both the British and the Bakgatla troops were dangerously placed, because when they fired at the laager their bullets landed on each other's positions. Another logistical problem was that the British troops could not cross the river quickly because there was no accessible drift.[33]

Holdsworth later claimed that it was for these reasons and his "belated realisation" that he and his men were in ZAR territory that he decided to withdraw his troops and return to Mochudi. This left the Bakgatla on their own and gave them an opportunity to settle their longstanding grievances against the Boers. In the ensuing fight, 14 Bakgatla were killed and 16 were wounded. The Boer casualties amounted to 20 dead, including J. H. Barnard, a member of the first *Volksraad* in Rustenburg. The Bakgatla also captured 100 oxen, 30 horses, and 18 women and children.[34] Bakgatla success in this attack must have been significant because "15 Burgers deserted the laager" and Commandant Kirsten admitted, after the war, that "the Kaffirs shot wonderfully well, in the same manner as the Boers, and their aiming was excellent, infinitely better than that of the English."[35]

At this early stage, the Bakgatla extended the war far beyond Derdepoort and used it entirely for their own purposes. The murder of a German trader, Sidney Engers, in Sikwane village, near Derdepoort, illustrates this. Ramono, a Bakgatla commander, ordered Engers arrested and imprisoned at Mochudi. The Bakgatla, however, killed Engers because they thought he was armed and intended to kill them, and because he was friendly with the area's Boer community. According to Linchwe and Ramono, he was also "a personal friend of Commandant Rickards [*sic*] of Derdepoort."[36] This was well known to the Bakgatla border communities of Derdepoort, Sikwane, Mathubudukwane, and Mochudi, whose residents considered Engers guilty by association. This opinion was reiterated by the Resident Commissioner at Mafeking, R. Williams, when he reported that the Bakgatla had killed Engers because he was a Boer sympathizer.[37] But even more serious in the eyes of the Bakgatla was that Engers had spied on Bakgatla and British troops on behalf of the Boers. The British commanders in the area also believed this from their intelligence reports and had therefore agreed, before the Derdepoort attack, that Engers should be taken prisoner. As Segale said: "Engers was friendly with the Boers and giving them information of the British Forces' movements. Mr. Surmon said he should be made a prisoner and brought to Mochudi."[38]

Despite European outrage at this incident,[39] none of the Bakgatla involved was punished,[40] presumably because the British military authorities considered the Bakgatla their allies. After all, Bakgatla military prowess in the Pilanesberg had enabled the British to leave the area entirely to their surveillance and could turn British attention to fighting the Boers elsewhere in South Africa. Finding the Bakgatla not guilty was a way of acknowledging their role. British officials, such as Ellenberger and Williams, consistently defended the Bakgatla in the Derdepoort episode.[41]

There were rumors of the murder of Boers and the destruction of their property by the Bakgatla among Boer communities of the western Transvaal.[42] Sensational stories of such "atrocities" were published both locally and abroad. A contemporary pro-Boer source, for example, recorded that "a German trader was disemboweled and otherwise tortured,"[43] while another reported that some of the Derdepoort Boer women and children taken captive were murdered by the Bakgatla.[44] The British fear (and the Boers' desire) that the Derdepoort episode might be publicized abroad was realized early in 1900 when a German journal reported that British and Bakgatla soldiers took turns raping Boer women *en route* to Mochudi.[45] These accounts, with their brutal images of Bakgatla and British atrocities, still linger in the consciousness of older Afrikaners in Rustenburg. In a popular account of white Rustenburg's experience in the two South African Wars of 1880–81 and 1899–1902, Wulfsohn recorded that at Derdepoort the Bakgatla "attacked civilians, women and children, looting, plundering and burning homes and shops and generally running wild," while the Boer women and children whom the Bakgatla took to Mochudi "walked the whole of the 25th and 26th without being offered food or water by their escort."[46]

These reports, however, were exaggerated and were contradicted by a number of sources. The Assistant Commissioner at Gaborone, W. H. Surmon, for example, reported that "not one of them [the Boer captives] ever mentioned to me that they had in any way been ill-treated by the Bakhatla beyond being required to walk from Sekwani to Mochudi."[47] Engers's housekeeper, De Villiers, who was one the prisoners of war "marched" by the Bakgatla to Mochudi, also refuted the allegations of Bakgatla brutality: "We were all together and I saw no outrage or violence of any kind committed on the Dutch women. They were insulted in no way by any one, to my knowledge as we were together the whole time."[48] De Villiers should be considered a credible witness because, with her employer and source of livelihood gone, she had nothing to lose by telling the truth. Moreover, she gave her testimony in Mafeking, geographically far removed from Derdepoort and any intimidating influences on her testimony. This, however, is not to exonerate the Bakgatla of all blame. They destroyed Boer property in Derdepoort by setting fire to a number of buildings, including Commandant Riekert's house.[49]

Issues and Repercussions Arising from the Derdepoort Episode

Key questions about the Derdepoort assault, which have previously been overlooked in the historiography,[50] need further explanation. Did Lt. Col. Holdsworth, for example, really not understand that by ordering the Bakgatla regiments onto a ridge overlooking the Boer laager, he was in effect telling them to cross into the Transvaal, against official instructions? Why did he and his troops withdraw from the battle as soon as it began? It seems implausible that he did not know the terrain around Derdepoort, which ignorance resulted in the Bakgatla entering the Transvaal.[51] Segale, who knew the area and its Bakgatla community well, gave Holdsworth information about Derdepoort, and especially "the position of the [Boer] laager and how to get there."[52] Holdsworth deployed his men, both Bakgatla and British, on this basis. Ellenberger, who was in the war party, recorded that Segale "gave Colonel Holdsworth *all* information as to the position of the laager."[53]

Holdsworth must have known that he was sending the Bakgatla into the Transvaal. Indeed, on December 30, 1899, following an official inquiry into the Derdepoort issue, Surmon revealed that he was prepared to prove that Linchwe's men "were instructed to cross into the Transvaal at Sequani on the 25th instant, and *that they did so contrary to orders is not true.*"[54] But why did Holdsworth act the way he did? Perhaps because the Bakgatla knew the local terrain and the British did not, Holdsworth decided to use the Bakgatla to save his British troops. According to Wulfsohn, the idea of using the Bakgatla as "cannon fodder" was conceived by Col. Nicholson, Holdsworth's superior, long before the Bakgatla-British departure from Mochudi.[55] This explanation is not far-fetched. Both the Assistant and Resident Commissioners "remained convinced throughout the war that Holdsworth had deliberately used the Kgatla to do his fighting."[56] The Bakgatla, no doubt, felt betrayed by the British action at Derdepoort, and Linchwe himself expressed his disappointment to Holdsworth.[57]

The Boers were also aggrieved and alarmed by the incident, and on November 26, 1899, a Boer survivor of the attack cycled to Rustenburg to alert the Boer military authorities, who immediately embarked upon reprisals. There was considerable panic in reaction to the exaggerated estimate of the danger; a large number of Boer troops were sent to Derdepoort from Rustenburg and Crocodile Pools and many others were mobilized from the Heks and Kgetleng Rivers districts, the Waterberg, Mafeking and even Johannesburg. By the beginning of December 1899, the combined number of Boer troops at Derdepoort was well over 400.[58] Boer fears generated rumors that spread rapidly throughout the Pilanesberg and Rustenburg areas and galvanized the Boers into action.[59] Commandant-General J. van Rensburg led a carefully planned offensive of six Boer commandos against the Bakgatla and heavy fighting ensued during the early hours of December 22, 1899. Bakgatla pressure on a Boer commandant made him so "desperate" that two more commandos were sent to his rescue. But by the end of the day, the Bakgatla had succumbed to Boer fire and had "scattered in all directions," leaving some 150 dead while the Boers reported only four killed.[60] The Boer commandos razed the Bakgatla border villages of Mathubudukwane, Malolwane, and Sikwane, and threatened to attack Mochudi itself to punish the Bakgatla and eliminate any further danger.[61] Sikwane, the closest settlement to Derdepoort, was "thoroughly ravaged" by the Boers to prevent its being used as a base against them.[62] As a precaution, Linchwe moved his people and their livestock along the border to the safety of Mochudi.

The Boers took three horses, several wagons, ploughs, pots, and other small items as booty and burned a large quantity of ammunition.[63] After pillaging the three villages, Van Rensburg and his commando were satisfied with the "telling punishment" and generally believed that the Bakgatla would "no longer [dare] to trouble the Boers."[64] The Boers were prevented from continuing the offensive early in 1900 by the vulnerability of their unprotected farms in the Transvaal.[65] Their actions, however, only spurred the Bakgatla to fight back.

Bakgatla Escalation of the War in the Pilanesberg

The Bakgatla now considered the war against the Boers to be completely their own, and it soon escalated throughout the Pilanesberg. As a result of Segale's complaint to the British authorities that "the Boers were mistreating Transvaal Kgatla loyal to his brother [Linchwe],"[66] the Bakgatla received a further one hundred Martini-Henry rifles in January 1900. To those Bakgatla who were most eager to fight the Boers, this must have appeared as a "go-ahead" signal from the British, which they seized with enthusiasm. Linchwe mobilized the Makoba and Mojanko regiments, commanded by Ramono and Motshwane respectively, on February 16, 1900. The regiments waited in an elaborately planned ambush at Kayaseput, halfway between Derdepoort and the Dwarsberg mountains, for a large convoy of Boer troop reinforcements and supply wagons bound for Derdepoort from Rustenburg. These reinforcements were intended for the defense of the Boers in Derdepoort. Many Boers were killed in the ensuing attack, and their wagons and supplies were captured.[67] The news of this was so unsettling that a Boer commando at nearby Sepitse abandoned its laager.[68] This incident in Bakgatla history has lived on in popular memory and is depicted in a praise-poem dedicated to the bravery of Ramono.[69] Soon after the Kayaseput ambush, Commandant P. Steenkamp and some of the Rustenburg commando went to Derdepoort to bring back *all* the remaining Boers. Derdepoort was abandoned and remained unoccupied for the remainder of the war.[70]

The Derdepoort and Kayaseput episodes were significant. They boosted Bakgatla morale and gave them the confidence to pursue the war more vigorously, as later military engagements were to show. The Bakgatla also proved that the Boers were not invincible; the Boer withdrawal from Derdepoort was highly symbolic. Furthermore, as Mohlamme has pointed out, the Boer military threat on the western Transvaal-Bechuanaland border had been considerably reduced; the Boers "now concentrated their attacks south of Gaborone towards Mafeking." The British reoccupied Gaborone, which the Boers had forced them to abandon in October 1899.[71] Soon after the Kayaseput incident, Linchwe sent the Mojanko regiment under Modise to assist the Bakgatla at Saulspoort. In a major engagement at Moreteletse in Mabeskraal, the Bakgatla "captured 300 Boer trek oxen, and 2 vehicles [wagons] and successfully brought them off." But it was also in this battle that Tlatsi, Linchwe's *Ntona* (confidential assistant), was killed in action.[72] The British supplied a further 250 Martini-Henry rifles in mid-1900,[73] which clearly put the Bakgatla on the warpath. In July 1901, Linchwe obtained permission from the Assistant Commissioner at Gaborone "to protect his people at Saulspoort who were in danger of attack," but he was told "not to attack outside his own country [i.e., Mochudi in Bechuanaland]," although the message added that "there is no reason why he should not send some of his men to assist Saulspoort."[74] By this stage of the South African War, the British needed the assistance of the Bakgatla and openly approved of and encouraged their military role in the Transvaal. They supplied Linchwe with an unspecified number of "rifles and ammunition" on two occasions.[75] The Bakgatla operated south of the Kgetleng River as far as Rustenburg, with the permission of the British Director of Military Intelligence. They were so effective that F. Edmeston, the Sub-Native Commissioner (SNC) at Saulspoort, commented that "the Military Authorities were relieved of all anxiety as to this district, which was held by these [Bakgatla] people, as far north as Palla."[76] The triumphant Bakgatla claimed all the lands "stretching from the Crocodile to the Elands River. They were so carried away by this that it was generally understood among themselves that no Boers would be allowed to cross the Elands River."[77] Krikler has aptly described the Bakgatla as the "scourge of the western Transvaal."[78] Apart from their role as soldiers, the Bakgatla also served as scouts, guides, and wagon drivers, and supplied the British forces with intelligence reports "on every occasion of Boer movements."[79]

The Bakgatla's large-scale looting of Boer cattle was a major feature of the war in the Pilanesberg. More than any other Africans in the western Transvaal who participated in the war, the Bakgatla looted Boer cattle on an enormous scale.[80] As the Native Commissioner (NC) in Rustenburg reported at the end of the war, it was mainly the Bakgatla who raided Boer cattle; there were "very few instances" of other ethnic groups in the Pilanesberg involved in such looting.[81] This was to be expected, as the Bakgatla were the Boers' main adversaries in this area during the South African War. As a senior British official noted, however, the raids were carried out "[in] the majority of the cases ... at the instigation and with the cognizance of the [British] military authorities,"[82] presumably to demoralize the Boers and "reward" the Bakgatla. But it is likely that this activity was beyond the control of the British authorities.

The looted cattle were taken to the safety of Mochudi because, as one Mokgatla source put it, once they were there, "it was the end of them, whatever the Boers did, they could never get them back."[83] During the war, the looted cattle were shared out in two ways. Linchwe "generously" distributed some of them among the heroes of the war, while some were slaughtered to feed his troops. After the war, some were given to the ward headmen, the poor, the gallant men of war, and the sons of those who had died in the fighting. The Saulspoort Bakgatla who had brought looted cattle to Mochudi were rewarded with more cattle to ensure their loyalty.[84] And Linchwe still had plenty of cattle for himself, as indicated in June 1904 by the NC for the Western Division, C. Griffith, who noted that "The chief, Lintsoe, has a great many herds of cattle running on farms along the Marico and Crocodile Rivers."[85]

The Bakgatla also looted cattle belonging to other Batswana groups in the Pilanesberg. During the war, they raided livestock worth £828 from the Baphalane.[86] The NC reported in November 1902 that the Bakgatla had

"looted stock from most of the natives residing within reach of Saulspoort."
He had received "numerous complaints" from "various tribes" in the Pilanesberg whose cattle had been "raided or stolen from them by the Bakhatla
(Lintsue's people) during the war" and, to ensure the cattle's safe-keeping,
"99% of it" was taken away to the Protectorate.[87] Why did the Bakgatla do
this to their fellow Batswana and neighbors? The Bakgatla rationalized this
as punitive action against people they considered to be collaborators of the
Boers. If Chief Linchwe's report of February 14, 1902, to the Resident Commissioner (RC) in Mafeking is to be believed, some African groups "on
the Marico and thereabouts are helping the Boers and are supplying them
with information."[88] During the war, the Boers gave their cattle to some
"friendly" Batswana groups in the Pilanesberg, especially the Bafokeng of
Chief Mokgatle, the Bakwena of Chief Lerotoli, and the Baphalane of Chief
Ramokoka, for safe-keeping while they were away fighting. The Bakgatla
alleged that these groups favored the Boers by feeding them and acting as
their faithful scouts.[89] But it is also possible that the general chaos of the war
and past internecine struggles allowed the Bakgatla to take action against
their neighbors.

The allegations made by the Bakgatla were not unfounded. There is some
indication that throughout the Transvaal the Boer guerrillas sometimes commandeered livestock from Africans. But generally they were offered food by
or bought it from "friendly" Africans, especially when Kitchener's scorched-
earth policy destroyed the Boers' food supply in the countryside. As one
Boer leader at the Vereeniging Peace Conference stated: "We must obtain
mealies from the Kaffirs by using nice words."[90] The works of Warwick,
Nasson, Manson, Mohlamme, and Pretorius indicate that the Boers also
used Africans in armed combat,[91] which is why the Bakgatla treated their
neighbors as they did.

The Engers incident at Sikwane illustrates the fact that the Bakgatla considered those who aided their enemies as accomplices unworthy of lenient
treatment. A few months after the outbreak of war, the property of a Jewish
trader from Saulspoort, M. Pieters, was looted by the Bakgatla while he was
out of town. Pieters had been trading in Saulspoort since 1890. Goods to the
value of £3,400 were "completely looted" and he demanded compensation.
In an investigation by the SNC at the end of the war, the Bakgatla leadership
in Saulspoort admitted to the looting by "unknown people" from their location.[92] Their spokesperson, Segale, insisted that Pieters had used his shop
"for the purpose of supplying Boers' [commando] camps at different places
during the late war" and alleged that he "was promised by the Boers that
all goods taken away from his shop for supplying their camps will be paid

again by their Government (as Compensation) after having conquered British Armies."[93] Citing precise dates and various Bakgatla witnesses, Segale described the occasions on which Pieters had supplied a wide range of foods and other resources to commando camps throughout the Pilanesberg between October 15, 1899, and April 11, 1900.[94]

Pieters's request to the SNC for compensation was rejected for four reasons. First, since Pieters kept scaling down his claim (from £3,400 at first to £1,750), the SNC became skeptical about his *bona fides* as a person who could not "forgo any legitimate claim." Second, the SNC, like the Bakgatla leadership, maintained that Pieters's shop had goods worth only about £50 at the time of the looting. Third, Chief Ramono argued, with the support of the SNC, that the Bakgatla as a group were not to blame for the raid since they had been away at war at the time and so "neither the absent tribe, nor its absent authorities can be held to be responsible for the protection of the store from criminals—such protection being the duty of the late Government."[95] Last, the suggestion to the SNC by Pieters's lawyers, Roux and Jacobsz, that "the matter is one that had better be settled out of Court by mutual agreement,"[96] implied a weak legal position—one the SNC rejected.[97] Following the failure of his claim for compensation, Pieters decided to leave Saulspoort, and sometime in May 1903 he settled in Selukwe, Southern Rhodesia.[98]

The looting of Pieters's property was not solely the action of irresponsible, criminal elements, as Chief Ramono suggested to the SNC and Pieters; rather, it was a calculated effort to avenge Pieters's material assistance to the Boers.[99] It was instigated by and condoned at the highest level of Bakgatla society. Some members of the royal family were even involved. According to Pieters, Ditlhake was in possession of some of his stolen sheep and goats at the end of the war,[100] while "one of the Chief's brothers" had some of his stolen furniture.[101] Yet Pieters's prewar relations with the Bakgatla were generally quite good. He had, for example, given his "doors, door-frames and all house furnitures" to one Headman Bafsyoe [*sic*] for safe-keeping, while "Headman Mokae kept clothes and other goods for him." Pieters also "gave the other goods to his native friends,"[102] apparently free of charge. This is evidence of Pieters's good will toward the Bakgatla generally. The friendly relationship between Pieters and some Bakgatla existed *before* the war, however. It is feasible, therefore, that the Bakgatla looted Pieters's property not because he was white or unpopular, but simply because of the enormous material assistance he gave to the Boers from the beginning of the war. The open way in which he did this may have worsened matters.

The Bakgatla's looting was accompanied by general lawlessness and the wanton destruction of property. In the western Transvaal, "the breakdown of military and civil authority" became "very worrying" to the British.[103] While British military operations were mainly confined to the largest settlements along the railway and main roads,[104] the Bakgatla sowed mayhem in the countryside. The extent of Bakgatla destruction in the Pilanesberg was much greater than has hitherto been acknowledged. The historiography has tended to dwell on Boer atrocities and/or Bakgatla looting of Boer cattle.[105] Virtually all the Boers in the Pilanesberg, however, fled to Rustenburg for safety as a result of the violent Bakgatla campaign. E. F. Knight, a British journalist who traveled to the Pilanesberg immediately after the war, conveyed the situation graphically: "The Dutch population had to fly, and not a Boer, man, woman or child was left in the land." Knight came across numerous cases of the destruction of Boer property, "*not* by our troops—for the British columns never operated in this region, though they occasionally skirted it—but by the Kaffirs of the Bakgatla tribe, whose work of destruction was far more complete than that effected by our own soldiery."[106] But this kind of violence and destruction was not confined to the Pilanesberg; it occurred in other parts of the Transvaal as well.[107]

Virtually all the destruction of Boer property in the Pilanesberg can be attributed to the Bakgatla.[108] Knight and his party regularly came across the Boers' "roofless, gutted homesteads" on the first day of their travel from Rustenburg to the Pilanesberg in 1903. At Zand Drift on the Kgetleng River, the party saw "two Boer homesteads, both in ruins and deserted." Throughout the area to the north of the Kgetleng River, "every [Boer] homestead had been razed to the ground," and, close to Saulspoort itself, there were "a few scattered, ruined, and abandoned Boer homesteads [which] told the tale of the Bakgatla raids." The Bakgatla also felled fruit trees and removed corrugated-iron sheets and bricks from the abandoned Boer homes to build their own houses.[109] Bakgatla looting and destruction was, however, only a part of their much larger war to take over Boer farms and reoccupy their ancestral lands.[110] Once the Boers had abandoned their farms, the Bakgatla took them over "as theirs by right of conquest."[111] They were convinced that this would be a permanent acquisition, since the British had promised to give them "the territory ... they had controlled during the war."[112]

The above account of the Bakgatla role during the war should not give the impression that there was no reaction from the Boers. The period from August to December 1901, which saw an escalation of Bakgatla activity, was also a time when Boer retaliatory raids were at their peak. The Boers achieved some military successes and the Bakgatla sometimes sustained heavy losses. In a major battle on December 12, 1901, for example, Commandant J.C.G. Kemp

and his commando attacked Saulspoort and raided northwards to the Bier-
kraal River. Some thirty herdsmen under Kgaboesele attacked the commando
"on its retirement" until they ran out of ammunition. Kgaboesele and five
others were killed and the rest were wounded. This engagement was very
significant because it "cost the tribe some 6,000 to 7,000 head of cattle,
without mentioning small stock," apart from the dead and wounded.[113] This
Bakgatla claim points to the severity of the Boer assault. It also shows that
however successful the Bakgatla were, they could not afford to underestimate the military skill of Boer forces.

The Boers also committed considerable excesses during the South African
War. Even neutral African communities bore the brunt of Boer and British
warfare. In the southwestern Transvaal, "Africans faced immense losses and
hardships" as their crops were destroyed, their livestock was stolen, and their
communities were displaced.[114] In the Pilanesberg, Boer retaliation was to be
expected, in view of the extent of Bakgatla violence against them. At the end
of the war, the SNC reported that there had been "summary executions" as
well as "numberless cases of cruelty by Boers [which] took place in public at
Saulspoort, amongst which the flogging to death of an invalid, Mogasoe
Segogoane is the worst case."[115] The Boers also flogged anyone they sus-
pected of giving information to the British, while "men and women were
wantonly shot down when ploughing their lands in the Pilandsberg [sic]."[116]
In contrast, as the SNC claimed, the Bakgatla "never mutilated the bodies
of the enemy, nor injured a Boer female or child."[117] These actions have
some resonance with Nasson's assessment of the South African War in parts
of the Cape as "a war between British imperialism and Boer republicanism
turned with abrupt and explosive force into a desperate, undeclared civil war
between rural whites and rural blacks."[118] But unlike the Cape, where blacks
and coloureds were mainly on the receiving end of the Boer forces' "gener-
alised repressive determination,"[119] the Bakgatla war against the Boers in the
Pilanesberg was much more effective. Soon after Commandant Kemp's attack,
the scales were once again tipped in favor of the Bakgatla when they received
a new batch of rifles from Kitchener. This allowed them successfully to engage
the Boers at Draaiberg and Janskop, after which they effectively controlled
most of the western Transvaal until the Boer surrender on May 31, 1902.[120]

The Bakgatla had achieved many of their objectives in the war. They had
driven many Boers off their farms in the Pilanesberg and had occupied
them. Although this turned out to be a short-term position, it was nevertheless symbolic of the Bakgatla's strong desire to reclaim their ancestral
lands. They had also succeeded in raiding many Boer cattle, which became a
source of community wealth. A number of factors contributed to Bakgatla

success. At least until March 1900, Boer forces were preoccupied with the sieges of major towns, such as Mafeking, where they were engaged in fierce, debilitating battles with the British. Those in the far western Transvaal and the northern Cape concentrated on disrupting the railway, leaving vast expanses of countryside, such as the Pilanesberg, undefended and open to Bakgatla attacks.[121] Moreover, the Bakgatla's high fighting morale was sustained by the belief that they would regain their ancestral lands from the Boers. This belief was so strong that the Pilanesberg SNC, F. Edmeston, wrote that it "served to keep every available man in the [battle] field."[122] Bakgatla success can also be explained by their unity of purpose and the resoluteness with which they fought the Boers. This determination was forged over decades of external threats from both the Bakwena and the Boers, and it was strengthened by Bakgatla access to British arms. Grundlingh has recorded that the Boer commandos were poorly motivated and "would not have hesitated to surrender their arms at the earliest opportunity." The lack of discipline among Boers on commando meant that they could go home to check on their family and property whenever they wished to. Boer defeatism and low morale worsened after February 1900, when General P. Cronjé surrendered to General Roberts. It deteriorated even more when the British occupied Bloemfontein in March 1900 and later invaded the Transvaal.[123] All this facilitated Bakgatla war gains in the Pilanesberg.

Results of the War

The Bakgatla gained enormously from the looted Boer cattle, which more than compensated for what they had lost to the Boers. Cattle were an all-important resource Linchwe used to boost his status and prestige and to buy his people much-needed additional land in the Pilanesberg after the South African War. Africans in the Transvaal generally believed that the Boer farms they had occupied during the war "would be confiscated and given to the natives," but the British authorities "lost no time in dispelling this delusion."[124] In June 1903, the Commissioner for Native Affairs (CNA) described the idea of Africans possessing Boer farms as "misguided" and called for a return to the prewar status quo. Race relations could be "healthy," he stated in chauvinistic terms, "if the higher race recognises its obligations to the lower, and the lower race realises its true position and ... owns towards the higher race a becoming respect."[125] Since one of their war objectives was to regain possession of their ancestral lands, the Bakgatla were greatly disappointed when they were ordered to vacate the Boer farms. The CNA was aware of Bakgatla despair when he wrote that the Natives are greatly disappointed at not being made grants of land in consideration of the services they rendered to our troops during the late war; they fully expected that the farms would be taken from the Boers and given to them. They anticipated the [Boer] farmers being dispossessed of all title to land.[126]

The Bakgatla, however, experienced a greater loss than expulsion from Boer farms. Although there are no statistics of Bakgatla war losses, they lost heavily in human resources. Morton suggests that the Bakgatla "probably suffered a higher casualty rate, because the Boer was more experienced with the rifle and therefore a better shot."[127] On one occasion, the Bakgatla "lost 52 men in action" while 44 others were subjected to "summary executions" by Boers.[128] But there were, of course, many more casualties from the battles between the two sides. Morton has estimated the number of Bakgatla men killed in action at some 200, not to mention those who survived the war permanently disfigured in one way or another.[129] The general insecurity caused by the war and the fear of being killed by Boer commandos also prevented the Bakgatla from cultivating their fields. The consequent famine had a profound impact on food production. A survivor recalled in the late 1920s that "All that they [the Bakgatla in the Pilanesberg] knew was famine. It was famine that scattered them hither and thither and not war."[130] This was compounded by the fact that "every available man" was sent to the battlefield[131] instead of the corn field.

Relations between the Boers and the Africans were transformed as a result of the South African War. Krikler, for example, has recounted how many farm workers all over the Transvaal deserted their Boer masters during the war, never to return to "their exploiters."[132] Even more striking was the changed nature of the Africans' attitudes toward whites in general. Africans had become, as the Boers and the British administrators put it, "disrespectful" to white people. The African attitude was unmistakably hostile and was reflected in the CNA's report for June 1903. He recorded that black people had developed "a spirit of independence and apparent aggressiveness which was a new and regrettable feature in relations between black and white."[133] In September 1903, C. Griffith, the NC for the western Transvaal, reported that "all" the Africans who had fought with the British in the war "were disposed to be very disrespectful to the farmers and were disinclined to go out and work for them."[134]

This attitude was even more pronounced among the Bakgatla. They had played a major role in the defeat of the Boers and their struggles "were probably the most effective and militant of all those waged by rural working people during the South African War."[135] They saw their role in the war as having placed them on a different, special level and they therefore expected better treatment. In September 1902, the SNC observed that "They look upon themselves as having been *very necessary allies* of the British Government during the late war and that they are entitled to be treated *on a different footing* to the other tribes."[136] Their military role had demonstrated a considerable measure of courage, confidence, and even arrogance. The journalist E. F. Knight, who visited the Pilanesberg in 1903, observed that "The recent successes of the Bakgatla have given these already sufficiently conceited people very swollen heads. They are waxing insolent and may become dangerous."[137]

In 1902, when the NC instructed the SNC at Saulspoort to obtain "100 boys" to do "Government work" on a public road, acting Chief Ditlhake, who was to find the labor, regretted that he could not carry out the order. The reason, he explained to the NC, was that because of the recent war, "we can't compel anybody to go to work. . . . Only I will try to tell them all about your sayings. So I say anybody will do his will."[138] Such "insolence" and "insubordination" by blacks after the war were common in other parts of South Africa too. Knight's eyewitness account of the Orange Free State, for example, recorded that

> The Kaffir seems to have lost his former respect for the white man, even for his once firm master the Boer. Thus, the transport riders with whom I was travelling had generally to repeat an order twice or thrice before it was unwillingly obeyed by their independent and insolent black followers. These boys sometimes flatly refused to do what they were told, and laughed in the faces of their employers, who dared not punish them.[139]

Refusal to work for their former masters also had to do with the meager wages Africans received before the war and which Boer farmers wanted to perpetuate afterwards. The British military authorities, however, had paid Africans relatively high wages during the war. As Knight put it, this had "spoiled them," and the Boers had "considerable difficulty in obtaining [black] labour."[140] After the war, farm laborers had the option of returning to their prewar landlord, working for another one, or negotiating favorable terms of tenancy.[141] The British, however, would not brook "insolence" from Africans, who had to "recognise that due respect must be paid to both Boer and Briton alike."[142] The new British administration was keen to restore the prewar master/servant relationship. The NC emphasized this in 1903 when he declared that "not a stone was left unturned to establish fit and proper relations between the white population and the natives settled on the land."[143] Africans were emphatically told in public meetings throughout the Transvaal that the farms they had occupied belonged to their prewar owners and that master/servant relations had been restored.[144]

The newly created South African Constabulary (SAC) was used to ensure a return to the prewar status quo. The British had established the SAC in June 1901 after the annexation of the Boer republics. They consisted of a military force of 7,500 men, mostly from Canada, Australia, and Britain.[145] The SAC was designated "a rural police force" after the declaration of peace in May 1902, with Major General R. S. Baden-Powell as its commander. It was based on a network of police posts throughout the Transvaal (including the Pilanesberg) and the Orange Free State and replaced the army personnel that had been withdrawn. Grundlingh has shown that the SAC's major purpose was to prevent the threat of African rebellion and insubordination in the two Boer colonies. It was used to coerce black workers to return to their prewar employers, protect the Boers and their property, and "promote their [Boer] material interest in the immediate post-war period."[146]

The SAC played a crucial role in providing physical and psychological security to the few brave Boer farmers who returned to the Pilanesberg at the end of the South African War. For nearly a year after the war, most Boer farmers did not dare return to their farms for fear of reprisals from the Bakgatla. In September 1902, the SNC for the Pilanesberg reported that "Not one family of farmers has returned to the Pilanesberg."[147] The handful who did return by the end of 1903 did so only if the SAC was present on farms or in the area.[148] When Knight traveled through the Pilanesberg at this time, he noted that few Boer homesteads were "under the shadow of a Constabulary station."[149] Boer fears of the Bakgatla at this time were, however, misplaced. In October 1902, Linchwe was at pains to assure the British Assistant Commissioner in Gaborone of his and *all* his people's loyalty when rumors of possible Bakgatla disturbances spread in the Transvaal: "It is the desire of my heart as a chief of the Bakhatla, that my people in the Transvaal and in the Protectorate should obey the Government and to [sic] be regarded as loyal subjects of His Majesty the King."[150]

Another important means of restoring prewar race relations was to disarm the African population.[151] Many Bakgatla secretly retained or "probably sent the best of their firearms across the border to Mochudi."[152] Martini-Henry rifles were a common sight there after the war; Knight noted that "every man" he met in Mochudi in 1903 "carried a Martini-Henry carbine."[153] These guns were used by the Protectorate Bakgatla to poach game in the Transvaal Game Reserve during the 1910s.[154] The Bakgatla were not disarmed by the British authorities because of their military role during the war and because they were not regarded as a security threat afterward. In 1903, the High Commissioner, for example, commented on the Bakgatla's "loyal attitude," which he decided to reward by not forcing them to return the Boer cattle they had looted during the war.[155]

Immediately after the war, the SNCs were mainly concerned with African claims of compensation for war losses throughout Rustenburg and the Pilanesberg.[156] Linchwe claimed compensation as early as November 26, 1901, well before the end of the war, when he asked the Assistant Commissioner in Gaborone for £10,248 13s for "my people in the Transvaal, whose cattle, sheep, goats and horses were taken by the Boers during the present war."[157] The reply was that the Transvaal Bakgatla "cannot be treated more favourably than loyal British Refugees who have also suffered loss there," but that "if similar claims are considered at the end of the war his will be considered among them."[158] In view of Bakgatla military support for the British and the favorable treatment Linchwe expected in return, he must have been disappointed by this rebuff.

On July 21, 1902, the government decided to compensate blacks for their war losses and NCs were instructed to investigate and determine African claims in their respective districts. It was also decided that only the loss of livestock, grain, seed, and agricultural implements would be compensated. Any other losses could only be considered on the recommendation of the NC or magistrate.[159] The Executive Council resolutions of July 10 and 21, 1902, record that £140,000 was to be paid to Africans in the Transvaal, but the method of assessing their claims was inevitably quite subjective. Commissioners and magistrates were to assess "and estimate to the best of their ability the losses of each individual." Claimants had to substantiate their claims in affidavits supported by evidence "if obtainable," while the commissioners and magistrates were warned by the Executive Council to be careful because "natives are very clever at putting up claims."[160]

The most contentious issue regarding compensation, however, was the Boer demand that Africans return looted Boer cattle. The NC pointed out, with some justification, that "the [British] Military who [had] armed and employed the Bakhatla against the Boers" should compensate them.[161] But the British feared that this would provoke armed conflict among the Bakgatla, so they left the matter in abeyance.[162] This issue was quite difficult to unravel, as the NC admitted in February 1903: "an intricate one to deal with,"[163] since it touched on relations of power. He managed, for example, to return "to the Boers over 100 Head" but failed to get the Boers to return African cattle.[164] It was problematic to force the Boers to give up African cattle because officially they were still armed and, as many of them were embittered by the war, conflict could easily have flared up again.

The British arranged for the Boers to go to the Protectorate "for the purpose of identifying any of their cattle" after further complaints. But the Boers were deterred by the condition that each farmer "should give Linchwe's people access to his farm for the same purpose and under a similar arrangement."[165] They rejected this condition and refused to return Bakgatla cattle.[166] The matter was finally settled by the High Commissioner's decision that, because of the Bakgatla's "loyal attitude" during the war and because they had not been rewarded by the British, it would be "an ungenerous act to take from them the comparatively small share of plunder with which they have recouped themselves for losses sustained at the hands of the Boers."[167]

Although neither the Boers nor the Bakgatla returned the looted cattle, each was compensated by the British. Bakgatla losses were assessed at 5,179 livestock, valued at £11,313,[168] while Chiefs Magato, Mamogale, and Ramokoka received a combined total of £2,000 for the loss of their wagons and oxen.[169] The Boers' compensation claims, however, far exceeded those of the entire Pilanesberg African community. The Pilanesberg Boer compensation claims in the Western Division totaled £23,127 15s—much more than the combined Boer claims from Lichtenburg, Rustenburg, and Marico, and the second highest after the Potchefstroom claim of £32,701 19s.[170] In addition, the Boer farmers were supplied with livestock, rations, building materials, and agricultural implements.[171] This was an important aspect of Milner's reconstruction program at the end of the war.[172]

The South African War was important for the Bakgatla, as it shaped their economic future. The cattle they had looted more than compensated for the prewar losses as a result of rinderpest and contributed to a general increase in Bakgatla prosperity, which lasted for almost two decades. Traveling through Saulspoort in 1903, Knight observed: "Many of the leading men live in well-built houses of red brick. Signs of considerable prosperity and a relatively civilised condition are everywhere apparent."[173] Cattle also became a significant source of capital for buying additional land in the Pilanesberg, which boosted Linchwe's chiefly authority among his people.

Politically, Linchwe gained enormous prestige and authority among the Bakgatla on both sides of the border. This allowed him to install his brother, Ramono, as chief in 1902 despite official British opposition. But the Bakgatla failed to repossess their ancestral land in the Pilanesberg and legally they still owned the same four farms as they had before the war. Although the Bakgatla were forced to vacate the Boer farms after the war, many Boers never returned until after the First World War,[174] for fear of the Bakgatla.

Consequently, there was ample grazing for Bakgatla cattle for about eleven years after the Bakgatla-Boer War.[175] The Bakgatla objective of reuniting their divided people also failed, but their efforts were resumed immediately after the South African War.

Notes

1. W. R. Nasson, *Abraham Esau's War* (Cambridge, 1991), xviii.

2. See, for example, H. T. Siwundlha, "White Ideologies and Non-European Participation in the Anglo-Boer War, 1899–1902," *Journal of Black Studies* (December 1984): 223–34; W. R. Nasson, "'Doing Down Their Masters': Africans, Boers and Treason in the Cape Colony, 1899–1902," *Journal of Imperial and Commonwealth Studies* 12, no. 1 (1983); J. S. Mohlamme, "The Role of Black People in the Boer Republics during and in the Aftermath of the South African War of 1899–1902" (Ph.D. thesis, University of Wisconsin-Madison, 1985); A. H. Manson, "The Hurutshe in the Marico District of the Western Transvaal, 1848–1914" (Ph.D. thesis, University of Cape Town, 1990), chap. 6.

3. This quotation is from Nasson, "Warriors without Spears: Africans in the South African War, 1899–1902," *Social Dynamics* 9, no. 1 (1983): 91.

4. See, for example, R. F. Morton, "Linchwe I and the Kgatla Campaign in the South African War, 1899–1902," *Journal of African History* 26 (1985): 169–91; "'Babolayeng BagaKgafela!' The Kgatla Campaign in the South African War, 1899–1902," seminar paper presented in the History Department, University of Botswana, Gaborone, 20 March 1984; B. K. Mbenga, "The Bakgatla-baga-Kgafela in the Pilanesberg District of the Western Transvaal from 1899 to 1931" (D.Litt et Phil. thesis, University of South Africa, 1996), chap. 3.

5. See, for example, the older explanations by J. S. Marais, *The Fall of Kruger's Republic* (Oxford, 1961); T. Pakenham, *The Boer War* (Johannesburg, 1979); P. Warwick (ed.), *The South African War: The Anglo-Boer War, 1899–1902* (Harlow, 1980), chaps. 1, 2. For more recent explanations, see I. R. Smith, *The Origins of the South African War* (London, 1996).

6. For a detailed and incisive account of this incident and the social-political context in which it occurred, see B. K. Mbenga, "Forced Labour in the Pilanesberg: The Flogging of Chief Kgamanyane by Commandant Paul Kruger, Saulspoort, April 1870," *Journal of Southern African Studies* 23, no. 1 (1997): 127–40.

7. Interviews in the Pilanesberg: J. Sefara, 29 May 1993; T. S. Pilane, 8 October 1993; chief T.S.R. Pilane, 16 September 1994; L. Phaladi and M. Phaladi, 6 February 1993; B.N.O. Pilane and S. D. Matshego, 7 February 1993. In Mochudi, Botswana: S. D. Pilane, 12 March 1993; M. Monametsi and M. Mabodisa, 13 March 1993.

8. E. F. Knight, *South Africa after the War: A Narrative of Recent Travel* (London, 1903), 270.

9. See Mbenga, "Forced Labour," and Morton, "*Babolayeng BagaKgafela!*" 9–10.

10. Morton, "Linchwe I," 180; L. W. Truschel, "Nation-Building and the Kgatla: The Role of the Anglo-Boer War," *Botswana Notes and Records* 4 (1972): 188–89.

11. This issue is fully dealt with in Mbenga, "Bakgatla-baga-Kgafela," chap. 4.

12. P. Warwick, "Black People and the War," in Warwick (ed.), *South African War,* 191–92. In the predominantly black reserves of the Eastern Cape, for example, the British feared "a serious danger of general agitation and rising of the natives." For details, see L. S. Amery, *The Times History of the War in South Africa,* vol. 3 (London, 1905), 96.

13. War Office, *Military Notes on the Dutch Republics of South Africa,* June 1899, 42.

14. Ibid. See also Siwundlha, "White Ideologies," 224.

15. Amery, *Times History,* 4.200.

16. E. Broos, "Die Noordelike Hooflaer in die Distrikte Zoutpansberg, Waterberg en Rustenburg, Vanaf die Begin van die Tweede Vryheisoorlog tot die Besetting van Pretoria" (M.A. thesis, University of Pretoria, 1943), 34. Another Afrikaans source that gives the same viewpoint is H. J. Botha, "Die Moord op Derdepoort, 25 November 1899. Nie-Blankes in Oorlogsdiens," *Militaria* 1 (1969): 57.

17. D. Will and T. Dent, "The Boer War as Seen from Gaborone," *Botswana Notes and Records* 4 (1972): 195–209. For details of the war within the Bechuanaland Protectorate, see A. Sillery, *The Bechuanaland Protectorate* (Cape Town, 1952), chap. 9.

18. Amery, *Times History,* 2.270. See also Knight, *South Africa after the War,* 271.

19. R. Ramolope and S. Molope, joint interview, Saulspoort, 17 February 1994.

20. A. K. Pilane, "A Note on Episodes from the Boer War," *Botswana Notes and Records* 5 (1973): 131. This Pilane, an amateur historian and a member of the Bakgatla royal family, was personally involved in the Bakgatla-Boer War but has since passed away.

21. Amery, *Times History,* 4.204. See Amery, *Times History,* 2.270–71 for the comparatively strong military position of the Boers at the beginning of the war.

22. Cited in I. Schapera, *A Short History of the Bakgatla-baga-Kgafela of Bechuanaland Protectorate* (Cape Town, 1942), 44.

23. Ibid.

24. Surmon to Holdsworth, 23 November 1899, cited in *The Battle of Derdepoort, 25 November 1899,* 8 (this is a collection of various primary sources in booklet form in the Bakgatla's Phuthadikobo Museum in Mochudi, compiled by R. F. Morton, n.d.); Schapera, *Short History,* 44.

25. Ellenberger, "Notes on the History of the Bakgatla," cited in Schapera, *Short History,* 46. Ellenberger was Assistant Commissioner for the Southern Protectorate during the war and, later, from 1923 to 1927, Resident Commissioner for the Protectorate. He was the English-Setswana interpreter between the British and Bakgatla troops during the Derdepoort assault.

26. Botha, "Die Moord," 59.

27. Amery, *Times History,* 2.124; for details of the deployment of both Boer and British troops in the western Transvaal and the rest of South Africa on the eve of the war, see 2.98–132, 132–37, 270–71, 298.

28. L. Wulfsohn, *Rustenburg at War: The Story of Rustenburg and Its Citizens in the First and Second Anglo-Boer Wars* (Rustenburg, 1987), 49.

29. Wulfsohn, *Rustenburg at War,* 48.

30. Quoted in Morton, "Linchwe I," 175–76.

31. Morton, "Linchwe I," 179; *"Babolayeng BagaKgafela!"* 18–19.

32. Ellenberger, "Bechuanaland Protectorate," 5.

33. Morton, "Linchwe I," 179; *"Babolayeng BagaKgafela!"* 18–19.

34. Morton, "Linchwe I," 179. The captured Boer women and children were all repatriated to the Transvaal at the end of November 1899. See Wulfsohn, *Rustenburg at War,* 51.

35. W. van Everdingen, *De Oorlog in Zuid Afrika. Eerste Tydvak: 11 Oktober 1899– Maart 1900,* quoted in Schapera, *Short History,* 41.

36. Botswana National Archives, Gaborone (hereafter BNA), RC 5/4, cited in copy of telegram from Harbor, Mochudi, to Col. Nicholson, Bulawayo, n.d. For a more detailed discussion and analysis of the murder of Engers, see Mbenga, "Bakgatla-baga-Kgafela," 120–24.

37. National Archives of South Africa, Pretoria (hereafter NASA), SNA 59 NA 2111/02, R. Williams to Sir G. Lagden, 23 May 1902.

38. BNA RC 5/4, Affidavit of Segale to Captain J. Griffith, Gaborone, 3 August 1901. In the same file, see also the affidavit of Ramono to H. J. Ratcliffe and G. H. Phillamore, Mochudi, 3 May 1900; telegram from Harbor to Lt. Col. Nicholson.

39. See, for example, BNA RC 5/4, T. H. Focke to Sir A. Milner, 12 February 1900.

40. BNA RC 5/4, Affidavit of Ellenberger to Acting Resident Commissioner, Mafeking, 19 July 1901.

41. See, for example, Resident Commissioner R. Williams's defense of the Bakgatla troops' treatment of the Boer women and child captives during their forced walk from Derdepoort to Mochudi in SNA 59 NA 2111/02, R. Williams, Mafeking, to Sir G. Lagden, Johannesburg, 23 May 1902.

42. See, for example, Wulfsohn, *Rustenburg at War,* 51–52.

43. M. Davitt, *The Boer Fight for Freedom* (New York, 1902), 174.

44. W. Fouché, *Pieter Stofberg: Zyn Leven, Arbeid en Afsterven,* cited in Schapera, *Short History,* 43. The quotation belongs to the Rev. P.B.J. Stofberg, a Dutch Reformed Church (DRC) missionary in Mochudi at the beginning of the war.

45. Cited in P. Warwick, *Black People and the South African War, 1899–1902* (London, 1983), 41.

46. Wulfsohn, *Rustenburg at War,* 50. For other highly biased pro-Boer and anti-Bakgatla accounts of the Derdepoort "massacre," see especially Botha, "Die Moord," 1–98; Davitt, *Boer Fight for Freedom,* chap. 15. See also Wulfsohn, *Rustenburg at War,* chap. 6; J. H. Breytenbach, "Ongepubliseerde Manuskrip: Die Moord van Derdepoort," typescript (April 1985), 24–41.

47. SNA 59 NA 2111/02, quoted in R. Williams, Resident Commissioner, Mafeking, to Sir G. Lagden, Johannesburg, 23 May 1902.

48. BNA RC 5/4, affidavit of De Villiers to C. Bell, Resident Magistrate, Mafeking, 11 July 1900.

49. Ellenberger, quoted in Schapera, *Short History,* 47.

50. Morton, for example, refers briefly to the issue in a footnote. See Morton, "Linchwe I," 178.

51. Morton seems to suggest this when he says: "Only after the Kgatla guns came into action did Holdsworth realise that they were positioned across the river and in the Transvaal." See Morton, "Linchwe I," 179. Similarly, Warwick has recorded that

"the assault was executed with considerable misunderstanding." See Warwick, *Black People,* 40.

52. Ellenberger, cited in Morton, footnote, "Linchwe I," 178.

53. Ellenberger, "Bechuanaland Protectorate," 4, emphasis added.

54. SNA 59 NA 2111/2, Ralph Williams, Resident Commissioner (R.C.), Mafeking, to Sir Godfrey Lagden, Commissioner for Native Affairs (C.N.A.), Johannesburg, 23 May 1902, 3, emphasis added.

55. Personal communication: 12, 4th Avenue, Cashan, Rustenburg, South Africa, 28 June 1993. See also Wulfsohn's updated 1992 edition of his *Rustenburg at War,* 61.

56. Cited in Morton, "Linchwe I," 179–80.

57. Ellenberger, "Bechuanaland Protectorate," 5.

58. For details, see Breytenbach, "Ongepubliseerde Manuskrip," 29–30, 34–35.

59. For details of the fear and panic among the Boers these rumors brought about, see Wulfsohn, *Rustenburg at War,* 51–52; Breytenbach, "Ongepubliseerde Manuskrip," 34; F. Pretorius, *The Anglo-Boer War, 1899–1902* (1980), 76.

60. Everdingen, quoted in Schapera, *Short History,* 42; see also G.H.J. Teichler, "Some Historical Notes on Derdepoort Sikwane," *Botswana Notes and Records* 5 (1973): 29.

61. Ellenberger, "Notes on the History of the Bakgatla," quoted in Schapera, *Short History,* 47; Teichler, "Some Historical Notes," 129.

62. Breytenbach, "Ongepubliseerde Manuskrip," 38; Schapera, "Bakgatla ba-ga-Kgafela," I. Schapera (ed.), *Ditirafalo tsa Merafe ya Batswana* (Cape Town, 1940), 181.

63. Breytenbach, "Ongepubliseerde manuskrip," 38.

64. Quoted in Schapera, *Short History,* 42 and 43, respectively.

65. Truschel, "Nation-Building and the Kgatla," 189.

66. Ibid.

67. Schapera, *Ditirafalo,* 182. For more details of this incident, see, for example, CAD, Van Warmelo Boxes S.292(24) K32/13, J. Masiangoako, "Military System and War," 3–4. Warwick records that there were forty-two commandos in this convoy. See Warwick, *Black People,* 45.

68. Schapera, *Ditirafalo,* 182.

69. Schapera, *Praise-Poems of Tswana Chiefs* (London, 1965), 98, 101.

70. Wulfsohn, *Rustenburg at War,* 63.

71. Mohlamme, "Role of Black People," 40–41.

72. SNA 116 NA 672/03, S.N.C. to N.C., 27 April 1903, 2; Schapera, *Ditirafalo,* 182; Schapera, *Short History,* 20.

73. SNA 116 NA 672/03, Petition by R. Pilane and others to A. Lawley, Lieutenant-Governor, Transvaal, 9 February 1903, 4.

74. SNA 59 NA 211/02, cited in R. Williams to G. Lagden, 23 May 1902.

75. SNA 59 NA 2111/02, Williams to Lagden, 23 May 1902.

76. SNA 116 NA 672/03, S.N.C., the Pilanesberg, to N.C., Rustenburg, 27 April 1903, 2.

77. SNA 106 NA 491/03, N.C. to S.N.A., 18 February 1903, 1–2.

78. Krikler, "Agrarian Class Struggle," 163.

79. SNA 71 NA 2482/02, S.N.C. to N.C., 7 November 1903.

80. Morton has recorded that, because of the Bakgatla's large-scale looting of Boer cattle, the Kgatla Reserve (in Bechuanaland) held "16,091, which was probably as much as ten times the number of cattle the Kgatla possessed after the rinderpest and before the war" and that "[i]n the years after the war, cattle was so plentiful in the Reserve that beasts were slaughtered almost nightly in Mochudi for feasting." See Morton, "Linchwe I," 187.

81. SNA 106 NA 491/03, N.C. to S.N.A., 18 February 1903, 5.

82. Ibid.

83. NASA Van Warmelo Boxes K32/13, S.292(24), J. Masiangoako, "Military System and War," 2.

84. For details, see Morton, *"Babolayeng BagaKgafela!"* 27.

85. NASA TKP Vol. 239, Annual Report by the C.N.A., 30 June 1904, Annexure "K," B.42. For details of how Linchwe used "his own" cattle in order to gain the loyalty of his people in the Pilanesberg after the war, see chap. 4.

86. SNA 71 NA 2482/02, N.C. to S.N.A., 11 December 1902.

87. SNA 71 NA 2482/02, N.C. to S.N.A., 6 November 1902. In the same file, see also Telegram, S.N.A. to N.C., 23 May 1903; N.C. to S.N.A., 10 November 1903.

88. SNA 17 NA 396/02, cited in R. Williams, R.C., Mafeking, to G. Y. Lagden, C.N.A., 14 February 1902.

89. SNA 116 NA 672/03, Petition by R. Pilane and others to Sir A. Lawley, 9 February 1903, 3–4. See also Mohlamme, "Role of Black People," 149–50.

90. J. D. Kestell and D. E. van Velden, *The Peace Negotiations* (London, 1912), 93, 55–56.

91. Warwick, *South African War,* 195–96; Nasson, *Esau's War,* 95 and especially chap. 6; Mohlamme, "Role of Black People," 67–69, 72–75; A. Manson, "The Hurutshe in the Marico District of the Transvaal, 1848–1914" (Ph.D. thesis, University of Cape Town), 232–35; Pretorius, *Anglo-Boer War,* 75. See also B. Viljoen, *My Reminiscences of the Anglo-Boer War* (London, 1902), 523–24; E. Lee, *To the Bitter End: A Photographic History of the Boer War, 1899–1902* (New York, 1985), 200.

92. SNA 125 NA 966/03, M. Pieters, Rustenburg, to S.N.A., 20 April 1903.

93. SNA 125 NA 966/03, Segale to S.N.C., 18 March 1903.

94. For details as to how plentiful these supplies were, see SNA 125 NA 966/03, S. K. Pilane to S.N.C., 18 March 1903.

95. SNA 125 NA 966/03, S.N.C. to N.C., 2 May 1903.

96. SNA 125 NA 966/03, Roux and Jacobsz to S.N.C., 16 April 1903.

97. SNA 125 NA 966/03, S.N.C. to N.C., 2 May 1903. S.N.C. Edmeston's decision was endorsed by the S.N.A. See the same file, S.N.A. to M. Pieters, 20 May 1903.

98. SNA 125 NA 966/03, S.N.C. to N.C., 16 May 1903; N.C. to S.N.A., 28 May 1903.

99. SNA 125 NA 966/03, cited in S.N.C. to N.C., 2 May 1903.

100. SNA 125 NA 966/03, Pieters to S.N.A., 20 April 1903.

101. SNA 125 NA 966/03, Pieters to S.N.C., 9 March 1903.

102. SNA 125 NA 966/03, S. K. Pilane to S.N.C., 18 March 1903.

103. Quoted in Warwick, *Black People,* 46.

104. By the beginning of July 1900, for example, the road from Rustenburg to

Ottoshoop "was seriously menaced" by the Boers. See L. Creswicke, *South Africa and the Transvaal War,* vol. 3 (Edinburgh, 1900), 70.

105. Krikler, Morton, Warwick, and Mohlamme say very little about this issue. Krikler, for example, although he acknowledges the Bakgatla as the "scourge of the western Transvaal,'" hardly discusses this aspect. See, for example, Krikler, "Agrarian Class Struggle," 151–76; "Social Neurosis and Hysterical Pre-Cognition in South Africa: A Case Study and Reflections," *South African Historical Journal* 28 (1993): 63–97; see also Morton, "Linchwe I," 169–91; "Chiefs and Ethnic Unity in Two Colonial Worlds"; A. E. Asiwaju (ed.), *Partitioned Africans: Ethnic Relations across Africa's International Boundaries, 1884–1984* (London, 1984), 127–53; Warwick, *Black People,* 186–209; Mohlamme, "Role of Black People."

106. Knight, *South Africa after the War,* 272, 264, emphasis added.

107. For details of this kind of violence in the Ohrigstad area of the northern Transvaal, see, for example, Viljoen, *My Reminiscences,* 533–34. But it should also be noted that the African destruction of Boer farms during the war was not completely universal. In the northern Orange Free State, for example, an African tenant took care of his Boer landlord's property, wife, and children following his capture and incarceration in a prisoner-of-war camp on St. Helena Island. See S. Motsuenyane, "A Tswana Growing Up with Afrikaners," *Munger Africana Library Notes* 47 (February 1979): 5.

108. See, for example, Morton, "Linchwe I," 179–91; Krikler, "Agrarian Class Struggle," 158–76.

109. Knight, *South Africa after the War,* 259–64.

110. See Krikler, "Revolution from Above," 29–31.

111. Knight, *South Africa after the War,* 272.

112. Quoted in Krikler, "Agrarian Class Struggle," 166.

113. SNA 116 NA 672/03, S.N.C. to N.C., 27 April 1903, 3.

114. For details, see M. Nkadimeng and G. Relly, "Kas Maine: The Story of a South African Agriculturalist," in B. Bozzoli (ed.), *Town and Countryside in The Transvaal: Capitalist Penetration and Popular Response* (Johannesburg, 1983), 93.

115. SNA 116 NA 672/03, S.N.C. to N.C., 27 April 1903, 2.

116. Knight, *South Africa after the War,* 270.

117. SNA 116 NA 672/03, S.N.C. to N.C., 27 April 1903, 3.

118. Nasson, *Esau's War,* 120.

119. For Boer commando activity and counteractivity, see Nasson, *Esau's War,* especially chap. 7.

120. SNA 116 NA 672/03, Petition by R. Pilane and others to A. Lawley, 9 February 1903, 4.

121. For details, see Amery, *Times History,* 4.205–6; Creswicke, *South Africa and the Transvaal War,* 4.206–12.

122. SNA 116 NA 672/03, S.N.C. to N.C., 27 April 1903, 3.

123. A. Grundlingh, "Collaborators in Boer Society," in P. Warwick (ed.), *The South African War: The Anglo-Boer War, 1899–1902* (Harlow, 1980), 260.

124. SNA 6 NA 519/02, *Native Affairs Department, Annual Report for the Year Ended 30 June 1906,* A.1.

125. NASA TKP Vol. 239, *Annual Report by the Commissioner for Native Affairs, Transvaal, for the Year Ended 30 June 1903,* A.1–2.

126. Ibid., Annexure "D," B.27.

127. Morton, "Linchwe I," 188.

128. SNA 116 NA 672/03, S.N.C. to N.C., 27 April 1903.

129. Morton, "Linchwe I," 186.

130. NASA Van Warmelo Boxes S.292(24) K32/13, Tsoabi, "Shields," cited in J. Masiangoako, "Military System and War," 6. It is likely that Tsoabi had witnessed the war.

131. SNA 116 NA 672/03, S.N.C. to N.C., 27 April 1903, 3.

132. For details, see Krikler, "Revolution from Above," 37–42.

133. TKP Vol.239, *Annual Report by the Commissioner for Native Affairs, Transvaal, for the Year Ended 30 June 1903*, A.1.

134. SNA 169 NA 2059/03, N.C. to S.N.A., 18 September 1903, 35.

135. Krikler, "Revolution from Above," 53.

136. SNA 62 NA 2160/02, S.N.C. to N.C., 26 September 1902. My emphasis. See especially the Bakgatla's lengthy petition to the Lieutenant-Governor, which clearly reveals their perception of their role in the war: SNA 116 NA 672/03, Chief S. K. Pilane and others to Sir A. Lawley, Lieutenant-Governor of the Colony of the Transvaal, 9 February 1903, especially 3–5.

137. Knight, *South Africa after the War*, 273.

138. SNA 62 NA 2160/02, Ditlhake to S.N.C., n.d. [1902], 18.

139. Knight, *South Africa after the War*, 88.

140. Ibid.

141. For details, see Krikler, "Revolution from Above," 96–101.

142. TKP Vol. 239, *Annual Report by the Commissioner for Native Affairs, 30 June 1904*, Annexure "K," B.41.

143. SNA 106 NA 491/03, N.C. to S.N.A., 18 February 1903, 4. See also TKP Vol. 239, *Annual Report by the Commissioner for Native Affairs, Transvaal, 30 June 1903*, Annexure "D," B.27.

144. For details, see Krikler, "Revolution from Above," 66–72.

145. For details of the origins and work of the SAC, see Grundlingh, "Protectors and Friends of the People?" in D. M. Anderson and D. Killingray (eds.), *Policing the Empire: Government, Authority, and Control, 1830–1940* (Manchester, 1991), chap. 10.

146. Grundlingh, "Protectors and Friends?" 175.

147. SNA 62 NA 2160/02, S.N.C. to N.C., 26 September 1902.

148. Knight, *South Africa after the War*, 273.

149. Ibid., 263, 273, 274–75.

150. BNA RC 8/8, L. K. Pilane, Mochudi, to Assistant Commissioner, Gaborone, 16 October 1902.

151. SNA 106 NA 491/03, N.C. to S.N.A., 18 February 1903, 7. For details of the mechanics of how blacks all over the Transvaal were systematically disarmed by the new British administration at the end of the war, see Krikler, "Revolution from Above," 76–87.

152. Great Britain, War Office, *The Native Tribes of the Transvaal* (London, 1905), 30.

153. Knight, *South Africa after the War*, 269.

154. BNA S44/3, sworn affidavits of S. Petu of Mochudi and Constable E. Holmes of Olifants Drift Police Post, 30 August and 27 September 1912, respectively.

155. SNA 71 NA 2482/02, High Commissioner to Lieutenant-Governor, n.d., January 1903.

156. SNA 106 NA 491/03, N.C. to S.N.A., 18 February 1903, 7.

157. BNA RC 6/13, L. K. Pilane, Mochudi, to Acting Assistant Commissioner, Gaborone, 26 November 1901. Most of the war losses, according to Linchwe, occurred around Saulspoort and Lesetlheng. In this source, see the "List of Property Taken from the Bakhatla in the Transvaal...."

158. BNA RC 6/13, High Commissioner, Johannesburg, to Resident Commissioner, Mafeking, 3 January 1902.

159. TKP Vol. 239, *Annual Report by the Commissioner for Native Affairs, Transvaal, 30 June 1903*, A.9.

160. TKP Vol. 239, *Annual Report by the Commissioner for Native Affairs, 30 June 1904*, Annexure "D," B.24–B.26. For details of the financial compensation, see B.25. During the war, the British army used to "requisition" or commandeer from Africans things like livestock and grain for their own use. The Africans were then given military receipts that were to be exchanged for money at the end of the war. Thus, from July 1902, the Native Refugee Department under Major de Lotbiere began the task of locating the Africans concerned in order to pay them. Some six months later, 2,948 Africans had been paid a total of £163,109 17s 8d, while many more were still to be paid. See TKP Vol. 239, *Annual Report of the Commissioner for Native Affairs, Transvaal, 30 June 1903*, A.10. However, it is unlikely that this practice would have occurred in the Pilanesberg because the British had left the area to their Bakgatla allies to deal with.

161. SNA 231 NA 2038/04, N.C. to S.N.A., 8 September 1904.

162. For details of the restitution of Boer cattle, see Krikler, "Revolution from Above," 60–65.

163. SNA 106 NA 491/03, N.C. to S.N.A., 18 February 1903, 5.

164. SNA 169 NA 2059/03, N.C. to S.N.A., 18 September 1903, 6.

165. SNA 71 NA 2482/02, Circular no. 15 of 1903, Secretary to the Law Department, to all Resident Magistrates, 17 April 1903.

166. Knight, *South Africa after the War*, 273.

167. SNA 71 NA 2482/02, High Commissioner to Lieutenant-Governor, n.d., January 1903.

168. SNA 116 NA 672/03, N.C. to S.N.A., 5 April 1903.

169. SNA 71 NA 2482/02, N.C. to S.N.A., 1 December 1902.

170. TKP Vol. 239, *Annual Report by the Commissioner for Native Affairs, 30 June 1904*, B.31.

171. Krikler, "Revolution from Above," 93–94.

172. For details of Milner's reconstruction program in the Transvaal, see D.J.N. Denoon, *A Grand Illusion* (London, 1973).

173. Knight, *South Africa after the War*, 267.

174. Morton, *"Babolayeng BagaKgafela!"* 28.

175. Morton, "Linchwe I," 188.

CHAPTER 6

"Loyalty Its Own Reward"

the South African War Experience of
Natal's "Loyal" Africans

JOHN LAMBERT

ON OCTOBER 11, 1899, the South African Republic and the Orange Free State declared war on Great Britain. The following day republican commandos invaded the neighboring colonies and in Natal swept through Klip River County within weeks. The small force of imperial and colonial soldiers were either trapped in Ladysmith or pushed back south of Colenso, and the whole of northern Natal was in the hands of republican burghers.

The South African War had a considerable impact on the inhabitants of the district, both black and white. Even before the war began, it had been obvious that the British army would not be able to defend northern Natal and the colonial government had advised the inhabitants to offer no resistance to the enemy unless attacked. The position was further complicated by the fact that so many whites were Afrikaners, stock farmers who had personal links with the burghers and possessed farms on both sides of the border. Many welcomed the invaders—according to the Transvaal Agency, three thousand Natal Afrikaners joined the commandos, fought on the republican side, and accepted annexation of the county.[1] For their part, most British inhabitants ignored the government's advice to stay on their farms or in the towns and fled in advance of the republican forces. While they were absent, their property was often looted and destroyed.[2]

The invasion was as disastrous for the Africans of northern Natal as it was for the British. Many fled behind the British lines, abandoning their crops and livestock. Those who stayed, particularly labor tenants on farms abandoned by their white owners, often had their crops requisitioned and their cattle and horses stolen.[3] Many Africans were press-ganged by the invaders to provide labor, which included the potentially dangerous job of digging trenches, sometimes within firing range of the British forces. Reports of Africans being flogged and even shot for refusing to obey orders were widespread.[4]

115

Natal African refugees from the gold mines also suffered. They were more fortunate, however, than those in the Cape because their return to the colony was organized by the Johannesburg agent of the Native Affairs Department, J. S. Marwick.[5] In addition to losing their work (and Natal homesteads depended on these wages), few returned to the colony with any savings. Since they had to pass through Boer lines in northern Natal, they were often relieved of any money or valuables they were carrying.[6] Some also found themselves commandeered into providing labor, such as pulling cannons at Laing's Nek and Ingagane.[7]

Zululand.

SOURCE: P. Warwick, *Black People and the South African War, 1899–1902* (Cambridge, Cambridge University Press, 1983), 81. Reprinted with the permission of Cambridge University Press.

Evidence in the Invasion Losses Enquiry Commission gives some idea of the losses incurred by Africans at the hands of the burghers and their Afrikaner allies.[8] Other sources tend to gloss over the extent of African distress while reporting in detail on the sufferings of whites. Yet African suffering was widespread both here and in the Nquthu district of Zululand as a result of raids from the Vryheid district of the South African Republic. Distress was heightened by the onset of drought in late 1899, which saw a dearth of crops in the homesteads and increased raids by commandos for produce. Harriette Colenso had appealed to the Pietermaritzburg Relief Committee for assistance for Africans in northern Natal and Zululand and for refugees from Johannesburg as early as December 1899.[9] Africans caught in Ladysmith during the siege suffered directly from the fighting. An estimated 2,440 Africans were within the British lines[10]; the first person killed was an African in charge of herding mules, while the shortage of food and medicines led to great suffering and many deaths, particularly of children.[11]

The attempts by the British forces to relieve Ladysmith and drive the burghers from the colony added to African woes. As the imperial army advanced, and particularly after the relief of Ladysmith on February 28, 1900, more destruction and theft took place, at the hands of British and colonial soldiers and of retreating burghers, who drove large numbers of stock before them.[12] The military took steps to help loyal white farmers and arranged for them to move their remaining stock south of the Thukela for safety until the republican forces had been driven out of the colony.[13] No steps were taken to assist Africans.

Some Africans used the retreat of the republican commandos to recoup their losses. Prominent among these were labor tenants on Afrikaner farms in the district. Many of the Afrikaner farmers who had assisted the burghers accompanied them in their retreat. While there were African labor tenants who remained loyal to these farmers, others used the opportunity not only to recoup their losses but also to settle old scores. There was a fair amount of looting and stealing on these farms. In the treason trials of rebel Afrikaners later that year, labor tenants were important witnesses against their landlords.[14] In at least one case during the British advance, a tenant was given a paper by the provost marshal that read, "The bearer is in charge of the property and effects of the rebel, J. T. Buys."[15]

This was surely an isolated case, but it would have horrified settlers. The anger felt by British Natalians at the actions of Afrikaner colonists was acute and widespread, and it left traces of bitterness in northern Natal for many decades. Few, however, would have approved of Africans benefiting from their flight. Settlers and officials alike shared the imperial determination expressed by the British government at the start of the South African War that Africans should not be involved in hostilities, that it was to be a "white man's war."[16] A contributor to the *Natal Witness* reflected the fear of what might happen should the Africans become involved in the fighting. Within days of the republican invasion, he wrote that the "present quarrel is a white man's quarrel, and wherever a native tribe rises to menace the whites, whether these be British or Boer, the guns of the white man must and will be turned on the black man."[17] Official policy in the colony concurred; it was based on the principle that the war was a "white man's war in which [Africans] should take no part beyond defending themselves and their property."[18]

With a settler population greatly outnumbered by Africans, the ministry was determined that Africans understand that their military support was not needed. To the prime minister, Colonel Hime, "employment of natives ... would be in opposition to the generally acknowledged trend of colonial public opinion, and would ultimately lead to the lessening of the prestige of the white man, and of the natives' respect for the power of the British government." To allow Africans to be combatants would "indicate vacillation and weakness, and give the natives an exaggerated idea of their own importance."[19]

This was in sharp contrast to the situation during the 1879 Anglo-Zulu War, when the Native Contingent had formed an integral part of the imperial forces. That, however, had been a war against an African rather than a white foe. Now Africans were to be kept out of the conflict and encouraged instead to supply labor for the war effort.[20] And indeed, for Africans outside the war zone, the increased demand for labor brought substantial rewards. Military needs and increased activity on railways and harbor works provided jobs for large numbers of men. There were also greater employment opportunities for both men and women in the towns, and as the price of agricultural produce soared, Africans benefited by planting extensively to meet the demand for vegetables and maize.[21]

African Participation in the South African War

Had the South African War not begun with such dramatic reverses in northern Natal, the ministry's determination to keep the conflict "white" and restrict African participation to the supply of labor might have succeeded. But the ringing success of republican arms and the establishment of *de facto* Boer administrations in Klip River County forced the government to accept African assistance. Commando raids into Zululand also brought the Zulu into direct contact with the fighting. The province had been annexed to Natal as recently as 1897, and had the British army not involved the Zulu in its defense, there would have been little to prevent the republican forces from sweeping through the territory and threatening Natal across the Mzinyathi (Buffalo) and Thukela rivers. Throughout the war, the *nongquai*, Zulu policemen, fought with imperial soldiers. Despite reaping the benefit of African cooperation and acknowledging that the Zulu had behaved loyally throughout the conflict, the government continually expressed its disapproval of the army organizing the Zulu to defend themselves.[22]

The government was more successful in preventing military involvement by armed Africans in northern Natal, although it did consider arming a small number of trustworthy Africans on at least one occasion. One of the most important chiefdoms in northern Natal, with a long record of loyalty to the Crown, was the Ngwane. It had been conspicuously loyal during the Anglo-Zulu War, and the government viewed its chief, Ncwadi kaZikhali, as one of its most reliable African allies. In August 1899, Ncwadi had been recruited to spy on the Orange Free State and to report to the army.[23] In October, he was told that if Natal were invaded, he should hold his own borders and prevent any burgher aggression. The magistrate of Upper Tugela was provided with two hundred rifles for Ncwadi, should commandos try to enter Natal through the Drakensberg passes, south of the Thukela, which led into his reserve.[24] As the Free State commandos entered the colony north of the river, it is unlikely that the guns were supplied, but Ncwadi proved a stalwart ally of the imperial forces, providing two hundred men for scouting and constable duties and contributing £366 toward the care of wounded soldiers.[25]

Other northern Natal chiefs proved equally loyal to the British. Like the Ngwane, the Chunu chiefdom in the Impafana reserve had been consistently loyal to the colonial authorities since the early days of British rule. Its chief, Silwana kaGabangaye, supplied the military with scouts.[26] Silwana and his neighboring chiefs, Mabizela kaMganu of the Thembu and Kula of the Qamu chiefdom, pleaded with the government to be allowed to raise levies for active service, pleas which for obvious reasons were turned down.[27] Another neighboring chief, Sibindi of the Mbomvu, served with forty of his followers as scouts,[28] while from Dundee, the Ngwe chief, Dumisa, sent the army a steady stream of secret messages about republican movements.[29] Other chiefs contributed money to war funds for the wounded; by the end of 1901, £921 had been given by Africans, most of which came from the chiefs.[30]

As had been the case during the Anglo-Zulu War, Christian Africans rallied to the imperial cause. In 1879, the *kholwa* of Edendale and Driefontein had played a prominent role with the imperial forces and the Edendale

Native Horse had distinguished itself in more than one battle. In the South
African War, leaders such as Lazarus Xaba and Luke Kumalo again volunteered for service. They were interpreters for the army and Kumalo acted
as General Buller's private interpreter and orderly—a position he had held
in 1879.[31]

The army realized the value of using Africans for intelligence and as early
as August 1899, General Penn-Symons appointed Jabez Molife and Simeon
Kambule to recruit spies.[32] On October 3, R.C.A. Samuelson, a member of
the Natal Carbineers and brother of the Under Secretary for Native Affairs,
was sent to Driefontein to raise a body of scouts.[33] As he had done in 1879,
the Driefontein chief, Johannes Kumalo, gave Samuelson his full support, and
by the time war started, a troop of two hundred *kholwa* scouts from Driefontein and Edendale had been raised under the leadership of the Edendale
chief, Stephen Mini, and of Jabez Molife and Simeon Kambule. The scouts
were organized into units and Molife and Kambule were commissioned as
sergeants-major.[34] The Native Scouts not only volunteered for service, but
unlike white volunteers, they provided their own horses and equipment.[35] In
addition to the *kholwa* scouts, those mentioned above who were supplied by
chiefs were used as spies and runners under the authority of their chiefs.
Molife also recruited a body of Sotho scouts from the Nquthu district to act
as guides and spies during the siege of Ladysmith.[36] By the end of the war, at
least 1,131 scouts had been recruited.[37]

Driefontein, in enemy-held territory north of Ladysmith, was an invaluable center from which the scouts operated. Lazarus Xaba coordinated
scouting activities from the farm. Scouts were hidden, housed, and fed at
Driefontein as they moved between Ladysmith and other places. Acts of
sabotage were also planned from the farm. Simeon Kambule's wife, Esther,
for example, provided George Xaba with weapons to attack the railway line
between Besters and Brakvaal stations.[38]

The role played by African scouts during the siege was particularly important. A corps of white Colonial Scouts had also been raised at the outbreak
of the war, but the Africans proved more effective as intelligence gatherers.
Unlike the Colonial Scouts, they came under fire regularly, but despite this,
they were not allowed to bear arms.[39] Not only did they carry dispatches
between the garrison and the relieving force; they also accompanied the military guides on reconnaissances[40] and were able in some instances to relieve
hardship in the town. For instance, a runner, at considerable risk to himself
under heavy fire, got through to the Intombi hospital carrying two sacks of
condensed milk for the patients.[41]

The scouts built up a wide network of African informers, both in occupied northern Natal and in Zululand. Scouts also captured armed Afrikaner rebels and handed them over to the British military authorities.[42] They continued to accompany Buller's troops as the burghers retreated from the colony, and they were often in the forefront of the army. They were, for example, the first on Laing's Nek as northern Natal was evacuated, before the stronghold was occupied by the Natal Carbineers.[43] Although the Native Scouts were officially disbanded at the same time as the Natal volunteer regiments, once Natal had been cleared of the enemy, many individual scouts continued to be employed by the imperial forces, both in northern Natal and outside the colony.[44] Writing at the end of December 1900, Lt. Col. David Henderson paid tribute to the contribution of the Native Scouts:

> their services have been of the utmost value. Although unarmed they have kept constant touch with the enemy's forces, and frequently penetrated their lines. A considerable number have been killed or wounded, some have been captured and flogged or otherwise maltreated.[45]

By 1901, the onset of guerrilla warfare forced the army to make increasing use of the African population throughout South Africa. Peter Warwick claims that as many as thirty thousand blacks were fighting with the British army in 1902.[46] Aware of the number of African scouts who had been killed and despite objections from the Natal government, the army began issuing rifles to Africans engaged on dangerous missions and most columns were accompanied by parties of armed African scouts. This, in fact, increased the danger to the scouts, as the Boers shot any armed Africans who fell into their hands.[47] Writing from Newcastle in late 1901, General Lyttelton referred a number of times to the shooting of African scouts in the Vryheid district and northern Zululand.[48] As Samuelson had been instructed to raise the force of Native Scouts again that year,[49] these could have included *kholwa* volunteers and members of Natal chiefdoms.

Despite strenuous objections from the Natal government, the British army used Dinuzulu kaCetshwayo, the son of the last Zulu king, to organize Zulu forces to protect the Transvaal/Zululand border and to carry out stock raids into the Transvaal. The government succeeded in ensuring that none except a few of the *nongquai* members who accompanied the levies were armed with rifles. This placed the Zulu at a disadvantage in the subsequent clashes with Boer guerrillas. In May 1902, weeks before the Peace of Vereeniging, the resulting frustration did much to precipitate an attack by the Qulusi on a Boer encampment at Holkrantz that left fifty-six guerrillas dead—an event that sent shock waves through British as well as Afrikaner South Africa.[50]

Reasons for African Participation in the War

With few exceptions, then, Africans in Natal responded positively and loyally to the British war effort in Natal. There were individual instances of Africans assisting the burghers during the occupation of northern Natal, but this was often because they had little alternative. Once the district had been annexed to the republics, burgher officials warned Africans of the consequences of noncooperation, yet there were few reports of Africans other than some members of the Qamu chiefdom siding with the enemy.[51] The only chief in the district who allegedly defected was Sandanezwe, the appointed chief of a branch of the Chunu chiefdom on the Transvaal border, but the charge was never proven.[52] And, as has been shown, the *kholwa* remained conspicuously loyal.

It can be argued, however, that there was little reason for Africans in Natal to be loyal to Britain by the end of the nineteenth century. From the 1880s onward, official policy toward Africans, both "traditionalist" and Christian, had been marked by an increasing attack on African institutions and a deliberate undermining of African independence. The gap between settlers and Africans in the colony was growing, and whichever way they turned, Africans found themselves hemmed in by restrictions and limitations.[53]

A general reason for African loyalty both in Natal and throughout South Africa can be found in the fact that most Africans considered British rule, harsh as it was, preferable to republican dominance. It was commonly held that a British victory would herald the dawn of a better era[54] and that loyalty to the imperial cause would be rewarded; that in Stephen Mini's words, "as a result of their behaviour ... certain concessions would ... [be] extended to them. They looked for an improvement in the administration, and that special consideration should be shown to them."[55]

This belief was encouraged by British and colonials alike. When the South African War began, the Secretary of State for the Colonies, Joseph Chamberlain, implied in the House of Commons that the treatment of Africans in the Transvaal would be very different after the war, an implication that was believed to hold good for Natal as well. Similarly, Milner claimed that his policies would protect Africans against oppression and wrong and that under the new dispensation political rights would be based on standards of civilization rather than on race or color.[56] In December 1899, the *Natal Witness* echoed these sentiments:

> It is evident then that the interests of the native populations are involved in this war, and a very little thought will convince even a casual student of

the certainty that the victory of the British troops must bring substantial benefits and large liberties within reach of the coloured peoples.[57]

During the occupation of northern Natal, the treatment many Africans received from the burghers and Afrikaner rebels would also have been a reason for opposing them. As already mentioned, confiscation and looting of property were common and reports of flogging and shooting were widespread.

There were financial rewards for assisting the British, despite the dangers involved. Runners between Ladysmith and the British army, for example, commanded high bonuses while some Zulu who looted Boer livestock in Vryheid and Utrecht would have been able to rebuild their herds.[58] Labor tenants who saw their landowners retreating with the burghers from northern Natal after the relief of Ladysmith must have congratulated themselves on their good fortune. With the farms abandoned there was no one to prevent them from recovering their losses. And for those Africans who either supplied labor to the army or capitalized on the need for produce, there was a chance to recoup the economic losses of the prewar years and even to prosper. Although this prosperity was a temporary phenomenon for most Africans, the import figures of goods specifically for African use indicate the extent to which they benefited—imports rose from £159,910 in 1899 to £271,450 in 1902.[59]

As far as the chiefdoms were concerned, those that most actively supported the British had a long history of collaboration. This was particularly true of the Ngwane, Chunu, and Thembu chiefdoms, whose chiefs had built a close relationship with the colonial state from its inception. In return, the interests of these chiefdoms had been promoted by the Natal government. By the time of the Anglo-Zulu War they had grown and prospered and their participation on the imperial side in that war had consolidated their position. In 1899 there was no reason for Ncwadi, Silwana, and Mabizela to suspect that their cooperation would not lead to further advancement. In addition, all three, and particularly Silwana, had seen the position of their chiefdoms threatened by the consolidation of settler farming around their reserves, and they may have seen their support of the British in the South African War as a way of strengthening their position *vis-à-vis* the mainly Afrikaner farmers.[60] Dumisa would also have had his reasons for siding with the British—since the Langalibalele rebellion of 1873, the Ngwe chiefdom had consistently tried to increase its landholdings by stressing its loyalty to the colonial state. Dumisa certainly expected that he would be rewarded for his assistance with rebel farms.[61]

Interestingly, of the great chiefdoms of northern Natal, the Qamu, whose loyalty was suspect, had most reason to be dissatisfied with British rule.

Although Kula remained the most powerful appointed chief in Natal, his position and that of the Qamu chiefdom had deteriorated steadily since the death of Kula's grandfather, Ngoza kaLudaba. Ngoza was Theophilus Shepstone's first appointment as chief of a specifically created "government tribe," the largest and most powerful chiefdom in the colony. Fear of its power had led Shepstone's successors to strip the chiefdom of its position and by 1899 it had been divided into nine separate units. Its members were overshadowed by the neighboring Thembu and Chunu chiefdoms and had been alienated from colonial rule. Perhaps in an attempt to regain the position his grandfather had held as principal African ally to the state, Ngoza offered to raise a levy of twenty thousand men.[62]

As far as the *kholwa* were concerned, the years before the South African War had seen the beginning of official attempts to undermine the position they had built up for themselves in earlier decades and to blur the distinction between Christian and "traditionalist." Yet despite the deterioration in their position, some *kholwa* continued to see advantages in British rule and offered loyalty and assistance in return. These included Jabez Molife, who was prepared to offer all in service to the Crown and who had a long history of loyalty, going back to the Bushman campaign of 1866.[63] Johannes Kumalo, the Driefontein chief, who was then almost a hundred years old and had prospered under colonialism, summed up the feelings of such men. In 1904 he told the South African Native Affairs Commission (SANAC) that he had always been loyal to the Queen because it "was not until we came under her beneficent rule that we knew any peace or safety at all ... and we now with all our hearts feel affection and loyalty towards the great lion in London, the King of the British."[64] Many of his Driefontein followers would have echoed these sentiments in 1899. Despite the deterioration in the *kholwa* position elsewhere in Natal, Christian Africans continued to prosper in northern Natal and particularly on the Driefontein farms.[65]

Many *kholwa* thus saw the South African War as an opportunity both to consolidate their position and to remind the British of their loyalty. Their efforts during the Anglo-Zulu War had brought them benefits, and they saw the Anglo-Boer War as offering similar opportunities. The years after the Anglo-Zulu War had seen the Natal government open the colony's Crown lands for auction and the *kholwa* had been encouraged to purchase them. By the end of the century, Africans were again experiencing a land shortage and many *kholwa* anticipated that their loyalty would be rewarded with land. P. M. Maling, a *kholwa* farmer, told SANAC in 1904 that as "our King has conquered everyone, I thought, looking upon us as his children, he would cut off a piece of meat and give to us and say 'Here—eat.'"[66]

Kholwa expectations are reflected in the resolutions passed in June 1900 when their leaders gathered in Durban to form the Natal Native Congress. The delegates included members of the Native Scouts, with Stephen Mini playing a prominent role. The stated purpose of the meeting was to "consider resolutions of devotion and loyalty to our great and gracious Queen," but the intention was certainly to use the war to strengthen their position by reminding the authorities of the promises made by the British. Thus Chamberlain was thanked for the "determined stand he has taken against class legislation," and Milner was praised for the excellent services he had rendered to "the cause of freedom, liberty and justice, and especially for the firm stand he took in the negotiations with the Transvaal government regarding the liberty and rights of the coloured people."[67] In both this and later meetings, the Congress stressed the benefits they hoped the new order in South Africa would bring—improved education, access to the franchise, and easier acquisition of land.

The Reward for African Loyalty

As was the case throughout South Africa, the hope and expectation that the triumph of imperialism would lead to an improvement in the position of Africans in Natal were soon shattered. Once the danger to the colony had passed, narrow settler interests again asserted themselves. Tributes to African loyalty continued to be made, but they proved little more than lip service and government actions were directed to ensuring that no long-term benefits accrued to Africans from the war, particularly gains that would be at the expense of the settlers.

This was clearly evident in the field of labor. The military presence saw a greater need for labor and an increase in its price to as much as £4 per month for unskilled workers. Since the inception of colonial rule, successive administrations had followed a cheap-labor policy, and the Hime ministry was determined that such a policy should not be overthrown by wartime demands. Clashes between the colonial government and the military over wages were endemic until 1902 when the civil authorities finally forced the army to agree to lower the "abnormal rate of wages" it was paying to 30s per month for unskilled labor and to end the supply to Africans of "demoralising" European rations.[68]

The Natal government was equally determined to prevent Africans from using the South African War to overturn the rights of property. Few issues caused more confusion and anger among labor tenants. During the invasion they had remained loyal in northern Natal and watched their Afrikaner neighbors and landlords welcome the commandos. Many had suffered considerable losses and believed that their loyalty would be rewarded at the expense of the rebels. Yet even as the commandos were withdrawing from the colony and the first trials of rebel farmers were beginning, steps were taken against them. Afrikaner farmers who remained on their farms, even those standing trial, began evicting labor tenants who had sided with the British. Although under martial law the administration took steps to prevent this from happening, ministers refused to take preventive measures once martial law had been lifted. On the contrary, they instructed magistrates to impress on labor tenants the fact that they remained subject to their contracts of service despite the treasonable actions of their landlords.[69] Since labor tenants on farms where the owners had accompanied the burghers on their retreat could not be expected to obey this instruction, the government arranged for them to be called out for *isibhalo* service with the military.[70] The labor tenants were, not surprisingly, bewildered by a turn of events that favored the interests of rebel farmers, despite their own loyalty and losses.

In 1903, Natal received the Transvaal districts of Vryheid and Utrecht as compensation for the losses suffered by the colony. The annexation of these districts increased the number of Afrikaners in Natal and deterred the government from taking steps that would alienate them from British rule. The government was particularly sensitive to the fact that Afrikaner sentiment had been outraged by the Holkrantz massacre of 1902 and was reluctant to be seen to side with African interests against those of whites. In northern Natal, the result was a decided deterioration for labor tenants, particularly after the passing of the 1901 and 1903 Native Servants' Identification Acts, which placed them in the absolute power of farmers.[71]

Drought in northern Natal and Zululand during the South African War contributed considerably to the suffering of Africans in these districts. Yet it was difficult for Africans to obtain relief, especially during the early months of the conflict. Funds had been set up both in the colony and in England to relieve distress, and donations had been made by Africans in Natal. These were intended to relieve white distress, however, as Harriette Colenso discovered when she tried to obtain relief for Africans from the Pietermaritzburg Relief Fund in December 1899. The government was supplying a limited amount of relief to Africans by early 1900 but its ministers were reluctant to admit that they could not cope. They turned down the Colenso request that they apply directly to the Mansion House Fund in London.[72] The government proved equally uninterested when an offer of assistance was made by the Aborigines Protection Society in February 1900.[73] Only in 1902 could the extent of distress among African refugees no longer be ignored, and monies from the Mansion House Fund were eventually allocated to them. Only eight hundred Africans, however, received relief during the war, out of the more than four thousand recipients throughout Natal.[74]

Africans who had suffered losses during the invasion also found it difficult to obtain adequate compensation. An Invasion Losses Inquiry Commission assessed claims, but it was more difficult for Africans to prove their case than it was for settlers. The Commission was also advised by the government not to give compensation for stock looted from the Zulu. This was ostensibly on the grounds that the tribesmen had benefited as a result of being used by the military for looting Boer stock. It is equally conceivable that the ministers' failure to prevent the military from using the Zulu rankled, while the possibility that the colony might be saddled with a larger compensation debt should the Vryheid Zulu be encouraged to make similar claims certainly carried weight with officials.[75] Requests by Dinuzulu for compensation for Zulu wounded or killed in action were also rejected;[76] in this case it is certainly conceivable that the ministry was trying to undermine his position once he was no longer of military use. Africans whose claims were accepted as *bona fide* usually received only 75 percent of each claim. This payment of a percentage of each claim applied to white claimants as well, but the fact that African claimants were seldom advised that the balance would not be forthcoming heightened feelings of alienation.[77]

After the end of the war in May 1902, drought conditions continued while a recurrence both of locusts and rinderpest and the outbreak of East Coast fever in 1904 added to African distress. At the same time, any lingering hopes that they might benefit from their loyalty were dispelled with the appointment of Sir George Sutton as prime minister in August 1903. Under Sutton and his successor, Charles Smythe, who took office in 1905, the prejudices of the farming community were blatantly pandered to. While failing to acknowledge any sense of obligation for African welfare, the ministries actively intervened to consolidate settler dominance in Natal.[78]

African chiefs found themselves particularly affected by the official determination to bolster settler interests. After the war, the thrust of official policy was to stress the role of the chiefs as government subordinates exercising authority at the government's pleasure rather than in their own right. This was a direct slight to the interests of the great hereditary chiefs, including those who had cooperated during the war. Indeed, it seemed the only things the chiefs who had provided scouts had received were individual presents of Lee Metford rifles and ammunition.[79] There is no indication of any chief or scout receiving any other recognition, and Dumisa's hopes of being given rebel farms were dashed.[80] The failure to issue war medals to Africans is discussed later in this chapter, but considering that those chiefs who fought in the Anglo-Zulu War received both recognition and increased salaries, their disenchantment after the South African War must have been great. After the war of 1879, chiefs had been allowed to buy Crown lands to alleviate the land shortage. Now, at a time when the need for land was even more acute, no attempt was made to make more land available. In Zululand the reward for siding with the British was the Zululand Delimitation Commission of 1904, which set aside more than a third of the province for white settlement.[81]

In the years following the war the government also intensified the campaign begun in the late nineteenth century against the *kholwa*. Those African Christians who had supported the war effort were bitterly disappointed by the lack of recognition for their services. In 1901, the government considered giving African scouts exempted from traditional African law Martini-Henry rifles and ammunition, and their leaders Lee Metford rifles and ammunition.[82] The final decision was delayed until the end of the war and there is no record of these being issued. The services of the Native Scouts were also downplayed. The official *Natal Volunteer Record* ignored them completely while paying tribute to the white Colonial Scouts who, unlike the Native Scouts, never came under fire.[83] Ironically, the only acknowledgment of the role of the Native Scouts is not in South Africa but in Britain, where the memorial to the Scottish Horse outside the castle in Edinburgh includes the names of four African scouts killed in action. A suggestion that the scouts be represented with other volunteer regiments at King Edward VII's coronation in 1901 was rejected by the prime minister on the grounds that they "would be spoilt by London girls, who were inclined to link arms with members of the black races."[84] Successive ministries also ignored a proposal made in 1899 by Colonel Royston, and later supported by the Governor, Sir Henry McCallum, that a permanent Native Corps similar to the old Edendale Native Horse be raised, based on the Driefontein men.[85]

The most damning indictment of the official failure to recognize the contribution of the Native Scouts was the fiasco surrounding the awarding of campaign medals. The Edendale Native Horse had received silver medals during the Anglo-Zulu War and the scouts expected no less for their services in the South African War. By late 1902, medals had been issued to the imperial and volunteer troops but not to any Africans. On December 30, 1902, a deputation of Native Scouts called on Chamberlain, who was in Natal at the time. He assured them that the Scouts were entitled to medals and a few days later he told a public meeting that he hoped that "we may be able to establish it as a fact that no man serves the British Government, or the

British Empire, and is otherwise forgotten."[86] Chamberlain took up the issue with the War Office and General Lyttelton was instructed to provide the Natal government with medals for the scouts. However, the Commander-in-Chief, Lord Roberts, countermanded the instructions and ordered that medals be issued only to scouts who had shown "conspicuous courage or skill" and that in line with army orders governing the issue of medals to non-enlisted men, they should receive bronze rather than silver medals.[87]

The Natal ministry was "opposed, on principle, to the granting of War Medals to Natives in connection with the Anglo-Boer War" as it wanted neither to admit an equality between the Native Scouts and the volunteer regiments, nor to alienate Afrikaners in Natal. According to Samuelson, George Leuchars (the Secretary for Native Affairs) objected to the scouts receiving medals because they would "parade their medals before the Boers and irritate them."[88] But ministers were aware of the anger that would be felt, particularly in light of Chamberlain's promises and the fact that the *kholwa* knew Samuelson had been told to draw up a list of scouts entitled to medals. To their credit, ministers did try to have bronze medals issued to all the scouts on Samuelson's list, but they came up against military insistence that only men who fulfilled Roberts's conditions should be considered.[89] Both the ministry and McCallum were prepared to take the issue further, to the King if necessary, but in negotiations that dragged on until late 1905 the Driefontein leaders refused to accept bronze medals, even should all scouts receive them.[90] The government, no doubt with a measure of relief, then allowed the question to drop.

The decision not to award silver medals to non-enlisted men and the controversy surrounding the issuing of bronze medals did much to destroy the trust of the *kholwa* in Natal. Although less important when compared to other ways in which the *kholwa* position was undermined, the medal fiasco symbolized for Christian Africans their rejection by the colonial state.[91] It is ironic that the Natal government was blamed for the non-issue whereas, despite its own feelings, it had tried to persuade the imperial army to accept the principle that all scouts should be treated equally. But in the light of the government's actions toward the *kholwa* it is not surprising that the issue should arouse resentment. Yet, had the British army shown more imagination and flexibility, the issue could have been resolved to the satisfaction of the *kholwa*. Silver medals were awarded, for example, to nurses who served with the army.

In its determination to conciliate Afrikaner opinion after the South African War, however, neither the army nor the British government was prepared to recognize the role played by Africans. The postwar ministries were equally reluctant to single out the *kholwa* contribution. In their view of the colony there was no place for a *kholwa* class that aspired to white cultural and socioeconomic status. As seen earlier, the Natal Native Congress had wanted better education, the extension of the franchise, and easier access to land. Despite its moderation, the Congress was regarded as a dangerous body[92] and the government took little notice of its petitions. In fact, official steps were taken to undermine the position already held by the *kholwa,* which reduced the gradations of privilege between them and other Africans. In the field of education, in 1903 the average grant per child to mission schools dropped to 13s 3d (from £1 2s 8d in 1893) and the requirements for grants were tightened to the point that a number of schools had to close.[93] A promise made by McCallum to Johannes Kumalo that a government school would be established at Driefontein in recognition of the scouts' services during the war was not fulfilled.[94]

Hopes of improved access to the franchise also proved groundless. Although there were many *kholwa* who could have qualified for the franchise, few who applied were successful; not even Stephen Mini's application was accepted.[95] It also became far more difficult for *kholwa* to obtain exemption from "traditional" authority, while the value of their status was eroded. Exempted Africans had been specifically included in discriminatory legislation from 1898, while in 1905 the Chief Justice, Sir Henry Bale, overturned an 1880 ruling that exemption extended to the children of a successful applicant.[96]

As far as improved access to land was concerned, by the end of the nineteenth century *kholwa* syndicates had become important purchasers of Crown land in Newcastle and Dundee divisions, a step that alarmed white farmers in northern Natal. Even before the South African War they had argued against African purchases of lands in "white" areas.[97] This demand now became more insistent and in 1903 the government bowed to pressure and barred all Africans, including exempted *kholwa,* from further purchases of Crown lands.[98]

～

The failure of both the imperial and the colonial state to recognize or reward African loyalty during the South African War had far-reaching repercussions among both "traditionalists" and *kholwa.* Four years after the end of the war, the Bambatha rebellion broke out and the response of the loyalists of 1899 was very different. Although Ncwadi was as loyal as he had been during the South African War and although a number of other great chiefs acceded to the request for levies, the enthusiasm of 1899 was lacking. It is possible that these chiefs identified with the government in order to retain (or even regain) the position they had held within the colonial state. Silwana obeyed the government's order reluctantly and was consequently deposed after the rebellion. Many of the chiefs who responded to the government's call found it difficult to find men willing to serve in the levies.[99]

The rebuff to the government came mainly from the *kholwa,* and the lack of volunteers from Edendale and Driefontein shook officials who took *kholwa* loyalty for granted. After the Bambatha rebellion, the Minister of Native Affairs consulted *kholwa* elders about the response and was told by Lazarus Xaba that broken promises in the past had caused disillusionment.[100] Stephen Mini concurred and told the 1906 Native Affairs Commission that the *kholwa* "had nothing to show for what they had done, and were ready to do." He repeated Xaba's comment that they had lost their faith in the government because "what they expected would take place in the form of a change for the better had not been realized."[101] Similarly, John Langalibalele Dube wrote of African disillusionment in an *Ilanga lase Natal* editorial: "You supported the English side most faithfully in their war with the Boers because you expected to be treated better by the English than by the Boers. But your faith brought disappointment. You have not found anything in respect of which you are better off than being under Boer rule, but in some respects it is worse than it would have been under the Boers."[102]

The treatment meted out to African loyalists after the South African War therefore ensured that the colony could no longer rely on a body of African support in the event of further conflict. More seriously, government policies and the contempt for African aspirations shown by officials led to widespread alienation and a realignment of African loyalties in the colony. After 1902, Africans realized that they could no longer look to either the British or the colonial government for redress of their grievances. The war had simultaneously increased the divide between Africans and settlers and narrowed the gaps between "traditionalists" and *kholwa* and between Africans north and south of the Thukela. The *kholwa* had been forced to accept that their attempts to establish a separate identity had failed, while "traditionalists" south of the river began to see themselves as Zulu. Increasingly disillusioned and frustrated, many chiefs and *kholwa* began to see the Zulu past as a common focus and, despairing of help from the British King, they were prepared to transfer their allegiance to Dinuzulu as the embodiment of Zulu national pride and sentiment. Dinuzulu's presence in Zululand, despite attempts by the government to minimize his role, had been strengthened by the military's use of his influence during the war. He was now regarded by many as a symbol of the survival of the Zulu royal house and provided an alternative focus of loyalty and opposition throughout the colony.[103]

Notes

1. *Natal Witness*, 21 November 1899.

2. Ibid., 12 February 1900.

3. Ibid., 27 November, 11 December 1899.

4. See *Natal Witness*, 11 November 1899 and 28 May 1900, which also refers to *kholwa* from the Normandien mission station who had been pressed into digging trenches on the Thukela for the burghers by the missionary, Rev. Prozesky.

5. According to Thomas Pakenham, neither Milner nor the Cape government made any provision for refugees trying to return to the Cape and Basutoland; see T. Pakenham, *The Boer War* (Johannesburg, 1979), 121.

6. *Natal Witness*, 18 October 1899; L. S. Amery (ed.), *The Times History of the War in South Africa, 1899–1900*, vol. 1 (London, 1900), 367.

7. *Natal Witness*, 17 October 1899.

8. Colonial Secretary's Office (CSO) [Natal Archives], 2917–2919, Invasion Losses Enquiry Commission, Native Claims.

9. Government House (GH) [Natal Archives], 1077, H. E. Colenso to Secretary, Pietermaritzburg Relief Committee, 6 December 1899, 78; 8 December 1899, 79.

10. Amery, *Times History*, 4.516.

11. *Natal Witness*, 8 November 1899; K. Driver, *Experience of a Siege Nurse (A Nurse Looks Back on Ladysmith* (Ladysmith, 1978), 13; CSO, 2917–2919, Invasion Losses Enquiry Commission, Native Claims.

12. CSO, 2917–2919, Invasion Losses Enquiry Commission, Native Claims.

13. *Natal Witness*, 23 April 1900.

14. GH 1302, Confidential, Governor to Secretary of State, 27 September 1900, 290.

15. *Natal Witness*, 20 March 1900.

16. P. Warwick, *Black People and the South African War, 1899–1902* (Johannesburg, 1983), 15.

17. *Natal Witness*, 14 October 1899.

18. GH 1040, Minute 2, Prime Minister to Governor, 13 February 1900, 99.

19. GH 1040, Minute 3, 14 February 1900, 102, 100. Although the British and Cape governments shared this attitude, circumstances elsewhere in South Africa forced them to agree to the arming of Africans, at first for self-defense. This was the case in the reserves of the eastern Cape, where armed African levies were organized under white officers in December 1899, and on the Transvaal/Bechuanaland border, where the Tswana were armed to protect the border and took part in the defense of Mafeking—see Amery, *Times History*, 3.96; Warwick, *Black People*, 20–21.

20. Africans played an equally important part in the Boer military system, acting as spies, transport riders, cattle herders, grooms, servants, etc. Approximately ten thousand were regularly employed in addition to those who were commandeered; see Amery, *Times History*, 2.87.

21. J. Lambert, *Betrayed Trust: Africans and the State in Colonial Natal* (Pietermaritzburg, 1995), 160.

22. GH 1040, Minute 2, Prime Minister to Governor, 13 February 1900, 99.

23. Secretary for Native Affairs (SNA) [Natal Archives], 1/1/316, 4/1905. Re Native Scouts' medals.

24. The guns had been sent to the Upper Tugela magistrate even before the outbreak of war; see CSO, 2580, c166/99, Prime Minister to Magistrate, Upper Tugela, n.d.

25. Natal, *Report on the Condition of the Native Population, 1901*, A81; Colonial Office (CO) 179 [Public Record Office], 217, no. 40, Governor to Secretary of State, 13 February 1901, 487.

26. *Natal Witness*, 21 November 1899.

27. Ibid., 11 November 1899, 23 February 1900; Natal, *Report, 1901*, B27/8.

28. S. Marks, *Reluctant Rebellion: The 1906–1908 Disturbances in Natal* (Oxford, 1970), 318.

29. Warwick, *Black People*, 82.

30. CO 179, 217, no. 40, Governor to Secretary of State, 13 February 1901, 487; 218, no. 104, 8 May 1901, 370; 220, no. 309, 13 November 1901, 267.

31. S. M. Meintjes, *Edendale 1850–1906: A Case Study of Rural Transformation and Class Formation in an African Mission in Natal* (Ph.D. thesis, University of London, 1988).

32. SNA, 1/1/316, 4/1905, Re Native Scouts' medals.

33. R.C.A. Samuelson, *Long, Long Ago* (Durban, 1928), 138.

34. Meintjes, *Edendale*, 380; SNA, 1/1/316, 4/1905, Re Native Scouts' medals.

35. Samuelson, *Long, Long Ago*, 146.

36. SNA, 1/1/316, 4/1905, Re Native Scouts' medals; GH 502, Report on Native Scouts by Lt. Col. D. Henderson, 31 December 1900, 146.

37. GH 1414, List of Scouts, 5 March 1903, 164.

38. Meintjes, *Edendale*, 382.

39. Samuelson, *Long, Long Ago*, 146.

40. SNA, 1/1/316, 4/1905, Re Native Scouts' medals.

41. Driver, *Experience of a Siege Nurse*, 30.

42. Meintjes, *Edendale*, 382; *Natal Witness*, 19 October 1899.

43. *Natal Witness*, 2 July 1900.

44. SNA, 1/1/316, 4/1905, Re Native Scouts' medals.

45. GH 502, Report on Native Scouts by Lt. Col. D. Henderson, 1 December 1900, 146.

46. Warwick, *Black People*, 5.

47. Amery, *Times History*, 5.249–51.

48. Lyttleton Papers [Liddell Hart Centre for Military Archives, King's College, University of London], NGL/KL, letters to his wife, 620, 10 September 1901; 625, 16 October 1901.

49. Samuelson, *Long, Long Ago*, 169f.

50. GH 1302, Confidential, Governor to Secretary of State, 21 September 1901, 443f.; 28 September 1901, 451f.; Warwick, *Black People*, 87f. provides the most authoritative discussion of the Holkrantz attack. It is also discussed by S. J. Maphalala, "The Murder at Holkrantz (Mtshashana) 6th May 1902," *Historia* 22, no. 1 (1977): 41–46.

51. GH 502, Enclosure, A. F. Henderson to Under Secretary for Native Affairs, 4 February 1901, 152.

52. Warwick, *Black People*, 81.

53. See Lambert, *Betrayed Trust*, passim.

54. This belief was widespread in African circles—see SNA, 1/1/1354, 3716/06, translation of "An Address to the Zulu Race" by J. L. Dube, *Ilanga lase Natal*, 2 November 1906.

55. Natal, *Native Affairs Commission, 1906–7, Evidence* (Pietermaritzburg, 1907), 909/10.

56. Warwick, *Black People*, 111.

57. *Natal Witness*, 4 December 1899.

58. Ibid., 1 and 30 November 1899, 8 January 1900.

59. Natal, *Report, 1901, 1902*.

60. J. Lambert, "Chiefly Collaboration in Colonial Natal: Case Studies of Phakade kaMacingwane and Thetheleku kaNobanda," in P. Alexander et al. (eds.), *Africa Today* (Canberra, 1996).

61. Warwick, *Black People*, 82.

62. For information on the Qamu, see SNA, 1/4/12, c96/03, USNA confidential report on the strength and combination of tribes, 15 June 1903.

63. SNA, 1/1/316, 4/1905, Re Native Scouts' medals.

64. *South African Native Affairs Commission (SANAC), 1903–1905*, vol. 3 (Cape Town, 1905), 489.

65. Lambert, *Betrayed Trust*, 146.

66. *SANAC*, 3.494.

67. *Natal Witness*, 11 June 1900.

68. GH 1546, Minutes of native labor conference held at Newcastle on 23 January 1902, 72f.

69. GH 1302, Confidential, Governor to Secretary of State, 27 September 1900, 290f; CO 179, 217, Confidential, Governor to Secretary of State, 21 January 1901, 118f.

70. Klip River Magistracy [Natal Archives], Minute papers, 3/3/14, 5 June 1900. See also 3/3/115, 25 February 1902. *Isibhalo* service required Africans to provide compulsory service on the colony's roads.

71. Lambert, *Betrayed Trust*, 167.

72. GH 1077, Enclosures, Secretary, Pietermaritzburg Relief Committee to H. E. Colenso, 9 December 1899, 80; Prime Minister to Governor, 22 January 1900, 76. This attitude was not confined to Natal; £29,000 was raised in Britain to relieve distress amongst whites in Mafeking during the siege. Africans received nothing—see Pakenham, *Boer War*, 418.

73. GH 190, 57, Secretary of State to Governor, 3 March 1900, 159f.

74. GH 1152, Mansion House Fund … report on operations to 30 June 1902, 6; 1100, Bale to Governor, 3 December 1903, 82.

75. GH 1302, Confidential, Governor to Secretary of State, 30 August 1902 and Enclosures, 525f.

76. S. J. Maphalala, "The Story of Compensation, Silver and Bronze Medals for the Zulus After the Anglo-Boer War," *Historia* 24, no. 2 (1979): 28.

77. Klip River Magistracy, Minute papers, 3/3/16, 1903–1905.

78. Lambert, *Betrayed Trust*, chap. 10.

79. GH 502, General C in C, Pretoria to Governor, 2 January 1901, 133f.

80. Warwick, *Black People,* 82.

81. A. Duminy and B. Guest, "The Anglo-Boer War and Its Economic Aftermath, 1899–1910," in A. Duminy and B. Guest (eds.), *Natal and Zululand from Earliest Times until 1910: A New History* (Pietermaritzburg, 1989), 365.

82. GH 502, Minute, HD Winter (for SNA), 31 January 1901, 135.

83. *Natal Volunteer Record: Annals and Field Service in the Anglo-Boer War, 1899–1900* (Durban, n.d.). An example of the way the scouts services were ignored is the credit given the Natal Carbineers for relieving Laing's Nek. In fact the scouts occupied the Nek, and finding it abandoned, signaled to the Carbineers to advance (*Natal Witness,* 2 July 1900).

84. Samuelson, *Long, Long Ago,* 185.

85. Ibid., 147; Meintjes, *Edendale,* 383.

86. SNA, 1/1/316, 4/1905, Re Native Scouts' medals; GH 1264, Enclosure 2, Speech by Chamberlain, 2 January 1903, 40.

87. GH 1264, Enclosure 1, Lyttelton to Bale, 20 February 1904, 39.

88. GH 1233, no. 112, Bale to Secretary of State, 6 June 1904, 128; Samuelson, *Long, Long Ago,* 150.

89. GH 504, General Officer Commanding, South Africa to Bale, 20 February 1904 and enclosures, 85f.

90. GH 1415, Précis of correspondence respecting War Medals to Natal Natives.

91. Sheila Meintjes sees it as the first real reversal of *kholwa* loyalty—see Meintjes, *Edendale,* 382.

92. GH 1085, Governor to Bigge, 19 December 1901, 86.

93. *SANAC,* vol. 3, Superintendent of Education, 235, 237.

94. Samuelson, *Long, Long Ago,* 148–49.

95. Natal, *Native Affairs Commission, 1906–7, Evidence,* Mini, 909.

96. *Natal Mercury,* 3 May 1905.

97. *LA Hansard,* vol. 28, Bainbridge, 20 June 1899, 260.

98. Lambert, *Betrayed Trust,* 164.

99. Ibid., 182.

100. Meintjes, *Edendale,* 387.

101. Natal, *Native Affairs Commission, 1906–7, Evidence,* 909.

102. SNA, 1/1/354, 3716/06, translation, 2 November 1906.

103. J. Lambert and R. Morrell, "Domination and Subordination in Natal, 1890–1920," in R. Morrell (ed.), *Political Economy and Identities in KwaZulu-Natal: Historical and Social Perspectives* (Durban, 1996), 87.

CHAPTER 7

The Role of the EmaSwati in the South African War

MANELISI GENGE

THIS CHAPTER EXAMINES the role played by the emaSwati in the South African War.[1] The involvement of the emaSwati was a contributory factor to the defeat of the Boers by the British in Swaziland. They entered the war with a specific agenda: to expel the Boers from their country in order to regain their independence. They also hoped to benefit from the spoils of war by capturing livestock from the Boers and looked forward to rewards from the British, for whom they had fought and gathered intelligence as scouts.[2]

The emaSwati royalists had contested Boer authority in Swaziland in 1894, when the convention between Britain and the Transvaal established a protectorate administered by the South African Republic. The emaSwati viewed the outbreak of the South African War as an opportunity to settle old scores with the Boers. The extent to which the emaSwati took part in the conflict invites a rethink of the impact of the war in the southern African region. The exclusion of the emaSwati and black South Africans from the Treaty of Vereeniging, signed by the British and the Boers in May 1902, has long obscured the diversity of combatants. By exploring the different theaters of conflict and the issues involved on each front, we can broaden our scholarly understanding of the war. This chapter also makes a further contribution to the growing literature on African involvement in the war.[3] Swaziland has a history of providing human resources for British imperialism in South Africa, for example, through its military alliance with Britain against the BaPedi in 1879. Yet, the extent to which Swaziland has contributed to the shaping of the South African past remains underrepresented in South African historiography.

Prewar Relations with the South African Republic

The emaSwati never accepted the establishment of the South African Republic (Transvaal) Administration in Swaziland by Britain and the Transvaal in

1894. A year later, King Bhunu vowed that "he would never on any account
agree to [the Transvaal administration] being established in his country."[4]
The emaSwati leaders did not accept administration by the Transvaal. From
1894 onward, the era of King Bhunu and Queen Mother Labotsibeni was
characterized by attempts to get rid of Boer administration from Swaziland.
Among the many grievances against the Boers, the emaSwati resented most
the denial of justice, violation of Article 2 of the Anglo-Transvaal Convention of 1894, which protected the rights of emaSwati rulers against Boer en-
croachment and interference and against flogging by Boer officials.[5] These
grievances were an aspect of emaSwati resistance to the establishment of

Swaziland.

SOURCE: P. Warwick, *Black People and the South African War, 1899–1902*
(Cambridge: Cambridge University Press, 1983), 105. Reprinted with the
permission of Cambridge University Press.

Boer rule in Swaziland. When the South African War broke out in October 1899, the emaSwati leaders were still negotiating the replacement of Transvaal administration by a British protectorate.

War means different things to different people. It sometimes means refashioning power relations among the combatants and allies both during and after the fighting itself; the acquisition of wealth in booty and reparations or indemnity; the redrawing of state boundaries; and even the creation of new states. During the 1880s, the independence of the Swazi state was guaranteed by Britain and the Transvaal largely because of the emaSwati alliance with them against the BaPedi chiefdom in 1876 and 1879. Some of these general features of war were applicable in Swaziland during the South African War.

Many whites (British and Boers) lived in Swaziland on the eve of the South African War. They had come to Swaziland during the era of mineral and grazing concessions in the early 1880s.[6] As rumors of the coming war increased, they repositioned themselves. Those who were considered Transvaal burghers (citizens) under Article 8 of the Convention of 1894, which established Transvaal Boer administration in Swaziland, reclassified themselves as British subjects by taking an oath of allegiance to Queen Victoria through the British Consul in Swaziland.[7]

The British and the Boers in Swaziland, as in the rest of southern Africa, wanted an exclusively "white man's war," at least in theory, which meant excluding Africans and other groups from even discussing or commenting on it.[8] On June 27, 1899, when J. Smuts, the British Consul in Swaziland, visited both King Bhunu (now called the Paramount Chief) at Ngabezweni, and the Queen Mother, Labotsibeni, at Zombodze, he was asked by Labotsibeni whether or not Britain was at peace. Labotsibeni also asked Smuts: "If the Boers are so widemouthed and say the English are cowards why don't you fight them?" Smuts told her that the current situation between the British and the Boers was neither her affair nor the emaSwati's, so there was no need to discuss it. With a typically paternalistic colonial attitude, he added, "H.M. [Her Majesty's] Govt. will be annoyed to hear you made a remark of that kind though your tone was not serious. All the Swazis have to do is to keep quiet. If you want news you can send to me and if I have any I can give you I shall do so."[9] Thus, neither Labotsibeni nor Smuts talked about the emaSwati position in the event of a war between the British and the Boers. Labotsibeni might have resorted to the time-honored Swazi strategy of giving "a bulldog a bone to chew then proceed to manuvre [sic] until you are established" or "lie down when a bulldog charges."[10] Smuts, for his part, had avoided the issue because he thought he "might thereby suggest what was not present to her mind. I also thought it well not to question her as to who were the boers who had spoken disparagingly of us [the British] but I think it is likely some of them had done so."[11] This is an example of what one scholar has referred to as a tendency by colonialists to perceive indigenous people as mere objects or victims of the colonial enterprise, those who did not influence the colonial settlement.[12] Smuts was deceiving himself by thinking that the emaSwati were not considering what their position might be in the event of a war. Later, Smuts heard from a storekeeper that the emaSwati believed that the British were afraid of the Boers.[13]

When informing Labotsibeni that the Anglo-Boer prewar negotiations were exclusively a "white man's affair," Smuts neglected to tell her that during the negotiations between May 30 and June 6, 1899, President Paul Kruger had revived old ambitions when he had proposed that the South African Republic be given complete control of Swaziland in exchange for a Reform Bill in the Transvaal, which would give *uitlanders* (foreigners) easier access to republican citizenship.[14] This was sufficient reason for Labotsibeni to be informed of Anglo-Boer negotiations, since Swaziland was seen as an item for bargaining between the Boers and the British.

The conversation between Labotsibeni and Smuts points in various directions. First, it shows that Labotsibeni was better informed than King Bhunu about matters of state and was deeply concerned with them, for it was she who questioned Smuts on Anglo-Boer relations. Second, it demonstrates that contrary to British wishes that the Anglo-Boer conflict be kept a "white man's affair," Africans followed the prewar negotiations with keen interest. For instance, apart from Labotsibeni's concern, regular meetings between a British magistrate and local chiefs were held at Mafeking to consider matters of armament and defense for the BaTswana against a possible Boer attack in Bechuanaland. The Boer Republics (the Transvaal and Orange Free State) had maintained an uneasy coexistence with neighboring African polities because the latter generally regarded Boer "native policy" as harsh.[15]

The emaSwati resented the taxes that the South African Republic imposed on them after 1898. Little wonder then that in November 1899, when Schalk Burger, a Transvaal burgher, asked the Paramount Chief to provide him with a hundred Swazi porters, Bhunu declined on the grounds that taxation had forced his men into the labor market.[16] The extent of the emaSwati's grudge against the Boers was indicated in John Gama's statement to Smuts that if war broke out between the British and the Boers it would mean "an assegai for each boer unless the Swazis [were] very firmly forbidden to take part in the matter."[17] This statement turned out to be a realistic assessment of the emaSwati attitude toward the Boers.

War and the Swazi Royal House

When the South African War began, J. C. Krogh, the Swaziland Special Commissioner for the Transvaal government, turned the reins of the country over to Bhunu and Labotsibeni. In an ingenious way, however, the South African Republic indicated that the restoration of independence was a temporary measure and that it still retained overlordship in the affairs of Swaziland. A letter by the Commandant-General, Piet Joubert, in which the Transvaal recognized Bhunu as the supreme political authority in Swaziland for the duration of the war, stated:

> You Bunu, are the only person who, *as long as the war lasts,* has power in Swaziland over everything. For so long you can do as you like, and it would be very good if *you guarded and took care of every house and work, so that no damage is done* ... you can tell all the remaining whites to go. If any woman, child or defenceless person, black or white, is injured or marauded, South African Republic Government will be dissatisfied.[18]

Although this letter purported to restore emaSwati independence, it was in fact a Boer attempt to persuade the emaSwati to remain neutral in the conflict and to make them responsible for the protection of Boer property and of those of whites who could not leave Swaziland because of age, health, or other reasons.

By this time concessions, which had been ratified by the court of law established by Britain and the Transvaal in 1890, had given whites a foothold in Swaziland.[19] They had acquired immovable goods and resources. Both the British and the Boer settlers aimed to return to Swaziland after the South African War. It was therefore important for them and their governments to make sure that their properties were protected. Many applied to return to Swaziland and claimed compensation for losses incurred during the war.[20] The British authorities made land ownership and other interests in Swaziland important qualifications when considering the applications of whites planning to return to Swaziland after the cessation of hostilities.[21] The handing over of political control of the country to the emaSwati leaders was therefore a way of avoiding anarchy after the withdrawal of the Transvaal Administration, and it was designed to ensure the protection of white property. The British were concerned about the maintenance of law and order.[22] But, immediately after the war, British officials in Swaziland and South Africa prepared for the eventual British takeover of Swaziland. By doing so, they hoped to end the emaSwati days of wartime independence. As early as 1902, one British official confidentially wrote, "It wont [*sic*] do for the Swazis to know there is a chance of their being in a temporary state of independence."[23]

Since the advent of Europeans in the interior of southern Africa, the emaSwati leaders had realized that they could not remain independent without cooperation under European "protection." As early as 1846, for example, the emaSwati had formed an offensive and defensive alliance with the Boers in the eastern Transvaal. They had collaborated with the Boers as well as the British in colonial wars against the BaPedi during the latter half of the nineteenth century.[24] Transvaal Boer support had been crucial in checking internal jealousies within the royal family during succession struggles, especially on the accessions to the throne of Mswati and Mbandzeni. The emaSwati leaders also asked Theophilus Shepstone Jr. from the Natal Colony to act as their agent in dealings with European mineral and land grazing concessionaires in the 1880s.[25] It is not accurate to state, therefore, that "the Swazi leaders did not quite understand what protection meant" when they pleaded for British "protection."[26] "Protection" simply meant different things to Swazi leaders and the British government.

The heightened Anglo-Boer tension in the Transvaal prompted the British and Boers, on October 4, 1899, to instruct their subjects to leave Swaziland or remain there at their own risk. However, burghers who were liable to be enlisted were allowed to remain in Swaziland.[27] Thus, the war marked a temporary suspension of European colonialism in terms of Transvaal administration of Swaziland. The Swazi rulers were not neutral in the South African War, as some would have us believe.[28] The emaSwati had always collaborated with Europeans in the wars against Africans in the interior of South Africa. They had used their involvement in such wars to bargain with Europeans. When the South African War broke out, the choice for the emaSwati rulers was not whether to be neutral, but which side to join. Until 1899 there had been no Swazi precedent for taking sides in a war in which the main protagonists were Europeans. Since the Anglo-Transvaal Convention of 1890, which had put Swaziland on the road to colonization, the emaSwati's diplomatic strategy of playing off the British against the Transvalers had been rendered ineffective.[29]

King Bhunu did not live to see the war. He died in December 1899, before the emaSwati became actively involved. His successor was his infant son, Nkonjani or Mona, who became known as Sobhuza II. Labotsibeni became Queen Regent until Sobhuza reached his majority. She effectively became the head of state to whom British and Boers communicated their views regarding the war in Swaziland.

When war broke out, Swaziland had just emerged from the rinderpest epidemic of 1896–97, which had killed many Swazi cattle and dramatically disrupted the economy. The coming of an Anglo-Boer administration to Swaziland in the early 1890s had put an end to the emaSwati's traditional cattle-raiding activities.[30] Withdrawal of the Boer administration at the outbreak of the South African War provided the emaSwati with an opportunity to rebuild their livestock through raiding. (Wealth in cattle was central to royal power. Swazi royalists used cattle to maintain client relations with their subjects by *sisa,* that is, placing cattle among them, and also for ritual purposes.)

In the letter in which the Transvaal purportedly returned power to the emaSwati rulers, Commandant-General Joubert reminded Bhunu of old traditions about how Boers "made" Swazi kings (such as Mbandzeni), of how they had protected the emaSwati against the amaZulu, and of Boer peaceful coexistence with the emaSwati. He also promised that the Boers would not use Swaziland as a battlefield in their fight against the British.[31] But the emaSwati rulers were obviously unhappy with Boer administration by the time war broke out; neutrality was not an option for the emaSwati, who could see that war "threw up its own opportunities."[32] The British made use of emaSwati services in so many ways that emaSwati neutrality became a farce. The emaSwati provided food for British soldiers and they also became scouts.

Chief Mavela Nkosi's war

During the early phase of the war, Lord Kitchener, Commander-in-Chief of the British Forces in South Africa, asked Labotsibeni to send her men to guard the Amsterdam border post against Boer infiltration. Labotsibeni refused because she had no men to send to the border.[33] She neglected to inform Kitchener that her *emabutfo* (army) had, since early 1900, been engaged in a purge of emaSwati who were perceived to be against the rule of the monarchy or were alleged to have been spying for whites on her activities.[34] So Kitchener turned to Chief Mavela Nkosi, whom he asked at an interview in Pretoria "to employ Scouts, and work along the Amsterdam border in conjunction with our [British] troops, promising a good reward."[35] Kitchener told Mavela to use his own Swazi men and gave him six rifles. Mavela was an influential chief in southwestern Swaziland. He organized thirty-two scouts, including himself, from his village and fed them at his own expense.[36]

Mavela also provided intelligence about Boer operations to Colonel Colville and Major Godman of the British army. He handed over to Colville Boer livestock captured by his Swazi scouts. Colville paid Mavela thirty cattle and Godman paid him in money for his services. Mavela also joined with British forces at Chievely who were marching on the Transvaal.[37] He was acutely aware of his precarious position, which had resulted from his siding with Britain in the war. He told a British commander, "I have been consistently on the side of the English and on that account have been *hunted* by the Boers in my own country."[38]

In 1903, the Special Commissioner vouched for Mavela's contribution to the British war effort when he said, "I believe that Mavela did good work & captured a number of Boers & a good deal of stock, which was handed over to various columns."[39] In the same breath, the commissioner pointed out that Mavela's services made him vulnerable to Boer hostility. The Boers destroyed his village, household property, grain, and horses, in retaliation for British intelligence officers crossing the border. Mavela's village was also plundered by British troops.[40] The commissioner recommended that Mavela's application for compensation be favorably considered, for "as far as I know the man appears to have done a lot of work under promise of reward, and if it is not recognized, he and the others will surely have reasonable grounds for charging us with a breach of faith." Two months later, the Special Commissioner for Swaziland explained Mavela's compensation: "I think that it would be only reasonable to pay him the £50, *to close the incident,* as Sir Thomas Cunningham suggests."[41] Cunningham had explained that the Intelligence Department in Pretoria was ready to pay Mavela £50 "*in order to bury the incident completely.*"[42] Mavela was finally paid £50 by the Department of Intelligence in Pretoria.[43] Cunningham's view prevailed, which is why Mavela's involvement in the South African War has remained obscure in Swazi historiography.

By 1903, Sir Thomas Cunningham paid Mavela £20 compensation for the grain destroyed by the Boers and £20 for intelligence he had sent to Cunningham. Cunningham told Mavela, however, that he was being compensated only on condition that he never again make a claim against the British government for the loss or destruction of property at the hands of the Boers.[44] Cunningham was trying to bury forever the fact that Mavela's village had suffered Boer attacks during the war.

Until February 1902, Mavela received some payment for his services from various British military authorities. But after that, Cunningham gave Mavela £15 per month, paid through the office of Queen Regent Labotsibeni, whose Secretary was Josiah Vilakazi.[45] The British alleged that £52 10s had been given to Vilakazi to pay Labotsibeni, who was supposed to pay Mavela and his men for their services to the British. Vilakazi denied that he had ever received such payment. The Special Commissioner for Swaziland speculated that the money had been taken by Labotsibeni: "it is a pity that these moneys were not paid directly to persons to whom they were due."[46] Whatever the reasons for Cunningham's changes to the way Mavela was paid for his military services, by channeling money through Labotsibeni, he had effectively widened the involvement of the emaSwati in the war. It was now no longer confined to individuals, but included Swazi leaders as well. That Mavela and his scouts were paid through Labotsibeni also gave the Regent a degree of influence over them. This boosted the image of Swazi royalists, who were recouping power after the departure from Swaziland of the Boer administration.

Mavela was not alone in rendering services to the British. His Swazi scouts had brought greater involvement in the South African War. Their actions were significant in the British defeat of the Boers. Apart from capturing Boer livestock, the scouts guarded and patrolled the Amsterdam border post and sent intelligence to the nearest British columns. Mavela and his village shouldered some of the economic burden of war on the border. By the end of the conflict, Mavela claimed £1,130 from the Special Commissioner for himself and his scouts. He told the Special Commissioner that his people were demanding reimbursement for their services.[47] In the eyes of most British military authorities, Mavela had an impeccable military service record. Thomas Cunningham congratulated him on his "splendid work, being practically the only loyal Swazi of influence in South Western Swaziland." Besides recommending that Mavela be paid £50 to bury the incident of his village's destruction by the Boers, Cunningham recommended that the British authorities in Pretoria not compensate the emaSwati scouts. He asserted that "if these boys were paid, I think the others similarly employed in other Districts would have similar claims. As there were nearly 1,700 in all, the amount of the claims would be very great, therefore I do not recommend that they should be paid."[48] Despite the Swazi scouts' important, if limited, contribution to the Boer defeat, the British military authorities did want to reward them.

Chief Ndabazezwe, who lived near the border of the Ingwavuma District, also played an important role in the South African War. He informed the British at Ingwavuma and in Natal of Boer military movements. Ndabazezwe's political services contributed to the Boers' defeat in the war. This was acknowledged by various British officials who, when the war ended, recommended that Ndabazezwe be given a Lee-Metford rifle in recognition of his loyalty, and that it be presented by the Special Commissioner for Swaziland in Mbabane. Other officials, however, recommended that Ndabazezwe be given cattle instead of a gun, in accordance with the law that disarmed

Africans in the Transvaal. As one British official remarked: "it would be embarrassing just now to issue a rifle in Swaziland."[49] Presenting Ndabazezwe with a gun and ammunition would have been only token recognition of his services. Certainly, it would be the cheapest way to reward a chief who had placed his life and that of his village in danger. A rifle or a few cattle would not bring about any material improvement in Ndabazezwe's village. That the British officials were more concerned with developments in the Transvaal than with recognizing emaSwati support shows that their motive was the establishment of a British imperial order in southern Africa. The suggestion that the Special Commissioner for Swaziland present Ndabazezwe with the gift was probably intended to win emaSwati loyalty. It was also part of a larger scheme to establish a layer of loyal chiefs who would be useful to the British administration immediately after the war.

Important as it was, the involvement of Chiefs Mavela and Ndabazezwe on the British side did not, however, bring about the commitment of the Swazi state in the person of the monarchy. The Regent became involved in the war only when the British gave her "orders and permission to seize and appropriate Boer cattle" in Swaziland. (Similar orders were also given by column commanders to various chiefs in the Transvaal.)[50] Some of these orders were given to Labotsibeni verbally in order to keep them secret.[51]

Chief Thintintha Dlamini's Regiment and the Battle at Hlatikhulu

After 1901, the war shifted from military battles to guerrilla attacks, which required intimate knowledge of the terrain. During this phase many Boers returned with their livestock to Swaziland, without the permission of Labotsibeni. These incursions prompted Major General T. E. Stephenson, Commander of British Forces in the Barberton District of eastern Transvaal, to write to Labotsibeni on February 2, 1901, to inform her that Lord Kitchener wished her to order the emaSwati to "defend themselves against all Boer incursions" into her country. He also informed her that Kitchener had issued orders that "all Boer cattle taken by your people will become their lawful property."[52] Labotsibeni sent a letter to the British military authorities on February 16, 1901, requesting protection for southern Swaziland. On February 21, 1901, Lieutenant-General J.D.P. French, who commanded the British forces on the Swaziland frontier, dispatched British troops to Swaziland. He told the Regent to attack any Boers who entered Swaziland and to keep their cattle for her "own use."[53] Captain Dudley Rideout wrote to Labotsibeni requesting permission for three white men on a special mission to remain in Swaziland for an indefinite period. He asked her to give them "all the

information they require" and assured her that the British were capturing Boer prisoners daily and that many Boer soldiers had surrendered. He
warned, however, that the Boer leaders were still steadfastly refusing to
capitulate. Rideout concluded his note by reminding Labotsibeni that she
should "of course prevent any supplies reaching the Boers and to stop all
letters coming through to them. Your people may take all cattle and sheep
they find belonging to the Boers."[54]

Armed with these orders and assurances, Labotsibeni directed Swazi chiefs
to organize their *emabutfo* (regiments) to expel Boers from Swaziland and
confiscate their livestock. She instructed chiefs that, should there be fighting,
Boer women and children were to be spared, for she had been ordered by
the British not to kill them.[55] The first target of the Swazi regiments was a
party of Boers that had reentered Swaziland without Labotsibeni's permission, apparently trying to escape British forces at Piet Retief. In February
1901, the Regent dispatched an *ibutfo,* under Chief Thintintha Dlamini, to
expel the Boers from Swaziland. Three Boers, Lodewijk Andries Slabbert,
Hendrik Slabbert, and Hans le Roux, were killed by Thintintha's *ibutfo* near
Umsheng's Drift on the Assegai River. According to an eyewitness, the regiments threw L. A. Slabbert's body into the river.[56]

By February 1901, Boers reentered Swaziland from many directions without permission from Labotsibeni. They evaded British forces by taking refuge
at Hlatikhulu Mountain. Chief Silele reported their presence to the Queen
Regent. On March 4, 1901, Labotsibeni sent Chief Siquza (alias Thintintha
Dlamini) and four other chiefs with eighty Swazi regiments to expel Boers
from Hlatikhulu Mountain. Thintintha told the Boers to leave their cattle
because they belonged to the Regent, who had been given them by the
British. Salomon Maritz told Thintintha that he was a resident of Swaziland and that he had never left the country. But on March 6, 1901, Chief
Ntshingila of Hlatikhulu advised Maritz and other Boers to leave because
Thintintha was about to attack them. Under pressure from the emaSwati *impi*
(military unit), Maritz, Joubert, H. Mey, H. van der Schyf, and D. Jordaan
left Hlatikhulu Mountain and surrendered to the British at Mahamba, under
Colonel Allenby's command. On their way to the British camp they told
other Boer parties, such as those of J. Engelbrecht and J. Rudolph, that they
were on their way to surrender. Maritz also warned them of what could
happen to them if they did not surrender. More than ten Boer families with
large herds of cattle ignored his warning.[57]

When Thintintha gave Labotsibeni's orders to leave Swaziland, the Boers
refused "in an insolent manner (it is said)" to cooperate. They declared that
"they recognised no Native Authorities and did not fear them."[58] A Boer also

poked Thintintha in the face and told him that "there was no Swazi King, he was dead," and therefore they would not leave the country.[59] He and his compatriots were quickly forced to swallow their words, when on March 9, 1901, Thintintha's regiment attacked and killed some of them. Several others, including Andries Breytenbach and Adriaan Pretorius, escaped to the eastern Transvaal near Bethal. Thintintha captured their cattle, which he sent to the Queen Regent. According to eyewitness accounts, six Boers, one "Cape boy," and two emaSwati were killed and six emaSwati were wounded in the skirmish. Others put the number of Boers killed at eight and reported that none of the emaSwati had been killed.[60] Some scholars who have briefly referred to this encounter are completely silent about casualties among the emaSwati.[61] The commanders of the *emabutfo* vehemently denied that white women and children were killed in this battle. Some British officials, however, believed otherwise.[62] Although the African men who were looking after the Boer livestock received blows from the emaSwati *impi*, they were not killed because their "orders are not to kill the Natives, we have got to clean the whitemen out."[63] When Colonel Allenby was informed of this attack, he did not immediately take action against the emaSwati. It was only after the British took over Swaziland that Thintintha Dlamini was imprisoned by the British for "exceeding his orders" by killing the Boers.[64]

Some Boers lost their families at Hlatikhulu Mountain and referred to the battle as a "massacre."[65] One British official reported it differently: "the incident can hardly be called a massacre, for plain warning was given, an attack made in day light and resistance offered by Boers who wounded several Natives and some were apparently killed."[66] The Hlatikhulu battle had far-reaching effects on the Boer community in Swaziland. Many, such as P.J.C. Venter, who could not trace their relatives in Swaziland after the South African War referred to the battle at Hlatikhulu as a starting point in their search for relatives.[67] It is probable that many people (emaSwati and Boers) died in this battle. Secondly, it was a major military encounter between the emaSwati and the Boers. It compelled the Boers to surrender to the British military authorities in Swaziland, or to flee the country.

For the emaSwati *emabutfo*, the Hlatikhulu incident conferred military distinction on Thintintha Dlamini, who "gained a great reputation as a warrior, while he was a favourite of the Ndlovukazi [Labotsibeni] for having sent the captured cattle to her." Since the days of the emaSwati military alliance with the British against the BaPedi in 1879, no Swazi army commander had distinguished himself on the battlefield. Thintintha did not live long enough to establish his newly earned military reputation. In about January 1907, he was shot while resisting arrest by Swazi police, who were employed by the

British administration. Labotsibeni was incensed by the news of his death; she "indulged in loose talk and threats against the particular Native Constables at whose hands Tintita met his death."[68] Such threats were popular among young Swazi, but Labotsibeni's advisers blamed Thintintha for his own death.

It can be argued that the capture of Boer livestock by the emaSwati was not limited to the Hlatikhulu battle. Long after, in May 1901, Labotsibeni and the Swazi Council received instructions from Smuts to capture Boer cattle. He told them:

> if the Swazis, when acting on their own accord in obedience to the foregoing instructions, (i.e. remaining loyal & keeping Boers out), capture stock belonging to Boers, they may keep them, but they must at once report to the nearest British Officer the number taken, and, if possible, the names of the Boers to whom they belong. If the Swazis capture stock when they are acting under the orders of British Officers, or when they are forming a part of a British force they are not entitled to keep such stock.[69]

Smuts also told the leaders that certain emaSwati were near the border guarding Boer cattle they claimed were theirs. This, in his view, amounted to assisting the Boers and he prohibited the emaSwati from doing so. He warned Labotsibeni and the Council that the emaSwati would not benefit from "hiding Boer stock," because when the war ended, any Swati found in possession of Boer cattle would be punished.[70]

Since cattle were highly valued by the emaSwati, Smuts's orders had a strong appeal. But, unlike those given by British military authorities, his instructions had a sting in the tail. By telling the emaSwati to keep a record of the number of confiscated cattle and the names of the Boers from whom cattle were captured, and by threatening that any Swazi deviation from his instructions would be punished by the British after the war, Smuts left the door open for British repossession of Boer cattle captured by the emaSwati. This was unusual for the emaSwati who were accustomed to increasing their livestock through war booty. (When they had given military assistance to the British against the BaPedi in 1876–79, they had been allowed to return to Swaziland with thousands of cattle taken from the enemy.)[71] Smuts's instructions also indicated that Swaziland would be under British control when the war was over. By forbidding the emaSwati from looking after the Boer cattle under *siza* arrangements, Smuts actually dissembled Swazi neutrality in the South African War, and ironically, he therefore inadvertently enlisted Swazi involvement on the British side against the Boers.

Indeed, through Labotsibeni's orders, the emaSwati captured large Boer herds during the war, which she "distributed at intervals" among her subjects.[72] The capture of Boer cattle was one of the major ways in which the emaSwati participated in the South African War. They captured Boer stock as far afield as the Piet Retief District of the Transvaal.[73] Some emaSwati suffered night raids for cattle and harassment by the British forces. For example, certain emaSwati who lived at Ngogweni in the Piet Retief District had their cattle raided by Gouman (given name unknown) and Charles Elisha King, of Mahamba, who worked for the British Intelligence Department, based in Hlatikhulu. This occurred immediately before the final surrender of the Boers. One night, Mgwayiza Mtungwa was awakened by the noise of horses. When he went outside he saw his brother, Nyunda, being taken by Africans who were with King. They beat him with a whip while interrogating him about whose cattle were in his kraal. They accused him of looking after Boer cattle. Although he told them that the cattle were his, they took them away. Many other households were raided in similar fashion and cattle were rounded up by King and another white man, known to the emaSwati only by his Swazi name, "Nomatshayinkonjana." King and "Nomatshayinkonjana" drove the cattle to Hlatikhulu.[74] Incidents like this were widespread, because when the war ended "most of the damage claimed for [by Africans] was done by the British Forces."[75]

Claims of Compensation for Loyalty

The irony of emaSwati involvement in the South African War, at least from their point of view, was most apparent when the conflict ended. Their reasons for entering the war proved unattainable. The British War Office was flooded with claims for war losses. The Central Claims Board outlined the conditions under which claims from Africans for compensation would be considered.[76] In the Transvaal, District Commissions handled claims from ex-burghers, whereas claims of British subjects and foreigners were dealt with by resident magistrates. In Swaziland, claims from the emaSwati were at first not entertained at all; then they were referred to the Military Compensation Board.[77]

From a loan of £2,000,000 for compensation claimed by Africans, only £200,000 was allocated for war losses suffered by those in the conquered territories. Swaziland submitted a claim of £2,231 17s 6d, of which only £1,109 2s 6d was earmarked for losses incurred by the emaSwati. However, Swaziland's claim was not paid from the above loan.[78] If compensation claims for war losses are anything to go by, they show the extent to which the emaSwati were either involved in or affected by the war. For example, Reuben Twala, a Swazi teacher who lived near the Mahamba Mission Station provided the British forces with five or six hundred bags of maize when they arrived at Mahamba. He also sustained losses from the war itself. He claimed compensation for animals: twenty head of cattle, ten goats, four riding horses, and three pigs; a three-room house with a thatched roof; furniture; and six maize fields.[79] Many emaSwati sustained losses but could not afford lawyers to present their cases, which meant that their claims were never documented.

The most controversial aspect of compensation for war damages, and one of the main reasons for emaSwati support of the British during the conflict with the Boers, was the retrieval of captured Boer livestock from the emaSwati as well as emaSwati cattle that had been captured by the Boers.[80] A circular issued on September 11, 1902, stipulated:

1. If it is proved that such stock was captured in war by the British Forces, and given to the natives by Military Authorities for services rendered it shall be restored to Government by delivery to the nearest Repatriation Depot, and compensation shall be given to the natives equal to the full value, as defined by section 4.

2. If it is proved that such stock was looted by natives under Military Orders, or advice, it shall be returned to the claimant upon his satisfying the Magistrate or Native Commissioner that he is the rightful owner, and compensation shall be given by Government to the natives equal to half the value, as defined in section 4.

3. If the stock cannot be shown to have been acquired by either of the foregoing method, or by any lawful means, it shall, on being identified, be returned to the rightful owner, without compensation to the natives.

4. For the purpose of compensation, the following tariff should be observed. All stock should be valued according to age and condition. The valuation shall not exceed in the case of horses £10, cattle £9, sheep & goats 15/-.[81]

This circular undermined one of the reasons that had spurred the emaSwati to join the war, namely to increase their wealth by capturing Boer livestock.

Although the British authorities had largely disregarded most claims for compensation from the emaSwati, it was not easy for them to implement their plans as spelled out in the circular. Officials were caught between two irreconcilable challenges: meeting Boer requests for raided livestock from the emaSwati, on the one hand, and the refusal of the emaSwati to surrender their booty under British military orders, on the other. Some Boers pointed out that since the recovery was proving difficult, "their" cattle were dying in the hands of the emaSwati.[82]

Labotsibeni dug in her heels, arguing that she had acted under British orders and the permission of Kitchener when she confiscated Boer cattle. Since she had already distributed the booty among her subjects, she was unwilling to return Boer livestock.[83] Godfrey Lagden conceded that the British had no right to demand restoration and issued a directive to the Special Commissioner for Swaziland that "to all enquires you must return reply that we have no power to reverse acts done under the written authority of the Commander-in-Chief."[84] Sir Richard Solomon, Attorney General, agreed that "it is quite impossible for us [the British officials] to ignore the instructions of the Military Authorities on which these seizures were made."[85]

The emaSwati were a significant factor in bringing about a British victory in the eastern Transvaal and in Swaziland during the South African War. They did not merely fight a British war, however; they had their own agendas around land and livestock, which they pursued tenaciously until the Boers surrendered.

Notes

1. This chapter uses the term "emaSwati" to refer to the Swazi people. The Swazi people call themselves "emaSwati" or "maSwati," instead of the anglicized version, "Swazis" (plural).

2. The financial assistance of the National Research Foundation toward this research is hereby acknowledged. The opinions and conclusions in this chapter are the author's.

3. A pioneering work on the role of Africans in the South African War is Donald Denoon's "Participation in the 'Boer War': People's War, People's Non-War, or Non–People's War?" in B. A. Ogot (ed.), *War and Society in Africa* (London, 1972), 109–22. Seminal on this subject is P. Warwick, *Black People and the South African War, 1899–1902* (London, 1983). See also the collection of essays in P. Warwick (ed.), *The South African War: The Anglo-Boer War, 1899–1902* (Harlow, 1980); W. R. Nasson, "'Doing Down Their Masters': Africans, Boers, and Treason in the Cape Colony during the South African War of 1899–1902," *Journal of Imperial and Commonwealth History* 12, no. 1 (1983): 29–53, and "Moving Lord Kitchener: Black Military Transport and Supply Work in the South African War, 1899–1902, with Particular Reference to the Cape Colony," *Journal of Southern African Studies* 11, no. 1 (1984): 25–51. See also note 8 below for further citations.

4. Letter from J. Stuart, Acting British Consul, Bremersdorp, Swaziland, to His Excellency the High Commissioner, Cape Town, 24 April 1895, Enclosure 2, African No. 499, *Further Correspondence Relative to the Affairs of Swaziland* (Colonial Office, 1895), 2.

5. H. S. Simelane, "Swazi Resistance to Boer Penetration and Domination, 1881–1898," *Transafrican Journal of History* 18 (1989): 134.

6. See P. Bonner, *Kings, Commoners and Concessionaires: The Evolution and Dissolution of the Nineteenth-Century Swazi State* (Johannesburg, 1983).

7. Confidential letter from J. Smuts, Her Majesty's Consul in Swaziland, to the High Commissioner, 13 September 1899, in Confidential Despatches and Telegrams, British Consul, 1897–1899, File No. S. 14 D, Swaziland National Archives, hereafter referred to as SNA.

8. See for example S.T.T. Plaatje, *Native Life in South Africa,* ed. B. Willan (London, 1916; repr. 1989), chap. 18; Warwick, *Black People,* chap. 1; I. R. Smith, "The Origins of the South African War (1899–1902): A Re-Appraisal," *South African Historical Journal* 22 (1990): 24–60; W. R. Nasson, "Warriors without Spears: Africans in the South African War, 1899–1902" (Review essay), *Social Dynamics* 9, no. 1 (1983): 91–94; R. F. Morton, "Linchwe I and the Kgatla Campaign in the South African War, 1899–1902," *Journal of African History* 26 (1985): 169–91; W. R. Nasson, "Moving Lord Kitchener," *Journal of Southern African Studies* 11, no. 1 (1984): 25–51; M. Tamarkin, "Milner, the Cape Afrikaners and the Outbreak of the South African War: From a Point of Return to a Dead End," *Journal of Imperial and Commonwealth History* 25, no. 3 (1997): 392–414, and J. Krikler, "Agrarian Class Struggle and the South African War," *Social History* 14, no. 2 (1989): 151–76. The view that the upcoming South African War was to be exclusively a "white man's war" raises the need for a comparative study of this war with the Civil War of the 1860s in the American South, during which slaveowners expected slaves to stay out of the war fought against the white Northerners, as if the issue of slavery were not one of the crucial causes of that war.

9. J. Smuts, British Consul in Swaziland, confidential letter to the High Commissioner, 28 June 1899, in Confidential Despatches and Telegrams, British Consul, 1897–1899, SNA.

10. Quoted in A. M. Dlamini, "Expansion and Survival Policy of the Swazi Nation," unpublished paper (University of Swaziland, Special Collection, n.d.), 2.

11. Smuts to the High Commissioner, 28 June 1899, in SNA.

12. R. Greenstein, "Rethinking the Colonial Process: The Role of Indigenous Capacities in Comparative Historical Inquiry," *South African Historical Journal* 32 (1995): 115.

13. Smuts to the High Commissioner, 28 June 1899, in SNA.

14. T. Pakenham, *The Boer War* (London, 1997), 67. For a discussion of the Transvaal's old ambition to possess Swaziland as a corridor to Delagoa Bay on the east coast for strategic reasons, see N. G. Garson, "The Swaziland Question and a Road to the Sea, 1887–1895," *Archives Year Book for South African History,* Vol. 2 (Pretoria, 1957), 267–434. See also D. Rhoodie, *Conspirators in Conflict: A Study of the Johannesburg Reform Committee and Its Role in the Conspiracy against the South African Republic* (Cape Town, 1967), 15.

15. For a discussion of the Boer "native policy" see J.A.I. Agar-Hamilton, *The Native Policy of the Voortrekkers: An Essay in the History of the Interior of South Africa, 1836–1858* (Cape Town, 1928), and C. H. Thomas, *Origin of the Anglo-Boer War Revealed: The Conspiracy of the 19th Century Unmasked,* 2d ed. (London, n.d.),

166–71. For African anti-Boer sentiment in the Cape Colony, see Nasson, "'Doing Down Their Masters,'" 29–53.

16. Warwick, *Black People*, 106.

17. Smuts's confidential letter to the High Commissioner, 13 September 1899, in Confidential Despatches and Telegraphs, British Consul, 1897–1899, File no. S. 14 D, SNA. Gama was a Swazi informant whom the British officials in Swaziland regarded as reliable.

18. Quoted in Warwick, *Black People*, 106. Emphasis added.

19. For a discussion of the establishment of the concession court, see M. Genge, "Law and the Imposition of Colonial Rule in Swaziland, 1890–1898" (M.A. thesis, Ohio University, 1992), 78–82. For more information about the concessions see Bonner, *Kings*, chap. 10.

20. For Boer applications for permits to return to Swaziland, see the following files in SNA: J154/02, J243/02, J166/02, J221/02, SCS 257/02, SCS 592/02, and SCS 878/03. For Boers or Burghers, as they were referred to, who returned to Swaziland without permission, see files J118/02 and SCS 196/03. For claims for compensation for war losses from both British and Burghers/Boers, see files SCS 254/03, SCS 941/03, SCS 575/02, SCS 549/02, and SCS 242/03. For applications for grants of relief to certain burghers who returned to Swaziland after the war, see file J236/05.

21. Minute Paper, D. Honey, Secretary for Native Affairs, Swaziland, to W. H. Moor, Assistant Colonial Secretary, 12 May 1902, file J243/02, SNA. See also a copy of a letter, E.H.M. Legget, Major R. E., Director of Burgher Camps Department, Pretoria, to the Colonial Secretary, Pretoria, 28 November 1902, J243/02, SNA.

22. See, for instance, Nasson, "'Doing Down Their Masters,'" 31; and for Bechuanaland, see Plaatjie, *Native Life*, 188.

23. Confidential letter, Sir Godfrey Y. Lagden, Special Commissioner for Native Affairs to Sir Neville Lyttleton, G.O.C. Transvaal and the Orange River Colony, 30 June 1902, J58/02, SNA.

24. For the British and Boer destruction of the BaPedi polity, see P. Delius, *The Land Belongs to Us: The Pedi Polity, the Boers and the British in the Nineteenth-Century Transvaal* (Johannesburg, 1983). For the role of the emaSwati in this destruction, see M. Genge, "The Role of the AmaSwazi in the Destruction of the BaPedi State, 1876–1879" (Seminar Paper in African History, Michigan State University, Fall 1993), 1–30.

25. J. W. Headlam (ed.), *Materials for the History of South Africa, 1890–1895: Being Selections from the Private and Official Correspondence of Lord Loch*, vol. 2 (London, 1898), 2; Bonner, *Kings*, chap. 5; J.S.M. Matsebula, *A History of Swaziland*, 3d ed. (Cape Town, 1987), chap. 8; and W. J. Leyds, *The Transvaal Surrounded: A Continuation of "The First Annexation of the Transvaal"* (London, 1919), ch. 34.

26. J. B. Mlahagwa, "Capital, Class and State in Colonial Swaziland: The Hegemony of Capital and the Demise of Dlamini Power" (Research Paper submitted to the International Development Research Center, Nairobi, April 1982), 7. (A copy of this paper is available at the University of Swaziland, Library, Special Collection.)

27. Government Notice issued to all white inhabitants in Swaziland by J. C. Krogh, Special Commissioner for Swaziland, 4 October 1899, J180/03, SNA.

28. For the neutrality view, see Matsebula, *History*, 172, and Warwick, *Black People*, 108. Crush has uncritically accepted Matsebula's and Warwick's view of the emaSwati's neutrality. See J. Crush, *The Struggle for Swazi Labour, 1890–1920* (Kingston, 1987), 48.

29. For a discussion of this, see Genge, "Law," 68–78. For the emaSwati's strategy of playing off the British against the Transvalers, see Headlam (ed.), *Materials*, 10.

30. R. M. Packard, "Maize, Cattle and Mosquitoes: The Political Economy of Malaria Epidemics in Colonial Swaziland," in J. Daniel and M. F. Stephen (eds.), *Historical Perspectives on the Political Economy of Swaziland: Selected Articles* (Kwaluseni, Social Science Research Unit, University of Swaziland, 1986), 84.

31. Quoted in Warwick, *Black People*, 106.

32. Crush, *Struggle*, 47. For opportunities created by the war for Africans elsewhere, see Nasson, "Moving Lord Kitchener," 25–51. For a discussion of the emaSwati's dissatisfaction with Boer administration see Simelane, "Swazi Resistance," 117–46.

33. Letter, Special Commissioner for Swaziland, Mbabane, to the Commissioner for Native Affairs, Johannesburg, 2 January 1903, SCS 612B/03, SNA, and a copy of a letter signed by Benjamin Nxumalo and Mavela Nkosi, to the Special Commissioner, 28 October 1902, J14/03, SNA. See also a letter from the Special Commissioner for Swaziland, Mbabane, to the Assistant Secretary, Swaziland Affairs, 3 March 1903, SCS 612B/03, SNA.

34. For more information on this see Statement by John A. Major, attached to a letter from J. A. Lawson, Captain, S. H., Komatiepoort, to Captain Gardyne, Adjt., S. H. Headquarter Office, Barberton, 11 March 1902. See also a letter from John A. Major, Lebombo, to A. C. Ross, British Consul Lourenco Marques, 2 April 1900; a reply letter from Y. R. Luke, Acting Vice Consul, British Consulate, Lourenco Marques, 15 April 1900; Mahleke Statement from Lebombo; Statement by Indabaningi; letter from John A. Major, East Lebombo, Portuguese Territory, to N.B.M. (British) Consul, Delagoa Bay, 5 May 1900; reply letter from J. R. Luke, Acting Vice Consul, British Consulate, Lourenco Marques, May 1900; Statement by Makalima; Magigenbanit Statement, and Ingagati's statement. All these are in J63/02, SNA.

35. Letter, Special Commissioner for Swaziland, Mbabane, to the Commissioner for Native Affairs, Johannesburg, 2 January 1903, SCS 612B/03, SNA and copy of letter signed by Benjamin Nxumalo and Mavela Nkosi, to the Special Commissioner, 28 October 1902, J14/03, SNA. See also a letter, Special Commissioner for Swaziland, Mbabane, to the Assistant Secretary, Swaziland Affairs, 3 March 1903, SCS 612B/03, SNA.

36. List of Swazi scouts included in a copy of a letter signed by Benjamin Nxumalo and Mavela Nkosi, to the Special Commmissioner, 28 October 1902, attached to Commissioner for Native Affairs' letter to Sir Thomas Cunningham, 14 January 1903, J14/03, SNA. For reference to Mavela as an influential chief, see copy of a letter from Thomas Cunningham, Staff Captain and late Intelligence Officer, Barberton District, to Sir Godfrey Lagden, Commissioner for Native Affairs, Johannesburg, 17 January 1903, J14/03, SNA. For Mavela's claim for raising and feeding the Swazi scouts at his own expense, see an extract from notes of message brought by a deputation sent by

the Swazi Queen Regent, to Enraght-Moony, attached to a letter from Enraght-Moony to the O. C., Intelligence Pretoria, 30 June 1902, J14/03, SNA.

37. Copy of a letter from Thomas Cunningham, Staff Captain, late Intelligence Officer, Barberton District, to Sir Godfrey Lagden, Commissioner for Native Affairs, 17 January 1903, J14/03, SNA. For Mavela's involvement with HM's forces, see a letter, Enraght-Moony, Special Commissioner for Swaziland, to the Commissioner for Native Affairs, Johannesburg, 2 January 1903, J14/03, SNA.

38. Extract from notes of message brought by a deputation sent by the Swazi Queen Regent, attached to a letter from Enraght-Moony, to the O. C., Intelligence Pretoria, 30 June 1902, J14/03, SNA. Emphasis added.

39. Letter, Special Commissioner for Swaziland, Mbabane, to the Commissioner for Native Affairs, Johannesburg, 2 January 1903, SCS 612B/03, SNA. See also a letter from Enraght-Moony, Special Commissioner for Swaziland, Mbabane, to the Commissioner for Native Affairs, Johannesburg, 2 January 1903, J14/03, SNA.

40. Letter, Special Commissioner for Swaziland, Mbabane, to the Commissioner for Native Affairs, Johannesburg, 2 January 1903, SCS 612B/03, SNA, and a letter, Special Commissioner for Swaziland, to the Assistant Secretary, Swaziland Affairs, 3 March 1903, SCS 612B/03, SNA. For the British troops' taking of livestock from Mavela's village, see the letter from Enraght-Moony to the O. C., Intelligence Pretoria, 30 June 1902, J14/03, SNA.

41. Letter, Special Commissioner for Swaziland, Mbabane, to the Commissioner for Native Affairs, Johannesburg, 2 January 1903, SCS 612B/03, and the letter from Special Commissioner for Swaziland to the Assistant Secretary, Swaziland Affairs, 3 March 1903, SCS 612B/03, SNA, respectively. Emphasis added.

42. Copy of a letter from Thomas Cunningham, Staff Captain, and late Intelligence Officer, Barberton District, to Sir Godfrey Lagden, Commissioner for Native Affairs, Johannesburg, 17 January 1903, J14/03, SNA. Emphasis added.

43. Letter, Staff Captain, for DAQMG, Intelligence Pretoria, to the Special Commissioner for Swaziland, Mbabane, 3 April 1903, J14/03, SNA. See also letter, B. H. Warner, for Special Commissioner for Swaziland, Mbabane, to DAQMG, Intelligence Pretoria, 15 April 1903, J14/03, SNA.

44. Copy of a letter from Thomas Cunningham, Staff Captain, and late Intelligence Officer, Barberton District, to Sir Godfrey Lagden, Commissioner for Native Affairs, Johannesburg, 17 January 1903, J14/03, SNA.

45. Ibid.

46. Letter, Special Commissioner for Swaziland, to the Assistant Secretary, Swaziland Affairs, 3 March 1903, SCS 612B/03, SNA.

47. Copy of a letter, Benjamin Nxumalo and Mavela Nkosi, to the Special Commissioner, 28 October 1902, attached to a letter, Commissioner for Native Affairs, to Sir Thomas Cunningham, 14 January 1903, J14/03, SNA.

48. Copy of a letter, Thomas Cunningham to Sir Godfrey Lagden, 17 January 1903, J14/03, SNA.

49. Copy of Minutes from A. P. Maritz, Magistrate, Ingwavuma District, to the CM and CC Eshowe, 14 July 1902, J197/02; Copy of Minutes from C. R. Saunders, CM and CC Eshowe, to the Secretary for Native Affairs, 2 August 1902, J197/02;

F. R. Moor, Secretary for Native Affairs, Pietermaritzburg, Natal, to the Commissioner for Native Affairs, Johannesburg, 6 August 1902, J197/02; and S. O. Samuelson, Under Secretary for Native Affairs, Pietermaritzburg, Natal, to the Commissioner for Native Affairs, Johannesburg, 9 December 1902, J197/02. For those who opposed a gift rifle, and instead suggested cattle, see Commissioner for Native Affairs, Johannesburg, to the Secretary for Native Affairs, Pietermaritzburg, Natal, 11 December 1902, J197/02; G. Y. Lagden, Commissioner for Native Affairs, Johannesburg, to the Secretary for Native Affairs, Pietermaritzburg, Natal, 14 August 1902, J197/02. The quotation is from Commissioner for Native Affairs, Johannesburg, to the Secretary for Native Affairs, Pietermaritzburg, Natal, 16 December 1902, J197/02, SNA.

50. Confidential letter, Sir Godfrey Y. Lagden, Special Commissioner for Native Affairs, Pretoria, to Sir Neville Lyttleton, GOC Transvaal, 30 June 1902, J58/02, SNA.

51. Confidential letter, Neville Lyttleton, Pretoria, to the Commissioner for Native Affairs, 2 July 1902, J58/02, SNA.

52. Copy of a letter from T. E. Stephenson, Major General, Commanding British Forces, Barberton District, to the Queen Regent, Swaziland, J180/03, SNA. For another view that orders from the military authorities resulted in the involvement of the emaSwati in the war, see letter from Enraght-Moony to the Acting Secretary, Swaziland Administration, 25 April 1904, J32/03, SNA.

53. Copy of a letter from J.D.P. French, Lt. General, Piet Retief, Transvaal, to Nabatibeni (Labotsibeni), Queen Regent of Swaziland, 21 February 1901, J180/03, SNA.

54. Copy of a note from Dudley Rideout, Cap. R. E. Intelligence Officer, 2nd Cavalry Brigade, Intombi, to Queen of the Swazi People, n.d., J180/03, SNA.

55. Sworn statement of Chief Thintintha Dlamini, who led the Swazi regiment that exterminated the Boers on Hlatikhulu Mountain in March 1901, before Bertram Nicholson, Sub-Commissioner for Natives, Hlatikhulu Division, Swaziland, 17 March 1903, J180/03, SNA.

56. Letter, R. Drake, Captain, Assistant Resident Magistrate, Piet Retief, to the Special Commissioner for Swaziland, Mbabane, 5 October 1903, SCS 2245/03, SNA. See also a copy of an affidavit by Macapikolo sworn before Thomas S. Dunn MB, Justice of the Peace, 30 September 1903, SCS 2245/03, SNA.

57. Sworn statement by Salomon Maritz, who fought for the Boer forces, before Bertram Nicholson, Sub-Commissioner, Hlatikhulu, Swaziland, 26 March 1904, J32/03, SNA. See also a sworn statement by Bulindhlela, Queen Regent Labotsibeni's royal messenger, who lived at the Zombodze Royal Palace, before Francis Enraght-Moony, Special Commissioner for Swaziland, 2 April 1904, J32/03, SNA.

58. Copy, confidential letter, F. Enraght-Moony, Special Commissioner for Swaziland, Mbabane, to the Assistant Secretary for Swaziland Affairs, 18 August 1903, J32/03, SNA.

59. Sworn statement by Thintintha Nkosi before Bertram Nicholson, Sub-Commissioner for Natives, Hlatikhulu Division, Swaziland, and witnessed by H. Raddon-Reed, 17 March 1903, J180/03, SNA.

60. Sworn statements by Sinyewana Nkosi, Thintintha Dlamini, and Mcaca Lukelo, respectively, before Bertram Nicholson, Sub-Commissioner for Natives, Hlatikhulu,

Swaziland, 2 March 1903, 17 March 1903, and 5 March 1903, J32/03, SNA. See also B. Nicholson to the Special Commissioner, Swaziland, 20 March 1903. The mere pressure of testifying before a British official might have contributed to different statistics in these eyewitness accounts.

61. See Warwick, *Black People,* 107; Matsebula, *History,* 176.

62. See letter, Enraght-Moony, Special Commissioner for Swaziland, to the Commissioner for Native Affairs, 28 March 1903, J32/03, SNA.

63. Sworn statement by Umzela before S. W. Jones (J.P.), 16 June 1903, Ermelo, J32/03, SNA. See also Sworn statement by Gentleman before S. W. Jones (J.P.), 2 June 1903, and Jack before S. W. Jones (J.P.), 15 June 1903, all at Ermelo, J32/03, SNA.

64. F. Enraght-Moony to the Commissioner for Native Affairs, 28 March 1903, J32/03, SNA. For Thintintha's going beyond Labotsibeni's orders, see Matsebula, *History,* 176. The circumstances pertaining to Thintintha's death are underresearched.

65. To label this battle a "massacre" is indicative of a Eurocentrism: see R. Wright, *Stolen Continents: The "New World" through Indian Eyes* (New York, 1992), x. This chapter, therefore, refers to the Hlatikhulu incident as a "battle," not a "massacre."

66. Confidential letter, F. Enraght-Moony to the Assistant Secretary for Swaziland Affairs, 18 August 1903, J32/03, SNA.

67. See for example letter from Leonard Bangley, Assistant Resident Magistrate, Bethal, to the Resident Magistrate, Standerton, 24 January 1903, J32/03; D. Honey, Assistant Secretary for Swaziland Affairs, to the Special Commissioner for Swaziland, 27 January 1903, J32/03; F. Enraght-Moony to the Commissioner for Native Affairs, 28 March 1903, J32/03; Confidential letter from F. Enraght-Moony to the Assistant Secretary for Swaziland Affairs, 18 August, 1903, J32/03; and J. P. Scallan to B. Nicholson, Sub-Commissioner, Swaziland, 18 February 1903, J32/03, SNA.

68. F. Enraght-Moony, Resident Magistrate for Swaziland, Mbabane, to the Secretary for Swaziland Affairs, Johannesburg, 26 January 1907, J8/1907, SNA.

69. Extract from a message delivered by Mr. Smuts in Swaziland to the Queen Regent and Council in May 1901, in G. Y. Lagden, Commissioner for Native Affairs, to the Special Commissioner for Swaziland, J10/03, SNA.

70. Ibid.

71. J. H. Lehmann, *The Model Major-General: A Biography of Field-Marshal Lord Wolseley* (Boston, 1964), 276.

72. Letter, G. Y. Lagden to Neville Lyttleton, 30 June 1902, J58/02, SNA.

73. Letter, Resident Magistrate for Swaziland, Mbabane, to the Secretary for Swaziland Affairs, Johannesburg, 15 June 1905, RMS 108/05, SNA.

74. See sworn statements by Mgwayiza Mtungwa, Nyunda Mtungwa, Somveli Mthembu, and Mgoduka Mthembu, before Bertram Nicholson, Sub-Commissioner for Natives, Hlatikhulu, Swaziland, 27 January 1903, and a covering letter for these sworn statements from B. Nicholson to the Special Commissioner for Swaziland, 28 January 1903, SCS 641B/02, SNA. See also a letter from Jones, Resident Magistrate, Piet Retief, to B. Nicholson, Sub-Commissioner for Native Affairs, Hlatikhulu, 29 December 1902, SCS 641B/02, SNA.

75. Memorandum on "Native Compensation Claims," J153/03, SNA.

76. A Minute with reference to Claims of Natives for Compensation for War

losses, from Col. French for President Central Claims Board, Pretoria, to Sir Godfrey Lagden, Special Commissioner for Native Affairs, 28 September 1902, J159/02, SNA.

77. Sir Godfrey Lagden's minute on "Compensation Claims," Johannesburg, 12 December 1902; and D. Honey to the Secretary for Native Affairs, 12 December 1902, J159/02, SNA.

78. Memorandum on "Native Compensation Claims," J153/03, SNA.

79. Letter from Hubert B. Cawood, attorney, notary public, and conveyancer, Ladysmith, Natal, to Captain T. S. Fox Strangways, A.P.M. Ladysmith Sub-District, Ladysmith, 29 May 1901, J153/03, SNA.

80. For a reference to stock taken by Boers from Africans, see Circular no. 1754/02, from W. Windham, Secretary for Native Affairs, Johannesburg, to the Native Commissioner District, 25 September 1902, J144/02, SNA.

81. Circular no. 1516/02, signed for Secretary for Native Affairs, Johannesburg, to the Native Commissioner District, 11 September 1902, J144/02, SNA.

82. H. Tennant, Secretary to the Law Department, Attorney General's Office, Pretoria, to the Secretary to the Native Affairs Department, Johannesburg, 20 August 1903, J180/03, SNA. See also a copy of a letter from Fred J. Smuts, Nooitgedacht, Ermelo District, to the Lieutenant Governor, Pretoria, 6 July 1903, J32/03, SNA. Smuts was one of the Boers who lost their stock to the emaSwati subsequent to the Hlatikhulu battle.

83. Copy of a confidential letter, Sir Godfrey Y. Lagden, Commissioner for Native Affairs, to Sir Neville Lyttleton, GOC Transvaal, 30 June 1902, J58/02, SNA; and a letter from Resident Magistrate for Swaziland, Mbabane, to the Secretary for Swaziland Affairs, Johannesburg, 15 June 1905, RMS 108/05, SNA.

84. Copy of a letter, G. Y. Lagden, Commissioner for Native Affairs, Johannesburg, to the Special Commissioner for Swaziland, 13 February 1903, J180/03, SNA.

85. H. Tennant, Secretary to the Law Department, Attorney General's Office, Pretoria, to the Secretary for Swaziland Affairs, Johannesburg, 3 September 1903, J180/03, SNA.

CHAPTER 8

British Nursing and the South African War

SHULA MARKS

IT IS A WIDELY ACKNOWLEDGED fact that during the South African War vastly more men, women, and children died of disease than of enemy fire. This is true even if one excludes the massive loss of life in the concentration camps and restricts one's gaze to the death toll on the British side: of the 22,000 deaths, two-thirds were from largely preventable disease. Nevertheless, until recently the medical history of the war has attracted comparatively little attention.[1] Even more scanty has been the attention paid to the history of nursing in the war;[2] two of the most comprehensive histories of British nursing—Robert Dingwall, Anne-Marie Rafferty, and Charles Webster's *Introduction to the Social History of Nursing* and Brian Abel Smith's *History of the Nursing Profession*—barely mention it.[3] Yet this was the first war in which large numbers of female nurses were employed and actually nursed in the field hospitals close to the battle front, and the deficiencies revealed in South Africa led directly to the transformation of British military nursing services evident in World War I. As Anne Summers concludes: "the post-Crimean reforms produced a tiny, marginal female nursing service. Those inaugurated in 1902 represented a major and irreversible public shift on the employment of female nurses in wartime."[4]

Thus, while the Crimean War and the colonial wars that followed it were obviously crucial in transforming the relationship between war and society, the acceptance of women as nurses at the front in the First World War owed more to the experience of the South African War than to any previous military encounter. The shortcomings of the hospital services and especially of nursing during the war led directly to the formation of Queen Alexandra's Imperial Military Nursing Service, a separate Army Nursing Department with an independent nursing board, in 1902. Sidney Browne, who had worked as Superintendent Sister of the base hospitals at Wynberg and Rondebosch

before being posted to Springfontein during the war, was appointed its first
Matron-in-Chief.[5] The redoubtable Mrs. Ethel Bedford Fenwick, suffragette,
vigorous campaigner for nurses' registration, and editor of *The Nursing
Record and Hospital World*,[6] who was to play a major role in attacking the
unorganized state of nursing during World War I, also led the outcry against
these same inadequacies in 1899–1902.[7]

If the South African War played a major role in gaining acceptance for
British nurses in battle and at the battle front, the war experience was also
important to the history of the profession elsewhere. Jan Bassett maintains,
for example, that in Australia, "The South African War was to become a
turning point, not only in the lives of the fifty or sixty Australian nurses
who served in South Africa, and in the development of Australian civilian
nursing, but also because it initiated the founding of Australian military
nursing."[8] This is true too in South Africa, where the repercussions of the
war for nursing, as in other spheres, were profound. The immediate postwar
years saw a considerable expansion in the number of British nurses in key
positions in South Africa, many of whom had served with the Army Nursing Service. It is at least arguable that the authoritarian character of much
twentieth-century nursing in South Africa and the intensifying demand
for the segregation of nursing practice arose from this influx of British military nurses. At the same time, the suspicion, if not downright hostility, with
which many English-speaking nurses were regarded by Afrikaner nationalists in the subsequent decades may also have resulted in part from wartime
experiences in the concentration camps.[9]

Finally, at a time when women's responses to imperialism are beginning
to attract increasing scholarly attention, the response of British nurses, and
especially of the British Nurses' Association, to the South African War also
provides a fascinating window not only on the ambiguities intrinsic to
military nursing anywhere and at any time, but also on the gendered and
fractured nature of late nineteenth-century imperialism.[10]

The South African War and the Nursing Profession

For all the celebration of Florence Nightingale's achievements at Scutari
during the Crimean War, at the outbreak of the South African War the role
of women in military nursing was still remarkably limited. It is not often
realized how few women actually served as nurses at Scutari and how limited their role was. And although Britain was engaged in a series of colonial
conflicts in the years after the Crimean War, these did not lead to any great
demand for the extension of women's participation in military nursing. On

the contrary, to expose British women to capture by a "savage" foe and the supposed attendant sexual dangers was clearly unthinkable to both the imperial military authorities and the nursing establishment: there were only two nurses, for example, from the Netley military training hospital in the war in the Anglo-Egyptian Sudan in 1898, and they were stationed hundreds of miles away from the front, at the base hospital in Cairo. As a contemporary journalist recorded, the army felt it was "too horrible to contemplate any of these Sisters, these Englishwomen, falling into the hands of an unscrupulous race like the Dervishes."[11]

Thus on the eve of the South African War there were still only seventy or eighty "intelligent and hardy" female nurses in the Army Nursing Service (ANS) at Netley.[12] An overall review of the armed forces in the mid-1890s had led, it is true, to renewed pressure for a reformed and expanded military nursing service. Nevertheless, despite the advocacy of a handful of military doctors and the British Nurses' Association, relatively little was done apart from the eventual launch by the War Office of the Army Nursing Reserve Service in March 1897. This was placed under the direction of Princess Christian, then President of the Royal British Nurses' Association, who had done much to encourage its formation over the previous three years.[13]

At the end of 1898 there were still only some one hundred women in the Reserve, accepted on conditions very similar to those applied to the Army Nursing Service.[14] To be considered for either the Service or the Reserve, an applicant had to be between twenty-five and thirty years of age and to have had at least three years' training in a general hospital; above all, however, the applicant had to "come of a family of 'respectability' and 'good standing' and show herself to be possessed of the 'tact, temper and ability' necessary for nursing."[15] What the member of Parliament, journalist, and nursing campaigner William Burdett-Coutts coyly referred to as "The Old Law, or what may be politely termed the sentimental difficulty—'philandering'" could only be avoided by the good character and conduct of carefully chosen nurses "accompanied by a good matron."[16] By the end of the century, the rules may have been slightly more relaxed, and "ladies" were "by no means ubiquitous in the service"; nevertheless, promotion still depended very largely on class.[17] In the army, as in the male wards of a general hospital, respectability and discipline were of the essence if all breath of scandal was to be avoided in a profession anxious to distance itself from the former public association of nurses with licentiousness and liquor.

The role of the Army nurses was also still remarkably circumscribed: both in the military hospitals in Britain during peacetime and in the base hospitals during war their main task was to train male orderlies, for female nurses did not go near the zone of battle; nor did they treat venereal disease—a major scourge in every army. According to Dr. Francis Fremantle, a civilian doctor who worked at the Wynberg Hospital in Cape Town for some months at the beginning of the South African War and who keenly advocated the use of women nurses even in field hospitals, the role of the Nursing Sisters was "not precisely defined"; they were "more like superintendents of nursing comparable to that of Night Sisters at a London hospital" than hands-on practitioners.[18]

When the war against the South African Republic broke out, the War Office was still steeped in an older and, as it proved, extremely inefficient system of nursing. As Fremantle, who soon found himself in hot water—or as he put it, "Stellenbosched" (i.e., moved sideways)—for raising the issue, stated in an article in the *Guy's Hospital Gazette* in January 1900:

> The whole system of female nursing in the Army is that it appears to have been clumsily grafted on to the old system of nursing by orderlies, purely in deference to public opinion and Miss Florence Nightingale. The graft has never taken root. The Nursing-sisters, as they are called, have no fixed position in the service. The orderlies often refuse to recognize their authority.[19]

Nor was this surprising, given the opposition within the Royal Army Medical Corps (RAMC) to the employment of female nurses, in what many of them regarded as a male domain to be manfully maintained.[20] When Sir Alfred Downing Fripp of Guy's Hospital, London, proposed taking a large contingent of nurses to South Africa to staff the largely upper-class rural voluntary hospital sent out by the Imperial Yeomanry, he was "solemnly" warned by someone on the headquarters staff of the Director General of the RAMC that his plan to use female nurses was going to be "a complete wreck":

> His last piece of advice to me was: "You are making an awful mistake about these nurses: they will all be tripping over each other's skirts; there will be nothing for them to do. Take my advice and lose them."[21]

Initially the lack of nurses was not seen as a major issue, except by the many women who wished to join the troops being sent to South Africa. Nursing the wounded was not believed to be particularly demanding, and the RAMC, with its 3,800 medical orderlies and some 1,000 reservists, was convinced it was well prepared for all eventualities. One of the few to think otherwise was Sir Walter Foster, a lifelong physician who, as secretary to the

Local Government Board, had had the main responsibility for dealing with the last cholera epidemic in the United Kingdom. At the end of October 1899, he wrote to the War Office, predicting the loss of life from outbreaks of "fever and other maladies more or less preventable by careful sanitary work." However, his suggestions that sanitary and medical experts be sent out and a small sanitary commission created, and the offer of his own services, were curtly rejected. According to the supremely confident medical authorities in the War Office, the RAMC already had the requisite knowledge of sanitary matters and needed no special assistance.[22]

Nevertheless, as early as the end of 1899, complaints began to seep into the British press about the shortage of nurses both at the front and in the base hospitals. In December 1899, for example, Fremantle was concerned that the influx of patients to the base hospitals at Wynberg after the battles of Belmont, Graspan, and Modder River revealed extensive insufficiencies in the nursing arrangements. His remarks, published in the *Guy's Hospital Gazette,* were rapidly disseminated in the general press.[23] These deficiencies were all the more deplorable because, as he said, there was no reason for the shortage, "since there are a thousand civilian nurses in England and the Cape willing and thirsting for the work."[24]

It was, in addition, a matter of some bitterness among South African nurses that initially, while nurses from Australia, New Zealand, Canada, and even the United States were able to join their British counterparts in South Africa, qualified nurses in the Cape Colony were not at that stage recruited by the army. Not only were South African nurses allegedly already suffering hardship because their wealthy white private patients had fled South Africa at the outbreak of war; they were all the more aggrieved as the Cape Colony was the only state in the world that registered trained nurses and thus had some uniformity of training and professional control.[25] Their complaints were supported by Bedford Fenwick, never loath to propagandize on behalf of nurses' registration, but also—to be fair—an internationalist in nursing matters and a champion of colonial nurses. Their exclusion was additionally unjust, South African correspondents of the *Nursing Record* indignantly pointed out, for local nurses had greater knowledge of local diseases and the "hardships of a rough and ready life on the veldt, and are accustomed to the eccentricities of a colonial commissariat"; moreover, the colonial nurse was "used to colonial ways" and had "colonial sympathies." Above all, one letter writer concluded,

> She is familiar with climatic peculiarities ... and with an intimate knowledge of the Kaffir and his ways, she can deal with the vagaries of the "black

and yellow boys" who constitute the domestic staffs of South African hospitals.... it would almost seem that the home authorities are labouring
under some misgiving as to whether or not the trained nurses of South
Africa may not be some sort of black women.[26]

Both the coded (but blatant) racism and the implied superiority of colonial
knowledge in dealing with the indigenous population characterized nursing
discourse in both Britain and South Africa at the time.

The furor over the nonemployment of South African nurses was not
abated by the intervention in this debate of the special correspondent of
the *British Medical Journal,* a local doctor, who justified the ban by arguing
that, in general, women submitted "far less kindly to discipline than men,
and the Colonial nurses ... have in most cases never been under even the
same discipline as that to which the British Sisters have to submit." It was,
he asserted, "a matter of common repute ... that, to put the case mildly, only
too many of the nurses from the Golden City are not so staid as the requirements of military discipline demand."[27] This released a flood of indignant
responses, although by April 1900 the issue had resolved itself because, as
Stone points out, the demand for nurses and, perhaps more importantly,
orderlies with any kind of training exceeded the supply and the War Office
was forced to recruit qualified (and, indeed, unqualified) nurses and orderlies wherever they could be found.[28]

Thus, whereas in the first months of the South African War some fifty
nurses and three thousand orderlies were thought to suffice for the needs of
the army, after "Black Week" and with the outbreak of the virulent typhoid
epidemic, this number was rapidly seen as inadequate. The public outcry
that accompanied the publication of a sustained critique of the RAMC's
medical and nursing services by the civilian doctors and nurses who went
to work in South Africa, and by Burdett-Coutts's less than temperate letters
in *The Times* on hospital conditions, forced the establishment of a Royal
Commission on the Care and Treatment of the Sick and Wounded in the
South Africa Campaign while the war was still at its height, and the RAMC
was forced to respond by sending out more doctors, nurses, and orderlies.[29]
By mid-April 1900, there were more than 500 nurses employed in South
Africa; by July 1900, there were 900 nurses, 7,000 orderlies, and about 1,000
medical officers to serve 224,000 men.[30]

According to the *Illustrated London News Record of the Transvaal War,*
their response showed that "the feminine half" had responded to the challenge of the war better than their male counterparts.[31] The newspaper exaggerated, although there were always far more women ready to volunteer as

nurses than were actually selected. According to the War Office, by mid-1900 about two thousand applications had been received from women seeking employment as nurses, but no record had been kept of those who offered their services free. The enthusiasm of the nurses who strove to be sent to South Africa can only be described as remarkable. In some hospitals all the nurses were reported to be anxious to join the war effort. Nevertheless, this has to be put into perspective. Some 450,000 men fought on the imperial side during the war, while even compared to the number of orderlies and civilian doctors, the number of nurses who served in the South African War remained small: by the end of the conflict, some 12,500 men had worked as orderlies and 15,000 doctors had been employed in South Africa.[32] The doctors, nurses, and orderlies were mostly from Britain, but there was also a sprinkling of volunteer doctors and nurses from Australia, Canada, and New Zealand, and a large contingent of Indian orderlies and stretcher bearers drawn both from the subcontinent and from the local Indian community. The latter were organized by M. K. Gandhi, anxious at that time to display his loyalty to the imperial cause, although the motives of the Indian volunteers may well have been both rather more mixed and more material.[33]

Gendered Victorian Assumptions about Nursing

Central to the argument of those who advocated the employment of more nurses in South Africa were profoundly gendered Victorian assumptions about the superiority of women over men as nurses. Week after week, the *Nursing Record* drummed out the message that a major (if not *the* major reason) for the high death rates in the South African hospitals and the unnecessary suffering of "Tommy Atkins" was the incompetence of male orderlies—who by definition were incapable of rendering the compassion and care proffered by women. Not only were the orderlies untrained; for the most part they were also not "the right class of man."[34] Callous and lacking in regard for their patients' welfare, they were also drunk, dishonest, and dissolute.

It was not only the nurses who dwelt on the limitations of the male orderlies. Answering those who argued that soldiers preferred being nursed by men, Burdett-Coutts observed tartly,

> Any man who has been seriously ill knows the difference between a rough-hewn orderly with horny hands and creaking boots, smelling of tobacco and other things, moving about his bed, tending him with a man's touch, and the real ministering angel, the female nurse. It is not the poor orderly's fault, he does his best; but he is built that way.[35]

Less partisan, perhaps, was Sir William Ogston, the surgeon at the Lord
Methuen's First Divisional Field Hospital at Modder River, who believed that

> The men who volunteer to enlist in the RAMC do so under the imagina-
> tion that their functions will be to take part in battles, carry wounded
> under fire, and so forth, and when they have to do dangerous and repul-
> sive duties in pest houses, [they] become for the most part disillusioned
> and inefficient. The quiet heroism required for the latter work is beyond
> most men.[36]

Unlike many of the more ardent advocates of female nursing, Dr. Fremantle
thought that the orderlies were "of a very high order, being drawn from a
somewhat more educated class than the ordinary soldier."[37] Nevertheless, he
also believed that, "owing to the natural chivalry of the common soldier and
the natural conscientiousness of a woman, the work would be far better
done and the discipline far better maintained than at present" if female
nurses were employed.[38]

The orderlies had little opportunity of answering back, although there
was a handful of medical men, members of the St. John's Ambulance
Brigade, and even army nurses, who pointed out that they were in fact the
backbone of the nursing service, both on the battlefield and in the hospitals.
W. S. Inder, of the St. John's Ambulance, for example, who worked at the
Wynberg Hospital and observed the orderlies at work for several months,
believed that the RAMC orderlies did "all in their power, tending the sick
and dying with the sympathy and tenderness of women."[39] As an orderly
himself he could perhaps be expected to say this. Yet his views were confirmed by a number of others, including some of the nurses who gave evidence before the Royal Commission in 1901. Nursing Sister Holmes was not
alone in praising their experienced care: "I have found them splendid fellows
and very hard workers," she declared.[40]

Nurse E. C. Laurence, of the Royal Red Cross, noted perceptively that
the inefficiency of the orderlies may in part have resulted from the overly demanding and bossy attitude of the female nurses. "Our sisters," she remarked,

> are working awfully well, but some of them don't get on well with the
> orderlies—a great mistake: they don't seem able to hide the fact that they
> think the orderlies very useless and incapable, and consequently the order-
> lies don't do their best in working with them; it is a great pity as the men
> are quite willing and anxious to learn, and are very patient in having to do
> many jobs that must be very trying to them.[41]

This places an interesting gloss on Sister Henrietta's criticism that the orderlies seemed to resent the nurses' energy and remarked of one that she was "as bad as a blooming Colonel," while another was said to be "a little beast for work."[42]

As Stone suggests, however, the claims that merely because the orderly was a male and therefore an inferior nurse seem to have been based purely on gender stereotypes.[43] Entangled with this were the claims made for female nurses on the grounds of class. "The orderlies failed ... in comparison with the nurses in gentleness to the patient and sympathy," argued the British Surgeon General, Dr. J. Jameson, before the Royal Commission. "Naturally a person in a superior social position must be a superior person."[44] Nor, given the army's casual attitude to prevention, was there much evidence that the rates of disease would have been reduced substantially had female nurses been employed instead of male orderlies, although good nursing could sometimes be the difference between life and death to an individual patient.

In many ways, then, whether men or women made up the bulk of the attendants was somewhat irrelevant. The basic problem was not one of gender but of training.[45] The army was loath to train male nurses "to meet even a modest emergency," and there was no civilian training for male nurses. Nursing orderlies in the RAMC at the beginning of the South African War generally had three or four months' training in "a wide range of topics," but only about a quarter of the orderlies were so trained. As the medical crisis worsened and the army was forced to draft anyone it could get into service, thousands of novices descended on the hospitals whose training, Stone remarks, "was perfunctory to say the least." This inevitably increased the workload of experienced staff and "the overall medical care provided during the war suffered in consequence."[46]

At the same time, the relationship between the nurses and the orderlies was in Stone's words "anomalous." While she superintended the ward and the orderly was supposed to obey her orders, the nurse lacked the final authority to enforce her commands and had to operate through the wardmaster, "himself an orderly who had risen through the ranks." Given the gender and class differences between the nurses and the orderlies, it is hardly surprising that on occasion the relationship was fraught.[47]

The Rush of Imperial Women to the War Front

Whatever the relationship between female nurses and male orderlies, there was certainly no great bond of "sisterhood" between the nurses and the many unqualified women who made their way to South Africa to participate in the war. That so many of those finding their way to South Africa were "society ladies" who "posed" as nurses drove Bedford Fenwick and the correspondents to her *Nursing Record* to a fury. Nor were they alone. So great was the flood of women that it became quite a scandal in both Britain and South Africa, and in April 1900, Queen Victoria herself was moved to raise the matter with Chamberlain and to "strongly disapprove" of "the hysterical spirit which seems to have influenced some of them to go where they are not wanted." In response, Chamberlain suggested to Milner that he issue a suitable notice "calling attention to the inconvenience of this unusual number of ladies visiting [the] seat of war."[48] In a personal letter to his longtime correspondent and confidante, Bertha Synge, Milner wrote in more unrestrained vein of the "frivollings of fashionable females," "their mutual jealousies, feuds, back-bitings and the total unsuitableness of a sort of quasi–Monte Carlo ... background to that grim tragedy going on in the Northern Veld."[49]

For the professional nurses, however, the issue was not simply the cavortings of the "scores of rich and idle women who went out to 'see some fun,' and who have not been at all squeamish in the selection of their amusements." Far more crucial were their claims to care for the sick and wounded, their appropriation of the nursing uniforms, and their undermining of the hard-won and still fragile professional respect and social respectability achieved by nurses over the previous half century. Within a week of the outbreak of the war, the *Nursing Record* cited reports that "ladies of title and distinction" were making their way to the Transvaal, offering their services and even going so far as to "take lessons in nursing." "The motive that inspires these ladies," it severely reminded its readers,

> is, no doubt excellent, but what our soldiers need and are entitled to, when sick and wounded, is skilled and efficient nursing—not amateur philanthropy, however well meaning. "Ladies of title and distinction," in common with those of more ordinary clay can only become efficient nurses by prolonged application and hard work. Sentimentalism and amateur assistance are out of place among the stern horrors of war.[50]

Averring to the antics of the likes of the Lady Jessica Sykes and her daughter—who were eventually expelled from South Africa—Bedford Fenwick remarked with heavy sarcasm:

> After the experience they have gained in nursing sick officers in South Africa, no doubt society dames will be prepared to "take a turn" in the

understaffed Workhouse Wards in the parishes in which they reside at home. We can assure them there are thousands of poor suffering old people and helpless children in the Unions of this England of ours, whose ailments are quite as heartrending as those of handsome young men at the front. Did we hear a sniff?

As news filtered back of society ladies flaunting their "chiffon and glitters" in Cape Town, and donning nurses' uniforms, the reaction became more and more hostile to "This class of woman—idle, vicious, parasitical ... our greatest enemy at home; in the tragic atmosphere of war she is an abomination; whilst pandering to the vanity and lusts of men for a *quid pro quo* she poisons the well-springs of his innermost nature" and as a result has made him contemptuous of women and their political aspirations.[51]

The involvement of the aristocracy and upper-class women in selecting nurses for service in South Africa, without calling on the expertise of serving matrons, and their role in decision-making in the Army Nursing Reserve and Central Red Cross Committee, also roused the indignation of professional nurses such as Bedford Fenwick.[52] Accusations of jobbery and favoritism in the selection of nurses for the front were rife; such preferential treatment allegedly led to the choice of candidates with neither the training nor the character necessary for military nursing.[53]

There was some irony in these confrontations: after all, in the mid-nineteenth century, it was the drunken working-class Sairy Gamp who had to be driven from the ranks of the profession while the columns of the *Nursing Record* carried constant and fulsome praise of aristocratic patronage of the nursing cause. Bedford Fenwick, who was always elegantly dressed and had a penchant for "priceless ... Chinese and English porcelain, mahogany furniture and miniature animals,"[54] "well understood the fine art of reducing British opposition to a minimum by persuading royalty to her cause."[55] As mentioned above, Princess Christian was enlisted as patron of the Royal British Nursing Association—although Florence Nightingale, who opposed the association's pursuit of state registration, did remark, "they are trying to make a Nurses' Republic with a Princess at its head."[56] Nevertheless, when it came to wartime nursing the pretensions of the "society ladies" had to be resisted.

Bedford Fenwick was equally censorious of young nurses who treated their South African assignment as a great and exciting adventure. She was appalled at the news that a number of nurses who had been chosen for service in South Africa had been seen in Harrod's "very busy buying evening gowns and shoes to take to the front!" where they were clearly intent on having "a real good time." Nursing, she admonished, was a serious vocation.[57]

Middle-Class Feminism, Nation, and Respectability

However much the virtues of women were applauded, in the nineteenth century middle-class feminists were as concerned with respectability as were their politically more conservative sisters. As George Mosse has remarked, nationalism—and, one might add, imperialism—fashioned new female symbols of the nation, which "embodied both respectability and the collective sense of national purpose." It

> used the example of the chaste and modest woman to demonstrate its own virtuous aims. In the process, it fortified bourgeois ideals of respectability that penetrated all classes of society during the nineteenth century. [Yet] ... If woman was idealized she was also firmly put into her place. Those who did not live up to the ideal were perceived as a menace to society and the nation, threatening the established order they were intended to uphold.[58]

Although Mosse is more concerned here with such female symbols of the nation as Germania, Britannia, and Marianne, Florence Nightingale and the new "lady nurse" were equally appropriated as female symbols of the nineteenth century, at least in the Anglophone world. To this female symbol of the respectable, "modern," bourgeois nation, upper-class "frivolity" was almost as threatening as working-class debauchery; a menace to the nation in peacetime, they were doubly so in war.

Nor were these concerns limited to the British middle class. Alice Bron, a well-connected Belgian social democrat and philanthropist who went to nurse in South Africa with a Dutch-Belgian Red Cross ambulance, soon found her modernizing feminist and bourgeois sensibilities outraged both by the Boer soldiers—whom she rapidly came to regard as a bunch of "ignorant and rapacious peasants"—and by their "semi-educated" sisters.[59] In Pretoria after the British occupation, she found Afrikaner "nurses" who were nothing but "damsels who love flirtations and adventure and have never cared for anything except their own toilettes." Out for a good time, they gallivanted with the British officers and "were a sight to behold" with "their high heels ... their hair rolled up in a bunch," or "frizzed and curled like so many French poodles, and laced with such appalling tightness that one wondered how they managed to breathe."[60]

Camp followers were not unique to the South African War, nor, clearly, were they confined to the imperial army. It is, however, more difficult to determine how extensive the problem was; at least in the Afrikaner case, it is unlikely that it went beyond a small handful of women in the capital. Despite the scandal caused by their presence, it is unlikely that many society women were involved.[61] By the late nineteenth century, travel by single women to the Cape Colony (and indeed to the other "margins of empire") in search of adventure had become almost commonplace,[62] and it was widely regarded as a congenial and healthy destination for British emigrants. The well-known "surplus women" problem in Britain may thus have disposed a handful of the more optimistic to make their way across the seas in the hope of finding a husband among the large number of single men now stationed in South Africa. Nevertheless, however attractive Cape Town and the Mount Nelson Hotel (where many of the society "ladies" disported themselves) might be in the summer months, there could not have been more than a dozen "society ladies" able simply to pull up stakes and move to Cape Town in the first six months of the war. Most of those who found their way to South Africa were probably the wives of servicemen, anxious to be near the action; and many of them rendered a variety of sensible and useful services to the wounded and sick soldiers. Despite the caveats in the *Nursing Record,* which did try to discriminate between the useful and the useless volunteers, these capable women tended to be lumped together with the highly publicized society drones who were scandalizing Queen Victoria and colonial society.

The reasons for the salience of "society ladies" would appear to lie elsewhere. Not only did the newly established popular press, with its eye on the respectable woman reader, make the activities of these "society ladies" far more visible than ever before;[63] late-nineteenth-century codes of respectability also undoubtedly made them all the more shocking a threat to order and discipline, drawing the attentions of men from their duty to empire even as they palliated the rigors of war. It is clear too that members of the RAMC found the presence of upper-class women on the wards insufferable, as the case of Mrs. Richard Chamberlain, who was barred from the Wynberg hospital for distributing oranges and other forbidden food to typhoid patients, demonstrates.[64] Whatever their number, the transgression of boundaries they represented is manifest and the passions aroused were commensurate with this.

Patriotism rather than Pacifism among Nursing Volunteers

The total number of women who made their way to South Africa—whether as part of the Army Nursing Service, the voluntary hospitals and ambulances, or on their own—may have been small, but it is nonetheless remarkable how enthusiastically women seem to have responded to the call of battle. "In this hospital all the more excitable nurses are suffering from war hysteria, and are bombarding the WO, the Reserve and Special Committees, to be sent out to nurse the soldiers, and many of the most unsuitable for this special work have been selected," complained one "Sister in a London Hospital" to the *Nursing Record.* "Surely something can be done to prevent this most undignified scramble to the front, before we are engaged in fighting united Europe."[65]

In part, of course, this had to do with the centrality of South African affairs to empire in the 1890s; in part it was because, unlike other countries in which Britain had fought since the Crimean War, South Africa was a "civilized country in which none can say the sanctity of womanhood is not recognized."[66] South Africa was a "white man's country" and the South African War a "white man's war," rhetorically if not in reality; as Anne Summers has noted, however "demonised" the Boers may have been, they were "Europeans" and therefore considered "safe" for "English women."[67]

That nurses were prepared to go out to South Africa is all the more surprising in view of the paltry pay they could expect for hazarding their lives in arduous and often dangerous work: clearly the War Office and Army Medical Department believed that patriotism should be its own reward for women, and many women shared their belief. As early as November 1900, the *Nursing Record and Hospital World* noted the huge discrepancies between the salaries of the "Big" Army Surgeons and the nurses who were sent on active service in South Africa.[68] While leading civilian surgeons, like Sir William McCormac, Sir William Treves, and Sir Makins, could expect salaries of £5,000 per annum—and huge popular adulation for their "noble self-sacrificing patriotism" and "their devotion to Queen and country"[69]—nurses were expected to serve for £40 a year—plus minimal allowances for board and lodging and clothing:

> To offer thoroughly trained nurses ... the astonishing sum of 2s 2d. a day! and to encourage the wicked and lavish luxury of expending £4 upon the adornment of her vile body *per annum,* not to mention those triennial garments, the winter and summer cloaks, calls for the instant passing of sumptuary laws whereby such wasting of the nation's substance may be curtailed![70]

Although the differentials between the pay of nurses and that of the average medical officer was by no means so vast, and by the end of the first year of the war nurses' salaries had increased considerably as the need to recruit more nurses became imperative, they remained low. Nevertheless, considerable numbers of women were prepared to volunteer for nursing service at the front. Some no doubt did so out of patriotic motives; the majority may have felt that, low as these wages were, they were better than anything they could expect to earn at home.

Thus, although a good deal of attention has been paid to the class basis of male support for the South African War, far less attention has focused on the class basis of the nursing volunteers for the War. Mitch Stone has suggested that while the rhetoric focused on the middle- and upper-class ladies with professional training, the majority of nurses were probably of working-class origin.[71] Some were undoubtedly so: in August 1901, Dr. Gregory wrote of a group of nurses employed in plague work in Port Elizabeth who wished to terminate their contracts and return to the United Kingdom, "With the nurses it is entirely a matter of £.s.d. They would be prepared to go home provided they were paid up to the end of their contract time and some of them would demand their board up to that time. This is the ruling spirit among them."[72]

In fact, however, given the numbers involved and the selection processes of the Army Nursing Services—which were for the most part in the hands of upper-class women and medical men who placed a premium on the family background of the nurses recruited—the majority were probably drawn from the aspirant lower middle class who formed the majority of trained nurses in Britain, and who came "from families with enough money to educate their daughters but not enough to support them all their lives should they never marry."[73] In this they resembled the many lower-middle-class men in the ranks, "desperately trying to maintain a middle-class appearance on a pitifully inadequate salary and even more desperately fighting to keep above the mass of the labouring population," and for whom "volunteering for war was a token and a proof of their commitment to the system."[74]

Young women were less likely to have been as deeply ideologically influenced by the "drill and discipline ... *esprit de corps,* and loyalty to the regiment" that formed part of male education and, we are told, imbued the men with a sense of nationalism and imperial destiny.[75] Nevertheless, it seems unreasonable to assume—as Bill Nasson has remarked more generally of working-class soldiers' decisions to enlist—"that some feelings of popular patriotism and militarism did not play a part" in the decision of women to offer their services to the war effort.[76] At the same time, the lure of adventure and the possibilities of escaping the constraints of late Victorian society should not be underestimated. However difficult and painful their experiences, for many of the women concerned, the war years remained the high point of their lives.[77]

It is undoubtedly also true, as Summers remarks, that the rush of women to join the war effort (whether in World War I or in 1899–1902) puts paid to any feminist notion that women automatically form "a natural constituency for pacifism," and indeed Helen Bradford's chapter in this volume on the role of Afrikaner women in the war forcefully makes the same point. Summers argues that this was as true of feminists before the First World War as it was of feminists in that war and that it arose from the desire of the majority of feminists (Emily Hobhouse is, of course, the notable exception) to be incorporated in the mainstream, however critical they may have been of male-dominated society. Ethel Bedford Fenwick, she maintains,

> however much she regretted the destruction of human life in other nations' wars ... uncritically supported the policy of her own government during the Anglo-Boer War. The majority of suffragettes gave unthinking endorsement to the existence of Empire: and this implied unquestioning assent to its maintenance by military means.[78]

As Summers has shown, Bedford Fenwick's attempt "to make her Association indispensable to the War Office" and the defense of the realm was part of a strategy to assert women's rights to citizenship and the franchise on an equal basis with men.[79] Bedford Fenwick was also convinced that if nurses were to gain professional recognition they had to show the usefulness of professional nursing to the state, and she used the South African War explicitly to advance the state registration of nurses. This meant that her support of imperialism could not be halfhearted and lent particular significance to the rhetoric around *Uitlanders'* rights. Thus, in 1896, the *Nursing Record* was quick to assert its sympathy with Jameson's "quixotic race for liberty" at the end of 1895, for

> it is only we British women—disfranchised and yet inexorably taxed—who can truly sympathise with the "White Kaffirs" in the Transvaal—men maddened by the boorish tyranny of an inferior race, who prefer death rather than a prolongation of a brute's life under the cutting lash of a degradation which the lack of self-respect inevitably entails.[80]

In the midst of the war, in June 1900, Bedford Fenwick returned to this theme: the government, having expended so much money on enfranchising the "British tax-payers in the Transvaal," she hoped, would now "turn its attention to removing from the women Uitlanders at home the indignity and degradation which they now suffer from disfranchisement."[81] To reinforce the point, she lauded the patriotism of the British nurse, ever ready to "follow the flag" and claim "her right ... to assist in the Empire-making which falls to the share of this country in the expansion of its borders, and in maintaining the rights of its subjects." "It is pleasant to think," she concluded, "that after all the slaughter of the past six months happier days are in store for the Transvaal, and that not the least of the benefits brought to it by British rule will be the health and healing which follow in the wake of the trained nurse."[82]

Yet there was a major ambiguity at the heart of the late nineteenth century demand that women be allowed to engage fully in military nursing: how to reconcile its professions to heal all regardless of race, color, or creed, and the ambitions of an imperialism that prided itself on its civilized standards, which included the marvels of modern medicine and nursing, with the realities of a war that vilified the enemy in order to justify the taking of life and the destruction of livelihood. These ambiguities run through the discourse of the journal of the British Nursing Association, Mrs. Bedford Fenwick's *Nursing Record,* and the memoirs and letters of the war written by the more thoughtful British nurses. They strike one as decidedly less jingoistic than the general literature of the period would lead one to expect.

Thus, in an editorial in the first month of the war, Ethel Bedford Fenwick was able to write:

> strongly as we disapprove of the settlement of national disputes by means of Maxim guns and cold steel ... yet there is one bright side to the overhanging cloud. The work of nurses, in caring for the sick and wounded, is one which must commend itself to all, whatever their politics ... and however strongly they may disapprove of the reasons which have led to the present crisis. The mission carried on under the shelter of the Red Cross flag is one which seeks, as far as possible, to alleviate the horrors of war, and knows no distinction of colour, creed, or nation, but strives only to render assistance wheresoever it may be needed.[83]

In the same issue, in the "Army Nursing Notes" that were a regular weekly feature of the *Nursing Record* throughout the war, she continued:

> There is now no longer any glory in warfare, when science and wealth combined must spell victory, irrespective of the rights of the case. Militarism, under these circumstances, develops tyranny, and the smaller nations of the earth barter their independence before its power, or die in resisting the force of gold.

But the duty of women is plain. They may disapprove of the policy which causes blood to be shed, but those who suffer are the innocent instruments of this policy, and their sacrifice rouses our deepest sympathies and desire to help them in their suffering. In this war we must no longer sit idle whilst those responsible for the care of our wounded soldiers fail through ignorance to provide the best for their recovery.[84]

As these quotations suggest, Bedford Fenwick's sympathies were not restricted to the British soldiers caught up in the conflict, and her jingoism was at least on occasion muted. On October 7, 1899, she demanded, "Have any English women offered their services to the Boers? Surely the Red Cross is an International Society—and it is bound to nurse the wounded irrespective of nationality."[85] News that the Central British Red Cross was proposing to form a committee of representatives of the English Red Cross Society, the St. John's Ambulance, and the Army Medical and Nurses if war were declared was greeted with dismay:

A question which seems to us to be of primary importance, and one demanding an explanation is, if the Red Cross becomes a subordinate department of the War Office, how is it to fulfil its duties as part of an international organization? ... will the War Office assist the Red Cross Society in organizing aid to the sick and wounded amongst the Boers, or will the society help only our own troops? The fundamental idea of the Red Cross is that its members shall render assistance to the sick and wounded wherever they are found, without distinction, and care for the enemy in exactly the same way as for the sick and wounded of its own nation. We hear of a hospital ship for the benefit of British soldiers; but so far, we hear of no organization for rendering aid to the wounded Boers. Yet the British Red Cross Society cannot be true to its foundation principles, unless it renders equal assistance to both sides. Whether it is prepared to do this, is the question which its supporters should ask.[86]

In the early months of the war, Bedford Fenwick was at pains to stress any evidence of fellow-feeling between British and Afrikaner combatants, to counter claims that the Boers had maltreated wounded prisoners or fired on personnel wearing the Red Cross,[87] and to praise the bravery of both sides:

In spite of the propaganda of international peace, during the past week, the world has witnessed man, "very much man," going out to kill and be killed as in primeval times. The British and Boer armies have come face to face in Natal, and have fought finely, with a desperate dash and courage worthy of admiration, with the net result of hundreds of deaths, ghastly wounds, miserable prisoners, and wailing women.[88]

Bedford Fenwick was also supportive of Emily Hobhouse's endeavors on behalf of the women and children in the concentration camps, hoping that the South African Women and Children's Distress Fund would help "soften" the bitterness caused by the war and alleviate suffering, although there is relatively little coverage in the *Nursing Record* of their plight.[89]

Internationalism, Compassion, and Racism

A rhetoric of internationalism and compassion toward the enemy was all very well from the distance of London. How widely Bedford Fenwick's views were shared by the women who went out to nurse in South Africa and how far British nurses were able to sustain these ideals in the field are far more difficult questions to answer. Manifestly it was far more difficult to maintain this balance on the battlefield or under siege. Sister Henrietta Stockdale, for example, widely regarded as the Florence Nightingale of South African nursing, was quite outspoken in her hatred of the "treacherous, implacable, cruel foe" who had surrounded Kimberley.[90] In her diary, written during the siege of Kimberley, she confided that the "Boers"

are not men, they are fiends—that is the way I love my enemy you see. People talk of their bravery. I can't see where it is. What is the bravery, of creeping up beside a hill and firing at cattle herds, firing again as soldiers come up, and running like rabbits into holes and behind stones. It has been a war of mere looting on one side and defence of property on the other as far as this part is concerned.[91]

And again, on December 3, the forty-ninth day of the siege,

what is all the war about if there is to be no better Government in the country. The Dutch have proved themselves utterly incapable of governing themselves or anybody else. To put such brutes into power again is only bring certain wretchedness on the country. I have seen cases enough in Hospital to make me ready to believe any tales of them. Things too sickening to speak of or write about.[92]

Eight months later, with the casual racism more usually associated with attitudes toward Africans than toward Afrikaners, she remarked of the nursing arrangements made for the Afrikaners wounded at Cronje's *laager:*

There was not one bedstead, only three mattresses, and an equal number of pillows ... but in both rooms there was a thoroughly good floor, and I don't think the men suffered, lying on it on folded blankets—of course, they couldn't undress, but that doesn't distress a Boer.[93]

Nevertheless, for the most part, Boer prisoners of war seem to have fared reasonably well at the hands of the British nurses, although Mary Kingsley's posting to nursing duties at Simonstown suggests there was no great enthusiasm among English-speaking nurses to undertake these duties. After an initial hiatus, English-speaking nurses were also found to work in the concentration camps, although as representatives of the aggressive imperial power they were rarely popular, if Emily Hobhouse is to be believed.[94] When in 1911 the King Edward VII Memorial Order of Nurses was launched to serve the rural areas, the nationalist-minded *Volkstem* was less than enthusiastic about the prospect of English nurses let loose in the South African countryside. As it sourly remarked:

If we correctly understand the scheme now submitted to the public, it will amount to this—the white nurse will continue to be imported "ready made" from overseas, and consequently there will be a continuance of the undesirable state of affairs which has prevailed in this part of the world for several years and against which there is a justly strong and growing dislike in Afrikander circles—Dutch as well as English.... So long as no energetic and sincere endeavor is made to train nurses of whom there is a great need from among South Africa's own young women, and as long as provision is not made in the scheme ... for the training of South African–born nurses, we do not believe that the establishment of the Order will be popular.[95]

Nor did the internationalism extend to South Africa's black population. Indeed, one of the more resounding silences at the heart of the war reminiscences by imperial doctors and nurses is the virtual absence of any mention of the "'black and yellow' boys who constitute the staff of South African hospitals,"[96] the Africans and Indians who served in the field hospitals and camps as cleaners, scrubbing the wards and latrines, or who were routinely employed as stretcher bearers and drivers. Yet, as we have seen, 1,000 Natal Indians volunteered as ambulance bearers, in which capacity, according to the *Illustrated London News*, "they were not surpassed even by the colonists of Natal."[97] Insofar as Africans were noticed by the nurses it was largely in their capacity—or, more frequently, lack of it—as servants.[98] For the most part, the black population remained invisible.

The postwar years saw an intensifying outcry by white policy makers and public against white women nursing black bodies. It is not clear whether the impetus for this came from those already practicing in South Africa as serious overcrowding in the profession after the war and postwar influx of nurses led to a fall in already low wages and fears of competition from black nurses,[99] from British nurses who were unaccustomed to nursing Africans, or from men who feared that the incoming British nurses, who were unaccustomed to colonial mores, would transgress racial boundaries. The calls to bar white women from nursing black patients were denounced in no uncertain terms by the *British Journal of Nursing,* ever anxious to proclaim the universalist nursing creed.[100] Yet, Bedford Fenwick's casual reference to "white Kaffirs" and overtly racist letters in the *Nursing Record* and *British Journal of Nursing* also provided a counterdiscourse to the more liberal attitudes espoused in the journal on the question of white nurses caring for black patients. "Are the flower of Britain's womanhood to emigrate to a new country to find themselves voteless ... classed with Kaffir criminals, the pauper and the insane of all nations?" nursing journals demanded indignantly and rhetorically on more than one occasion.[101] In a series of articles in 1905–6 that managed simultaneously to insult everyone from Australian nurses ("not so well-trained or so conscientious in their work as English nurses"), to the "Colonial character" ("with its happy-go-lucky carelessness, and its cheerful, grumbling acceptance of the second best in everything"), to the inhabitants of Durban (which "must have been a lovely place before there were houses and people"), the effortlessly offensive Henrietta Kenealy also warned English nurses about the hazards of nursing "natives." This, she asserted, was "a very real drawback to hospital life in South Africa":

> The Englishwoman at home can have no idea what it means to nurse Kafirs. She probably thinks the colour of the black man is only skin deep, and physiologically she is right. One should not wish to destroy amiable illusions, but after twelve hours, or at most a week, in a male native ward the English nurse abandons the English notion that the native is "a man and a brother." ... As a rule Kafir wards are put in charge of the colonial nurses, who understand and manage natives better than we have ever been able to do.[102]

While it would be manifestly wrong to generalize from this example and attribute the heightened racism of the postwar years solely to the new contingent of racially conscious British nurses, their presence does seem to have increased colonial (largely male) fears that racial boundaries would be more readily transgressed, and to have contributed greatly to the intensifying demand for segregated nursing services.[103]

Whatever the ambiguities of wartime service and the complexities within South Africa of its legacy, the lessons of the South African War for military nursing were inescapable, and the years following the war saw its total reform. Their experiences during the conflict finally persuaded the RAMC that the female nursing service had to be expanded and the training of orderlies properly organized—although no one could have foretold that the next war would see some 50,000 civilian nurses at the front. The ambiguous right of British women to participate in war was essentially won on the battlefields of South Africa.

Notes

1. Recent contributions have included E. Lee, *To the Bitter End: A Photographic History of the Boer War* (Harmondsworth, U.K., 1985), chap. 3, and M. Stone, "The Victorian Army: Health, Hospitals and Social Conditions as Encountered by British Troops during the South African War, 1899–1902" (Ph.D. thesis, University of London, 1993).

2. By far the most important are Anne Summers's outstanding *Angels and Citizens: British Women as Military Nurses, 1854–1914* (London and New York, 1988) and an excellent chapter in Stone, "Victorian Army," on which I draw heavily in what follows. These, with the chapters in Charlotte Searle's magisterial *History of the Development of Nursing Services in South Africa* (Epping, Cape Town, 1965), one paragraph on British nurses in the war in S. B. Spies, "Women and the War," in P. Warwick (ed.), *The South African War: The Anglo-Boer War, 1899–1902* (Harlow, 1980), and a scattering of short articles in the *South African Nursing Journal,* as well as in the British and Australian nursing journals, virtually exhaust the coverage in the secondary sources.

3. London, 1988 and London, 1960, respectively.

4. Summers, *Angels and Citizens,* 205–6.

5. S. McGann, *The Battle of the Nurses: A Study of Eight Women Who Influenced the Development of Professional Nursing* (London, 1992), 82–84.

6. Founded in 1888, *The Nursing Record* was "written by nurses for nurses" and supported the registration of nurses. At the end of 1893, when it was taken over by the Bedford Fenwicks, it was retitled *The Nursing Record and Hospital World.* Ethel Bedford Fenwick used her position as editor to advocate vigorously the state registration of nurses and to attack its opponents equally vehemently. In July 1902 she changed its name to the *British Journal of Nursing,* in order "to represent in its title its relation to Greater Britain ... and thus proclaim its relation to those nurses throughout the British Empire who, with ourselves are working for the consolidation and welfare of their profession" (see McGann, *Battle of the Nurses,* 38–39). Much of what follows draws on *The Nursing Record,* and for the sake of simplicity, I have referred to it as the *Nursing Record* until its last change of name.

7. For more on Bedford Fenwick see McGann, *Battle of the Nurses,* chap. 2, "Mrs Bedford Fenwick: A Restless Genius." Curiously she does not mention Bedford Fenwick's role as editor-agitator during the war.

8. J. Bassett, "Turning Point: Australian Nurses and the South African War," *Journal of the Australian War Memorial* 13 (October 1988): 3–8. I am grateful to Judith Bember for drawing this to my attention and to Liz Dimock for putting us in touch.

9. See S. Marks, *Divided Sisterhood: Race, Class and Gender in the South African Nursing Profession* (Basingstoke and Braamfontein, 1994), 66–68, 74–76, for some of these tensions.

10. See, for example, C. Midgley (ed.), *Gender and Imperialism* (Manchester, 1998).

11. "The Nurses of Her Majesty's 'Tommies.' What the Queen Saw at Netley," *Sketch,* 7 December 1898.

12. Summers, *Angels and Citizens,* 122 for the epithets.

13. Summers, *Angels and Citizens,* 190–92. The British Nurses' Association received its royal charter in 1893.

14. Summers, *Angels and Citizens,* 183–92.

15. "Nurses of Her Majesty's 'Tommies.'"

16. Letter by William Burdett-Coutts MP to *The Times,* cited in the *Nursing Record,* 21 July 1900, 56.

17. Summers, *Angels and Citizens,* 119; Stone, "Victorian Army," chap. 10.

18. F. E. Fremantle, *Impressions of a Doctor in Khaki* (London, 1901).

19. Ibid., 116.

20. British Parliamentary Papers (B.P.P.) 1901, vol. 29, Cd. 453, *Report of the Royal Commission to Consider and Report upon the Care and Treatment of the Sick and Wounded during the South African Campaign* (London, 1901), 7. See also Stone, "Victorian Army," 266–78.

21. Evidence of Sir A. Downing Fripp, C.B., C.V.O., M.S., M.B., F.R.C.S., to the *Royal Commission on the War in South Africa,* cited in *The British Journal of Nursing,* 2 January 1904, 10. The description of the hospital is from M. D. Blanch, "British Society and the War," in Warwick (ed.), *South African War,* 227.

22. This correspondence, dated 31 October and 9 November 1899, was republished in the *Nursing Record,* 28 July 1900, 75.

23. January 1900, cited in R. W. Marshall, "A Doctor at War: The Boer War Writings of Francis Fremantle," submitted for "Anatomy C7" as part of the intercalated B.Sc. in the history of medicine, U.C.L., May 1993. Fremantle also published these views in his *Impressions,* 72, which appeared the following year.

24. January 1900. Cited in Marshall, "Doctor at War." The passage also occurs in Fremantle, *Impressions,* 72.

25. *Nursing Record,* 17 February 1900, 133–34.

26. "South African War Nurses. From a Colonial Point of View," *Nursing Record,* 17 February 1900, 133–34.

27. *Nursing Record,* 24 February 1900, 151–52: reprint of an article by "The Special Medical Correspondent of the *British Journal of Medicine.*"

28. See the following letters to the editor of the *Nursing Record:* from "An Indignant Colonial," 3 March 1900, 182–83; "Trained at Wellington Hospital," 10 March

1900, 203; and to the editor, 17 March 1900, 213–14 and 7 April 1900, 275. For the reasons for the acute shortage of orderlies, see Stone, "Victorian Army," 279–83.

29. See B.P.P. 29 and 30, Cd 453 and Cd 455 for the report of the Commission, the evidence given before it, and the appendices attached. (Reference henceforth is the Cd. number, *Royal Commission*.)

30. Cd. 453, *Royal Commission*, 10.

31. Stone, "Victorian Army," 299–300.

32. Cd. 1791, *Royal Commission*, 39, also cited in Stone, "Victorian Army," 264.

33. Cd. 455, *Royal Commission*, Appendix to Minutes of Evidence, 14–15. By the middle of 1901, Australia, New Zealand, and Canada had sent 51 Medical Officers, 77 nursing sisters, and 214 "subordinates"; India sent no fewer than 502 stretcher bearers. In addition, several nursing sisters came from different colonies of their own accord and were engaged in South Africa.

34. *Nursing Record*, 4 August 1900, 120, "Notes on Nursing in War Time," by the "Florence Nightingale of South Africa," Sister Henrietta Stockdale, writing from St. Michael's Home, Kimberley.

35. Burdett-Coutts's letter cited in the *Nursing Record*, 21 July 1900, 55–56.

36. Sir Alexander Ogston, *Reminiscences of Three Campaigns* (London, 1920), 119.

37. Marshall, "Doctor at War," 17.

38. Fremantle, *Impressions*, 117.

39. W. S. Inder, Orderly and 2nd Class Supernumerary Officer, *On Active Service With the S.J.A.B. South African War, 1899–1902* (Kendal, 1903).

40. Cd. 454, *Royal Commission*, 279 *et passim* for the positive remarks of other nurses.

41. E. C. Laurence, *A Nurse's Life in War and Peace* (London, 1912) 173.

42. Sister Henrietta Stockdale, "Notes on Nursing in War Time," *Nursing Record*, 4 August 1900, 121.

43. Stone, "Victorian Army," 324–26. I have addressed this issue elsewhere. See my "'We Were Men Nursing Men': Male Nursing on the Mines in Twentieth Century South Africa," in W. Woodward, G. Minkley, and P. Hayes (eds.), *Deep Histories: Gender and Colonialism* (Amsterdam, 2002).

44. Cd. 1790, *Royal Commission*, 498.

45. Stone, "Victorian Army," 324–26.

46. Ibid., 266, 289–90.

47. Ibid., 323–24.

48. Telegram from Mr. Chamberlain to Sir A. Milner, 3 April 1900; and Telegram, Sir A. Milner to Mr. Chamberlain, 10 April 1900, in C. Headlam, *The Milner Papers (South Africa) 1899–1905*, vol. 2 (London, 1933), 73–74.

49. Milner to Bertha Synge, 15 April 1900, in Headlam, *Milner Papers*, 2.74. Also cited in Spies, "Women and the War," 180.

50. *Nursing Record*, 14 October 1899, 315, and 21 October 1900.

51. Ibid., 18 November 1899; 10 February 1900; 24 February 1900; 3 March 1900; 7 April 1900; 21 April 1900.

52. Ibid., 4 November 1899; 6 January 1900; 10 February 1900; 24 February 1900.

53. Ibid., 10 February 1900, on the selection of nurses for the Yeomanry Hospital.

54. McGann, *Battle of the Nurses,* 53.

55. Searle, *History,* 160.

56. B. Abel-Smith, *A History of the Nursing Profession* (London, 1960), 71. At one stage royal patronage of rival nursing organizations even threatened "an embarrassing split in the royal family itself." A. M. Rafferty, *The Politics of Nursing Knowledge* (London and New York, 1996), 62.

57. *Nursing Record,* 14 July 1900, 35; Summers, *Angels and Citizens,* 199.

58. G. L. Mosse, *Sexuality and Nationalism: Middle-Class Morality and Sexual Norms in Modern Europe* (Madison, 1985), 90.

59. A. Bron, *Diary of a Nurse in South Africa* (London, 1901), 146.

60. Bron, *Diary,* 76, 93.

61. Summers, *Angels and Citizens,* 198.

62. See M. Adler, "Skirting the Empire. Women Travellers and Travel Writers in South Africa, 1799–1900" (Ph.D. thesis, University of London, 1996).

63. See, for example, R. Bourne, *Lords of Fleet Street: The Harmsworth Dynasty* (London, 1990) on Alfred Harmsworth's attitude toward women—"he put women on their Victorian pedestal—modest, demure, non-swearing" and "had a good nose for what interested women" (25)—and the importance of women readers and the South African War to the revival of the *Daily Mail* under Harmsworth (29–31).

64. See Cd. 454 *Royal Commission,* evidence pp.

65. Letters to the Editor, *Nursing Record,* 10 February 1900, 123: "We don't want matrons."

66. Letter from Burdett-Coutts cited in the *Nursing Record,* 21 July 1900, 55–56.

67. Summers, *Angels and Citizens,* 214–15.

68. For the attack on nurses' pay, see the *Nursing Record,* 11 November 1899, 18 November 1899, 6 January 1900, 14 April 1900, and 21 July 1900.

69. Letters to the Editor, "The Price of Army Nurses," *Nursing Record,* 18 November 1899, 412. This letter from "Another Loyal Nurse" was in response to a letter from "A Loyal Nurse" who had attacked the line taken by the *Nursing Record* on pay.

70. *Nursing Record,* 21 July 1900, 45.

71. Stone, "Victorian Army."

72. Cape Colony, Medical Officer of Health Archives, MOH 27/231, Dr. A. J. Gregory to Dr. Roscoe, 2 August 1901.

73. M. Vicinus, *Independent Women: Work and Community for Single Women, 1850–1920* (Chicago, 1988), 97.

74. Blanch, "British Society and the War," 228.

75. Ibid., 214.

76. W. R. Nasson, "Tommy Atkins in South Africa," in Warwick (ed.), *South African War,* 123–24.

77. Summers, *Angels and Citizens,* 203. See also, for example, the letter of a member of staff of the Portland Hospital to the *Nursing Record,* 1 September 1900: "Altogether, it has been an experience that none of us would have liked to miss, and we shall always look back on the South African campaign with feelings of great affection, in spite of all the difficulties and trials." Bassett, in "Turning Point," makes a similar point.

78. Summers, *Angels and Citizens*, 8.

79. Ibid., 182.

80. "Outside the Gates: Women: 'White Kaffirs,'" *Nursing Record*, 11 January 1896, 39.

81. Editorial, "Following the Flag," *Nursing Record*, 9 June 1900.

82. Ibid.

83. Editorial, *Nursing Record*, 21 October 1899, 325.

84. Ibid., 330.

85. *Nursing Record*, 7 October 1899, 303.

86. Editorial, *Nursing Record*, 14 October 1899, 305–6.

87. See for example "The Red Cross in War," *Nursing Record*, 1 September 1900.

88. *Nursing Record*, 28 October 1899, 351. See also 11 November 1899, 392: "From all sources comes the confirmation of the statement that the Boers have treated wounded prisoners with the greatest goodwill and kindness."

89. *Nursing Record*, 15 December 1900.

90. Sister Henrietta Stockdale, "Notes on Nursing in War Time," from St. Michael's Home, Kimberley, *Nursing Record*, 4 August 1900.

91. Kimberley Hospital Files 3/5/2, "Transcript by an Unknown Person of a Diary Kept by Sister Henrietta during the Siege of Kimberley, 15 October 1899–23 February 1900," entry for 26 November 1900, 9. (I am grateful to Matron Niemann, then at the Kimberley Hospital, for allowing me to see the transcript of Sister Henrietta's diary in 1991.)

92. Ibid., 12.

93. Ibid., 11 August 1900, 119–20.

94. See, for example, the experiences recounted in Emily Hobhouse, *War without Glamour* (Bloemfontein, 1924). See also Summers, *Angels and Citizens*, 203–4. It would need another paper to do justice to nursing in the concentration camps; fortunately, that topic is addressed in Elizabeth van Heyningen's chapter in this volume.

95. *Cape Argus*, 8 May 1911; *Volkstem*, 8 May 1911, both from the Royal Commonwealth Society scrapbooks of cuttings on the Order; the translation of the *Volkstem* article was also in the scrapbook.

96. See note 95.

97. *Illustrated London News*, special issue, "The Transvaal War 1899–1900," by Spenser Wilkinson.

98. One of the few exceptions I have found was a feature letter by A.E.W., "Off Duty among the Kaffirs," to the *British Journal of Nursing (B.J.N.)*, 1 September 1905, 218–20, which is unfortunately both patronizing and offensive. On 23 September 1905 (Mary Murray, "An Echo of the South African War," 255–56) readers were regaled with a tale of an attack on nurses by "a half lunatic [African] with distinctly homicidal tendencies."

99. The columns of the *B.J.N.* are full of warnings to women not to rush off to South Africa after the war because of the lack of available work. See, for example, *B.J.N.*, 1 October 1904, 272 and 5 August 1905, 119.

100. See for example the editorial, "A Colour Line," *B.J.N.*, 8 September 1906, and comment in *B.J.N.*, 9 February 1907.

101. *Nursing Record,* 6 April 1901, 277, and 11 January 1902, 37; see also 29 March 1902, 257, and the letters from "Trained in Ireland," *B.J.N.,* 26 June 1909 and from Miss Flora Gaythorne from Natal cited in "Outside the Gates," *B.J.N.,* 28 August 1909.

102. *B.J.N.,* 17 March 1906, 216, for the last quotation. The earlier quotations are from her article "Private Nursing in South Africa," *B.J.N.,* 30 December 1905; see also her letters in *B.J.N.:* 24 March 1906, 245–46, which adds the Scots to those insulted ("English and Colonials"); 7 April 1906, "A Physiological Reason," which adds early Dutch settlers; and 4 August 1906 ("Australians in South Africa"), which adds "Colonial medical men." It is interesting that Bedford Fenwick published the articles without comment and then defended Kenealy against her critics as someone who has "had great opportunities for observation" in South Africa, having held "important hospital appointments before the War, and worked there altogether for eight years, including her work with the Army Reserve" (*B.J.N.,* 9 March 1906, 226).

103. See Marks, *Divided Sisterhood,* chap. 3.

CHAPTER 9

Women and Disease

The Clash of Medical Cultures in the
Concentration Camps of the South African War

ELIZABETH VAN HEYNINGEN

To such a shelter I was called to see a sick baby. The mother sat on her
little trunk with the child across her knee. She had nothing to give it and the
child was sinking fast.... There was nothing to be done and we watched
the child draw its last breath in reverent silence. The mother neither moved
nor wept. It was her only child. Dry-eyed but deathly white, she sat there
motionless looking not at the child but far, far away into depths of grief
beyond all tears.[1]

The neglect I specially refer to is the result of a certain fatalism which is
common among them, only I suppose they would call it by a different
name. "It is God's will" is the excuse, or reason, they give for sitting by a
sick child and never moving as much as a finger to give it food or the
medicine ordered by the doctor.[2]

Two voices, two different perspectives. The rights and wrongs of the mortality in the concentration camps of the South African War have generated
much heat and a considerable literature.[3] The fact that the mortality rates
were exceptionally high is not in question, nor are the immediate causes, but
there have been surprisingly few modern studies on the camps themselves.
The conflict between the British doctors and the Boer women was not
entirely the result of the war but arose partly from a confrontation between
different traditions of healing. As a result the British authorities considered
the Boer women benighted, superstitious, ignorant, and culpably careless in
sanitary matters. To the women, on the other hand, the doctors were inhumane and lacked the skills or the desire to deal with camp mortality. Since,
for the Boers, the locus of medical care was in the home, contributing to the
standing of the woman in Boer society—an aspect of the nurturing role of

the *volksmoeder*[4]—their situation in the camps, where they were expected to send their sick children to hospital, was particularly disempowering. For their part, the doctors, who were in the invidious position of defending a policy that gave rise to massive mortality, tended to shift the responsibility for the deaths to the women and to see the camps partly as educational, teaching the women the basics of hygiene and childcare.[5] In both cases medicine was an element of ethnic and gender identity in which each society had a considerable emotional investment.

The Background to the Camps

The concentration camps, or "refugee" camps, as the British authorities called them at the time, came into being at the end of 1900 during the guerrilla phase of the South African War. After their homes had been burned and their stock destroyed or seized, old men, women, and children, together with substantial numbers of black people, were rounded up and incarcerated in camps hastily erected along the railway lines, usually outside small country towns. This policy was directed largely at country people who might provide sustenance and information to the Boer commandos. It was a deliberate military decision to conduct a scorched-earth policy against civilians as a means of forcing the Boer commandos to lay down their arms.[6] By October 1901 there were about nineteen camps in the Transvaal, including Mafeking, which was administered as a Transvaal camp,[7] and fifteen in the Orange River Colony (ORC), as the Orange Free State had become, including Kimberley, administered as an ORC camp.[8] In addition there were four in the Cape[9] and several others in Natal.[10] Some of the camps were small and temporary, but many contained larger concentrations of population than most Boer towns. The Bloemfontein camp, for instance, Dr. G. Pratt Yule observed, contained 6,426 white people, 2,000 more than the ORC capital.[11]

Initially the camps were administered by the military authorities at a time when supplies of all kinds, from tents to food, were limited and the railway lines from Cape Town and Durban were regularly attacked by Boer commandos.[12] Moreover, although the army had considerable experience in camp life, it had an extremely poor record in providing healthy conditions for its own soldiers; for the frail and the elderly military control was lethal.[13] In January 1901 it was decided to put the camps into civilian hands, but the High Commissioner, Sir Alfred Milner, had neither full control nor full information about the management of the camps until May, and it was only after November 8, 1901, that the civil authorities assumed complete control.[14]

There were a number of problems associated with the administration of the camps. The first was to find suitable superintendents. In the end they were drawn either from Cape colonials or from the Uitlanders and were a motley collection including accountants, surveyors, an architect, and a merchant.[15] While some were both capable and humane, others were neither and were eventually replaced. Supplies of tents, food, and other necessities including fuel and water were lacking, particularly in the beginning. Suitable medical personnel were equally hard to find and on occasion the local town doctor doubled as the camp doctor; matrons and nurses, too, were not available and a number of camps were assisted, at least for a while, by volunteer workers from the towns. Initially the camp authorities were willing to use Boer assistants, but in time these were often dispensed with as they were objects of suspicion, believed to be aiding the enemy.[16] Young Boer women, however, were recruited to help in the hospitals. Later they were described as "probationers" and, it was sanctimoniously claimed, they thus received a training "which may be of service to them in after life, and enable them to be of good service to their suffering kinsfolk."[17]

In the early stages, when tents were scarce, refugees were often housed in a wide variety of accommodation ranging from houses in the nearby towns to the grandstand of Johannesburg racecourse. In some camps attempts were made to construct wooden, mud, or reed huts, but in the end bell tents were usually used.[18] These were often old and barely waterproof. The inhabitants were generally not strictly confined. They were sometimes free to visit the nearby town, to forage in the veld for fuel, and occasionally to grow their own crops. Few made any attempt to escape, mainly because they had nowhere to go. They could not return to their homes, they would be a liability to the commandos, and they were often strangers in the area in which their camps were located and consequently could not find refuge with friends in the towns.

Reports and Testimony on the Camps

Public attention was first drawn to the conditions of the camps when Emily Hobhouse visited some of the ORC camps between January and April 1901. Although this was before mortality had reached its peak and she only visited a few of the camps,[19] she saw them before they had been properly organized. She was shocked by the poor quality and scarcity of the food, by the shortage of clothing, bedding, and other necessities, and by the callousness of the officials. Her letters and reports to her influential friends and relatives forced the British government to take action.[20] Emily Hobhouse was not the only pro-Boer to visit the camps. Accompanying her to South Africa were two Quakers, Isabella and Joshua Rowntree. They visited the Pietermaritzburg and Port Elizabeth camps, which were not as disorganized as those in the ORC.[21] In May 1901 two other Quakers, Frances Taylor and Anna Hogg, were sent out to South Africa by the Friends South African Relief Fund Committee. Traveling with them, but independently, was Helen B. Harris, who subsequently joined the Quaker movement; another Quaker, Georgina King Lewis, went later. For various reasons, however, their reports were not as widely disseminated as those of Hobhouse.[22]

The growing realization of camp conditions led the authorities to take action. Apart from transferring the camps to civilian control, Dr. Kendall Franks, an Irish-trained doctor who had come to South Africa in 1899, was instructed to report on the Transvaal camps.[23] In addition a Committee of Ladies (Fawcett Committee), led by Millicent Garrett Fawcett and including two doctors, Dr. E. C. Scarlett and Dr. Jane Waterston of Cape Town, were sent out to investigate camp conditions.[24] It was the tone of these reports that angered the Boers so much for, while admitting the faults in camp organization, they evidenced little pity for the victims, and the women were largely blamed for the deaths.

The South African War is unusual in that the testimonies of a substantial number of Boer women have also been collected and published, while some women kept diaries that were retained by their families. These records are not without their problems, however. One significant source is the stories collected by Emily Hobhouse and published either in *The Brunt of the War* or *War without Glamour*. Hobhouse had two purposes—to publicize the sufferings of the Boer women and, as a pacifist, in *War without Glamour* to emphasize the sufferings of civilian populations in wartime. She was not, therefore, going to publish anything that reflected disadvantageously on Boer women. Moreover, as she came from the middle classes herself, middle-class perspectives pervade her work both in her choice of interviews and in the standards by which she saw them. Almost all her testimonies come from women of some wealth and standing in the community. The same is true for many of the surviving diaries and memoirs, since they were usually produced by educated women. The voice of the *bywoner* is much more difficult to find. The partial exception is the evidence produced by M. M. Postma, who collected testimonies from a very wide range of people.[25]

Disease and Death

Starting around the end of March 1901 the British began to publish statistics on the camps and for a time fairly detailed records were kept. Emily Hobhouse collated morbidity and mortality statistics, which were published as appendices to *The Brunt of the War*.[26] Historians have made little attempt either to analyze the statistics or to explore the implications of the diseases occurring in the camps, with the exception of B. Fetter and S. Kessler who have produced two papers based on the registers of the Barberton and Nylstroom camps.[27]

The very high death rates, the worst occurring during the months from August to December 1901, were acknowledged by the British themselves. Some camps were far worse than others and there was no obvious correlation with the size of the camp. Nylstroom and Vredefort Road, with fairly small camp populations, still had extremely high mortality rates, while Potchefstroom, with a population reaching 7,538 in September 1901, for instance, had a relatively lower average death rate in that month: about 133 per 1,000 per annum.[28] At times mortality rates rose to heights of more than 1,000 per 1,000 of population per annum, at which rate the entire population would have died by the end of the year.[29]

High though these mortality rates were, as the authorities pointed out at the time, they were comparable with mortality rates in some parts of the Cape Colony. Charles Simkins has calculated that there was a crude death rate in the colony as a whole between 1891 and 1906 of about 14.8 per 1,000 per annum for whites and 33.6 for blacks. Infant mortality rates (IMR) were 150 per 1,000 per annum for whites and 304 for blacks.[30] On the diamond fields rates were always higher, and during the siege of Kimberley the IMR for children under one year of age in 1900 reached 430.86 per 1,000 per annum for Africans, 626.96 for coloured children, and 260.87 for whites. In the same year the IMR for neighboring Beaconsfield (essentially a working-class district of Kimberley) rose to the appalling height of 693.49 per 1,000, with 915.73 for coloured babies and 216.87 for whites.[31]

Although the camps varied considerably in the quality of the administration and in living standards, there were common denominators in the causes of mortality. Despite the variable quality of diagnoses in the camps, the main causes of death are clear enough.[32] Between the beginning of June and the end of December 1901 the most significant causes of death in the Transvaal camps, in descending order, were:[33]

Measles	3,483
Pneumonia and bronchitis	1,507
Diarrhea and dysentery	1,074
Enteric	747
Marasmaus[34]	266
Whooping cough	230

Convulsions	207
Malaria	151
General debility and weakness[35]	106
Heart disease	81
Influenza	65
Fever	36
Old age and senile decay	36
Meningitis	28
Gastro-enteritis	26
Bright's disease and nephritis	23
Croup	22
Premature and still births	16
Phthisis and tuberculosis	15
Diphtheria	11
Richitis[36]	10
Scalds and burns[37]	10

Measles is a highly infectious viral disease, transmitted mainly by droplet infection and needing a continuous chain of human contacts to survive. In the era before vaccination, measles was endemic in many societies, with epidemics occurring every two to five years. It is primarily a childhood disease, but because babies up to the age of six to nine months acquire a passive immunity from their mothers, it appears usually in children over that age. Where populations are isolated, however, and contact has not provided immunity, all ages may be affected. On a number of occasions measles has appeared as a classic example of a "virgin soil epidemic"; in South America it followed smallpox as one of the diseases that destroyed the Amerindian populations after the Spanish conquest, and it was equally devastating in the Pacific Islands in the mid-nineteenth century. Malnutrition makes people particularly vulnerable to the disease, which also weakens the natural immune system and leaves sufferers open to secondary infections. Pneumonia is a common complication in susceptible societies. Diarrhea is also a common phenomenon and is one of the most important causes of measles-associated mortality.[38] British doctors were partly aware of some of these features, as Dr. Yule explained:

A very important factor in the production and propagation of disease is the susceptibility of the Afrikander Dutch to almost every infection. This is particularly noticeable with regard to measles. Europeans enjoy a certain immunity from measles acquired by the frequency of epidemics at home, and it seems as if the Dutch by their long sojourn in South Africa and the isolation of their dwellings had practically lost this immunity. When measles attacks a susceptible population it is one of the most fatal of diseases, and that the Dutch have lost that degree of immunity possessed by Europeans is abundantly shown by the extremely malignant type the disease assumes in the camp.[39]

The devastating measles epidemic, therefore, was not one the British authorities could have anticipated and they were not directly responsible for its rapid spread through the country. However, the conditions in the camps contributed to the vulnerability of the camp populations and the movement of people from camp to camp encouraged the spread of the disease. Camp residents were given standard rations similar to those that might be found in prisons and other institutions at the time. They varied slightly from camp to camp and in the different colonies, and they were modified in the light of criticisms and improvements of supply. Initially, voluntary internees and *hendsoppers* were given a better diet, but this system was soon abandoned and no political distinction was made between the burghers.[40]

Despite these variations, the same problems occurred in all the diets. One was the quality of the meat. Camp inhabitants complained constantly that the meat was thin, tough, and slimy and the camp authorities often admitted that it was not up to standard. The other feature about the rations was the almost complete lack of fresh fruit or vegetables, except occasionally potatoes, and of fresh milk. Milk was almost always in a dehydrated form, and as the camp authorities felt that the mothers used too much, they dispensed it already diluted, with the result that it was sometimes too thin.[41] The British placed little importance on the nutritional value of vegetables, commenting about one group who were brought to Nylstroom that

These people seem perfectly happy and contented, and the Superintendent informed me they were Bywoners, who lived in much worse condition in their own homes and lived mostly on fruit and vegetables, so that the fare they received in the camp was to them novel and luxurious. Some of the people in the camp had never seen white bread until they were brought into Nijlstroom. These facts, the circumstances under which the different classes of Boer lived in ordinary times, should be considered when trying to establish the hardships or otherwise of their lot in these camps.[42]

The Boers, however, were accustomed to a diet that usually included ample fresh fruit and vegetables. Dietary studies suggest that at first glance the Boers were receiving an adequate supply of calories, but much of this was in the form of flour. The protein (mainly meat) came to 143 percent of the recommended daily allowance (RDA) but was often rejected because of its poor quality. The fat intake was low and the diet was severely deficient in vitamins and other essential nutrients.[43]

The body adjusts to undernutrition mainly by keeping its activity to a minimum, possibly an explanation for the lethargy and apathy the concentration camp population often displayed.[44] Famine and disease have always been closely related.[45] Recent studies exploring the effect of malnutrition on individuals and societies have pointed out a number of factors that may have been at work in the concentration camps. General starvation, it has been suggested, increases susceptibility to a variety of pathogens.[46] Famine has social consequences as well.[47] Initially a catastrophe may create a "disaster utopia" in which the community shows unusual mutual care and assistance. As starvation increases, however, and individuals become more apathetic, "social atomization" may occur in which this caring and sharing may disappear, replaced by an increasing hostility to friends or relatives who make demands on limited resources. The testimonies of the women often emphasize their mutual assistance, but social atomization may perhaps also have occurred in the camps, interpreted by the British as a lack of gallantry or an unwillingness to help one another:

> The idea of helping the helpless does not exist in consciences of the stalwart burgher, over and over again a woman whose husband is fighting or a prisoner of war has to sit and nurse her children and ask in vain of a fine well-built, noble "patriot" to chop her wood or fetch her rations or her medicine, his reply is "I have no time," or something to that effect. There is no such thing as gallantry among these creatures, unless paid for, when another name will cover the term gallantry.[48]

There was another factor at work as well, although its impact is difficult to measure. This was the effect of trauma arising from the destruction of homes and farms. Old people probably suffered most. The mortality of the old rarely receives the attention infant mortality does, but old men as well as old women were swept up into the camps. Humiliation, grief, confusion, and uncertainty about the future must all have weakened the health of the elderly.

The blue books and camp registers only noted cause of death, so there is little information on diseases that were prevalent but not fatal. Ophthalmia was one and there are photographs of flies on children's heads, perhaps a source of this problem. Scurvy is also mentioned occasionally, while those at the Johannesburg camp in February 1901 were "looking hopeless, helpless, sick, and vermin-ridden."[49] On the other hand there are some diseases that were less common than might be expected. Despite the doctors' strictures on midwives, there were few deaths in childbirth and the incidence of puerperal fever was low. Tuberculosis, already a scourge in the Western Cape, was rare. What stands out is the combination of maladies related to malnutrition, combined with epidemic disease.

Western versus Boer Medical Practice

The British doctors associated with the camps came from a tradition of medicine that had evolved during the preceding century partly as a result of scientific advances and partly in response to the high mortality industrialization and urbanization had produced in British cities. The realization, well before the germ theory of disease had been propounded, that polluted water supplies and inadequate sewage disposal were major causes of urban infectious diseases had profoundly affected their thinking about the control of disease. The development of the germ theory of disease from about 1859 on and of antiseptic and aseptic surgery from the 1870s on had reinforced their belief that cleanliness was the key to good health. As this message was absorbed by the Victorian middle classes, cleanliness came to be equated with moral health, and the notion was propagated by Victorian moralists as well as doctors. In South Africa, the young Dr. John Ross, son and grandson of Eastern Cape missionaries, encapsulated these views in a pamphlet on public health:

> Hygiene is a study of all the conditions and influences which affect mankind for good or evil. These influences may be mental, moral or physical, and they must be studied not only as they affect individuals or families, but also as they have an influence on communities and nations.... Attention to the laws of health is a public as well as a private duty.... People must be taught that attention to public health is a moral duty, that cleanliness, avoidance of excess, and health preservation go hand in hand with mental and moral training, and that morality consists as much in a hearty submission to the precepts of health as to the observation of creed.[50]

The emergence of an organized medical profession in the nineteenth century was closely associated with the evolution of the middle classes whose norms and standards they tended to express. By 1900 their status in society had been largely established. Doctors were claiming, and were often accorded, the right to pontificate on a variety of topics, not necessarily medical.[51] Thomas Carlyle was one of those who was instrumental in elevating the status of the medical profession, which he described in one of his essays: "the profession of the Human Healer being radically a sacred one and connected with the highest priesthoods."[52]

Such doctors rarely challenged the class hierarchy or the central beliefs of Victorian middle-class society; rather, they tended to reinforce contemporary prejudices and existing stereotypes. In the colonial world the role of the medical profession in reinforcing colonial conquest has been widely discussed.[53] More extreme jingo doctors readily condemned any society that was not northern European. During the plague epidemic in Cape Town in 1901 Professor W. J. Simpson, the imperial plague expert, had liberally condemned Africans, coloured people, Malays, Portuguese, Italians, and Levantine and Polish Jews as unsanitary.[54] Some doctors had been active in promoting British imperialism, and most who were seconded into the camps supported the British cause at least partially.[55] It was an easy step, therefore, to transfer prejudices about sanitation and cleanliness to Boer society; medical criticisms in the camps were very similar to those condemning slum societies, whether they were coloured and African people in Cape Town, Irish in Manchester, or the urban poor of Australia.[56]

There was another aspect of the medical ethos that had developed more recently, associated with the acceptance of the germ theory of disease. Historians have pointed out that this shift in the understanding of the origins of disease contributed to a move away from preventive medicine, based on the health of the community, to curative medicine in which the focus was on the individual pathogen at work in the individual body. It also placed a greater emphasis on the hospital as the locus of curative medicine; trained nurses, aseptic surgery, and the belief that the hospital was also an active instrument in sanitary education all contributed as well to a higher valuation of the hospital in the health care system toward the end of the nineteenth century.[57] Added to this was the gendered nature of Western medical practice, in which midwives and nurses were increasingly subordinated to the doctor, usually male, and patients, particularly female patients, were expected to be obedient to the will of the doctor.[58]

To Dr. Kendall Franks and other British doctors the Dutch tents were comparable to British slums. In an overcrowded camp "the squalor and dirt would equal, if not surpass, some of the residences of the poor in the British Isles, such as Whitechapel, St Giles, and the Liberties in Dublin."[59] Like British slum dwellers, the Boer women needed constant surveillance and coercion to ensure that they maintained sanitary habits in their homes and in their persons:

> I am informed that though the refugees are orderly in a sort of a way, that nevertheless they are not too obedient as to the keeping of animals, and some minor points of discipline. It is very necessary that rules and regulations should be made, and should be adhered to. We have bye-laws in towns. Why not in camps? Moreover, penalties are attached to bye-laws and enforced against offenders, and some power of this kind is necessary here. The refugees must be made to understand that, in the interests of themselves and their neighbours, rules must be obeyed and the defaulters will be punished.[60]

The accusations leveled by the British authorities against the Boer women were wide-ranging and were repeated by doctors, camp superintendents, visiting commissions, and the military and civil authorities. The Boer women were dirty and unsanitary, their tents were untidy, and their children were rarely washed. They closed up the tents and lived in a fetid atmosphere. They ignored the instructions of the doctors and persisted in using their own medicines, from "Dutch medicines" to more unsavory home remedies. They preferred their own midwives. They refused to enter the hospitals and concealed their children when they were ill.

Two documents were particularly responsible for publicizing these iniquities—a British command paper, Cd. 819, published partly in response to Emily Hobhouse's report, and the report of the Fawcett Committee. What angered the Boers was the way in which, in both cases, responsibility for the mortality rates was shifted from the actions of the British to the behavior of the Boer women. In addition Boer life was seen through middle-class eyes. Untidiness was equated with uncleanliness and unfamiliar tastes and social practices were interpreted as unsanitary.

Franks's reports were particularly striking. His choice of words is suggestive. The poor were usually "ignorant" or "dirty." A woman who complained about the meat was "loud-voiced." On the other hand, where people were more docile, as in the Johannesburg camp, they displayed "a general air of contentment." Children were "healthy," "chubby," and played with "happy peals of laughter."[61] Franks also had a passion for mathematical accuracy in the pitching of the tents.[62] Conversely one of the deficiencies of the Middelburg camp, Franks felt, was the lack of system in pitching the tents; the Middelburg inmates had the habit of moving their tents where they chose, to be near their friends.[63]

Middle-class judgments were even more pervasive in the report of the Fawcett Committee. At Norval's Pont, a well-run camp, camp residents were found playing tennis.

> There was a much better and more cheerful and pleasant spirit in this camp than in any other we had seen. Both men and women had a self-respecting bearing, they were busily employed with their daily work, and were not for ever gossiping in one another's tents.[64]

The Fawcett Committee, in its role as lady-of-the-manor, demanded the right to inspect the most intimate belongings and practices of the women. In the Klerksdorp camp Lady Knox and the camp matron had no hesitation in ordering a woman to display even the clothes she was wearing:

> In the first tent we found a woman—with one small child—who said she had no clothes and wanted underlinen badly. Miss Moritz promptly asked, "What have you on now? Show me," and the woman revealed, first, a scarlet flannel petticoat; secondly, a petticoat made out of a thick white blanket; and thirdly, a dark stuff petticoat all under a dirty stuff dress (temperature in tent must have been between 70° and 80°). Miss Moritz next pointed to a box ... and begged leave to see the contents. There were shifts, rags, dirty kappies, more petticoats, books, a handkerchief full of coffee beans, and another full of sugar. A big sack was next opened; it contained a dirty cotton dress, more underlinen, dirty, but with much embroidery, and a large bundle of men's coats and trousers, which she said belonged to a father-in-law long since deceased.[65]

In these middle-class eyes sanitary behavior was closely allied to order and to taste. Another family who met with disapprobation from Lady Knox possessed "five straw hats trimmed with artificial flowers, cotton and silk blouses covered with lace, a length of broad black satin ribbon, bead trimmings ... a very gorgeous empty cigarette case, and any amount of tawdry rubbish."[66]

By June 1901 the destitution of the new arrivals in the camp was also turned against them, despite ample evidence that women were often given no opportunity to rescue even the barest minimum of household necessities before their homes were destroyed:

> The condition of most of the families was most deplorable; their clothing was tattered and threadbare, and scanty as well. Bedding was of the

poorest description, whilst cooking utensils and conveniences of all sorts
were often conspicuous by their absence. The men who come in with the
convoys declare that the people are most improvident, and that if they are
possessed of better clothing &c., they neglect to have it brought out of the
houses and loaded on to the wagons when they are called upon to come
into camp.[67]

The British indictment of the Boers was undoubtedly partly the rhetoric
of war. Not only had the war to be justified, but the enemy had to be demon-
strably inferior, fit objects for the improving civilization British conquest
would bring. Even in the camps the few British inhabitants could be held
up as examples of the benefits of British rule. In Balmoral camp Brit was
contrasted with Boer:

> In the first tent there were English-speaking burghers engaged upon mak-
> ing a stove—a most ingenious contrivance—out of corrugated iron. The
> flaps of the tents were all fastened up, and the bedding was rolled up for
> the day. The interior of the tent was very clean and tidy. The people seemed
> very interested in their occupation, and explained the construction of the
> stove to us. In the next tent there was a child ill with pneumonia. Every-
> thing was untidy and dirty, and the air in the tent was stuffy and evil
> smelling. The child, for a wonder, was in a nightgown instead of its ordi-
> nary clothes. I examined its chest, the skin was grimy with dirt. The
> sickness in the tent would excuse the flaps being down and the want of
> ventilation, but nothing but dirty habits and ignorance would explain the
> filthy condition of tent and its inmates. They seemed not to understand
> what cleanliness is, and to care less.[68]

Of the "inept" and "slow" young women working as "probationers" in the
camps, Franks observed that

> It is obvious to all those who have had any experience of these camps that
> not only the probationers but the people generally must in future bene-
> fit by the education and discipline in these matters which a residence in
> these camps affords them, but the probationers benefit to an exceptional
> extent.[69]

The British reaction to Boer practices also indicates how far the modern
medical profession had abandoned preindustrial medical practice, for the

Boer tradition of healing was derived in part from an earlier European system, although they may have had difficulty in articulating this. Frontiersmen from at least the middle of the eighteenth century, the Boers had had little access to developing scientific thought and still less to doctors trained in modern medical schools. When the Boers trekked north they had no doctors with them and even at the end of the century few had access to trained practitioners. In 1898 there were 260 doctors registered in the South African Republic, with a ratio of 1 doctor to 1,328 whites. But these figures are misleading, for the majority were probably clustered in the areas of Uitlander settlement.[70] Even before the Boers left the Western Cape magical practices, carried over from Europe, were also probably incorporated into their healing system.[71] Furthermore, over 150 years of medical practice had been modified by the South African environment, by some limited access to European medicines, and by contact with the healing practices of the indigenous people.

Boer medicine had its origins in seventeenth-century Europe, when the humoral philosophy of medicine, derived from the Greeks (although questioned by some scientists), had by no means been discarded. Central to this system was the belief that the body and the environment formed a whole, and that health or disease was a product of the relationship between the two. The body consisted of four parts or "humors"—blood, phlegm, yellow bile, and black bile—each of which was associated with a particular part of the body and a specific season of the year and consisted of two fundamental qualities; so, for instance, blood was hot and moist, and was associated with the liver and with spring. C. Rosenberg notes that by the eighteenth century the fundamental principles were rarely articulated, but given the lack of diagnostic tools, treatment was still primarily concerned with bringing these humors into balance through a management of the excretions and secretions of the body. Bleeding and purging were favored nostrums but it was the result by which this balance was obtained, rather than the means, that was of significance.[72] Medical practice was concerned not with the diagnosis of a specific disease, since individual pathogens were not recognized, but with the identification of the cause of the imbalance and with restoring that balance.

Among the customs of the Boers that the British most abhorred was that of keeping the tents closed.[73] Ironically, the British passion for fresh air was also derived from an increasingly outdated belief that atmospheric pollution (miasma) was a source of disease. This view had been powerfully reinforced by Florence Nightingale in her *Notes on Hospitals* (1859), and it lingered on in the consciousness of both the medical profession and the British middle classes, despite the fact that the germ theory of disease emphasized the role of the individual pathogen as the causative agent of disease.[74] Repeatedly the women were ordered to tie up the flaps of the tents, at least for part of the day:

> When the children were sick the women kept draughts even more assiduously at bay. When ill nothing in the world will induce the mother to take off or change the child's clothing. The child is laid down on his clothes on mats of skin or rugs. The higher the fever rises, the more clothing or rugs are piled on. They keep the tents very close and admit as little air as possible. The sick child is kept in an overheated state, which renders it practically sensitive to the extreme variations of temperature which occur at this season.[75]

This notion of sweating out a fever was one of the most straightforward examples of the humoral system of healing, and was a long-established practice among the Boers. Louis Trigardt, one of the first of the Voortrekkers, had promoted sweating to break the fever of his son, using herbs, vinegar, and aloe.[76]

Franks and others were also critical of the use of "Dutch medicines," patent medicines that had been widely employed by the Boers at least since the eighteenth century. The original Halle medicines had been produced and distributed by an orphanage in Halle in Germany and were in use at the Cape until the early nineteenth century. The opening paragraphs of the diary of Louis Trigardt were devoted to an explanation of the value of these medicines, especially *Essentia dulcis*.[77]

By 1900 the Halle medicines had been largely replaced by the *Huis Apotheek*, a similar product that came in a box together with instructions for the use of the various items (although, it had been noted, few could read them and the family relied on the appearance of the bottles and their places in the box in order to identify them).[78] Old people, it has been observed, "het presies geweet wanneer Groen Amara of Wit Vometief die aangewese middel was, wat die werking van Rooi Veventel of Balsem Sulphuris moet wees op 'n siekte."[79] Mrs. Nicholson of Pietersburg, whose entire family survived in the camps despite severe illness, attributed her good fortune to the fact that they were able to buy nourishing food and to her use of the Dutch medicines. These, she explained, were extremely effective in experienced hands.[80] But camp stores were discouraged from stocking these medicines and the Fawcett Committee urged that they be prohibited entirely.[81] Boer women,

however, clung to their trusted remedies and, when they could not buy them
in camp stores, smuggled them in.

Veral aan Hollandse medikamente was daar 'n groot behoefte. Die verbod
op die invoer hiervan het dan ook by baie, miskien ten onregte, die sus-
pisie gewek dat dit met opset onthou word om die sterfte aan te moedig.
Planne moes dus beraam word om 'n eie voorraad te kry. Maklik het dit
nie gegaan nie. In die eerste plaas kon niemand die kamp verlaat of inkom
of die stad bereik sonder om hom by die dubbele wag aan te meld nie.
Sonder om dus al die slim planne om medisyne te kry hier to herhaal, wil
ek net die volgende paar hier noem: Tandepoeier vir kinders en ander
kleiner pakkies is eenvoudig in die hare versteek, terwyl groter pakkies oral
in die klere weggesteek is.[82]

Franks objected to the Dutch medicines on a number of grounds. They
were used without any understanding of their properties. Sometimes a
number of such remedies were administered all at the same time "without
any doctor's orders."[83] Franks disliked not only the medical self-sufficiency
involved but also the content of the medicines, including Hoffman's drops,
which contained ether, and *Essentia dulcis,* which had opium.[84] But Franks
was not the first doctor to oppose the use of the Dutch medicines. Cape
doctors had waged war against the *Huis Apotheek* for many years largely
because they were sold by unqualified traders and *smouses* who competed
financially with country doctors struggling to survive in a tough economic
environment.[85] Despite the strictures of the doctors, Dutch medicines were
as reputable as the patent medicines that were widely available in Britain,
and it was only in the authoritarian circumstances of the camps that their
use could be prohibited.[86]

Herbal remedies using indigenous plants also had a long and respectable
lineage but they must have been less readily available to the camp residents.
Even if they were allowed to forage in the veld for fuel, inmates were often
in an unfamiliar environment and would not know where herbs grew.[87]

Another aspect of Boer medical practice that was less acceptable, however,
and was certainly employed in the camps, was the use of animal parts,
blood, or dung. Burrows notes suggestively that "The intestinal contents of
different animals or their excreta were believed to possess almost magical
healing qualities."[88] However, pro-Boer sources are silent on this practice
and one is reliant on British evidence. There are probably good reasons for
this omission. Emily Hobhouse was not going to mention practices that
might alienate her readers and, middle-class herself, she probably dismissed

these stories as occasional and confined to a few of the most backward Boers. Educated Boer women probably disregarded them for the same reason and the testimony of those most likely to use such therapies was neither collected nor published.

A common example was a tea made of goats' dung as a popular remedy for measles, "administered by the mother with deplorable results."[89] Even more bizarre was the practice described by Franks in the Bloemfontein camp:

> Dr. Pern, the Principal Medical Officer, told me that he was once sent for to see a child who was ill in one of the tents. When he entered the tent, for some moments he could not make out what he saw. He then discovered that the parents had killed a goat and cut it open, removing all its internal organs. They had then put the child bodily inside the goat, with its head protruding through the opening made by removing the breastbone.[90]

Dr. G. B. Woodroffe of Irene camp reported a wide variety of such practices including "pieces of raw meat ... bandaged over each eye in acute conjunctivitis, and most of these cases ... caused by dirt." "An endless variety of rubbish" was inserted into babies' ears and "rags wetted with human urine are used for open flesh wounds."[91]

The use of animal parts as a form of therapy had a long tradition in Europe and appeared even in some of the early editions of Culpeper's pharmacopeia.[92] Folklore practices continued into the late nineteenth century in Britain, so it was not surprising to find them in South Africa among isolated Boer communities.[93] At the same time it is possible that this was a therapy that had been assimilated from or reinforced by the African healers, for dung was widely used at least in Xhosa healing practices.[94]

The silence of the Boer sources makes it difficult to assess whether it was particular sectors of the population who were most attached to folk medicine. In part it may have been a matter of class. According to General Maxwell, the Military Governor in Pretoria, the wealthier Boers had retired to Europe or had sufficient resources to maintain themselves in the towns. It was, he asserted, the *bywoners* who formed the bulk of the camp population and gave the most trouble as far as hygiene and sanitary practices were concerned.[95] Franks disagreed. In Europe, he claimed, such practices were confined to the most backward sectors of the population but among the Boers they were widespread in every class. He cited the example of President Kruger's nephew in the Bloemfontein camp, who had asked Dr. Baumann to give his wife a cow-dung bath for rheumatism.[96]

Where possible the women also preferred their own practitioners. Tant Alie Badenhorst complained that the British doctor in the Klerksdorp camp was unable to help her ailing child. Eventually she obtained permission to send for her old "herb-doctor":

> as he had no diploma, he could not really take doctor's work, but he doctored the Kaffirs. He had, anyhow, twice saved Wollie from death ... and I clung fast to him as my last straw.... Well, Mr Steyn gave the child a powder and ten minutes after that he was damp with sweat and we could hope.[97]

Maria Fischer was equally dubious about the efficacy of British medicine: "Ek het die doktor ingeroep om moeilikheid te voorkom, maar ek was bang om sy medisyne te gebruik. Ons gebruik die gewone huismiddels...."[98] Midwifery was still women's business in Boer society. Like many doctors of the period who were attempting to assert control over the female practice of medicine, Franks waged war against midwives with familiar horror stories:

> Although there is a maternity marquee I find the same ignorant prejudice prevails among the women, they prefer being attended in their own tents by their own wives, a set of untrained and ignorant women; the consequence is that the mortality in childbirth is very high among them. In one case, when the woman was attended by one of these midwives, the doctor was sent for because it was found that something had gone wrong. On arrival he found that the energetic midwife had removed not only the infant and the afterbirth but the entire womb as well.[99]

By far the greatest complaint of the authorities was the reluctance of the Boers to enter hospital. Given the growing importance of the hospital to modern medical practice, and their view of this environment as both educative and healing, doctors were particularly concerned. Franks reported that the uneducated Boer had a great objection to going into hospital. He attributed this to the same causes that were to be found in Britain among the lowest classes and he noted that "Miss Van Warmlo," one of the Pretoria volunteers in the Irene camp, believed that the resistance arose partly from the fear that they would have to pay to go into hospital and partly because they thought that they would be starved there.[100] Frequently mothers concealed sick children in order to prevent their being taken away.[101] Women were alienated by the coldhearted environment of the hospital[102] and by the fear that their children would die in hospital—"'n Moordhospitaal," young P. van Zyl called the Bloemfontein hospital.[103]

En wanneer kan sy tog uit die hospitaal gaan? So het daar twee bitter lange maande omgegaan dat ek my arme kind daar moes sien vergaan—doodsbleek, uitgeteer, verhonger, geen kos maar net kondensmelk en water, en ek kon daar niks aan doen nie.[104]

There was another factor as well. The custom of nursing babies as old as two years was also deplored. A. A. Aymard, the superintendent of the Krugersdorp camp, noted, "Many of these infants [who died in the tents of pneumonia] are thus nursed up to two years of age, whereas it is well known that mother's milk is nearly valueless after nine months."[105] Similarly, G. Pratt Yule, the ORC medical officer of health, remarked:

Dutch mothers have no ideas as to how a child ought to be fed, and none as to how it ought to be nursed when sick. They cook their food very badly, and it is common to see a baby feeding on meat, heavy dough bread, and stewed black coffee. The children are suckled up to the age of two years, so that it is impossible in the generality of cases to take children into hospital.[106]

～

The title of this chapter refers to "medical cultures" on the grounds that the practice of medicine is never based purely on empirical knowledge. Healing is an activity that is central in many societies, not least our own, and plays a number of religious, economic, and social roles. In Western society in the nineteenth century it was often the medical profession that provided a rationalization of middle-class beliefs such as the inherent characteristics of masculinity and femininity and their appropriate place in society.

But, although the Western medical profession had made considerable scientific advances by 1900, the therapies available to them were still very limited. The tools to control the measles epidemic and other diseases in the camps were confined largely to such traditional methods as isolation and the improvement of sanitation. Since quarantining was usually impracticable, it was not surprising that the doctors should have laid such emphasis on cleanliness, particularly when, in Victorian society, cleanliness had become so closely associated with the moral worth of women above all.[107] There were other issues involved as well. British doctors in the camps were usually loyal participants in an imperial war against an enemy portrayed as backward and undemocratic, yet it was the British who had chosen to conduct war against civilian society in a way that gave rise to massive mortality among women, children, and the old; and it was the doctors who were confronted with the consequences of this policy.

Faced with dilemmas to which they had no easy solution—disease they could not cure and a war conducted against those whom a gender-bound Victorian society usually defined as innocent—it is hardly surprising that the authorities in the camps looked for scapegoats. Boer women represented the domestic face of the enemy, the epitome of sluttishness, ignorance, and unmotherliness. For this reason their reports often combined a tempered criticism of camp management by the British authorities with a deliberate recitation of the more bizarre practices of the Boer women and an emphasis on their failure as mothers.

For their part Boer women in the camps struggled to retain control over some of the central elements of their lives. Given the inability of the doctors to save their children, they were suspicious of therapies that seemed more ineffective than their own and that inhumanely separated them from their children, who died in the inhospitable and uncaring environment of the hospital. Their ability to care for their children, using familiar and, they believed, proven remedies, was one means by which they could confirm their maternal role within the family and within the nation. Their traditions of healing were an integral part of the culture that was being destroyed by British imperialism and that seemed more appropriate to a rural life than was a system that placed emphasis on urban, middle-class values.

Yet, despite themselves, in the camps they were influenced by modern healing practices, through the regimen of the camps, through the camp officials, through their daughters working as "probationers" in the hospitals, and through the Boer women like Henrietta Armstrong or Johanna Brandt–van Warmelo who acted as intermediaries between the British doctors and the Boer women.[108] In the postwar years the social workers of such organizations as the Afrikaanse Christelike Vrouwe Vereniging, operating their own brand of "welfare feminism," taught working-class Afrikaans women the basics of childcare, nutrition, hygiene, and the like.[109] Young Afrikaans women moving into the nursing profession also absorbed these values.[110] By the 1960s the growth of hospitals and associated medical schools attached to the Afrikaans universities had become symbols of a modernized Afrikaner nationalism that claimed the right to be counted as part of Western civilization.

Notes

1. R. van Reenen, *Emily Hobhouse: Boer War Letters* (Cape Town, 1984), 112. This scene was used as the model for Anton van Wouw's sculpture at the Women's Monument in Bloemfontein, commemorating the victims of the concentration camps. See A. Grundlingh, "The National Women's Monument: The Making and Mutation of Meaning in Afrikaner Memory of the South African War" (chap. 2 of this book,

based on a paper presented at the "Rethinking the South African War" Unisa Library Conference, 3–5 August 1998, 5–6) for a fuller discussion of this usage.

2. British Parliamentary Papers (B.P.P.) 1901, Cd. 819, 299, Report of Dr. Kendall Franks on Heidelberg camp, 7 September 1901.

3. E. Hobhouse, *The Brunt of the War and Where It Fell* (London, 1902) was the first work to offer a pro-Boer perspective. Early attempts to examine the camps as a whole from opposing points of view were N. Devitt, *The Concentration Camps in South Africa during the Anglo-Boer War of 1899–1902* (Pietermaritzburg, 1941); S. J. Thomson, *The Transvaal Burgher Camps South Africa* (Allahabad, 1904); A. C. Martin, *The Concentration Camps* (Cape Town, [1957]); J. C. Otto, *Die Konsentrasiekampe* (Cape Town, [1954]). S. B. Spies, in *Methods of Barbarism: Roberts and Kitchener and Civilians in the Boer Republics: January 1900–May 1902* (Cape Town, 1977), analyzes British policy. J. L. Hattingh, "Die Irenekonsentrasiekamp," *Archives Yearbook for South African History* 1 (Pretoria, 1967): 72–201, and J. Brandt–van Warmelo, *Het Concentratie-Kamp van Iréne* (Amsterdam, 1905), both discuss the Irene camp. A substantial number of women's testimonies have also been published, including E. Hobhouse, *War without Glamour or Women's War Experiences Written by Themselves, 1899–1902* (Bloemfontein, 1924); A. M. Badenhorst, *Tant Alie of the Transvaal 1900–1902*, ed. E. Hobhouse (London, 1923); M. A. Fischer, *Tant Miem se Kampdagboek Mei 1901–Augustus 1902* (Cape Town, 1964); E. Neethling, *Should We Forget* (Cape Town, 1902?); M. M. Postma, *Stemme Uit die Vrouwekampe Gedurende die Tweede Vryheidsoorlog Tussen Boer en Brit van 1899 tot 1902* (1925?), republished later as *Stemme Uit die Verlede* (Johannesburg, 1939); and G. E. Bezuidenhout, *Uit die Donker Woud* (Johannesburg, 1946).

4. E. Brink, "Man-Made Women: Gender, Class and the Ideology of the *Volksmoeder*," in C. Walker (ed.), *Women and Gender in Southern Africa* (Cape Town, 1990), 273–92; M. du Toit, "Women, Welfare and the Nurturing of Afrikaner Nationalism: A Social History of the Afrikaanse Christelike Vroue Vereniging, c. 1870–1939" (Ph.D. thesis, University of Cape Town, 1996).

5. See C. Rosenberg, *The Care of Strangers: The Rise of America's Hospital System* (Baltimore, 1987), 189, for the educational role of the hospital; also M. van Wyk Smith, "Telling the Boer War: Narrative Indeterminacy in Kipling's Stories of the South African War," paper presented at the "Rethinking the South African War" Unisa Library Conference, 3–5 August 1998, 6, for an elaboration of this notion of the war as an educative experience.

6. S. B. Spies, "Women and the War," in P. Warwick (ed.), *The South African War: The Anglo-Boer War, 1899–1902* (Harlow, 1980), 164–65. Spies discusses these policies more fully in *Methods of Barbarism.*

7. Balmoral, Barberton, Belfast, Heidelberg, Irene, Johannesburg, Klerksdorp, Krugersdorp, Lydenburg, Mafeking, Meintjies Kop, Middelburg, Nylstroom, Pietersburg, Potchefstroom, Standerton, Vereeniging, Volksrust, Vryheid.

8. Aliwal North, Bethulie, Bloemfontein, Brandfort, Harrismith, Heilbron, Kimberley, Kromelleboog, Kroonstad, Ladybrand, Norval's Pont, Orange River, Springfontein, Vredefort Rd, Winburg.

9. East London, Port Elizabeth, Uitenhage, and Kabusi.

10. Apart from Howick, Pietermartizburg, and Merebank in Durban, there were a number of others of shorter duration.

11. B.P.P., Cd. 853, *Further Papers Relating to the Working of the Refugee Camps...*, 115, Dr. G. Pratt Yule's report, 9 November 1901.

12. D. Cammack, *The Rand at War 1899–1902: The Witwatersrand and the Anglo-Boer War* (London, 1990). It was for this reason that, when Milner was anxious to see some of the Uitlanders return to the Rand, the decision was taken to transfer many of the concentration camp inhabitants to the Natal camps, notably Merebank. Spies, *Methods of Barbarism,* 223–24.

13. In South Africa 13,250 soldiers died of disease, compared with 8,692 who were killed in action or died of other causes. L. S. Amery (ed.), *The Times History of the War in South Africa 1899–1902,* vol. 7 (London, 1901), 25. An inquiry into conditions in the military hospitals confirmed the poor standards of army medicine. W.L.A.B. Burdett-Coutts, *The Sick and Wounded in South Africa: What I Saw and Said of Them and the Army Medical Service* (London, 1900). S. Marks's "Imperial Nursing and the South African War" and "'We Too Were Soldiers': The Experiences of the British Nurses in the South African War," papers presented at the "Rethinking the South African War" Unisa Library Conference, 3–5 August 1998, both contribute more nuanced perspectives on this issue.

14. Spies, *Methods of Barbarism,* 193–96.

15. Ibid., 195.

16. Irene camp, for instance, had six volunteer workers from Pretoria but they were turned away after the Fawcett Committee reported unfavorably on them.

17. B.P.P., Cd. 819, *Reports, &c. on the Working of the Refugee Camps,* 46, W. R. Tucker's report on Krugersdorp camp, 23 May 1901.

18. Ibid., 23, 24.

19. Bloemfontein, Aliwal North, Norval's Pont, Springfontein, Orange River, and Kimberley.

20. Van Reenen, *Emily Hobhouse,* 121–33; J. Fisher, *That Miss Hobhouse* (London, 1971), 139–72.

21. H. H. Hewison, *Hedge of Wild Almonds: South Africa, the Pro-Boers and the Quaker Conscience 1890–1910* (Cape Town, 1989), 190–91.

22. Ibid., 207–24.

23. Prior to his arrival in South Africa, Franks had had an outstanding professional career in Dublin, where he had pioneered the use of antiseptic and aseptic surgery. He came to South Africa because of his wife's health and, when war broke out, was attached to the British forces as a consulting surgeon. In 1904 he was knighted for his services. *Dictionary of South African Biography* [*DSAB*], vol. 5 (Pretoria, 1987), 277–78.

24. B.P.P., Cd. 893, *Report on the Concentration Camps in South Africa by the Committee of Ladies Appointed by the Secretary of State for War* (London, 1902).

25. Postma, *Stemme Uit die Vrouwekampe.*

26. Spies, *Methods of Barbarism,* 364, considers Hobhouse's tables to be accurate; Otto, *Die Konsentrasiekampe,* also includes statistics, while Thomson, *The Transvaal Burgher Camps,* has figures for the Transvaal in 1902.

27. Fetter and Kessler, "Death by Concentration: The Burgher Camps at Barberton and Nylstroom" (unpublished paper, n.d.), and "Scars from a Childhood Disease" (unpublished paper, n.d.).

28. Camps with the Highest Death Rates (per 1,000 per annum):

Kroonstad	347.58
Bloemfontein	338.67
Heilbron	290.00
Bethulie	289.58
Nylstroom	287.50
Klerksdorp	271.58
Brandfort	270.33
Standerton	265.33
Vredefort Road	225.83
Mafeking	225.83
Middelburg	220.42
Springfontein	214.75

29. Camps with the Highest Mortality Rate per Month (per 1,000 per annum):

April 1901	Johannesburg	347
May 1901	Bloemfontein	1,554
June 1901	Potchefstroom	453
July 1901	Middelburg	622
August 1901	Kroonstad	1,173
September 1901	Vredefort Rd	634
October 1901	Brandfort	1,256
November 1901	Nylstroom	675
December 1901	Bethulie	779
January 1902	Bethulie	408
February 1902	Winburg	145
March 1902	Heilbron	234

30. C. Simkins and E. B. van Heyningen, "Fertility, Mortality, and Migration in the Cape Colony, 1891–1904," *The International Journal of African Historical Studies* 22, no. 1 (1989): 96–97.

31. B.P.P., Cd. 902, *Further Papers Relating to the Working of the Refugee Camps*, 27. These figures were supplied by Dr. John Gregory, M.O.H. for the Cape Colony. The British government played up the fact that comparative figures for Cradock in 1900 were 814.05, with a coloured infant mortality rate that exceeded births.

32. Fetter and Kessler suggest that "most of these reports were limited to the level of mortality rather than the cause of it"; see their "Scars from a Childhood Disease," 3. In fact from May until the end of December 1901 causes of death in the Transvaal were published. Although diagnoses varied in quality, they are sufficient to glean a picture of the main diseases of the camps.

33. B.P.P., Cd. 819, Cd. 853, Cd. 902. These figures are tentative since diagnoses varied wildly from camp to camp.

34. "Wasting away of the body"—*Concise Oxford Dictionary*, 1964.

35. This was a particularly vague category appearing under a variety of headings

including congenital debility, inanition (*Concise Oxford Dictionary*, 1964: "Emptiness, especially from want of nourishment"), malnutrition, and asthenia (*Concise Oxford Dictionary*, 1964: "Loss of strength, debility").

36. Rickets, caused by a deficiency of vitamin D, which is supplied by (among other sources) sunlight. It was common in European industrial cities but also occurred in sunny countries where children were too completely protected from the sun. K. F. Kiple, *The Cambridge World History of Human Disease* (Cambridge, 1993), 978–79.

37. These are now common causes of mortality in South African shanty towns where, lacking gas or electricity, paraffin is widely used as fuel.

38. Kiple, *Cambridge History of Disease*, 871–75.

39. B.P.P., Cd. 853, 114.

40. Spies, *Methods of Barbarism*, 185–86. Rations varied slightly depending on time and place, but daily standardized rations in the ORC in March 1901 were as follows (Cd. 819, 37): 1/2 lb fresh or tinned meat, 3/4 lb meal, rice, samp or potatoes, 1 oz coffee, 1 oz salt, 2 oz sugar, 1/12 tin condensed milk. Condensed milk was not included in the Transvaal rations, but otherwise the portions were similar.

41. B.P.P., Cd. 819, 15.

42. Ibid., 216.

43. My thanks go to Ingrid Schloss of the Department of Nutrition at the University of Cape Town for doing this analysis on the ORC ration scale above. She adds that calcium was particularly deficient, as were vitamins A, C, E, and riboflavin. Her analysis was based on the assumption that all the rations were eaten, but there is considerable evidence that the meat, particularly, was frequently rejected. The addition of milk and potatoes considerably improved the diet.

44. See the epigraphs that open this chapter.

45. For the problems and complexity of the issues involved in the relationship between malnutrition and epidemic disease see R. I. Rotberg and T. K. Rabb (eds.), *Hunger and History: The Impact of Changing Food Production and Consumption Patterns on Society* (Cambridge, 1985), especially 305–8, and A. G. Carmichael, "Infection, Hidden Hunger and History," 51–66. According to this latter source the relationship between malnutrition and measles and pertussis (whooping cough), two diseases that were prevalent in the camps, has definitely been established, along with diarrheas, most respiratory infections, most intestinal parasites, cholera, leprosy, and herpes.

46. Kiple, *Cambridge History of Disease*, 160.

47. Ibid., 158.

48. B.P.P., Cd. 819, 241. See also Cd. 819, 137; Cd. 893, 119.

49. B.P.P., Cd. 819, 27, 23. Despite this reference to vermin, there is little evidence for typhus outbreaks, a disease associated with malnutrition and lack of sanitation.

50. J. Ross, *A Few Chapters on Public Health: Adapted for South Africa* (King William's Town, 1887), 1; see also K. Figlio, "Social Roots of Medical Ideas: Disease and Civilisation in the 19th Century," *Bulletin of the Society for the Social History of Medicine* 21 (December 1977): 17–18.

51. There is a wide literature on this subject including N. and J. Parry, *The Rise of*

the Medical Profession: A Study of Collective Social Mobility (London, 1976), and W. J. Reader, *Professional Men: The Rise of the Professional Classes in Nineteenth-Century England* (London, 1966); for the Cape see H. Deacon, "Cape Town and 'Country' Doctors in the Cape Colony during the First Half of the Nineteenth Century," *Social History of Medicine* 10, no. 1 (1997): 25–52; E. van Heyningen, "Agents of Empire: The Medical Profession in the Cape Colony," *Medical History* 33 (1989): 450–71.

52. T. Carlyle, *Latter-Day Pamphlets* (London, 1903), 160.

53. R. Mcleod and M. Lewis (eds.), *Disease, Empire and Medicine: Perspectives on Western Medicine and the Experience of European Expansion* (London, 1988), and D. Arnold (ed.), *Imperial Medicine and Indigenous Societies* (Manchester, 1988), were the first of major publications on the subject. See also D. Arnold, *Colonizing the Body: State Medicine and Epidemic Disease in Nineteenth-Century India* (Berkeley, 1993), and M. Vaughan, *Curing Their Ills: Colonial Power and African Illness* (Cambridge, 1991).

54. Cape Archives, M.O.H. 46 f668, Prof. Simpson's report, 22 May 1901.

55. Dr. L. S. Jameson, Rhodes's personal doctor, and Dr. Darley Hartley, who was the founder of Milner's propaganda body, the South African League, are obvious examples of politically active doctors, although neither served in the camps.

56. A. Mayne, *Representing the Slum: Popular Journalism in a Late Nineteenth Century City* (Melbourne, 1990), provides an interesting explanation of the reasons why slums were represented in this way.

57. Rosenberg, *Care of Strangers*, 189.

58. S. Marks, *Divided Sisterhood: Race, Class and Gender in the South African Nursing Profession* (London, 1994), 3–4, 33, 44.

59. B.P.P., Cd. 819, 216.

60. Ibid., 27, Dr. G. Turner's report on Irene camp. Turner had previously been medical officer of health for the Cape and subsequently transferred to the same position in the Transvaal.

61. Ibid., 167–69.

62. Ibid., 326.

63. Ibid., 331.

64. B.P.P., Cd. 893, 50.

65. Ibid., 138.

66. Ibid., 138–39.

67. B.P.P., Cd. 819, 66.

68. Ibid., 325.

69. Ibid., 331.

70. *Staats-Almanak Voor de Zuid-Afrikaansche Republiek,* 1898. The size of the ZAR population is extremely problematic, but the almanac gives a figure of 345,397 for whites. The place of residence of about half the doctors is not included, but 72 were listed for Johannesburg. Only four other towns—Krugersdorp, Potchefstroom, Rustenburg, and Wakkerstroom—are listed as having white populations of more than 10,000. See also E. H. Burrows, *A History of Medicine in South Africa Up to the End of the Nineteenth Century* (Cape Town, 1958), 230–32; B. Spoelstra, *Ons Volkslewe* (Pretoria, 1922), 123.

71. N. Worden, V. Bickford-Smith, and E. van Heyningen, *Cape Town: The Making of a City* (Cape Town, 1998), 30.

72. Rosenberg, *Care of Strangers,* 71–75; Kiple, *Cambridge History of Disease,* 11.

73. Others had also commented on this practice, including Dr. W. G. Atherstone in 1857. N. Mathie, *Dr. W. G. Atherstone 1814–1898: Man of Many Facts: Pseudo-Autobiography,* vol. 1 (Grahamstown, 1998), 253.

74. Rosenberg, *Care of Strangers,* 130.

75. B.P.P., Cd. 819, 163–65, Franks's report on Irene camp.

76. See also B.P.P., Cd. 819, 240; A. W. Sloan, *English Medicine in the Seventeenth Century* (Durham, 1996), 62–63; G. S. Preller (ed.), *Die Dagboek van Louis Trichardt (1836–1838)* (Cape Town, 1938), 45.

77. Preller, *Dagboek van Louis Trichardt,* 45.

78. J. F. Juritz and Co., *List of Halle Medicines* (Cape Town, 1870); and "Pharmaceutical Notes from the Cape Colony," *The Chemist and Druggist* 27, 15 October 1885, 600; both cited in M. Ryan, *A History of Organised Pharmacy in South Africa 1885–1950* (Cape Town, 1978), 3; Burrows, *History of Medicine,* 190–91. Today these products are manufactured by Lennon of Port Elizabeth and are widely available in pharmacies as a form of alternative medicine.

79. Spoelstra, *Ons Volkslewe,* 124.

80. Hobhouse, *War without Glamour,* 55.

81. B.P.P., Cd. 893, 10.

82. Van Zyl, *In die Konsentrasiekamp,* 39. For other references to the preference for Dutch medicines see Neethling, *Should We Forget?* 110–11; Fischer, *Kampdagboek,* 44.

83. B.P.P., Cd. 819, 193. Apparently this was common practice. See Spoelstra, *Ons Volkslewe,* 124.

84. Ibid., 193. Opium was widely used in patent medicines in Britain, particularly in the popular children's medicine, "Godfrey's Cordial." Despite some legislative restrictions, Smith believes that its use continued to be widespread until 1914. F. B. Smith, *The People's Health 1830–1910* (London Burrows, 1979), 95–97.

85. Burrows, *History of Medicine,* 155.

86. Smith, *People's Health,* 343–45. Smith points out that the production of patent medicines in Britain had become an extremely lucrative industry by the middle of the nineteenth century. Although the medical profession waged war against their indiscriminate use, the British government was reluctant to ban such a prosperous business and the doctors were able only to prevent the use of the more dangerous substances.

87. For a list of herbs commonly used by the Voortrekkers see Burrows, *History of Medicine,* 192–93; also Spoelstra, *Ons Volkslewe,* 125–28.

88. Burrows, *History of Medicine,* 192.

89. B.P.P., Cd. 819, 50, 240. Tantalizingly, Burrows claims that Louis Trichardt referred to the use of goat dung for measles, but I have been unable to verify this claim. Preller, *Trichardt Dagboek,* 145, cited in Burrows, *History of Medicine,* 192.

90. B.P.P., Cd. 943, 7. Burrows, *History of Medicine,* 192, also cites a similar practice in the treatment of pneumonia.

91. B.P.P., Cd. 819, 240.

92. Sloan, *English Medicine,* 61.

93. Smith, *People's Health,* 109–10, 334–42.

94. J. W. Appleyard, *The War of the Axe and the Xhosa Bible. The Journal of the Rev. J. W. Appleyard,* ed. J. Frye (Cape Town, 1971), 11; J. FitzGerald at the Grey Hospital in King William's Town refers to this practice on a number of occasions, for instance, Kaffrarian Museum, J. FitzGerald *Letterbook,* vol. 1, J. FitzGerald to the Chief Commissioner, Fort Murray, 6 December 1856.

95. B.P.P., Cd. 934, 50. See also Cd. 819, 58.

96. Cd. 934, 7. M. Groeneveld, "The Role of the Nurse in the Military Medical Services in the Republican Forces during the Anglo Boer War," paper presented at the "Rethinking the South African War" Unisa Library Conference, 3–5 August 1998, is a useful reminder that modern medicine was sometimes acceptable to the Boers. In Heidelberg, Transvaal, the wife of the British district surgeon, together with local Boer women, established a small hospital to care for the wounded. Transvaal Archives, A432. Such examples reinforce the possibility that traditional healing practices were more prevalent among lower-class or more isolated communities.

97. Badenhorst, *Tant Alie,* 239.

98. Fischer, *Tant Miem Fischer,* 44.

99. B.P.P., Cd. 819, 163, Franks's report on Irene camp. As noted above, mortality from this source was fairly low.

100. Ibid., 162, Dr. K. Franks's report on Irene camp. "Miss Van Warmlo" was Johanna van Warmelo, better known as Johanna Brandt, whose experiences were published in *Het Concentratie-Kamp van Iréne.* Ironically, Franks was clearly impressed by this lively young woman whom he mentions on several occasions. The fear of starvation, commonly expressed, arose from the practice of feeding enteric cases only on milk.

101. Van Zyl, *Uit die Konsentrasiekamp,* 22; Free State Archives, A 248. Mrs Bessie Venter, Diary, 1899–1902, 42.

102. Neethling, *Should We Forget?* 110; Postma, *Stemme Uit die Vrouwekamp,* 15.

103. Van Zyl, *Uit die Konsentrasiekamp,* 21.

104. Postma, *Stemme Uit die Vrouwekamp,* 18.

105. B.P.P., Cd. 819, 364.

106. Ibid., 114. Extended nursing was often a means of spacing births in preindustrial societies.

107. One has only to look at descriptions of perfect domesticity in the works of authors such as Dickens or Trollope to see how neatness and cleanliness are used to define the feminine ideal.

108. H.E.C. Armstrong, *Camp Diary of Henrietta E. C. Armstrong: Experiences of a Boer Nurse in the Irene Concentration Camp, 6 April–11 October 1901* (Pretoria, 1980).

109. Du Toit, "Women, Welfare"; "Maria Elizabeth Rothmann," in *DSAB,* 5.661–63.

110. Marks, *Divided Sisterhood,* 68–70.

CHAPTER 10

The Politics of War

Lord Kitchener and the Settlement of the
South African War, 1901–1902

KEITH SURRIDGE

IN JAMES MORRIS's concise yet quintessential pen-portrait, Lord Kitchener is described as a man "powered by an overriding and ceaseless ambition," who consequently "maddened many colleagues by his ruthless determination to succeed."[1] Morris's evaluation is a familiar one, but Kitchener's single-mindedness was successful: he attained the highest honors and offices and died a national hero.

A substantial literature has been generated by the Kitchener legend, and most of it has focused on his career during the First World War. From the 1930s, once the mythology surrounding Kitchener had largely evaporated, appreciations of his life and work became more critical, and this remained the tenor of the historiography until quite recently. Now the tide has turned somewhat, and Kitchener has received the attentions of revisionists, who have gone some way to rehabilitate the reputation of the fallen idol.[2] So far, however, there has been little reconsideration of Kitchener's tenure as commander-in-chief in South Africa in 1901 and 1902.

In his memoirs, Lloyd George remarked that "there is no greater fatuity than a political judgment dressed up in a military uniform,"[3] an opinion of Kitchener's political ability that has held good ever since. Historians of the South African War have generally regarded Kitchener in this light and believe that his military decisions were made with complete disregard for their political consequences. Kitchener is viewed as inconsiderate and motivated solely by his desire to succeed to the command of the Indian army. In 1952, Edward Crankshaw took a rather critical view of Kitchener, who, he believed, "was not interested in the political future of South Africa. He was a soldier of genius. He wanted to shut down and have done with this war which was no longer a war, and get away to India, where there was work to be done of the kind he understood."[4] Writing at the same time, Leo Amery felt that Kitchener "was desperately anxious to get away and was little concerned with the political consequences." A decade later, G. H. Le May stated that the enormous armies employed by the British during the war "were handled by their commanders with a disregard for the political consequences of their operations" and reiterated that Kitchener was desperate to take up the Indian command. In subsequent decades this view has been perpetuated by Donald Denoon and Thomas Pakenham.[5] So far, historians have been too ready to see the flawed Kitchener rather than the discerning one.

This chapter intends to show that Kitchener's thinking was more considered than such scholars supposed, something that so far has not been emphasized within the context of the South African War. Although it cannot be denied that Kitchener was intensely ambitious, he was, nevertheless, guided by a genuine political and diplomatic foresight, and his wartime pronouncements and decisions were based on an intuitive grasp of the situation in South Africa. I argue that there was more to Kitchener than a desire to succeed to a less exacting and more glamorous post in India. Kitchener was very much aware of the social complexity of Anglo-Boer relations, and he realized from an early point that some form of accommodation would have to be made with the Boers. Thus, throughout his tenure as commander-in-chief, Kitchener not only conducted a military campaign, he strove also to secure a settlement that would ensure that Anglo-Boer hostilities would never occur again. Consequently, Kitchener's outlook brought him into dispute with his colleague Sir Alfred Milner, the High Commissioner, who did not want to see an accommodation reached with the Boers. Thus, an ideological edge was added to the basic differences engendered by the various demands of guerrilla warfare. For Kitchener, this meant that his military decisions did have a political aspect to them, one that would affect South Africa after the peace. Therefore to understand the postwar settlement, and some of the difficulties encountered by Milner during the war and after, it is necessary to appreciate the role played by Kitchener beforehand.

Empire and the British Army

In his recently published Lees Knowles lectures, Hew Strachan has drawn attention to the importance of the empire as "the most consistent and most continuous influence in shaping the army as an institution."[6] The empire gave soldiers not only experience of several types and styles of warfare, but also political responsibility. In South Africa, throughout the nineteenth century, soldiers were often appointed as governors, which office was often combined with that of commander-in-chief: Sir George Napier, Sir Harry Smith, and Sir George Cathcart fulfilled these dual roles during the Cape frontier wars against the Xhosa, while Sir William Butler assumed the mantle of high commissioner when Sir Alfred Milner took leave between late 1898 and early 1899. On two occasions, during troubled times in South Africa, the British government utilized the prestige of one of the Victorian era's most famous soldiers, Sir Garnet Wolseley. In 1875 and then in 1879–80, Wolseley was made first governor, then high commissioner, of Natal, Zululand, and the Transvaal in order to overawe recalcitrant colonists and Boers and defeated Zulus. Elsewhere in Africa, soldiers such as Lord Cromer went on to assume high political office after leaving the army. In other instances, serving officers took up minor administrative posts in newly acquired territories: for example, Henry Brackenbury (later quartermaster-general of the army), when one of Wolseley's junior officers in Cyprus, organized a military police force and reformed the island's prison service.[7] Thus, wherever one looked, army officers, both serving and retired, were vital to the smooth running of imperial administration.

During a campaign, army commanders were usually free from political scrutiny and often combined sweeping political powers with those of their military position. For example, Wolseley was given full responsibility in the Gold Coast/Ashanti campaign in 1874, owing to the lack of imperial government locally and the need for comprehensive powers to ensure that the demands of the campaign were met. In northern Nigeria Brigadier-General Sir Frederick Lugard was made high commissioner in 1899 and subsequently used his position and authority to launch an attack against the Sokoto Caliphate, which by 1903 was absorbed into the British Empire. Lugard then set about constructing a political settlement in the area, which later became the future imperial policy of indirect rule.[8]

In Kitchener's case, his first real taste of administrative duties came when he was made governor of the eastern Sudan in 1886, which at that time comprised the port of Suakin and its environs. Kitchener's main responsibility was to defend the town against the forces of the Mahdi, who had earlier conquered the Sudan and killed General Gordon in Khartoum. Here he soon realized that brute force alone would never succeed in pacifying a determined and recalcitrant enemy. Kitchener used a "carrot and stick" approach by dealing with friendly Sudanese, and those wishing to repudiate Mahdism, in a straightforward and diplomatic manner, while at the same time enforcing a trade blockade with the interior in order to induce the more resilient followers of the Mahdi to surrender. In 1889, Cromer, then Sir Evelyn Baring, acknowledged that "Colonel Kitchener's view of the situation a year ago was more correct than my own." It was reported to him that "no one possessed so much influence with the heads of tribes as Colonel Kitchener."[9] From the outset, therefore, Kitchener already appreciated that the conduct of military operations also required sound administrative judgment and a capacity to "know your enemy."

Kitchener's first major military command, also in the Sudan, between 1896 and 1898, was characterized by the continual interference of his political superior, Lord Cromer. Only when the conquest of the Sudan was complete did Kitchener manage to shake off Cromer's restraining hand. Kitchener ruled the conquered province himself, brooking no interference and determined, as Philip Magnus has written, not to be "scolded like a schoolboy by Cromer."[10] Kitchener's governorship of the Sudan was fairly short-lived owing to the conflict in South Africa, but in some ways (although not in others) he revealed his appreciation of local conditions and the need for British officers and officials to show initiative and consideration. He advised them to exercise a paternal outlook, to respect religion and to frown on slavery. Nevertheless, his actions toward the southern areas of the Sudan, which until November 1899 concealed the last remaining Mahdists, gave an early indication as to how he would deal with the Boer commandos. In the southern Sudan, Kitchener did little to alleviate famine conditions in order that the Mahdists might be starved of not only supplies, but also local support. In the end, the Mahdist leader, the Khalifa, was betrayed, hunted down, and killed.

Up to the outbreak of the war in South Africa, Kitchener's experience of politicians had not been a particularly pleasant one. At times Cromer had been overbearing, and to a man of Kitchener's disposition—ambitious, self-obsessed, and self-important—the shackles imposed by political requirements had sometimes been too much and had led to occasional bouts of histrionics. During an episode when Cromer tried to forbid the final advance on Omdurman and Khartoum, Kitchener was beside himself and told a friend that he wished he were dead.[11] Consequently, when Kitchener was ordered to South Africa in December 1899, he was given a new arena in which to acquire military glory, but this time with full knowledge of the pitfalls of civil-military relations.

Rethinking Milner's Role

By the time Kitchener became commander-in-chief in late 1900, Sir Alfred Milner had already been in South Africa for three years and had acquired set views regarding the future settlement of the country. These had two important aspects: first, to ensure the gold-mining industry was able to function smoothly and profitably, so as to provide the wealth necessary for the reconstruction of South Africa; second, as he explained to Major Hanbury Williams, to safeguard the new South Africa by relying on the British element, which he hoped to sustain through the encouragement of immigration, and by anglicizing the Boers as far as possible through the medium of an English education.[12] Milner's policies have come under thorough scrutiny from historians in the recent past, which should come as no surprise considering that he was the personification of British aims and expectations before, during, and after the war. In two articles, Shula Marks and Stanley Trapido paid particular attention to Milner's policies during his time as high commissioner between 1897 and 1905. The second article, written in 1992, was more concerned with the debate on the centrality of the gold-mining industry in the origins of the war and engaged forcefully with the views expressed by Andrew Porter and Iain Smith.[13] It is not my intention to enter that already overcrowded debate; rather, I intend to add to the discussion contained in the first article, written in 1979. This dwelt more on the view, forwarded by historians such as G. H. Le May, Leonard Thompson, and Donald Denoon, that Milner apparently won the war but then lost the peace. According to Marks and Trapido this proposition is wrong: Milner's policies were ultimately successful because under his guidance postwar South Africa became a viable and thriving capitalist state. Milner, expertly supported by his "kindergarten" of Oxford graduates, "laid the foundations for a state which not only reflected the demands of twentieth century imperialism but also fulfilled them." His achievement, it is argued, should not however be ascribed to the "idiosyncrasies of a single individual, but has to be located in the context of late-nineteenth century British history and its articulation with the imperatives of southern African capitalist development." For Marks and Trapido that context is to be found in the "pervasive ideology of social imperialism," which incorporated ideas of social and economic planning designed to ensure the survival of Britain and the British race as a great imperial power and people. Thus Milner's preoccupation with securing a stable, capitalist state in South Africa, in alliance with the gold-mining industry before, during, and after the war, can be contextualized within the need to secure the British empire from rivals without and from social decay within. Basically, Milner's interventionist government in South Africa was to be a precursor of what he hoped to achieve in Britain at some future date.[14]

Although this objective formed a central part of Milner's grand design, it also had a significant political dimension that needs to be stressed in any discussion of his policy aims. To Milner, each was vital to the other if his schemes were to succeed overall. In the same letter to his former military secretary cited above, Milner explained that

> On the political side, I attach the greatest importance of all to the increase of the British population. British and Dutch have to live here on equal terms. If ten years hence, there are three men of British race to two of Dutch, the country will be safe and prosperous. If there are three of Dutch to two of British, we shall have perpetual difficulty.[15]

Milner realized subsequently that social reconstruction on this scale was unfeasible, but he insisted nevertheless "that the institution of responsible government must await the establishment of a population with some experience of free institutions and clean justice, and the development of an electorate which had had time to settle down and to learn to differ on other than racial lines."[16] Milner hoped that imperial authority would last long enough for his plans to be realized, but here too his political hopes were dashed; the former republics were granted responsible government before he felt his plans had matured. If Milner saw this concession as a failure of his policies, a point Marks concedes, then it is worth inquiring as to why this happened.[17] Basically, this can be answered by stating that self-government was achieved largely due to the efforts of the Afrikaner political leadership, which was provided by those who had led the military effort against the British: Louis Botha, Jan Smuts, Christiaan de Wet, and J.B.M. Hertzog. In this respect, therefore, Leonard Thompson is right to suggest that "in white ethnic terms, Milner's grand design did not succeed. He failed to create the conditions he had considered essential before it would be safe to establish self-government in the former republics."[18]

Changing the Political-Military Equation

When Kitchener succeeded Roberts as commander-in-chief, the guerrilla war was well underway and not going too well for the British. The primary task before the new commander, therefore, was the defeat of the Boer commandos. An invading army that seeks to subjugate enemy territory often has to confront resistance in the form of guerrilla warfare. One of the major requirements in the fight against guerrillas and their near cousins, insurgents, is the close cooperation of the civil and military authorities; this means the generals ought to be intimately attuned to political objectives.[19] Both sides should be thoroughly agreed on what their forces need to do to defeat the guerrillas and to ensure the acceptance of the new order. This implies, however, that the military are subordinate to the politicians, because the army is pacifying the occupied area so that tangible political aims can be realized. In essence, the military are being directed by the political authorities. This perception of civil-military relations has a long pedigree not only during a war against guerrillas, but in warfare in general, and is, according to Strachan, "a reflection of the degree to which we have been brainwashed by Clausewitz, or rather by the glosses of others on Clausewitz." Too much attention has been focused on Clausewitz's famous dictum, that "war is not a mere act of policy but a true political instrument, a continuation of political activity by other means." This suggests that in the conduct of military operations, the soldiers are beholden to the considerations of the politicians. However, Strachan explains that this is Clausewitz theorizing, but there was also a practical side to Clausewitz, who argued that "war in general, and the commander in any specific instance, is entitled to require that the trend and designs of policy shall not be inconsistent with the means." In light of this remark, Strachan suggests that "Strategy is at once *both* political *and* military. The political objectives in war have to be moderated by what is militarily feasible: the formulation of a practicable plan must be bounded by military capabilities. Thus the notion that politics is the superior and stronger element in the equation distorts the reality."[20] In South Africa, though the military objectives were plain enough—the defeat of the Boer commandos— the political objectives were not so clear-cut because the British government was unable to decide on a policy beyond the idea of "unconditional surrender." This left Milner to formulate his own schemes, and he then tried to persuade the government of their utility and to enforce their consideration on Kitchener. However, Kitchener needed reassurance that the commandos would not try to hold out indefinitely because they were outraged by the prospect of what awaited them if they gave in, while Milner demanded the army conduct its operations to suit his views. Therefore Kitchener was given scope to consider the political ramifications of his actions, and Milner was left to discover, as S. E. Finer has remarked, that warfare enables soldiers to augment their political authority, which becomes apparent usually when politicians challenge the soldiers' conduct of operations.[21]

If Milner's views are to be interpreted within the social context in which they were formulated, in this case social imperialism and national efficiency, then it is equally necessary to consider Kitchener's views in the same light, because opinion within the army was also influenced by these anxieties and the debates they generated. At the time, army officers were deeply concerned about the health and condition of recruits, and ultimately about the fitness of the British race to fight a major European war. Many of them regarded the

Boers as superior specimens because of their rural upbringing and military skills honed on the veld. Indeed, the Boers were often seen as replenishment stock and a welcome addition to the empire.[22] We should not be surprised to find, therefore, that Kitchener also shared this outlook, although how far is difficult to judge owing to a paucity of evidence. Kitchener, it seems, never waxed lyrical about the Boers as some officers did. According to his first major biographer, Sir George Arthur, his former personal private secretary, Kitchener knew quite well what was at stake in South Africa:

> The cause for which Kitchener had worked till physical energy was nearly exhausted, and nerves strained almost beyond snapping point, was neither that of the Kimberley diamond dealer nor that of the Uitlander on the Rand. He looked and laboured, for a South Africa *pacificata*, a South Africa *amica*, who would harness all her energy to England's effort in the years when that effort would surely be made.[23]

Leaving aside the hyperbole and the hindsight, Arthur's remarks do carry a grain of truth. Kitchener was aware that the Boers would never agree to a settlement in which they were subordinated to capitalist interests. In other words, the Boers had to be made to realize that after their military defeat there was still an important role for them to play in South Africa. As he explained to the Secretary of State for War, St. John Brodrick, in January 1901, the Boers would not want to be ruled by capitalists and would want some guarantee that they would be granted self-government in the future: "They are I believe absurdly afraid of getting into the hands of certain Jews, *who no doubt wield great influence in this country.*"[24] In Kitchener's case his views were not based on a romantic, nostalgic, or emotive perception of the Boers, unlike those of many of his officers. His thinking was predicated on a more straightforward, logical, one might say cold-blooded appreciation of South Africa's, and ultimately Britain's, requirements. What has tended to obscure this view of Kitchener is the almost illogical way he presented his arguments to the British government. Nevertheless, for Kitchener, the idea that the Boers would still have to play a major role in South Africa after the war was a basic, self-evident truth.

To find the first real intimation of Kitchener's political thinking it is necessary to start with the abortive peace talks between Kitchener and Louis Botha in March 1901. Basically, these talks, despite Kitchener's enthusiasm for them, were always tentative owing to the fact that the Boer leadership had no intention of surrendering and the British government had no desire to be lenient. Unsurprisingly, the negotiations broke down, the crux of the problem being the failure to agree on an amnesty for the Cape Colony rebels. Kitchener's exasperation at this failure was made apparent to Brodrick. In his dispatch of March 22, 1901, Kitchener commented at length on the talks and concluded:

> My views were that once the Boers gave up their independence and laid down their arms the main object of the Govt. was attained, and that the future civil administration would soon heal old sores and bring the people together again. After the lesson they have had they were not likely ever to break out again.

Then he made rather an ill-considered remark, suggesting why the war was being fought. "We are now carrying the war on," he wrote, "to be able to put 2 or 300 Dutchmen in prison at the end of it. It seems to me absurd and wrong and I wonder the Chancellor of the Exchequer did not have a fit."[25]

This letter confronted the issue that now began to drive Kitchener and Milner apart: what were the government's war aims? From this point, Kitchener began to undermine the links between the Cabinet and Milner, who then were more or less at one over the desire to see the Boers surrender unconditionally. Kitchener's willingness to talk to the Boer generals provided an alternative scenario, one to which the British government later succumbed, and one to which Milner remained opposed to the very end.

It is clear that the failure of the Middelburg talks rankled with Kitchener for some time afterward and influenced the tone of several of his subsequent dispatches, which were noted for their bitterness and absurd proposals. The anger Kitchener dissipated in his correspondence should not influence our judgment of his state of mind, however. Kitchener was letting off steam and his suggestions should not, therefore, be taken at face value, which some historians have done. At a second glance, it is possible to see some purpose in Kitchener's pronouncements, absurd though they seem. On April 26, 1901, he vented his anger at Botha by describing him as an "excellent actor" with the mind of a "pettifogging attorney," although he then went on to give what Thomas Pakenham has described as "sound political advice":

> If you had unconditional surrender tomorrow I think you would have to follow very closely the lines laid down in the abused terms of peace in dealing with the Boers, that is to say, if you really want to live in peace and security with them and be able to give them self-government later. The strain on the empire will be very great if we are to have our Alsace 6,000 miles away instead of next door as Germany has.[26]

In a subsequent dispatch, dated June 21, 1901, Kitchener's invective was given added piquancy because he was being pressured by the government to make concrete declarations about his military aims and the resources at his disposal. At that time Milner was in London working on the government to accept his scheme, the aim of which was to make future negotiations unnecessary. The Boers would be made to surrender unconditionally or wither away in the inhospitable regions of the old republics.[27] Kitchener's reactions at this time were borne on the back of immense frustration, even anger, at this political interference, although the tenor of his message remained clear amongst the absurdities of the dispatch. Here, Kitchener said, the government had two choices if they wanted to see an end to the war: first, he famously suggested that the entire irreconcilable population be deported to either Madagascar or Fiji; second, he proposed they should make peace with terms, and that once the Boers had given up their independence they should be left to quarrel among themselves. As Kitchener remarked, the objections raised against the peace terms in England and South Africa (by the Cape loyalists) had "made it almost impossible for Boer and Briton to settle down peaceably, so this course having failed, we are, as far as I can see, forced into the more objectionable first course proposed." Although Kitchener also went on to describe the Boer population as "savages with a thin white veneer," there is, nevertheless, plenty in the dispatch indicating that by and large Kitchener admired the Boers and rated them far more highly than he did the other South African whites (the colonists and the Uitlanders). He considered the Boer to be superior in courage, knowledge of the country, horsemanship, work hardiness, and determination, and added "I know this is not the view of the loyal colonist, but when have they ever told us one single thing that turned out to be true?" In conclusion, Kitchener feared that "the so called loyalists will never live at peace with the Boers, though we may force the latter into a cessation of hostilities, we shall I fear never bring them down to consider themselves thoroughly defeated, and to be ready to crouch and lick the feet of the local white settler whom they despise. In South Africa, it may be said, with more or less truth that 'the tail wags the dog.'" And to ensure that the government was fully aware that a long, unedifying war was before them, he added, "I have therefore very little hope in a permanent settlement by any intermediate course between the extreme ones above mentioned."[28]

All this revealed the general line of Kitchener's thinking, one that consistently advocated the necessity of some form of negotiated peace in order to preserve the future security of postwar South Africa and the empire. It was a line to which other soldiers were attached as evidenced by the Intelligence

Division, which, in answer to some questions from the Colonial Office on the sagacity of confiscating the property of the Boer leaders, stated that "To enforce confiscation in the case of particular men only, such for example as Louis Botha, would be unjust and would put against us in the future those leaders whose support is necessary to the peaceful settlement of the country."[29]

Joseph Chamberlain subsequently attacked Kitchener's ideas in a letter to Brodrick in August 1901. Although he saw the weaknesses in Kitchener's ideas, Chamberlain recognized them for what they were—threats and bluffs—and remarked that "I am afraid Lord Kitchener attaches too much importance to bluff, but it is a very dangerous game when you do not hold all the cards." Chamberlain felt that to issue a series of proclamations to which Britain could not give effect would make the government look ridiculous "in the eyes of the Home and Foreign nations."[30] While Chamberlain was right to be skeptical about implementing wholesale schemes of banishment and confiscation, Kitchener had, nevertheless, made a telling point; without these threats and bluffs the only alternative would be a bitter, hard-fought campaign that might leave the Boers implacable enemies of Britain forever. Kitchener's expedients were meant, first and foremost, to complement his military operations and were not designed to be alternative strategies. They were meant to add venom to the sweep-and-scour policy pursued on the veld and were expected to be the straw that finally broke the Boer camel's back.

However, in July 1901 Milner and Kitchener reached a consensus on the issue of banishing the Boer leaders from South Africa. The original idea was Kitchener's, and its endorsement by Milner gives an insight into his thoughts and intentions. Milner had stood out against the Botha peace talks because they went against virtually everything he aimed for. He had prefaced his rejection by earlier declaring that surrendered Boers, who from "disgust at the continuance of the present aimless and ruinous resistance would stand by us, ought to be encouraged to resist those still out on commando."[31] As mentioned earlier, during the Botha talks he had completely rejected calls for a rebel amnesty, believing such a concession would have "a deplorable effect" upon opinion in the Cape Colony and Natal.[32] Milner had conspicuously refused to treat with the Boer leaders and had signaled his disagreement with Kitchener's own outlook. However, after rejecting Kitchener's wild idea to banish the irreconcilable population, even though as Kitchener told Lord Roberts, "a little bluff now would finish the war," Milner opted instead for a modified version—the banishment of the Boer leadership.[33] His support of Kitchener carried the government, and on August 7, 1901, a proclamation was issued that threatened Boer officers and "leaders of armed bands" with permanent banishment if they had not surrendered by September 15. This expedient, like many others, was a failure; few, if any, Boer commandos were intimidated by it. Nevertheless, as a statement of intent it provides ample evidence as to who Milner thought were his main enemies.[34] In fact, later in December, Milner clarified his position in a terse statement to Chamberlain: "I never lose sight of the fact that the 'conciliation' of our former enemies ought never to be our *first* object. Our first object, & duty, is to make sure of the position by strengthening the British element, whether the Boers like it or not."[35] Ironically, on that very same day, December 20, 1901, Kitchener informed Brodrick that the army had in fact promised Boer leaders they would not be banished if they surrendered with their men.[36]

Kitchener versus Milner

The peace negotiations that began in April 1902 and concluded with the signing of the Treaty of Vereeniging on May 31 provided the final battleground for the competing views of Milner and Kitchener. Earlier, Milner laid his cards firmly on the table by declaring to the Johannesburg business community that "it is no use to wheedle, the only thing is imperturbably to squeeze, and to keep our clemency and our conciliation ... for the Boers who surrendered, instead of lavishing our blandishments on those who still continue to fight."[37] Milner was now convinced that the military situation was efficacious, that the Boers were actually losing the fight and given more time would surrender voluntarily. As he told Clinton Dawkins: "The advantage for the future of a war ending as it is ending is enormous. I can see my way to settlement with a free hand, but if we are to be hampered by terms, I shall be happy to hand the impossible tangle to somebody else."[38]

Milner soon discovered that he would be hampered by terms, but he decided to soldier on rather than resign. Between April and May 1902, he tried unsuccessfully first to scupper the talks that had begun with a meeting on April 12 between Kitchener and the Boer generals at Pretoria, and then to hold out for terms he believed would provide some hope for the future. Milner, however, continued to remain pessimistic even when the British government offered the Boers terms. When the Boer generals took these to their men in mid-April 1902, Milner clarified his misgivings:

> No doubt the policy of general immediate forgiveness has great disadvantages, especially for the new governments. To have not [only] the more conciliatory Boers like Botha & Delarey [*sic*], but bitter enemies, like Steyn & Smuts, living in our midst from the outset, will be a great handicap.[39]

On the other hand, terms were exactly what Kitchener believed to be necessary to end the conflict and provide a lasting settlement. The peace talks at Vereeniging gave Kitchener the opportunity to converse with fellow soldiers in the same way he had dealt with Major Marchand at Fashoda—firmly but fairly. After the successful conclusion of that incident, when France withdrew from the southern Sudan, Lord Salisbury praised Kitchener's "chivalrous character and diplomatic talents."[40] At Vereeniging, the government put their faith in these abilities once again.

That Kitchener fulfilled this commission with some diplomatic aplomb was remarked on soon after by Erskine Childers, in the fifth volume of *The Times History,* which covered the Vereeniging talks. On the whole, Childers's views have been rather neglected despite the insight they provide into the reasoning behind Kitchener's methods during the South African War. In his analysis, Childers alluded to the same argument used by Kitchener in April 1901, and asked a profound question about the whole nature of British aims and policies during the war, one the British government had been reluctant to face until the very end. "Was it not true," Childers asked, "and was it not generally felt to be true, that the Middelburg terms only represented what, in the last resort, we should be compelled under any circumstances to grant?" In other words, whether the Boers surrendered unconditionally or not, the terms Kitchener had offered Botha at Middelburg in 1901 would still have to provide the foundation upon which British policy in South Africa would be based thereafter. This in fact was what Kitchener had been telling the British government since those talks collapsed. To him, the idea of unconditional surrender was a fallacy and a dangerous one. Childers acknowledged this in his account: if there had been no terms some Boers would have continued to fight; some might have invaded the Cape Colony again, which would have made the task of capturing them very difficult, as had been the case before. The British would, of course, still win, but they would have gained little advantage from doing so, and in the process they would have expended more time and money the British public would be ill-disposed to part with.[41]

Thus by 1902 the British government had come to acknowledge the value of many of Kitchener's earlier pronouncements—hence the Cabinet's desire to see substantial talks take place.[42] The war was not going to be won by the British trying to crush the Boers and their lifestyle. Indeed, Kitchener had never had any faith in Milner's schemes in this respect, especially the bid to anglicize the Boers. As early as April 1901, Kitchener had argued that the split between the bitterenders and the handsuppers was one that might be exploited in the future, but the attempt to silence the Afrikaner language was ill-advised: "if they are not treated fairly they will come together again. Take the Dutch language for instance; if you absolutely and openly attempt to suppress it entirely they will start their own schools and keep up the language as a national sentiment." Furthermore, Kitchener had written that "I think the only safe way for the future is to put in as many English and oversea colonials as possible and give them self-government as soon as possible."[43] By November, however, during one of his pessimistic phases, Kitchener revealed that his outlook had altered—the result, no doubt, of a greater awareness of South African social realities. Kitchener now questioned whether the return of the irreconcilables after the war would really bring peace and there might be the possibility of another rebellion. Yet there was little that could be done. "Sending out British colonists will I fear hardly change the situation; a few may be isolated on farms but the great majority will be massed in Johannesburg and will greatly increase the anxiety of any military authority that has to deal with the situation."[44] Thus on two major policy issues, which were attempted after the war, Kitchener had already signaled his disagreement and fundamental mistrust. He, at least, had already seen the inherent weaknesses in "Milnerism."

Unsurprisingly, therefore, during the talks at Vereeniging, Kitchener and Milner disagreed.[45] From the start, Kitchener believed that the Boer leaders would have to be treated with some generosity because "none of them like the idea of being handed down to posterity as traitors who gave their country away."[46] Consequently, Kitchener was prepared to be lenient over two major conditions: an amnesty for rebels and money for the rebuilding of farms, both of which points had political ramifications for Milner's schemes, because they threatened to upset the loyalists upon whom Milner counted heavily. Indeed, Milner and Kitchener differed openly on the financial compensation question, with Kitchener willing to see that the Boer leaders' promissory notes were honored in order that they should keep their prestige.[47] The implications of this financial settlement being accepted disturbed Milner, who felt that such a "gift" would be received badly by the Transvaal loyalists, who would have to bear the costs themselves. That is, Milner felt that the mining industry would be reluctant to see their taxes spent on rehabilitating irreconcilable Boers. Politically, the grant had wider implications because if the Boer leaders handed out British money, it might cement their political leadership afterwards. Knowing that he might lose on this issue, Milner tried to get the grant distributed through his office. Indeed, Milner was thwarted on this point by Chamberlain himself, his main backer in the Cabinet, who was unwilling to see the talks fail over a monetary dispute.[48]

Although Milner managed to gain amnesty terms acceptable to the colonial governments and the promise that the money would be distributed by a special commission, he nevertheless felt he had lost out at the talks. He never accepted the Vereeniging settlement and knew that it had weakened his position in postwar South Africa because the Boer generals remained as leaders of Afrikanerdom. A year later he told Spenser Wilkinson that the South African struggle continued:

> It has changed its character: it is no longer war with bullets, but war it still is. It is quite true we hold the winning cards, but it is not true we have won the game, and we cannot afford to lose a single trick.[49]

Against Anglicization

As the peace talks got underway, Milner let slip some of his pent-up feelings in a letter to his former military secretary:

> I hate all negotiations, but having to negotiate, I recognize that one must give up something which one need not have given up.... The obvious principle seems to be, that the man who is going to run the whole show should arrange the conditions.[50]

The conditions however were not arranged by Milner, and Kitchener's victory in this sense was a truly damaging one. It has been said by one historian that "we may confidently exclude the peace negotiations and the treaty of Vereeniging as having any major bearing upon the failure of [postwar] imperial policy."[51] Yet this was not how Milner regarded it; indeed, one might say Milner's subsequent troubles stemmed from it. An essential prerequisite for Milner's future policies was that the British should quickly and decisively defeat the Boers and by so doing discredit the Boer authorities and leave the population bewildered and leaderless. This of course did not happen, and the guerrilla war ensured that the Boers gained a credible leadership after many had fled to Europe or had been captured. Milner regarded these leaders as potential maggots in an otherwise healthy apple, and the idea of negotiating with them was anathema. His desire to banish these men by the proclamation of August 7, 1901, showed his determination to ensure that potential obstacles were removed from a future British South Africa. The sort of leadership Milner envisaged would be provided by the likes of J. G. Fraser, an English-speaking, longstanding resident of the Orange Free State, who had actually worked his way through the administration of this Afrikaner-dominated republic. Fraser had implored Milner not to forget the handsuppers and not to discontinue English education in the concentration camps. This was, more or less, the language Milner liked to hear, and Fraser was "one of the men whom we must rely upon in the future."[52]

This was not the view of Kitchener, who might not have stated his case as eloquently as Milner had, but who nevertheless had a clear picture in his mind's eye of the future development of South Africa. For the British to succeed, they would have to work in tandem with the Afrikaners. Kitchener, like many of his army contemporaries, was a political general whose skills had been honed in the empire, either through confrontation with imperial or local politicians or through the exercise of political responsibility. It was a facet of leading Victorian soldiers that is often neglected by historians, and in Kitchener's case ridiculously so. It is worth remembering that the army did much to fashion the nature of British rule throughout the empire. When we also remember the concerns in Britain at the time about national decline and racial degeneration, then with all this in mind Kitchener's desire to placate the Boers after their military defeat is readily understandable, as are the sentiments expressed in his farewell speech from South Africa:

> There may be individuals amongst our former opponents whose characteristics and methods we do not like or approve of; but, judged as a whole, they are, I maintain, a virile race and an asset to the British Empire, for whose honour and glory they may I hope before long be fighting side by side with us.[53]

Consequently, Kitchener knew what was feasible and dismissed Milner's ideas and aims to reconstruct South Africa socially—anglicization was not a workable policy. Kitchener felt first and foremost that the Afrikaners had to be defeated militarily, then they would be amenable to suggestion afterward. Otherwise, as he told ministers in 1901, extreme measures would have to be utilized if the British were not only to defeat the Boers, but to secure peace thereafter. While he was in control of the campaign, Kitchener pursued it with relentless energy and determination. Yet it was not done simply to win glory, although that aspect was always welcome to Kitchener. To achieve lasting fame, Kitchener also felt that he had to secure a lasting victory; he did not want to end up like Roberts, who in 1900 had proclaimed loudly that the war was over. This was acknowledged by Milner, who told Chamberlain that "K won't go, unless he can do so with glory & saying that he has finished the war. But the war can only be formally finished, either by a compact—wh. Heaven forbid!—or by his catching the last Boer, wh. may take years." All this meant, as Milner suggested earlier in the same letter, "that there is an honest, complete fundamental difference of view between us, on the whole

SA question, wh. necessarily leads to our taking opposite views on almost every practical issue."[54]

What did this mean then for the political side of "Milnerism"? First, it meant that the Boer generals provided the leadership for the political struggle against Milner, as he feared it might. Milner's myopic attitude toward the handsuppers certainly closed a breach in the nationalistic armor of the Afrikaners. Denoon suggests that Milner never believed the Afrikaners could be divided and that it did not matter whether the generals were acknowledged as postwar leaders or not.[55] If that was the case then why did Milner want to secure their banishment? Could it be that knowing he had failed to destroy the leadership, Milner accepted that there was now very little chance to perpetuate the schism within Afrikaner society?[56] The activities, real or imagined, of the Boer generals seemed to haunt Milner. In 1903, he tried to co-opt them onto the Transvaal legislative council in an attempt to undermine their credibility, but it backfired when they refused, merely reinforcing their image as national leaders. The following year, Milner became increasingly concerned about their activities. He explained to Chamberlain's successor, Lyttelton, "that a political movement is afoot among the Boers of both new colonies [and] is engineered by the leaders of the men who surrendered at Vereeniging and the 'deputation' sent to Europe during the war."[57] In 1905, following his resignation, Milner sought to put his successor, Lord Selborne, in the picture and advised him against the "political" Boers, "who will leave no stone unturned, to make you see through their spectacles. They are 'British citizens,' and fully prepared to take advantage of that position, yet they are working against everything British."[58] When the former Boer republics were granted self-government in 1907, by Campbell-Bannerman's Liberal ministry, everything Milner had apparently worked for, from the political perspective, appeared to have fallen apart. He had demanded at Vereeniging that the issue of self-government be a dead letter and not open for discussion for he did not envisage such a concession until his plans had matured. Now this had come to pass, and under the leadership of those he had identified earlier as his and Britain's implacable enemies. For this of course he had Kitchener to thank. Thus the Treaty of Vereeniging had played a part in influencing imperial policy because it provided for an alternative political vision of a British South Africa, one opposed to that envisaged by Milner, who remained ungracious in defeat. In the end, all he could say was "I think it all sheer lunacy."[59]

Notes

1. J. Morris, *Pax Britannica* (Harmondsworth, 1969), 239.

2. For a brief review see J. Bourne, "Goodbye to All That? Recent Writing on the Great War," *Twentieth Century British History* 1 (1990): 93–97.

3. D. Lloyd George, *The War Memoirs of David Lloyd George,* vol. 1 (London, 1938), 451.

4. E. Crankshaw, *The Forsaken Idea: A Study of Viscount Milner* (London, 1952), 96.

5. L. Amery, *My Political Life,* vol. 1 (London, 1953), 165; G. H. Le May, *British Supremacy in South Africa* (Oxford, 1965), 36, 127; D. Denoon, *A Grand Illusion: The Failure of Imperial Policy in the Transvaal Colony during the Period of Reconstruction 1900–05* (London, 1973), 23; T. Pakenham, *The Boer War* (London, 1982), 561.

6. H. Strachan, *The Politics of the British Army* (Oxford, 1997), 74.

7. Ibid., 76; E. Spiers, *The Late Victorian Army 1868–1902* (Manchester, 1992), 158–59.

8. See for example J. Lehmann, *All Sir Garnet: A Life of Field-Marshal Lord Wolseley 1833–1913* (London, 1964), chap. 8; B. Vandervort, *Wars of Imperial Conquest in Africa 1830–1914* (London, 1998), 190–95; M. R. Lipschutz and R. K. Rasmussen (eds.), *Dictionary of African Historical Biography* (London, 1978), 126–27.

9. Cited in Sir G. Arthur, *Life of Lord Kitchener,* vol. 1 (London, 1920), 160.

10. Philip Magnus, *Kitchener: Portrait of an Imperialist* (Harmondsworth, 1968), 183.

11. Ibid., 139.

12. T.R.H. Davenport, *South Africa: A Modern History,* 4th ed. (London, 1991), 204; Milner to Hanbury Williams, 27 December 1900, in C. Headlam (ed.), *The Milner Papers,* vol. 2 (London, 1933), 242–45.

13. S. Marks and S. Trapido, "Lord Milner and the South African State Reconsidered," in M. Twaddle (ed.), *Imperialism, the State and the Third World* (London, 1992), 80–94.

14. S. Marks and S. Trapido, "Lord Milner and the South African State," *History Workshop Journal* 8 (1979): 54–55.

15. Milner to Hanbury Williams, 27 December 1900, in Headlam (ed.), *Milner Papers,* 2.242.

16. The quote is from Headlam (ed.), *Milner Papers,* 2.244.

17. S. Marks, "Southern and Central Africa, 1886–1910," in J. D. Fage and R. Oliver (eds.), *The Cambridge History of Africa,* vol. 6 (Cambridge, 1985), 488.

18. L. Thompson, *A History of South Africa* (London, 1990), 145.

19. T. Mockaitis, *British Counter-Insurgency, 1919–1960* (London, 1990), 2–3; Strachan, *Politics of the British Army,* 173–74.

20. Strachan, *Politics of the British Army,* 1.

21. S. E. Finer, *The Man on Horseback: The Role of the Military in Politics,* 2d ed. (London, 1988), 64.

22. For more on this see K. Surridge, "'All You Soldiers Are What We Call Pro-Boer': The Military Critique of the South African War 1899–1902," *History* 82, no. 268 (1997): 582–600.

23. Arthur, *Life of Kitchener,* 2.105–6.

24. Kitchener to Brodrick, 25 January 1901, Kitchener Papers, Public Record Office, Kew (hereafter KP PRO), 30/57/22/Y18. For more on civil-military relations see K. T. Surridge, *Managing the South African War, 1899–1902: Politicians v. Generals* (Woodbridge, 1998).

25. Kitchener to Brodrick, 22 March 1901, KP PRO 30/57/22/Y33–36.

26. Kitchener to Brodrick, 26 April 1901, KP PRO 30/57/22/Y48; Pakenham, *Boer War,* 500.

27. "Conversations with Lord Milner," Memorandum by J. Chamberlain, 31 May– 2 June 1901, Birmingham University Library, Joseph Chamberlain papers (JC), JC 13/1/144. This was circulated to the Cabinet on 12 June.

28. Kitchener to Brodrick, 21 June 1901, KP PRO 30/57/22/Y62.

29. Notes by the Intelligence Division, c. 13 June 1901, PRO, Cabinet Office Papers (CAB), CAB 37/57/58.

30. Chamberlain to Brodrick, 20 August 1901, JC 11/8/40. See also S. B. Spies, *Methods of Barbarism? Roberts and Kitchener and Civilians in the Boer Republics: January 1900–May 1902* (Cape Town and Pretoria, 1977), 235–37.

31. Milner to Chamberlain, 11 December 1900, PRO, Colonial Office papers, CO 417/296/fos. 429–30.

32. Milner to Chamberlain, 3 March 1901, PRO, CAB 37/57/34.

33. Milner to Chamberlain, 26 July 1901, JC 13/1/166. Kitchener cited in Spies, *Methods of Barbarism?* 237.

34. Spies, *Methods of Barbarism?* 238–39.

35. Milner to Chamberlain, 20 December 1901, JC 13/1/206.

36. Kitchener to Brodrick, 20 December 1901, KP PRO 30/57/22/Y113(b).

37. Quoted in Headlam (ed.), *Milner Papers,* 2.319–23.

38. Milner to Clinton Dawkins, 16 January 1902, Bodleian Library, Oxford, Milner Papers, MP IV/B/221/fos. 172–76.

39. Milner to Chamberlain, 21–23 April 1902, JC 13/1/235.

40. Cited in Magnus, *Kitchener,* 176; also T. Royle, *The Kitchener Enigma* (London, 1985), 186.

41. L. Amery (ed.), *The Times History of the War in South Africa,* vol. 5 (London, 1907), 573–74.

42. Marsh, *Joseph Chamberlain: Entrepreneur in Politics* (London, 1994), 519–22.

43. Kitchener to Brodrick, 26 April 1901, KP PRO 30/57/22/Y48.

44. Kitchener to Brodrick, 15 November 1901, KP PRO 30/57/22/Y102.

45. *The Times History,* for example, stated that Kitchener's conciliation and Milner's intransigence were "a curious inversion of the roles usually assumed by the soldier and the statesman respectively." Amery (ed.), *Times History,* 5.575.

46. Kitchener to Brodrick, 30 March 1902, KP PRO 30/57/22/Y136.

47. See Headlam (ed.), *Milner Papers,* 2.349.

48. Milner to Chamberlain, 21 May 1902, JC 13/1/254–55; Chamberlain to Milner, 22 May 1902, PRO, CAB 37/61/95.

49. Milner to Wilkinson, 27 April 1903, NAM, Spenser Wilkinson Papers, 9011/42/17.

50. Milner to Hanbury Williams, 30 April 1902, in Headlam (ed.), *Milner Papers,* 2.341.

51. Denoon, *Grand Illusion,* 230.

52. Milner to Chamberlain, 23 April 1902, JC 13/1/235.

53. Cited in Arthur, *Life of Kitchener,* 2.106.

54. Milner to Chamberlain, 8 February 1902, JC 13/1/209.

55. Denoon, *Grand Illusion,* 25–26.

56. On this point see J. Benyon, *Proconsul and Paramountcy in South Africa: The High Commission, British Supremacy and the Sub-Continent 1806–1910* (Pietermaritzburg, 1980), 295–98.

57. Milner to Lyttelton, 22 February 1904, in Headlam (ed.), *Milner Papers,* 2.518; Benyon, *Proconsul and Paramountcy,* 303.

58. Milner to Selborne, 14 April 1905, in Headlam (ed.), *Milner Papers,* 2.550–53.

59. Milner to Sir H. F. Wilson, 17 April 1907, in Headlam (ed.), *Milner Papers,* 2.534.

CHAPTER 11

Hobson's *The War in South Africa*

A Reassessment

ALAN JEEVES

MOSTLY WRITTEN IN THE months before the Anglo-Boer War began, J. A. Hobson's account of the crisis was one of the first critically to assess British war aims and to argue that the conflict had little, if anything, to do with asserting the political rights of British subjects in the South African Republic (ZAR).[1] He based his findings on personal research and observation during an extended visit to the region in mid-1899. After a period on the Rand, he traveled to Bloemfontein for the Kruger-Milner negotiations and was in Cape Town when war was declared. A correspondent for the *Manchester Guardian,* he compiled the first part of the book from his letters to that newspaper. His preface described the second half as an "economic and political analysis" aimed at assessing the prospects for a "stable" postwar settlement. To a limited extent, the arguments outlined in this journalistic work anticipated parts of the theory famously advanced in his later *Imperialism: A Study* (1902).[2] Looking back, the author himself thought his time in South Africa was "a turning point in my career and an illumination to the understanding of the real relations between economics and politics."[3]

Completed in great haste to catch a market and to influence events, Hobson's book has many deficiencies. Little more than a crude polemic, its account of the origins of the war is notable for an unsavory blend of anti-Jewish comment and unsubstantiated conspiracy theories. However, it also included an astute assessment of the likely future impact of the conflict on South Africa's political economy.

Hobson's Jews of Johannesburg—An Alternative Interpretation

Like most visitors then and now, Hobson found that Johannesburg made a "powerful impression." One came upon the city after a rail journey through a thousand miles of wasteland in which only Bloemfontein had any claim to be a town. The Rand was a "weird mixture of civilisation and savagedom." Concerning its white population, Hobson was struck by the absence of significant numbers of Afrikaners. Beyond government officials and their families, they had "hardly a presence" in a city that was "dominantly, and even aggressively British," but British with a difference that was "mostly due to the Jewish factor." "So far as wealth and power, and even numbers are concerned," he wrote, "Johannesburg is essentially a Jewish town."[4] The Jewish character of the place, he implied, was enough to suggest that its jingoistic character was a sham.

While aware of ethnic and other differences among the mine controllers, he emphasized that, apart from Cecil Rhodes, Charles D. Rudd, and a few others, they too were "chiefly German in origin and Jewish in race."[5] Once "British arms have established firm order," he warned, "this foreign host will return with enhanced numbers and increased power."[6] Whereas in other places and countries such interests mostly kept themselves clear of politics, in the Transvaal they had dominated the political scene through "bribery and other persuasive arts." Not only imperial policy and British public opinion, but also the Transvaal government and the Volksraad, were manipulated by this alien group of financiers. After the South African War, Hobson asserted, "the judicious control of the press and the assistance of financial friends in high places will enable them to establish and maintain a tolerably complete form of boss-rule in South Africa."[7]

Hobson's disparaging comments about Johannesburg's Jewish population were no mere matter of personal prejudice; they also served a definite political purpose. Hobson's assessment was a means both to discredit the Randlords in the minds of his British readers[8] and to challenge the legitimacy of the whole strident campaign for Uitlander political rights. By making the Uitlanders into un-British aliens and strangers, he could call into question the legitimacy and honesty of their political demands and open the way for an alternative interpretation of why the Empire was at war in South Africa. The private profit of grasping Randlords rather than the political rights of British subjects was, in his telling, the real governor of the engine of imperial intervention.

Controlling the Press

Apart from control of Uitlander political organizations, the capitalists, according to Hobson, chiefly exercised their influence through a captured press. Most of the English-language dailies, he wrote (correctly), were under the financial control of Rhodes and Wernher, Beit/Eckstein[9] through their domination of the Argus company. Even the pro-Kruger English press was under capitalist control, he asserted, citing the case of the *Standard and Diggers News*. In his view, none of the Argus company's papers in Johannesburg, the Cape, or Rhodesia had any editorial independence. They existed to promote a conflict that would serve their owners' "business interests."[10]

Quoting John Hays Hammond, Percy FitzPatrick, and others, Hobson used statements of the mining leaders themselves to establish his case that profit rather than politics was at the root of the conflict. He had noted that even some of the ZAR's former friends in the mining industry, notably J. B. Robinson, had predicted a large addition to dividends (Hobson estimated two and a half million pounds) once a more efficient and honest regime was established in Pretoria: "Here is something worth spilling the blood of other people for."[11] Greater profitability was the primary motive of the Randlords in unleashing their press against the Kruger government in a disingenuous campaign for political reform.[12]

Since the Jameson Raid, Hobson insisted, the "entire weight" of the capitalist press had been used to this end. The Randlords recruited W. F. Monypenny as editor of the Johannesburg *Star* and made him one of their instruments for this purpose. To the same end, they later set up a new morning paper, the *Transvaal Leader*. Money was no object; to get its propaganda message home to Britain before the war, the *Leader* alone ran up cable bills of three thousand pounds per month. In support of this thesis, Hobson cited many examples of irresponsible journalism designed to manipulate British politics and public opinion and to provoke the Transvaal government. The London papers got their information mainly from the South African "kept press." At the *Star*, Monypenny fed the line dictated by his financial masters directly to *The Times* itself. Together the *Star* and the *Leader* promoted a plethora of falsehoods that were directly responsible for bringing on the conflict. They vastly exaggerated the political disabilities of the Uitlanders, vilified the Transvaal government unjustly, promoted the cause of British intervention, and agitated against efforts to promote a peaceful settlement. Their objective was to destroy republican independence by both inflaming British jingoism and pushing the ZAR into "defiance and despair."[13]

To establish the illegitimacy of the Uitlanders' political campaign, Hobson emphasized that their main political organizations, the South African League (SAL) and the Uitlander Council, were dominated by mining industry employees and were "distinctly to be regarded as the mouthpieces of the great capitalist groups."[14] His argument that officers of these political organizations were merely servants of mining bosses was wide of the mark, but he correctly saw that much of the agitation was more a creation of a rabid press and SAL jingoes than an expression of real popular sentiment.[15] Once peace was established he expected these elements to continue their efforts to dominate Transvaal politics. Their role extended beyond South Africa to Britain, where they aimed to shape public opinion "by representing the Outlander movement as the passionate appeal of an oppressed and outraged multitude of our fellow-subjects against the tyranny of a Boer oligarchy."[16]

The War for a Racialized State

Hobson was particularly critical of the idea that the South African War was in any sense about securing better treatment of Africans. He pointed out that the one area of broad agreement between British and Boers concerned race policy. While accepting that Downing Street and imperial officials in southern Africa tried to conduct a native policy based on "consideration and humanity," he insisted that they did not call the shots and would not do so in future. Imperial policy, he asserted, would fail completely if it tried seriously to challenge the "strong deep-rooted general sentiment of inequality."[17] Like Milner, Hobson saw that any such effort would promote the unity of the now disrupted white races and probably lead to the separation of South Africa from the empire.

While white South African racial thinking was in part the product of fear and irrational antipathies, it was based fundamentally, Hobson argued, "in solid economic sentiment." Racial domination served the prosperity of the whites and hardly any of them wanted to see changes that might threaten their economic well-being. The most that even the best-intentioned could rise to was a sort of "kindly paternalism" that saw the natives as "permanent inferiors," as "children who can never grow up." The war, he concluded, "may procure for us more gold and more cheap labour, but there is not much likelihood that it will issue even incidentally in any gain to the natives."[18]

Behind Hobson's discussion of South African native policy and his emphasis on the mining industry's economic and political domination lay the germ of an idea that has been hugely influential in South African historiography since the 1960s. His analysis of the South African political economy in 1899 emphasized the essential modernity and economic rationality of white domination. Second, he predicted an intensification of inequality after the war and even more oppressive labor policies, and he saw both as the result of the growth of the mining industry. The primary beneficiary of the harsh labor regime that would follow the war, and its main architect, was the modern industrial system the mines had created. In insisting that the industry's overriding need for cheap labor was the primary motive of the capitalists in fomenting the war, Hobson was thinking less of the immediate situation in the post–Jameson Raid period and more of what he knew about the mining companies' future intentions.[19]

Aware of the high levels of investment in the development of new mines, Hobson understood that a major expansion of mining output was in prospect once hostilities ceased and that the labor needs of the companies would grow correspondingly. The war would serve two purposes. It would sweep away the inefficient Boer oligarchy that had been unable to modernize sufficiently to meet even the mines' current reform demands. More importantly, it would be the means to extend imperial influence and control across southern Africa. By promoting subcontinental unification under British auspices, the war would give the mining capitalists unimpeded access to the labor resources of the entire region. That was why, he wrote, "we are fighting in order to place a small international oligarchy of mine-owners and speculators in power at Pretoria."[20]

Not only did the mines intend drastically to cheapen the cost of black labor, Hobson insisted; they were also determined to reduce white wages. Before the war, the perceived need to maintain political unity among the Uitlanders had led most of the mining companies to refrain from any systematic effort to cheapen the cost of white labor, whether by reducing wages or by substituting blacks for whites in underground work. No such constraints would operate once a pro-capitalist regime was established in Pretoria, and white labor, like the black migrants, would be among the certain losers under the new dispensation.[21]

Despite the centrality of the cheap-labor system in his assertions about the real causes of the war, Hobson was able to produce very little direct evidence to back it up. He did refer to testimony of the mining industry to the 1897 Industrial Commission. He emphasized the companies' complaints about the maladministration of the pass and liquor laws and he cited ongoing complaints of labor shortages on the mines in the months before the war.[22] If he was aware of the modernizing efforts of the Transvaal government and its largely successful reforms to support the gold industry's labor demands, he simply omitted them from consideration, presumably because they did not fit the requirements of his argument. Similarly, while emphasizing the expansionist recruiting ambitions of the companies, he did not see the significance of the Transvaal-Mozambique agreement of 1897 and the Portuguese conquest of southern Mozambique. Together these policies and developments led to a major increase of migrant labor from that source and did much to satisfy the industry's short-term labor needs.[23]

There was no reference either to the importance of these reforms in enabling the mines to reorganize their recruiting system and successfully to impose a 30 percent reduction in black wages.[24] Partly Hobson's cheap-labor thesis emerges by default. It followed from his belief that the campaign for Uitlander political rights was both phony and the product of capitalist manipulation. Since he did not doubt that the mining industry had conspired to launch the war, he had to find a motive sufficiently powerful to offset the threat to the industry's immediate interests that the war, and the cessation of production, profits, and dividends resulting from it, represented. Certain that a vastly expanded recruiting system was their paramount objective, he simply jumped to the conclusion that in that need lay their motive for gross manipulation of the prewar political agitation.

Debating Hobson's Cheap-Labor Thesis

Pointing out that Hobson's cheap-labor thesis as the primary motive for the South African War was more asserted than demonstrated, new research in the 1980s sought to discredit the argument by emphasizing the extent to which the Transvaal government had modernized its economic and administrative policies in direct response to the demands of the mining industry. The conclusion of this work was that the Kruger government had been so successful in meeting the companies' demands for reform in labor policy that "mining capitalists had little reason to intrigue with British Imperialists in a destructive war. By the end of the 19th century the mine owners had no reason to regard the African labour supply as an obstacle to the development of the mining industry; even less was it a *casus belli*."[25]

This finding and other work emphasizing the modernizing efforts of the Kruger state in its last years[26] make a considerable case against the labor dimension of the Hobson thesis. However, as the quoted passage suggests, complete dismissal of the idea that the imperatives of the cheap-labor system played an important role in precipitating the war depended more on what the researcher concluded was objectively the case than on evidence of what the mine controllers themselves thought. If the industry's dissatisfaction with Kruger's labor policies remained great, as Hobson believed, then the mine controllers were likely to act on that perception, however much the government might in fact have done (as shown in recent research) to meet their actual labor needs.

Evidence of the extent of the mining industry's involvement in the prewar political campaign is readily available in the correspondence of the leading company. The letterbooks of Wernher, Beit/Eckstein fully document that firm's political activities in support of economic and political reform in the year before the war while leaving lots of room for differences of interpretation about the firm's motives. At the forefront of the industry from the beginning and managing at least half of its output by 1899, the company's partners did take important steps to revitalize the English-language press. As Hobson correctly noted, they brought in W. F. Monypenny as editor of the *Star*, paid him a huge salary,[27] and gave him a mandate to promote the cause of Uitlander rights in both South Africa and Britain. There is no evidence in company correspondence that they tried to dictate editorial policy to Monypenny or their other editors on a day-to-day basis. However, before the offer was made, extensive discussions with Milner and officials in London took place.[28] The partners knew what they were getting when they appointed him and Monypenny had a very clear idea of what was expected of him. The same firm also authorized the heavy expenditure needed to set up the *Transvaal Leader*, which became a more outspoken critic of Kruger's republic and more jingoistic even than the *Star*. Its mandate was to build Uitlander unity, support the South African League, and broadcast virulent propaganda against the ZAR in South Africa, in Britain, and around the empire.

Partners in H. Eckstein and Company took a number of other steps designed to strengthen the political campaign of the South African League and to give the appearance of spontaneity and general support that the political agitation for Uitlander rights had mostly lacked before 1899.[29] Since some of its partners had been sentenced to death for their involvement in the conspiracy that preceded the Jameson Raid, the firm had been notably cautious in the political arena (as a result of the Raid, some of them were subject to a three-year ban on political involvement). Its senior partners in London had been especially outspoken against direct involvement in the campaign for political rights and in advocating negotiations with the Kruger administration for the sort of economic changes that it did introduce in 1896–97. Though with considerable misgivings, particularly on the part of the senior London partner, Julius Wernher,[30] those cautious policies were largely abandoned in the year that preceded the outbreak of war.

On the basis of the Wernher, Beit/Eckstein correspondence in 1898–99 and other evidence, it can be argued that recent work has gone too far in its complete dismissal of Hobson's cheap-labor thesis. Despite the reforms of the immediate prewar period, most of the leading capitalists, including those previously friendly to the Kruger state, remained dissatisfied with its labor and other economic policies and practices.[31] It is true that labor issues did not figure prominently in the publicly stated demands of the Chamber of Mines in 1899.[32] Nor was black labor anywhere to be found in the so-called

Great Deal negotiations (February–April 1899) when the ZAR offered economic and other concessions to the mining companies in return for their
agreement to withdraw from the political campaign against the republic.[33]
Nevertheless, there is good evidence that the Chamber of Mines remained
concerned that the republic was not doing enough to enforce its pass and
liquor laws or to extract cooperation from the Portuguese and bring to heel
the industry's own rogue recruiters and mine managers who, despite orders
from the top, continued to compete for labor and to bid up recruiting costs.[34]

   Running through the correspondence of Wernher, Beit/Eckstein is also a
set of concerns about governmental structures and priorities, not only in the
Transvaal but also in the subcontinent as a whole. The partners seem to have
understood that a divided white South Africa, with its weak, feuding, and
parochial local governments, would be incapable of serving the long-term
needs of a modern mining industry. Even a reformed and efficient Transvaal
republic would not be sufficient and was likely, they probably realized, to
remain an impediment to wider intercolonial cooperation. Moreover, they
certainly thought that the reforms introduced in 1896–97 did not go far
enough. These reforms did not come close to meeting the agenda the industry laid out before the Industrial Commission in 1897 or even the part of it
accepted by the commission in its recommendations. While impressed with
the improved administration, particularly of the liquor law, introduced by
Jan Smuts when he became Transvaal's Attorney General in mid-1898, they
continued to doubt that such improvements were sufficiently entrenched to
outlast their author, whose political authority and prospects looked uncertain.[35] The Jameson Raid had produced an environment of suspicion and
distrust between the industry and the government that neither side had been
willing or able to dispel.

The Interests of Wernher, Beit/Eckstein

Significant elements in the Volksraad and probably the State President himself quite understandably saw the dominant part of the mining industry
grouped around Wernher, Beit/Eckstein as the enemy of their independence.
Among the mine controllers, what was most alarming was the unpredictable
character of policy making in the ZAR. Politics involved a complex process
of influence peddling and bribery. Fully involved in these intrigues themselves, they found it infuriating that politicians and officials once bought
refused to stay bought and soon sold themselves again to a higher bidder. The
letterbooks of Wernher, Beit/Eckstein in these years are full of complaints
about the machinations of the liquor interests, the dynamite monopolists,

and rival mining companies, most of whom seemed consistently able to out-maneuver and outbid the company in Pretoria.[36] Far from being the masters of the situation, as Hobson thought, the partners were always moaning among themselves about their political ineffectiveness in Pretoria. Beyond actual corruption, politics among the Boers seemed to them completely opaque and produced a government not of settled law but of arbitrary policy making and tyrannical administrative practice at the whim of capricious oligarchs.

An example of the sort of action that most concerned them was the government's new 5 percent profit tax introduced with very little warning at the end of 1898. Although not enforced, the new tax was taken as evidence that the government, despite the efforts of Smuts, remained unpredictable and unable or unwilling to develop an environment favorable to modern industry. Confiscatory measures might be expected at any time. Fearing that the new tax might be applied retrospectively, Georges Rouliot, the ranking Eckstein partner in Johannesburg, wrote to his principal, Julius Wernher, that he expected the worst:

> People will be scared beyond limit and will chuck everything overboard to get out of a country where things of that nature are possible. You will witness the biggest slump the market has ever seen; and if such are the intentions of the government, I personally would be inclined to get out of everything.... These measures will raise such a storm among European shareholders that Kruger will find himself in a bad hole.... But meanwhile it will be the industry that will have to pay for everything. Anyhow all this looks most unhealthy, and I am afraid that '99 will not be a very pleasant nor a very prosperous year.[37]

Even before the new tax was introduced, the partners in Wernher, Beit/Eckstein had been debating among themselves whether they should bother to try to get a reform candidate elected in place of Kruger in the 1898 election, or instead simply hope that the president's arbitrary and intransigent policies would soon bring down the whole structure.[38]

Driven by their labor needs, the mining companies were also beginning to think about issues of law and governance in the region as a whole. With so many of their workers coming from outside the Transvaal, they saw the need for a uniform system of law that could enforce recruiting agreements and labor contracts on a subcontinental basis.[39] They needed a stronger political system that could induce the Transvaal's neighbors, including particularly the Cape, Natal, and Portuguese Mozambique, to admit or better support the industry's recruiters so as to increase the flow from those supply areas. Writing to Julius Wernher in 1898 about continuing difficulties with the labor supply, Percy FitzPatrick exclaimed: "If we had *only* a common law in South Africa, how easy it would be!"[40]

What the Wernher, Beit/Eckstein partners probably hoped to see resulting from a resolution of the South African crisis was a process of governmental consolidation and renovation very much like the one on which they were embarked in their own business. By 1899, they were in the midst of a rigorous effort to restructure and reorganize their holdings on the Rand. To varying degrees, similar efforts were underway throughout the industry, and the so-called group system was already assuming its modern form. At the same time, the agreements made in 1896–97 to reduce black wages marked a major step toward the establishment of the industry's long-sought recruiting monopoly.

For Wernher, Beit/Eckstein this process of reorganization and consolidation eventually transformed what had been a highly successful entrepreneurial partnership into the industry's most bureaucratic and one of its least enterprising firms. In the last years of the nineteenth century, windfall profits through stock-market operations had ceased to be the major source of cash that they had been before the collapse of gold share prices prior to the Jameson Raid.[41] The Rand's dominant producer took the lesson that it should institute efficient modern administrative systems to manage the investments, equipment, and personnel to develop low-grade mining on the vast scale required. Reorganization was also the means by which the company could pull money out of South Africa and diversify its holdings through investment in non-mining, non-speculative bonds and shares, particularly in public utilities.[42] The risk-taking and gambling of earlier years were out; the search was on for stability and steady profits. It seems likely that this shift in priorities also influenced the way the company looked at the political environment.

In summary, the thinking of the partners in the dominant mining house about South Africa's future development was probably driven at least in part by this underlying, though never well-articulated, sense that modern industry in South Africa required a unified and modern political, legal, and administrative system. A stable political order, beyond what they expected would ever be possible under the ZAR, would be a guarantor of future profits and a potential partner in the expansion of the labor system. Reform of the Transvaal state was important but by 1899 was perhaps not enough; also needed was an effort to pull together and renovate the ramshackle political structures of the subcontinent as a whole. Cooperation with the British government as it began to intervene very directly and forcefully in South

African affairs in 1899 may have seemed the most likely means to achieve that result. In any case, as the crisis developed, it was important to become allied with the probable winning side. A British successor government might tax them more heavily but would offer more stable conditions for business, an established legal framework and administrative system across the region, a better guarantee of enhanced flows of labor, and greater security of revenues and profits.

Rereading Hobson's War

Hobson's assessment, despite its many shortcomings, revealed the significance of these longer-range developments very effectively. His fondness for anti-Semitic conspiracy theories probably explains why later historians have mostly tended either to dismiss or to disregard his interpretations.[43] That his research tended to be superficial and his use of evidence selective did not help his credibility. Yet he did capture a major direction of change in the mining industry and in the trajectory of the subcontinental political economy overall. Particularly important was his insistence on the modernity of South African racial policies and their congruence with industrial development. He predicted large-scale mining expansion after the South African War and saw that it was likely to produce an intensification of inequality, an even more ruthless application of labor controls, and further impoverishment of the black working class.

Based on the Randlords' increasing involvement in the political struggle through their control and use of the press, Hobson concluded that they had written off Kruger's government. Although recent scholarship has argued that the government had fully met the mines' most important reform demands and removed labor as a *casus belli,* that was not Hobson's conclusion. Despite the findings of his recent critic, there is good evidence for his insistence that reorganization and further development of the regional labor supply remained very high on the Chamber of Mines' political agenda and that dissatisfaction with labor policies and administration in the Transvaal remained great. If his suggestion that labor issues made the mine controllers expanders of the British Empire was an overstatement,[44] he saw that a regional labor empire was in prospect. Its maintenance and development, he accurately predicted, would require ever greater interference beyond established imperial frontiers.[45]

Of course, Hobson in his polemical attack on the Randlords made claims far beyond his evidence. He was writing as much to influence public opinion and the direction of imperial policy as to inform. Since he had concluded that the rapid expansion and intensification of the mines' coercive labor system was likely to be the major outcome of the war, he simply asserted that achieving this result must have been their main motive in promoting the conflict. He drew his account of the causes and motives of the war from his predictions of its likely effects and outcomes. That fallacy, however, should not detract from his suggestive assessment of the modernity of the South African racial system, its essentially industrial character, and the impact of the War of 1899–1902 on its probable course of future development.

Notes

1. J. A. Hobson, *The War in South Africa: Its Causes and Effects* (London, 1900).

2. The question of how much Hobson drew from his South African experiences for the later book has generated a growing literature, including: R. V. Turrell, "Finance ... the Governor of the Imperial Engine: Hobson and the Case of Rothschild and Rhodes," *Journal of Southern African Studies* 13 (1987): 417–32; N. Etherington, "Theories of Imperialism in Southern Africa Revisited," *African Affairs* 81 (1982): 385–407; P. J. Cain, "J. A. Hobson, Financial Capitalism and Imperialism in Late Victorian and Edwardian Britain," *Journal of Imperial and Commonwealth History* 13, no. 3 (1985): 1–28, 5–6.

3. Quoted in M. Freeden (ed.), *J. A. Hobson: A Reader* (London, 1988), 19.

4. Hobson, *War in South Africa,* 10–11.

5. Ibid., 189.

6. Ibid., 195.

7. Ibid., 196.

8. T. Lloyd, "Africa and Hobson's Imperialism," *Past and Present* 55 (1972): 130–53, 150.

9. That is, Wernher, Beit and Company (Julius Wernher; his partner, Alfred Beit; and their associates), the London partnership, and H. Eckstein and Company (named for Hermann L. Eckstein, a founding partner, who died in the early 1890s), their Johannesburg subsidiary, also a private partnership.

10. Hobson, *War in South Africa,* 206.

11. Ibid., 229–30.

12. Ibid., 230–31, 239–40.

13. Ibid., 206–28.

14. Ibid., 204–5.

15. A conclusion confirmed in the research of D. Cammack in *The Rand at War, 1899–1902: The Witwatersrand and the Anglo-Boer War* (Berkeley, 1990), 32.

16. Hobson, *War in South Africa,* 205.

17. Ibid., 291.

18. Ibid., 295.

19. Ibid., 229–40.

20. Ibid., 197.

21. Ibid., 240.

22. Ibid., 231–32.

23. P. Harries, "Capital, State and Labour on the 19th Century Witwatersrand: A Reassessment," *South African Historical Journal* 18 (1986): 25–45; A. H. Jeeves, *Migrant Labour in South Africa's Mining Economy: The Struggle for the Gold Mines' Labour Supply, 1890–1920* (Johannesburg, 1985), 43–44.

24. Harries, "Capital, State and Labour," 42.

25. Ibid., 45.

26. P. Harries, *Work, Culture and Identity: Migrant Labourers in Mozambique and South Africa, c. 1860–1910* (Portsmouth, 1994), 129–37; C. van Onselen, *Studies in the Social and Economic History of the Witwatersrand, 1896–1914,* vol. 1: *New Babylon* (Johannesburg, 1982), 13.

27. Barlow Company Archives (B.C.A.), Sandton, H. Eckstein Collection (H. E.), H. Eckstein and Company to W. F. Monypenny, 26 January 1899.

28. A. N. Porter, *The Origins of the South African War: Joseph Chamberlain and the Diplomacy of Imperialism, 1895–99* (Manchester, 1980), 180–82.

29. A. H. Jeeves, "The Rand Capitalists and the Coming of the South African War, 1896–1899," in S. Jones and J. Inggs (eds.), "Business Imperialism in South Africa," *Journal of South African Economic History* 11, special issue (1996): 55–81, 77–80 (reprint of a 1974 article); Cammack, *The Rand at War,* 32.

30. R. V. Kubicek, *Economic Imperialism in Theory and Practice: The Case of South African Gold Mining Finance, 1886–1914* (Durham, N.C., 1979), 70.

31. B.C.A., H. E., G. Rouliot to J. Wernher, 10 December 1898, reporting on discussions during a meeting of the Chamber of Mines' executive committee; also Rouliot to A. Beit, 19 November 1898, and to J. Wernher, 20 February 1899; National English Language Museum, Grahamstown, Sir Percy FitzPatrick Papers, FitzPatrick to A. Beit, 27 October 1898; to J. Wernher, 28 November 1898 and 4 March 1899.

32. Chamber of Mines, Annual Report (C.M.A.R.) for 1899, 39.

33. Speech by FitzPatrick at meeting of Uitlander leaders, 13 March 1898, in A. H. Duminy and W. R. Guest (eds.), *FitzPatrick: South African Politician: Selected Papers 1897–1906* (Johannesburg, 1976).

34. For example, C.M.A.R. for 1898, 79–86, and 1899, 84, and *passim* in both reports.

35. B.C.A., H. E., G. Rouliot to J. Wernher, 20 February 1899.

36. For example, B.C.A., H. E., G. Rouliot to J. Wernher, 8 February 1897 and 10 December 1898.

37. B.C.A., H. E., G. Rouliot to J. Wernher, 19 November 1898.

38. A. Duminy and B. Guest, *Interfering in Politics: A Biography of Sir Percy FitzPatrick* (Johannesburg, 1987), 47–48.

39. C.M.A.R. for 1898, 68.

40. FitzPatrick to J. Wernher, 30 July 1898, in Duminy and Guest, *FitzPatrick: South African Politician.*

41. Kubicek, *Economic Imperialism,* 70–72.

42. M. Fraser and A. Jeeves (eds.), *All That Glittered: Selected Correspondence of Lionel Phillips, 1890–1924* (Cape Town, 1977), 13–15.

43. Harries, "Capital, State and Labour," 45; I. R. Smith, *The Origins of the South*

African War, 1899–1902 (London, 1996), 398; A. N. Porter, "The South African War (1899–1902): Context and Motive Reconsidered," *Journal of African History* 31 (1990): 43–57, 44; N. Etherington, *Theories of Imperialism: War: Conquest and Capital* (Beckenham, 1984), 40–83; J. S. Marais, *The Fall of Kruger's Republic* (Oxford, 1961), 324; but for more sympathetic approaches see Turrell, "Finance," 419, 431; and Cain, "J. A. Hobson," 5–6.

44. Hobson, *War in South Africa,* 233.

45. J. Crush et al., *South Africa's Labor Empire: A History of Black Migrancy to the Gold Mines* (Boulder, Colo., 1991), 33–54.

CHAPTER 12

The Jewish War

Anglo-Jewry and the South African War

RICHARD MENDELSOHN

WRITING IN THE *Contemporary Review* in January 1900, J. A. Hobson, the radical journalist and future theorist of imperialism, made his famous accusation that the South African War was in large part Jewish in origin.[1] This charge was repeated and elaborated upon in *The War in South Africa: Its Causes and Effects,* the polemical volume he published during the same year, which drew on his experiences as a visitor to South Africa during the crisis months in mid-1899. Hobson charged that behind the war's patriotic façade lurked a conspiracy of mining capitalists, mainly Jewish, who sought the overthrow of the Boer republic and its replacement by an administration more supportive of their needs, particularly for a supply of cheap and docile black labor. Hobson's evidence for the Jewish character of this war-making conspiracy was what he took to be the prevalence of Jewish names among the Randlords.[2]

Hobson was not the first to claim publicly that this was a Jewish war. John Dillon, the member for East Mayo, had suggested as much in the parliamentary debate in October after the outbreak of the South African War. So had the *Catholic Times* and the socialist Henry Hyndman, who on the eve of the Boer ultimatum had published a piece about "The Jews' War in the Transvaal."[3] But Hobson, it appears, was the most influential of the accusers. The views he expressed in his prominent article and his widely reviewed book were directly echoed in Liberal pro-Boer circles and in Labour. For the Labour MP, John Burns, speaking in the House of Commons in February 1900, "the British Army, which used to be for all good causes the Sir Galahad of History, has become in Africa the janissary of the Jews.... Wherever we examine there is the financial Jew operating, directing, inspiring the agencies that have led to this war."[4] "Jewish financiers," and their coded equivalents, "cosmopolitan capitalists," were stock villains in the Liberal pro-Boer

pamphlet campaign against the war, while trade unionists at the TUC meeting in September 1900 expressed their concern that the war was being fought
to secure the gold fields for "a number of cosmopolitan Jews, most of whom
had no patriotism and no country."[5]

These widespread views and oft-repeated charges, which drew on contemporary anti-Semitic fantasies of the operation in the world of an insidi-
ous and overweening Jewish power, were perceived as both defamatory
and threatening by the established Jewish community of Britain. Through
its preeminent journal, the weekly *Jewish Chronicle,* the self-styled "Organ
of Anglo-Jewry,"[6] the community contested what were seen as outrageous
claims. The *Chronicle* denounced the general proposition of a sinister and
overwhelming Jewish mastery: "Jews," it stated categorically, "possess no
disproportionate amount of financial power."[7] It also rejected the specific
notion of a Jewish capitalist conspiracy manipulating the course of events in
South Africa; "the story of the Transvaal Jews setting the match to the Transvaal powder magazine is an idle and malicious fiction," it insisted.[8] It held
up to ridicule Hobson's evidence for such a conspiracy. Hobson's claim that
the Randlords were predominantly Jewish, based on his cataloguing of their
Jewish-sounding names, was mocked:

> We have always contended that though many of the capitalists of the Rand
> may, as the joke has it, "speak in broken accents," it did not follow that they
> were therefore Jews.... many of the capitalists have nothing but a German
> cognomen to justify the ascription to them of Jewish blood; whilst several
> of the German financiers who were Jews, have long ago left their people for
> their people's good, and yielded their immortal souls unto the care of the
> Roman-Catholic Church.[9]

Furthermore, while the Randlords were not necessarily Jewish, the Jewish
Randlords were not necessarily anti-Kruger: "some of the wealthiest Jewish
capitalists like Lewis and Marks ... are among Kruger's most determined
friends." Albu was a "strong pro-Boer," while Emanuel Mendelssohn was
the proprietor of "the Government organ," the *Standard and Diggers' News.*
Contrary to Hobson's view, "many Jews, chiefly of Continental origin, were
so far from soliciting the interference of England that they rallied to President Kruger."[10]

Contesting Hobson's Accusation

Behind the ridicule, however, lay a very real anxiety about the damage the
Hobson accusation might do. The reason for concern was that the charge—

and the South African War itself—coincided with a crisis within the relation-ship between the Jewish community and the host society. Anglo-Jewry had been a settled community that had achieved full civil and political equality by the last quarter of the nineteenth century, a community that was fully anglicized and, for all its religious distinctiveness, comfortably integrated into British life despite the residual prejudices of British society. This calm was shattered in the 1880s and 1890s when Czarist persecution and economic hardship sent a wave of Jewish refugees westward. The arrival of many of these "alien" Jews in Britain, and their concentration in the East End of Lon-don, with all the attendant problems of overcrowding, of "sweated" labor, and of perceived competition with native workmen, precipitated an ugly and menacing anti-Semitic clamor—dressed up in England as anti-alienism—of the sort Anglo-Jewry had hoped it had long since escaped (and which, it was painfully aware, was reaching a new crescendo in continental Europe). An anxious Anglo-Jewry's solution to the problem was to encourage the onward migration of these refugees, and to accelerate the acculturation of those who chose to stay in England by means of a range of anglicizing agencies—schools, clubs, welfare organizations, and charities.[11]

Anglo-Jewish behavior during the South African War was conditioned by this crisis. As we shall see, Anglo-Jewry seized upon the distant imperial war as an opportunity to demonstrate the depth of its patriotism and of its embed-ment in English society, to give the lie to those who, witnessing the influx of exotic eastern European Jews into Britain, saw the Jew as alien and therefore essentially unpatriotic and unassimilable. The South African War became for Anglo-Jewry a great exercise of affirmation of its Englishness, a Jewish war certainly, but not in Hobson's negative sense, rather in the wholly positive sense of signaling Anglo-Jewry's full membership in the national community.

Preaching Jewish Patriotism

At the start of the war, the Chief Rabbi, Dr. Hermann Adler, whose politi-cal views it appears were close to those of the government, gave the lead. He composed a special War Prayer, which he directed should be recited every sabbath for the duration of the conflict in every synagogue in the British Empire falling under his spiritual jurisdiction. This instruction carried con-siderable weight—in religious terms Anglo-Jewry was more centralized than its great Russian and American counterparts—and the Chief Rabbi's auth-ority was far-reaching, though not unchallenged. The prayer, in Hebrew and English, called on the divine to "shield" the army "in the day of battle" and to "gird them with victory, so that the war may be speedily ended."[12]

In a widely publicized sermon delivered in the North London Synagogue on the fourth (Jewish) sabbath of the war, Adler reiterated his call for "a speedy and decisive victory" and enthusiastically endorsed the war policy of the government.

> our statesmen have anxiously striven for the maintenance of peace. But they also recognised the fact, that of all policies none is more danger-ous, none more calculated to sap a nation's greatness than the advocacy of peace at any price. There are dangers even worse than war with all its horrors. If we would permit the Continental powers to entertain the idea, that England only cares for the counter and the till, that, absorbed in her race for wealth and lapped in smooth prosperity, she were indifferent to the interest of her sons in distant lands, and that she could accept insults with equanimity, then the end of her greatness would be in sight. Hence it was that the Government of our Queen had no alternative but to resort to the fierce arbitrament of war, with the view of restoring just and righteous government to the Transvaal, and to vindicate the honour of England.

Adler ended with a ringing appeal for generous contributions by all Jews to the various war funds. Specially bound copies of the sermon were sent to the Queen, the Prince of Wales, Salisbury, Balfour, and Chamberlain. Six hundred copies were distributed to the press throughout the country. The prayer was also "considered of sufficient public interest to be put on the 'tape' at the House of Commons."[13]

Adler's lead was taken by his subordinate rabbis. It would seem that even those who before the war had questioned the wisdom and justice of British policy in the Transvaal, duly conformed. One who had privately threatened to omit the routine Prayer for the Royal Family from his services if Britain went to war with the Transvaal now dutifully read out the War Prayer.[14] The prayer was also promptly adopted by those synagogues outside the direct authority of the Ashkenazi Chief Rabbi, including the historic Spanish and Portuguese Jews' Congregation, the seat of Dr. Moses Gaster, the Haham or spiritual leader of the Sephardi community. Dr. Gaster, a Romanian who had lectured at the University of Bucharest and was an expert on Romanian literature, expressed public views on the war that differed very little from those of the English-reared Adler.

> England is fighting now the battle for justice, equality, peace and righteous-ness.... We Jews who have lived long enough under the regime of different laws for us and different laws for the other inhabitants, must fully appreci-ate the righteousness of the cause for which England has drawn the sword.[15]

Patriotic prayers were also read out in the *chevras* of the East End, the small and informal places of worship where Yiddish-speaking immigrants prayed in an intimate and fervent style alien to their more formal Anglo-Jewish brethren. Here the prayers in English were carefully transliterated into Hebrew characters to enable the prayer leader "to recite them correctly."[16]

The only rabbinic dissent of note, and that only a muted dissent, came from Dr. Solomon Schechter, a brilliant German-Jewish scholar who was Reader in Rabbinic and Talmudic Literature at Cambridge and Professor of Hebrew at University College, London, and was later to found the Conservative Movement in Judaism. According to his biographer, Schechter once walked out of a service in Cambridge when the War Prayer was being recited. "The less God Almighty knows about this dirty business, the better for all of us," he explained.[17]

The Jewish community, including the newcomers from eastern Europe, favored Adler's view over Schechter's. They saw England, despite the upsurge of anti-alien sentiment, as a bastion of tolerance, decency, and fair play, where Jews could escape the *Judenhetze* and discrimination so rife in continental Europe.[18] Anglo-Jewry demonstrated its gratitude and intense patriotism—its Jewish jingoism—in a variety of ways. These included the conspicuous acts of generosity of the wealthy elite, the Cousinhood, who provided the secular leadership of the Jewish community. The *Jewish Chronicle,* eager to publicize Jewish patriotism, kept a careful tally of the substantial Jewish contributions to the various war funds—and boasted that these formed "a striking proportion" of the donations.[19] It also detailed the gifts made by wealthy individuals and firms. Thus it noted in October 1899 that Lord Rothschild had presented every guardsman who left for South Africa with a briar-wood pipe, a tobacco pouch, and a quarter pound of tobacco, and that in December, J. Lyons and Co. gave the War Office ten thousand—ten tons of—'old-fashioned' Christmas puddings for distribution to the troops at the front.[20] Alfred Mosely spent some £25,000 on equipping a base hospital in South Africa. The *Jewish Chronicle* reported that he had "modestly refrained from attaching his name to the hospital," calling it instead the Princess Christian Hospital. Mosely's reward was a mention in dispatches and being made a Companion of the Order of St. Michael and St. George in 1901.[21]

When the volunteer units were raised for service in South Africa, the *Jewish Chronicle* published lists of Jewish financial contributions to these. Jewish individuals and firms, particularly those with strong South African ties, contributed generously to the fund for equipping the City Imperial Volunteers (CIV). The Dünkelsbuhler firm gave £3,000, Barnato Brothers £1,000.

The *Jewish Chronicle* noted that the firm of Wernher and Beit, "which is often described as a Jewish one, owing to Mr. Julius Wernher being the son of an Israelite, has given the munificent sum of £50,000." Captain J. Waley Cohen, a member of one of the leading Anglo-Jewish families and a prewar volunteer officer, offered to equip at his own expense and take out to South Africa a detachment of thirty signalers for the CIV.[22] Similarly generous contributions were made to the Imperial Yeomanry Hospital Fund by the Mosenthal and Neumann firms.[23]

The anglicized Jewish middle classes contributed as enthusiastically, if not on the same grand scale. Special services were held in synagogues throughout the country at which rabbis delivered patriotic sermons before sizeable collections were made for war funds. Fund-raising concerts were organized that typically culminated in an emotional recital of Kipling's "The Absent-Minded Beggar." Jewish schools and associations, including a Zionist group, made their contributions.[24]

The immigrant East End showed a similar enthusiasm and generosity, the *Jewish Chronicle* claimed. As its "chevra reporter" wrote in January 1900,

The excitement occasioned by the outbreak of hostilities in South Africa among East End Jews is still as great to-day as it was when war first began. Besides the fact that there are hundreds of families having relatives in South Africa, especially in the Transvaal, a fair number of Jewish soldiers at the front hail from East London. There are few, if any, "Little Englanders" amongst the foreign Jewish population, and the general opinion is that England must win and that Jews must pray, for her success in gratitude for the freedom enjoyed in this country. It is, therefore, not surprising that in many a Chevra synagogue, a chapter of Tehilim [psalms] is specially chanted. This sympathy is not mere lip-loyalty. No sooner was the Soldiers' Widows and Orphans Fund opened by the Lord Mayor, than East End Jews set about collecting as much as was possible. Committees were formed, and even at weddings, Bris Milahs [circumcision ceremonies] and Confirmations, the Fund was not forgotten, to the detriment of the Talmud Torahs [religious classes] and other East End charitable institutions. In the task of swelling the Fund, the Friendly societies take a leading part.... These manifestations are all the more noteworthy considering the widespread distress now prevailing in the East End. Dear provisions and slackness in trade have not lightened the burden, but, not-withstanding all this, the Ghetto Jews have given cheerfully and willingly towards the fund raised for the succour of "the little things" left behind by those who are fighting for England's honour and glory.[25]

The Jewish East End's response to the news of the relief of Mafeking is further testimony to the eagerness and speed with which the immigrants had taken on the patriotic coloring of the host society, which, for all of its anti-alien murmurings, was seen as far more welcoming than the hostile eastern European societies from which they had come. The relief of Mafeking was greeted with the same euphoric exuberance in the Jewish East End as elsewhere in the empire, though with a day's delay necessitated by strict observance of the sabbath. While the news was received on Friday evening, rigorously orthodox East Enders delayed their mafficking until Saturday evening, extending the *Simcha* (celebration) until late on Sunday. As the *Chronicle*'s chevra reporter noted, the celebrations took a peculiarly Jewish form. "East End Jewry has a method of its own in commemorating any auspicious occasion. First comes the religious ceremony and then the civil celebration." On the Saturday afternoon, in all the small synagogues of the East End the preachers discussed the great news in their homilies. The moment the sabbath ended, on the Saturday evening, the patient worshippers surged into the streets, which were soon bedecked with bunting and flags. "Old men, young men, staid matrons and gay young girls vied with each other in parading the joy they evinced at the success of the British arms, which moreover so many Jews bore." Every barrow in Petticoat Lane bore a flag. Hawkers sold "Mafeking fish," "Mafeking oranges," "Mafeking lemons," "Mafeking cakes." "Yiddish bands" played patriotic music. "All were happy. The sentence, 'Mafeking is relieved' was like an abracadabra, opening the way to joy, levelling the rich and poor, ending the terrible anxiety. Mafeking relieved. Mazal Tov, Mazal Tov." Typically, the relief of Mafeking was given a Jewish spin by the *Chronicle* and its East End correspondent. The Jewish East Enders' celebrations had an added edge, it was tortuously argued, "because they themselves knew fully well the misery and wretchedness of being caged up for months and months in a small area, for what after all is the Pale of Settlement of Russia but a large Mafeking with the eager foe watching and waiting outside the gates?" Mafeking itself had been saved, the *Chronicle* insisted, through the foresight of the Weil brothers, who had laid in large stocks of provisions before the siege began.[26]

Celebrating Jewish Soldiering

While the *Jewish Chronicle* made great play of patriotic display and generosity, what mattered more, it proudly noted, was that "at the seat of war itself, Jewish patriotism is being vindicated in still more substantial fashion—at the sword's point."[27] Jewish military service in the South African War was perceived to be Anglo-Jewry's principal response to the anti-Semitic charges of a lack of patriotism and of culpability in the war. It was Jewish soldiering in particular that made it a Jewish war, not in Hobson's negative sense, but in the positive sense of full participation in the country's struggle. As the *Jewish Chronicle* pointed out, this was the first war in English history in which Jews had played a full part:

> But this is the first time that Jews have taken a really considerable part—vastly more than proportionate share, in fact—in the active military work of the Empire, and as such, the present war, which is in many respects a turning point in the history of the Empire, marks also a considerable stride forward in the annals of English Jewry. A Jewry has arisen one in heart and interest with the Imperial people among whom its lot is cast, indistinguishable in aims and character from the Western race with whom its fortunes are united, and triumphantly refuting by its spirit and sacrifices the rhodomontade of the anti-Jew. No finer object-lesson has been displayed to the world of the success which waits upon a policy of wise toleration and justice.[28]

The *Jewish Chronicle* served as a drummer throughout the war for Jewish soldiering. Week by week for the duration it listed the names and units of Jewish regulars and volunteers. It kept a record of all Jewish casualties. For many months it carried a regular weekly page of photographs of Jewish soldiers in uniform. It also printed lengthy extracts from the letters Jewish soldiers had written home to their families. ("I hope there will be no 'grousing' about the seating accommodation at the Chanucah Service this year. If any do grumble, ask them to think of their Jewish brethren whose only seating accommodation is the cold, wet ground, and whose Chanucah party consists of bully beef and hard biscuits.... I believe we are getting a pipe, some tobacco, and a pudding as a Christmas gift (Mazzoltoff!). I would rather have a piece of good old fried fish.")[29]

The lists, letters, and photographs were published with the explicit purpose of demonstrating the extent of Jewish participation in the South African campaign. The *Chronicle* attempted to identify all Jewish soldiers serving in the British army as well as in the volunteer units raised in South Africa and elsewhere in the empire. The *Chronicle* scoured the lists of recruits for Jewish-sounding names. Some of its guesses led to embarrassing errors. It claimed, for example, that Colonel Aubrey Woolls-Sampson, founder of the Imperial Light Horse, was Jewish, and was then forced to print a retraction: "From the name and other circumstances, this gallant officer has often been supposed to be of Jewish extraction, but we now have the highest authority to say that the belief is unfounded." It also laid claim to those of even the remotest Jewish ancestry. Thus it gave an honorable mention to a trooper killed at Ladysmith who belonged "to a branch of the Mocatta family that left Judaism some generations back."[30]

Right through the war the *Jewish Chronicle* kept a running tally of the number of Jewish soldiers in the imperial army. The figures were never complete, the *Chronicle* always hastened to add, because of the anonymity preferred by some Jewish soldiers. Many, it appears, signed up under assumed, gentile names—thus Berkovich became Davis (and was killed in action at Spionkop), Isaacs became Ingram, and Van Dantzig became Downs. Aaron Myers, educated at the Jews' Hospital and Orphan Asylum, Norwood, became Robert Harvey of the Naval Brigade in South Africa, while Abraham Harris became Sidney Fillis of Brabant's Colonial Scouts. Some claimed to be members of Christian denominations. "I have met several Jewish soldiers since I have been on service," Private Safferty of the 2nd Middlesex wrote, "who have enlisted as 'Church of England,' 'Roman Catholic,' &c. I have often wondered why they do so, as their physiognomy always gives them away at first sight." The reticence and subterfuge are testimony to the recruits' anxieties about their fellow soldiers' possible reactions to their being Jewish. "It is well recognised," wrote the *Chronicle*, "that the still numerous 'crypto-Jews' remain silent as to their origin, rarely from any motive beyond the avoidance of the good-humoured banter, which their features nevertheless usually bring them."[31]

Drawing on its figures, which it insisted were undercounts, the *Jewish Chronicle* (and others) engaged in an intricate ethnic calculus, the purpose of which was to demonstrate that Jews were playing a disproportionate part in the war effort, and in this way to counter the sort of allegation that had appeared in the *Daily Chronicle*, that the number of Jews serving in South Africa was "quite insignificant." A good example is the calculation in January 1900 by the controversial Rabbi Hertz, formerly of Johannesburg, that if the white population of the British Empire was approximately sixty million, of which only 156,000 were Jews, and there were 60,000 troops in South Africa, then there ought only to be 150 Jewish soldiers. Instead there were, he said, at least 750. (By the last months of the war, the total number of Jews who had fought on the British side had risen to 3,000 by one estimate, but this figure would presumably have included colonial volunteers and the many Jewish members of the Town Guards in the Cape Colony.)[32]

Who were these Jewish soldiers? Few were regulars of whom only a handful were officers of any seniority. The great majority were volunteers, many of whom joined during the crisis period in late 1899 and early 1900. While Jews served in a very wide range of units, both in the British army and in those raised in South Africa and elsewhere in the empire, the CIV, with its London base, became a natural focus for Jewish volunteering (and, as a result, for the *Jewish Chronicle*). Those young Jews who volunteered in "marked numbers" for the CIV represented the "very pick" of the community; "they were naturally all native Jews, and in physique, efficiency and bearing worthily ranked with their Gentile comrades. Among them were numbered sons of our leading families, our middle classes and our artisans, animated all by the same self-forgetting spirit of patriotic zeal."[33]

The Imperial Yeomanry also included "a due representation of militant Judaism." Some of those volunteering were "the rawest Jewish immigrants," but these were largely turned away. "We are not raising a Yiddish regiment" was the "half-scornful remark" of one of the recruiters.[34]

As these comments indicate, the Jewish volunteers, like their gentile counterparts during this phase of the war, were mainly middle-class.[35] Significant numbers, however, came from lower down the social scale, from the children of eastern European immigrants. That they volunteered was seen as testimony to the efficacy of the anglicizing institutions created to integrate the immigrant population as speedily as possible. The *Jewish Chronicle* identified many of these soldiers as products of the Jewish schools, the Jewish Lads' Brigade (modeled on the Church Lads' Brigade), and the Jewish Working Men's Club.

Constructing Jewish Heroes

The most prominent of the Jewish regulars was Colonel Albert Edward Goldsmid, founder of the Jewish Lads' Brigade. He was one of a set of Jewish participants in the campaign who were singled out for special attention by the *Chronicle* and held up as heroic examples of the Jew at war. Colonel Goldsmid, who served in South Africa mainly as a staff officer—though he had a narrow escape at Paardeberg, where "two shots wounded his horse, a third smashed his water-bottle, and a fourth penetrated into his saddle bag"[36]—was a particular source of communal pride. His rather dull activities were the subject of close and admiring attention in the *Chronicle*. This was in part because he was the most senior Jewish officer serving in the regular army. It was also because of his quintessential Englishness; in appearance and manner he was "an almost archetypal Indian colonel." But it was above all because of his personal history. Goldsmid was born in Poona to a father who was a member of the Indian Civil Service. His parents had converted to

Christianity, which fact he only discovered as a young man. To their con-
sternation, Goldsmid himself chose to return to Judaism (at a time when
the traffic was mainly in the opposite direction). He also chose to play a very
active and creative role within the Jewish community. He was the founder of
the Jewish Lads' Brigade, an organization modeled on its Christian counterpart, and directed at "ironing the Ghetto bend" out of East End youngsters.
He was also a leading English Zionist at a time when Zionism was highly
suspect within the Anglo-Jewish elite to which he belonged.[37]

The flavor of Goldsmid's patriotic Anglo-Jewishness, which the Jewish
community so admired, is captured in a letter he wrote from the *Dunnottar
Castle* en route to South Africa:

> The Lads' Brigade I beg most urgently to bring to the favourable con-
> sideration of Jews of all classes, who wish to see the members of their
> race imbued with the high feeling of honour and discipline that distin-
> guishes the best side of the English character. At a time when all Eng-
> land is making unheard-of sacrifices for the promotion of patriotic
> objects, let the Jewish community not fall behind, but continue to train
> up their lads so that, when their age permits of it, they may take their
> share in the defence of England's empire.[38]

A less respectable hero was "the Jewish scout Morris," whose adventures the
Chronicle avidly followed, and who epitomized the manly, fighting virtues
it professed to admire. Popularly known as "Darkie Morris" or the "Fighting Jew," Morris's earlier career as recounted in the *Chronicle* reads like a
combination of Zelig and Flashman. Son of the Beadle of the St. John's
Wood Synagogue in London, he ran away from home at the age of thirteen
after his bar mitzvah and joined the Royal Navy. His subsequent military
service included the Sudan and Ashanti campaigns, and the Benin expedition where he "had the luck to have the fall of the King's nephew to his
rifle." Discharged from the navy in 1895, he moved to Johannesburg, where
he joined the Fire Brigade and served as a diver, recovering bodies from
Wemmer Pan. Later in the year he trekked to Bulawayo and joined the
British South African Police, just in time to serve in the Jameson Raid.
Morris escaped capture and made his way to Johannesburg, where he was
fêted by the Jewish community. On his return shortly after to Rhodesia he
served as Baden-Powell's "special scout" during the 1896 "rebellion." When
the Spanish-American War broke out, he fought as an irregular in Cuba,
"just to keep his hand in."

During the South African War he served as a scout with Kitchener and

French and took part in numerous engagements. He was a "born scout"; so highly did the Boers rate him that they promised a reward of £500 for his capture. Morris was "a man of fine physique," the *Jewish Chronicle* noted approvingly, and "a very great favourite" with both Baden-Powell and Rhodes: muscular Judaism married to gentile affirmation.[39]

The most singular of the *Jewish Chronicle*'s chosen heroes was Rose Lina Shappere, an Australian nursing sister who served in South Africa through much of the war—and who probably confounded the *Chronicle* readers' expectations of what was an appropriate role for Jewish women in wartime. Born in Ballarat, she had first worked as a schoolteacher in New Zealand. But, as she recounted to an admiring interviewer from the newspaper, "teaching was not to her taste. The desire seized her to become a nurse. For one thing, she wanted to show that Jewish girls do not mind how hard they work." Her family, who shared the current Jewish middle-class prejudices against nursing, strenuously objected "to her adopting a laborious career." Ignoring their objections, she trained as a nurse in Melbourne, and subsequently worked in Perth, Kalgoorlie, and Adelaide. Sister Shappere, who was of an adventurous disposition, went to the Transvaal in 1899, on the advice of a friend who wrote "that he was sure war would break out presently." She served at first in the Boer Ambulance at Standerton, but when she discovered, as she told her interviewer, that only the Boer wounded would be treated, she decided to leave, despite a handsome pay offer from one of President Kruger's Eloff grandsons. She made her way to Ladysmith, where she nursed through the siege under "terrible" conditions:

> We saw our men dying around us, and could do nothing for them.... The tents were badly pitched, they were blown away by the wind, and the pelting rain came through, drenching the patients as they lay in their beds. We nurses had to go from tent to tent under the enemy's fire, because there were so few orderlies to attend to the men. And to make matters worse the food was bad and there was nothing like sufficient comforts for the sick and wounded. No one will know all that we suffered during that terrible time. We thought we should never come out alive, and in moments of despair some of us almost hoped that the Boers would come and take us prisoners, for then we should have been better cared for.

Nursing as many as 84 patients at a time, many of them with enteric fever and dysentery, with an acute shortage of drugs, took a severe toll: "the sufferings and privations I underwent completely ruined my constitution. When the siege was over I broke down, and had to be invalided to the coast."

She took a hospital ship to England and after a very brief rest returned to South Africa to continue her nursing with the Princess Christian's Army Nursing Reserve. As she proudly told the *Chronicle* interviewer, she was the only Jewess in the Army Nursing Reserve—unsurprising, given the reluctance then of Jewish women to enter the nursing profession.

The *Chronicle* reporter was overwhelmed by this "almost romantic career" and by Sister Shappere herself, who "is so fair of countenance with features of so Saxon a type, that no one would take her to be a Jewess"—a "compliment" most suggestive of the mindset of the interviewer and his readership. The nonconformist Sister Shappere, who chose an active, public, and unsheltered life at odds with the ideology of domesticity the *Chronicle*'s Anglo-Jewish middle-class readership shared with their gentile peers, would for all her social "abnormality" still have met the enthusiastic approval of at least a part of the readership. Besides being a certified war heroine, mentioned in Lord Roberts's dispatches, Sister Shappere was also one of a growing number of Jewish women at the turn of the century who were redefining what was socially acceptable. She nursed through the ordeal of the siege of Ladysmith and was just a more radical example of those middle-class Jewish women who at the end of the nineteenth and the beginning of the twentieth century "had stepped out of the private sphere of the home and begun to move into the public arena."[40]

The common denominator for these three heroes is their (mild) exoticism in contemporary Anglo-Jewish terms. Goldsmid, Shappere, and Morris all behaved in ways unexpected of English Jews. Part of their attraction for the *Chronicle*'s readership was that they confounded stereotypical views of the Jews, both those held by others and those held by the Jews themselves. Jewish soldiering at large during the South African War did the same.

Challenging Anti-Semitic Stereotypes

Jewish opinion attached a range of meanings to Jewish soldiering in the South African War. It was seen, firstly, as giving the lie to the chronic anti-Semitic charge of Jewish shirking, cowardice, and lack of genuine patriotism:

> The deplorable fiction about human rubbish shot upon the English dumping ground should be one of many doomed to go by the board, thanks to the war. There are others destined, we hope, to a like fate. The theory of the impossibility of Jewish patriotism is one of them. The conception of the Jew as the weakling of Europe who leaves the rougher work of patriotism to the Gentile, the while he plies his trade, is another.[41]

Jewish soldiering was also seen as representing the revival of a long-dormant warrior tradition. The volunteers were imagined as modern-day Maccabees, spiritual descendents of the Hasmoneans who had successfully fought the Syrian-Greeks in the second century B.C.E. The Jewish Festival of Hanukkah—the Festival of Lights, the celebration of Judah the Maccabee's victory over Antiochus and rededication of the Temple—was given special prominence during the war. As the *Jewish Chronicle* explained in December 1900, the festival's "increasing appeal and popularity are due ... to the spirit of martial ardour that has become lately intensified in the general community."[42]

Beyond confuting anti-Semitic canards and reviving an ancient warrior tradition, Jewish soldiering in the South African War was also seen as an assertion of a new "muscular Judaism" diametrically opposed to the physical frailty and passivity of a ghetto past, a reassertion of a long-submerged Jewish manliness. One of the major concerns of the established Anglo-Jewish community in the 1890s was the physical condition of the new immigrants from eastern Europe who had crowded into the East End of London. As Chief Rabbi Adler put it graphically at a wartime school awards ceremony, "for many generations, Jews had been victims of all the grievous disabilities of Ghetto life, with its cramping and deteriorating influence upon their physical development. This was particularly marked in our foreign brethren who were frequently narrow-chested and dwarfed in stature."[43] Consequently, energetic efforts were made through agencies such as Goldsmid's Jewish Lads' Brigade and the Jewish schools to "iron out" this "ghetto bend."

Soldiering in the South African War was represented as a continuation of this process of Jewish physical improvement. The *Jewish Chronicle* made much in its reporting on Jewish soldiers of their physical prowess and competence in the military skills, traditionally regarded by Jews as well as gentiles as beyond Jewish capability. Charles Aarons of the Salford Fusiliers "is a splendid type of muscular Judaism. Standing five feet, nine inches in height, he turns the scale at twelve stone, and was declared by the regimental surgeon to be the fittest and best built man in the whole battalion. He is twenty-three years of age, and is a splendid shot with the rifle, having won many prizes by his skill with that weapon." Lieutenant Alex Granger, serving in the Intelligence Department in the Transvaal in 1902, was "one of the finest representatives in the field of those qualities which we love to call British. He is a crack shot, perfect horseman, and skilled naturalist, and has the brightest of futures to look forward to."[44]

Private Joseph Freedman of the 3rd Battalion Grenadier Guards, who was wounded at Belmont, was "of splendid physique, a good type of the crack regiment to which he belonged." The *Jewish Chronicle* noted that though Freedman's parents were "of foreign birth," they had "always viewed the fact that they had a son in the British army with pride." It also noted with satisfaction that Freedman, who was educated at the Manchester Jews' School, had retained his "Jewish predilections," and that while he was in Manchester had taken "every opportunity to encourage physical culture amongst his co-religionists."[45]

The final meaning attached to Jewish soldiering was that it had cemented the bond between Anglo-Jewry and the nation—that it had "helped once for all to seal the union between the Jewish and Gentile subjects of the Queen," that it had resulted in "the irrevocable weaving of the Jewish element into the national fabric."[46] Writing at the Jewish New Year in September 1900, after close to a year of active Jewish soldiering, the *Chronicle* declared that

> The year that has gone has, indeed, marked a new stage in its [Anglo-Jewry's] relationship to the rest of the English people. The war, which had a unifying influence on the scattered members of the British race, has also established once for all the complete political solidarity of English Jews with their Christian fellow-subjects. Never before have Jews fought for the flag in such numbers.... Jewish loyalty and oneness with the nation are once more proved in the eyes of the world.[47]

The ultimate significance of Jewish soldiering—and indeed of the war—for Anglo-Jewry is splendidly encapsulated in a poem that achieved wide currency among Jews during the South African campaign. Entitled *The Jewish Soldier,* it was first published anonymously in the *Jewish Chronicle* in March 1900. The author was later revealed to be Alice Montefiore (Mrs. Henry Lucas), sister of Claude Montefiore, president of the Anglo-Jewish Association and one of Anglo-Jewry's principal lay figures, and herself a poet, a Hebrew scholar, and a translator of traditional Hebrew hymns. "This admirable exposition of the feelings of British Jews for the British flag" was very well received: the Chief Rabbi applauded "the thrilling words with which a sister in faith has voiced the sentiments of Anglo-Judaism"; it was published in the *Times,* reprinted in pamphlet form, and even set to music, both as a song and as a march for pianoforte solo.

The Jewish Soldier distills the meaning of the war for Jews, an understanding of the conflict wholly at odds with that of J. A. Hobson. The poet's—and Anglo-Jewry's—Jewish war, unlike Hobson's, is glorious, self-sacrificing, and patriotic, not mercenary and meanly conspiratorial:

Mother England, Mother England, 'mid the thousands
Far beyond the sea today,
Doing battle for thy honour, for thy glory,
Is there place for us, a little band of brothers,
    England, say?

Dost thou ask our name and nation, Mother England?
We have come from many lands,
Where the rod of the oppressor bowed and bent us,
Bade us stand with bated breath and humble gesture,
    Suppliant hands.

Long ago and far away, O Mother England,
We were warriors brave and bold,
But a hundred nations rose in arms against us,
And the shades of exile closed o'er those heroic
    Days of old,

Thou hast given us home and freedom, Mother England,
Thou hast let us live again
Free and fearless midst thy free and fearless children,
Sharing with them, as one people, grief and gladness,
    Joy and pain,

Now we Jews, we English Jews, O Mother England,
Ask another boon of thee!
Let us share with them the danger and the glory,
Where thy best and bravest lead, there let us follow
    O'er the sea!

For the Jew has heart and hand, our Mother England,
And they both are thine to-day—
Thine for life and thine for death, yea, thine for ever!
Wilt thou take them as we give them, freely, gladly,
    England, say![48]

Notes

1. This chapter is part of a larger project on Jews and the South African War that will include, as this discussion does not, the wartime experiences of South African Jewry, including their expulsion from the countryside as part of Kitchener's anti-guerrilla strategy. This, in turn, is part of a still larger project, a new history of South African Jewry I am working on with Professor Milton Shain of the Kaplan Centre for Jewish Studies at the University of Cape Town.

2. J. A. Hobson, "Capitalism and Imperialism in South Africa," *Contemporary Review* 77 (January 1900): 1–17; and Hobson, *The War in South Africa: Its Causes and Effects* (London, 1900), 189–97. For a discussion of Hobson's views on the Jews, see C. Holmes, *Anti-Semitism in British Society, 1876–1939* (New York, 1979), 20–21, 67–68; Holmes, "J. A. Hobson and the Jews," in C. Holmes (ed.), *Immigrants and Minorities in British Society* (London, 1978), 125–57.

3. *Jewish Chronicle* (hereafter *JC*), 13 October 1899, 15; Holmes, *Anti-Semitism,* 69.

4. S. Koss (ed.), *The Pro-Boers: The Anatomy of an Antiwar Movement* (Chicago, 1973), 94–95.

5. Holmes, *Anti-Semitism,* 68; J. S. Galbraith, "The Pamphlet Campaign on the Boer War," *Journal of Modern History* 24 (1952): 119–21.

6. For a fine, critical account of the history of the weekly, see D. Cesarani, *The Jewish Chronicle and Anglo-Jewry, 1841–1991* (Cambridge, 1994).

7. *JC,* 25 May 1900, 17.

8. *JC,* 19 January 1900, 15.

9. *JC,* 20 April 1900, 14–15.

10. *JC,* 10 November 1899, 12; 20 April 1900, 12; 19 January 1900, 15. For Sammy Marks's close relationship with Kruger, see R. Mendelsohn, *Sammy Marks: "The Uncrowned King of the Transvaal"* (Cape Town and Athens, Ohio, 1991). For Emanuel Mendelssohn's support of the Boer state, see R. Mendelsohn, "Oom Paul's Publicist: Emanuel Mendelssohn, founder of the first congregation," in M. Kaplan and M. Robertson (eds.), *Founders and Followers: Johannesburg Jewry, 1887–1915* (Cape Town, 1991).

11. The Jewish population of England, some 60,000 at the start of the 1880s, more than trebled during the following thirty years as a result of Eastern European immigration. For the history of Anglo-Jewry at the turn of the century, see G. Alderman, *Modern British Jewry* (Oxford, 1992); E. C. Black, *The Social Politics of Anglo-Jewry, 1880–1920* (Oxford, 1988); D. Cesarani (ed.), *The Making of Modern Anglo-Jewry* (Oxford, 1990); S. A. Cohen, *English Zionists and British Jews: The Communal Politics of Anglo-Jewry, 1895–1920* (Princeton, N.J., 1982); T. M. Endelman, *Radical Assimilation in English Jewish History, 1656–1945* (Bloomington, 1990); D. Feldman, *Englishmen and Jews: Social Relations and British Culture, 1840–1914* (New Haven, Conn., 1994). While the recent academic literature is particularly rich, an older work, Lloyd Gartner's classic study, *The Jewish Immigrant in England, 1870–1914* (London, 1960), remains essential reading.

12. *JC,* 27 October 1899, 11. For Adler, see Black, *Social Politics,* 26–29.

13. *JC,* 10 November 1899, 13; 3 November 1899, 11.

14. *JC,* 11 January 1901, 10; 18 January 1901, 9.

15. *JC,* 3 November 1899, 11; 17 November 1899, 12. For Moses Gaster, see Black, *Social Politics,* 29–31.

16. *JC,* 31 January 1902, 9.

17. N. Bentwich, *Solomon Schechter: A Biography* (Cambridge, 1938), 104; G. Saron and L. Hotz, *The Jews in South Africa: A History* (Cape Town, 1955), 211.

18. The Jewish view of Britain is captured in a sermon given at a Thanksgiving service in a Glasgow synagogue in March 1900 in celebration of the "recent victories" in South Africa: "We Israelites have this additional cause for gratitude—that it has pleased our Almighty Father to assign this land as an asylum from oppression, where we may mingle with other citizens as their equals in constitutional rights and as brothers in love of country and devotion to its institutions and laws. This is emphatically the land where Israelites in their captivity, can dwell securely, whilst its liberties remain uninjured by popular violence or by tyrannical usurpation. Here the spirit of Judaism can shine forth without let or hindrance from the malign influence of political disqualifications; and here can we devote our energies to our moral, educational and physical improvement without dread of molestation from our neighbours. Should not Israel's sons, therefore, love this land? Should they not defend it in time of need; foremost amongst its stoutest defenders? Should they not associate themselves with everything that concerns its social, political and national life and conditions?" (*JC,* 9 March 1900, 28).

19. *JC,* 20 October 1899, 17.

20. *JC,* 17 November 1899, 11–12.

21. *JC,* 22 February 1901, 19; 4 October 1901, 10.

22. *JC,* 12 January 1900, 10; 26 January 1900, 16.

23. *JC,* 12 January 1900, 10.

24. *JC,* 1 December 1899, 10, 28–29; 8 December 1899, 13; 22 December 1899, 12; 12 January 1900, 24–26; 1 December 1899, 29.

25. *JC,* 19 January 1900, 10.

26. *JC,* 25 May 1900, 10–11, 16–17.

27. *JC,* 20 October 1899, 17.

28. *JC,* 26 January 1900, 16–17.

29. *JC,* 20 December 1901, 14.

30. *JC,* 31 January 1902, 21; 26 January 1900, 10.

31. *JC,* 9 March 1900, 10; 24 January 1902, 22; 26 January 1900, 10; 18 October 1901, 14; 6 July 1900, 12; 23 November 1900, 13; 6 April 1900, 17.

32. *JC,* 16 March 1900, 8; 9 February 1900, 12; 24 January 1902, 22.

33. *JC,* 26 October 1900, 12.

34. *JC,* 26 October 1900, 16; 27 April 1900, 17.

35. For the class basis of volunteering, see R. Price, *An Imperial War and the British Working Class* (London, 1972); W. R. Nasson, "Tommy Atkins in South Africa," in P. Warwick (ed.), *The South African War: The Anglo-Boer War, 1899–1902* (Harlow, 1980).

36. *JC,* 6 April 1900, 10.

37. For biographical information, see J. Springhall, *Youth, Empire and Society:*

British Youth Movements, 1883–1940 (London, 1977), 152; C. Bermant, *The Cousinhood* (London, 1971), 242–43. For the Jewish Lads' Brigade, see Springhall, *Youth*, 41–43, and R. A. Voeltz, "'... A Good Jew and a Good Englishman': The Jewish Lads' Brigade, 1894–1922," *Journal of Contemporary History* 23 (1988): 119–27.

38. *JC,* 5 January 1900, 8.

39. *JC,* 23 February 1900, 10; 9 March 1900, 10; 25 May 1900, 13; 15 February 1901, 12; 31 January 1902, 21.

40. *JC,* 15 March 1901, 12; 10 January 1902, 10; 15 February 1901, 12. For the position of Jewish women in England, see L. Marks, "Carers and Servers of the Jewish Community: The Marginalized Heritage of Jewish Women in Britain," in T. Kushner (ed.), *The Jewish Heritage in British History: Englishness and Jewishness* (London, 1992); the quotation is from p. 119. G. Alderman, *Modern British Jewry* (Oxford, 1992), 197–200; L. G. Kuzmack, *Woman's Cause: The Jewish Woman's Movement in England and the United States, 1881–1933* (Columbus, 1990).

41. *JC,* 26 January 1900, 17.

42. *JC,* 8 December 1899, 24; 6 April 1900, 14; 14 December 1900, 18.

43. *JC,* 6 July 1900, 27.

44. *JC,* 2 February 1900, 10; 14 March 1902, 12.

45. *JC,* 1 December 1899, 10.

46. *JC,* 5 October 1900, 12–13.

47. *JC,* 21 September 1900, 15.

48. *JC,* 9 March 1900, 11; 23 March 1900, 20; 13 July 1900, 16; 16 November 1900, 3. For the poet, see Bermant, *Cousinhood,* 314.

CHAPTER 13

Taming the God of Battles

Secular and Moral Critiques of the
South African War

DAVID NASH

THE CONSCIENCE OF nineteenth-century Liberalism in Britain, at its furthest limits in matters of free speech and the issues of citizens' rights, has often been linked to the Secular Movement as much as to Protestant Nonconformity. Certainly this was the shade of libertarian thought that had, in the generation represented by its leader and noted republican Charles Bradlaugh, almost singlehandedly carried the torch for the extension and defense of the liberty of the citizen.[1] In particular, many prominent Liberals who sympathized with the aims of Secularists and in some cases actively supported their campaigns felt themselves to be fulfilling a vital role as guardians of liberalism's conscience.

While the campaigns of secularists in these areas have ostensibly done much to promote this view, it would be a mistake to see the operation of this "liberal conscience" as completely consistent, coherent, or indeed in any way homogeneous. Behind this is the perception that Secularists in particular could still find the implications of standing on principle riddled with contradiction. The South African War of 1899–1902 was perhaps the most striking instance of this, and attempts to resolve this significant divergence of views should be appreciated as an important anticipation of twentieth-century forms of peace politics. The dilemma this war presented for the influential Secularist minority and its long-term implications have generally been neglected by historians.[2]

Although Olive Schreiner described Secularists as the pro-Boers' most consistent supporters, this observation has been allowed to dissolve the actual differences of opinion among individual Secularists and Freethinkers. These differences are themselves an extremely useful window through which to see some of the debates that were represented in wider liberal circles during the war. Any homogenization of their views undervalues the breadth and complexity of their contribution to broader liberal critiques of both empire and the imperial state. Accepting Olive Schreiner's comments at face value (without unpacking the various reasons for what she describes as "support") and considering Secularists as simply another species of pro-Boer is profoundly misleading. Indeed, it casts a long and rather unhelpful shadow over the contribution of this group and its cohorts to the development of anti-militarist and peace politics in the twentieth century.

Secularists and Anti-Imperialism

One important strand shared by most Secularists and Freethinkers (to varying degrees) was a fundamental distrust of imperial motives that appeared to flout openly abroad rights that were only grudgingly accepted at home. Imperial adventures and expansionist policies were not simply wrong; they carried within them the justification of war—for conquest and the subjugation of infidel peoples. These policies were also the medium through which the conquerors could justify their own actions and seek sanction of and praise for their victories. The Secularist conception of an enlightened, rationalist "Spirit of the Age," which they frequently cited in other campaigns and circumstances, was, they believed, a standard by which the behavior of civilized nations toward the uncivilized should be exemplary. What is significant about this particular response is its radical departure from the earlier belief that colonial wars were essentially policing actions undertaken in the name of civilization.[3]

An example of this unambiguous critique is the following widely publicized piece from the *Freethinker* that "commemorated" the battle of Omdurman through a rewriting of the hymn "Abide with Me." Two verses read thus:

I fear no foe with Thee at hand to bless—
If he be savage, poor, and Maxim-less—
I give Death's sting and Grave its victory,
And triumph still if thou abide with me!

Hold Thou Thy cross before my dreaming eyes;
With pious thoughts imperial visions rise!
With sleep restore my strength to fight for Thee,
In charge, in massacre, abide with me![4]

However, the outbreak of the South African War brought Christians in the empire into conflict with one another for the first time since the Crimean conflict. The period between these wars witnessed a transformation in popular attitudes toward soldiering: shunned in the early century, soldiers were now embraced across class and ethnic boundaries.[5] Thus, the war in South Africa provided the British nation with the first struggle in living memory between adherents of the same religio-moral system.

These two facts become even more important when we consider the development and startling impact of more popular forms of journalism that were a product of the 1880s. The newspapers and periodicals of this era could, for the first time, genuinely claim to be molders as much as conveyors of opinion. As such, many were to hold them responsible for the glorification of imperial expansion and its development as a narrative with widespread popular appeal.[6] This aspect of social and cultural change had, however, not gone unchecked, since it also raised questions about the maintenance of civil rights and free speech, as well as the theory and practice of morality. It was precisely these questions that forced individual Secularists to create a range of philosophical and ideological positions that drew inspiration from, but were also ultimately to inform, liberalism more widely.

The range of this diversity and its implications can be gauged by contrasting the views of a number of Secularist voices—in particular those of George W. Foote, Hypatia Bradlaugh-Bonner, and William Stewart Ross, all editors of Secularist newspapers; J. M. Robertson, the celebrated journalist, literary critic, and author; and the Positivists, represented by the voices of Gilbert Murray, J. H. Bridges, and Frederick James Gould.

The *Freethinker* newspaper was edited by George William Foote, who had succeeded Charles Bradlaugh as president of the National Secular Society upon Bradlaugh's death in 1889. Foote was a noted Liberal individualist who brought the logic of these sentiments to bear upon the issue of imperialism. Emphasizing the realities of having to act in office—"If you have an empire you must be imperial"—Foote was representative of a small minority of Secularists who supported Britain's position in the South African War for its entire duration. Despite this, Foote was wary of endorsing the conduct of the war and the use of religion to justify military actions or to endorse victory. The latter sentiment was well illustrated in an article that saw religion as the root cause of the conflict:

> The Boer has a Mauser rifle in one hand and a Dutch Bible in the other, while the Britisher has weapons in both hands and a Bible behind his back. Each relies upon the God of that book. Each prays to the God of that book. Each informs the God of that book which side he ought to take in the quarrel. And what does this God do? He sits silently in heaven and does

nothing. He lets both sides take his name in vain. He reads them no lesson in honesty and charity; he does not bid them try justice and mutual toleration instead of fighting. He simply goes to sleep and leaves word for the victor to call him when the fight is over. Such a God is only fit for a museum. Some will say he is hardly fit for that.[7]

But if the war had to be fought—Foote was adamant—Britain should be triumphant. He saw the Uitlanders' grievances entirely as a civil rights issue, invoking the infamous Helot dispatch and condemning the Boers' treatment of the native population. In a series of editorials he regularly castigated the Boers' "simple" approach to religion as a dangerous anachronism, their apparent obsession with the minutiae of the Old Testament representing, to his mind, a bizarre pageant of scripture imitating art. Worse still, he saw them as misled by skilled and dangerously fanatical politicians. In Foote's view, Kruger—as an instrument of policy—encouraged Boers' conception of themselves as a "chosen race" by suggesting that the hand of the Almighty was behind the Great Trek, Majuba, and the delivery of Jameson into their hands.[8] In the realm of international politics this led them to become arrogant, misguided, and unnecessarily combative.

Foote accepted that confronting this religious form of imperialism with a flawed but nonetheless partially modernizing version was the lesser of two evils. However, his contributions hereafter fell into a rather myopic and one-dimensional pattern that policed press reports for their—in his view—anachronistic religious content. Thus he attacked the day of national humiliation and argued that the text of "turning the other cheek would mean that the British should offer Maritzburg once their 'offer' of Ladysmith had been accepted."[9] Overall he saw Britain's actions as a series of legitimate responses, which he could justify, sometimes with stunning banality.[10] His remaining contributions to the debates involved sniping at the procession of thanksgivings that concluded the South African War and the rush of victory parades that followed the peace.

In part, Foote's reaction was that of a liberal individualist whose moral and philosophical distaste of Christianity dictated his particular stance. There were, however, other aspects of liberal individualism that allowed Secularists to take such libertarian ideology in a fundamentally different direction. The Leicester Secular Society, which had held an open platform for many years, argued quite vociferously for the maintenance of free speech, which it felt was becoming still more fragile in the context of the war. When it became known that Samuel Cronwright-Schreiner was in the country arguing the Boer case, he was invited to speak at the Secular Hall in Leicester. An earlier meeting, at which Emily Hobhouse had spoken, had passed without incident largely due to the presence of forty police constables. Cronwright-Schreiner's visit required his host, Sydney Gimson, the Society's president, to make special provision for his safety against hostile mobs prepared to stalk him around the city.[11] Similarly, Secularists who supported the war saw the defense of free speech as fundamental to the protection of the liberalism debate. An otherwise hostile correspondent to the *Reformer* in 1900 considered it his "duty as a Freethinker to stand by any paper which I find courageous and independent in its own views, for an honest press is a safeguard of freedom."[12]

William Stewart Ross, the veteran editor of the *Secular Review*, now involved with the *Agnostic Journal*, initially saw Britain as pursuing just ends in the face of Kruger's obstinacy. Like Foote, Ross wrote disparagingly of the Boer Republic's status as the most "Christian" of nations. Ross, however, did not link this with modernization but rather with inconsistency. He drew attention to reports by Christian missionaries who deplored the Boers' treatment of Africans and its sanction by scripture; if the Boers were the chosen people of God, Ross argued, then Africans were treated with the same barbarism reserved for the Canaanites. Similarly, a missionary's account that the Boers had categorically denied that Africans had souls was used as a stick to beat Christianity and its failure to promote civilized behavior amongst its most pious adherents in Africa.[13] This sort of rhetoric was also advanced by other Secularists in wider contexts. A correspondent to the April 1900 issue of *The Reformer* chided Secularist pro-Boers for having neglected the civil rights issues involved in the conflict with the Boer Republics and suggested that Charles Bradlaugh himself had taught liberalism valuable lessons about how it should deal with those who denied basic civil rights to others.[14] This indicates a clear departure from conventional pro-Boer opinion, which is often considered to have neglected the interests of Africans.[15] Stewart Ross's interpretation of the invocation of Christianity by both combatants—"The God of Battles is invoked in the name of the Prince of Peace"—was again indicative of a common strand that indicted Christianity as an accomplice of war. The escalation of the war, however, eventually persuaded Ross to change his view.

Atheist Opposition to the War

J. M. Robertson was probably the most famous atheist Secularist to speak out in opposition to the war. He was a literary critic, journalist, and anti-imperial theoretician, and an associate of J. A. Hobson through their mutual attendance at the South Place Ethical Society. In 1886, Robertson had attacked imperialism as "the practice of international burglary," concluding that Britain's relations with so-called uncivilized states were "almost wholly barbarous."[16] By the outbreak of the Boer War in 1899, his critique had been published as *Patriotism and Empire,* an analysis echoed in Hobson's subsequent works. Hobson himself took a leading part in the ethicism of Secularism through his editorship of the *Ethical World,* and his concern with the potential and actual damage wrought by forms of unrestrained individualism is a current that has been recognized in his work.[17]

In some instances, the motif of "progress" and the belief in social and moral "reform" administered by enlightened forces influenced by reason to follow scientific "methods" makes interesting reading alongside the approaches associated with Comtean positivism. In his writings on the South African War, Hobson's work complements that of Robertson. Indeed, their combined works on the Boer War and imperialism should be read in counterpoint to one another. Hobson presented a primarily social, political, and economic critique of the imperial project with clearly spelled out moral consequences. His critique of the British imperial mission was influenced by the peculiar changes of the last quarter of the nineteenth century. Economic expansion was seen as a cause of chaos rather than the stability propounded by the free-trade ideology of Richard Cobden. At least some of this shock was caused by the Indian Mutiny, as paternalism replaced partnership as the main mode of imperial economic and social relations. The enemy that Hobson identified was not the honest trader or provincial businessman that Cobden represented, but the metropolitan financier who had intimate connections with the aristocracy and the military. Hobson was anxious that the logic of economic imperialism would lead to the manufacturing industry of the empire being relocated to the eastern colonies. This would impoverish Britain's industrial work force, leaving the empire prey to the acquisitiveness of the aristocratic financier. This pessimistic model of the future led Hobson to equate Britain's decline with that of the Roman Empire.[18]

Robertson's critique differed in emphasis since it furnished a philosophical and moral critique that had economic, social, and political consequences.[19] He argued in *Patriotism and Empire,* written a matter of months before the war, against what appeared to him to be the armory of a whole range of rhetorical weapons and attitudes that made a bloody, outsized colonial war not only possible, but to some influential interests a dangerous certainty. His analysis was erudite and to the point: "To put the case shortly, if nationalism is bad, imperialism is worse. If to intoxicate one's self on fatherland be unwholesome, to grow drunken on empire is pestilent."[20]

Implicated in the wholesale rush to embrace "drunken" patriotism were a number of imperial writers, among whom Kipling was singled out for special Secularist ire. He dismissed Kipling as a barbarian sentimentalist and a man who "passes for a prophet with the unprophetical," and to whom "all political philosophy begins and ends in the literary picturesque." He wrote on Kipling's "Recessional": "we figure for ourselves in the rest of the new gospel as the Dominant Race, beside whom Baboos, Home Rulers, and Russians, are as creeping things."[21] Most presciently of all, Robertson assessed this contribution to the growing levels of religious moral armament in somewhat chilling terms: "it needs only a sufficiently evil conjuncture of circumstances to enable a Moses of the Music-Hall, with perhaps a few Aarons of the Aeropagus, to start a Jingo crusade in which the nation may march as straight to dire disaster as ever did any ... fanatics in the Dark Ages."[22]

In this respect Robertson also echoed an important strand in Secularist culture that lamented the almost inevitably barbaric nature of modern culture. This in particular could be scathing about the interest that the populace at large had in semi-barbaric diversions. Secularists hoped that the marginalization of religious forms would bring an uplifting interest in philosophy and autodidact forms of learning. When the Church and chapel were seen to be losing ground to the music hall and beer shop rather than to the lecture and reading room, then the worst fears of some Secularists were realized. Positivists also noted that the coming of democracy had created a society that was more inclined to "acquiese in war and in preparations for war."[23]

Hypatia Bradlaugh-Bonner echoed Robertson's critique and noted with considerable alarm that members of the military establishment actively promoted war as essential to the advance of civilization. She heavily criticized a speech delivered by Viscount Wolseley to the Edinburgh Philosophical Society which, to her incredulity, quoted Ruskin to promote the view that "peace brought sensuality, selfishness and death, and that truth and strength, the arts and virtues, were founded and nourished in war." Wolseley then suggested that the desire of the Romans to conquer Britain had brought the country the benefits of civilization, which Britain was in turn exporting to indigenous populations throughout the world. Bradlaugh-Bonner noted drily that the recognition of militarism as an exemplar of civilized behavior liable to advance the moral and material prosperity of society was still some way off, since

If we are to accept the claim that military life tends to make the perfect citizen then the soldier has been a terribly misunderstood man. Only the other day a member of Parliament commented upon the fact that a discharged

soldier finds it almost as hard to get work as a discharged convict. His former life is a certificate only to such employment as requires an automatic
obedience to orders and a machine-like regularity of movement.[24]

From Robertson's attack on the cultural predispositions that made imperialism unavoidable, his critique dismantled what he called "The Militarist
Regimen" in a manner reminiscent of the Cobdenite critique that had been
influential in liberal circles earlier in the nineteenth century.[25] He attacked
the arguments of Wolseley and others that foot soldiers were better housed,
fed, and educated than their civilian counterparts; that the mingling of
classes in the military and an inculcation of discipline was desirable; that
the military had an elevated respect for state institutions; and finally that
arming a nation automatically gave it a deterrent.[26]

Once again, this argument spoke directly to a deep-seated liberal distrust
of militarism and the soldiering profession that emerged elsewhere in the
speeches of individuals such as Henry Campbell-Bannerman. Quite apart
from the traditional liberal distaste of all things military—especially professed military values—those in the Secularist wing of liberalism had their
own critiques of the military. Many, including Charles Bradlaugh himself,
had lost their faith partly as a result of religious compulsion in the army.
Moreover, the surrender of reason and individuality involved in the practice of soldiering was anathema to a philosophical position that argued for
responsibility and considered ethical judgments. Moreover, the purpose of
maintaining a standing army was presumed to be a means of terrorizing and
conquering that, in an imperial nation, modern strategists would describe as
a "first strike weapon."

Increasingly this use of force in what many Secularists and some liberals
considered to be dubious circumstances was a feature of mid- and late Victorian England. Secularists saw Christianity as a fundamental cause of this
change. The work of evangelists within the armed forces, the spread of missionary work, the cult of muscular Christianity with its attendant literature
about military figures (perhaps reaching its zenith in the heroic portrayal
of Gordon of Khartoum), and the very "militarization" of Christianity itself
(with the growing vogue for uniformed organizations) all provided examples
of Christian culture underpinning imperial and military adventure.[27] This
also marked a new and worrying development, in contrast to the earlier
part of the century, which had seen Christian culture marshaled to advance
the welfare of small nations and individuals whose causes could be shown
to be both civilized and moral. Hinton suggests that support for Kossuth,
the North in the American Civil War, and Gladstone's Bulgarian Agitation

were all examples of this phenomenon. Such sympathy for independent struggle and nationhood resurfaced as a form of undiluted pro-Boer feeling.[28]
The fear of coercion, the apparent vulgarity of modern culture, and the distrust of a uniformed army had spectacularly come together for Secularists
in the previous decades with the actions and campaigns of Samuel Booth's
Salvation Army. This organization constituted a fundamental public-order
problem for a number of local chief constables and the Home Office and
provided evidence to Secularists that Christianity had entered a new and
aggressive phase.

The fact that British culture itself had adapted to allow brutal imperial
adventures to become part of popular culture and the entertainment industry was also of considerable concern to Robertson. Whilst the music hall
preached revenge for "Black Week," there were other ways in which the
British nation was being made to feel not only supportive of the war but
comfortable with its involvement in the conflict.[29] In particular, many criticized the way the war was being commodified. Both Robertson and William
Stewart Ross criticized the idyllic pictures that were painted of British soldiers in South Africa. While they could be thankful that the worst excesses
of the muscular Christian panegyric had gone out of fashion, it had been
replaced by the consumption of popular books and pamphlets that eulogized
the campaigns and exploits of Britain's military commanders. Such works,
however, also began to focus more intently upon the exploits of the common
soldier. The British public was treated to a comfortable image of Tommy
Atkins sitting on the veld munching his bar of chocolate, thoughtfully provided by his generous monarch—all captured on film by the latest Kodak Box
Brownie camera. In such circumstances Secularists argued the reality of war
and the notion of motive in the conflict was being swept under the carpet.

In the last part of his *Patriotism and Empire* Robertson astutely admitted
that those who argued against imperialism did not have a clearly viable
alternative to offer:

> The "sane" imperialist, then, if he would hinder further expansion, must
> make out a case against that ideal of imperialism which primes expan-
> sionism; and if he does this, he will find that he must condemn the theory
> of imperialism in the lump, while recognising the exigencies of the situa-
> tion it has thus far created.[30]

Robertson then moved rapidly toward proposing an alternative route that
social development, freed of the shackles imposed by the exigencies of imperialism, should follow:

against racial swagger, scientific social development. Against arms expenditure, bettering the lives of the population and education. Against forced union, intelligent federation [this was a clear allusion to the equally unsatisfactory answers to the Irish question offered by prevailing definitions of imperialism—D.N.]. Against perpetual domination, the development of the tendency to self government.... Against downfall of empire, the construction of alternative bases for society. And lastly, as against a barbarian cult, which alternately chants a hypocritical hymn of propitiation to a God of War and bares venomous fangs towards the rival worshippers of the same deity, an ethic of reason and fraternity of human goodwill, that guards against supernaturalist vitiations.[31]

Robertson's critique of the South African War took on even greater significance because he was not simply a journalist or commentator writing from a distance—he was also involved in the war as an eyewitness, as was Hobson. Sent to South Africa as a reporter for the *Morning Leader,* Robertson sent regular accounts home that appeared under the *nom de plume* "Scrutator." He was one of the first to alert domestic opinion to the indiscriminate burning of farms as a military tactic, and he was condemned by *The Times* for his lack of patriotism.[32] He also appeared at meetings on his return from South Africa. In December 1900, at London's Westminster Palace Hotel, Robertson began his address by suggesting that the suppression of news had effectively turned the more jingoistic elements in the British press into election agents for the Conservative Party. He also alleged that stories of British troops being fired upon from Boer farms flying the white flag were being systematically exaggerated to extend the scorched-earth policy. He was also anxious to scotch fears that the Boer republics constituted any threat to the security of the Cape Colony. Of particular note were his reports that many in the Cape Colony were convinced that peace in Southern Africa would only be possible if the independence of the Boer republics was assured.[33]

Robertson's reports for the *Morning Leader* were subsequently collected in a controversial book, *Wrecking the Empire,* which was published in 1901. This book, boycotted by many booksellers, contained what one review described as

one long record of arbitrary proceedings on the part of the military authorities towards the Dutch in Cape Colony and Natal; of unjustifiable arrests and imprisonment of innocent men; of warring upon women and non-combatants; of a systematic policy of humiliating the Dutch throughout South Africa, and acts of the grossest injustice perpetrated under the license inseparable from Martial Law; the whole constituting a damning indictment of the war ... of a nature to cause every fair-minded Englishman to blush with shame at the infamies which have been perpetrated in his name in South Africa.[34]

Contemporaneous with the publication of this book, Robertson took his lantern slides of wartime atrocities on a tour. These exhibitions were, for many who opposed the war, the first point of contact with its graphic reality. Robertson was nonetheless pragmatic enough to realize that the empire was an obligation that could not be avoided or shirked. If anything, his experiences of the South African War sharpened this realization, and he pressed fellow anti-imperialists to accept imperial responsibility. Robertson hoped that imperial nations would henceforth embrace the duty to promote and encourage self-government among former colonies. Even when the war had ended, Robertson attacked both the glorification of empire and the compulsive need to popularize it to galvanize patriotism. These two tendencies came together in the person of Sir Arthur Conan Doyle, whose monumental *War in South Africa* was aimed at both audiences. It was an attempt to refute this twin imperative that spurred Robertson to write an open letter denouncing what he saw as the surrender of reason Conan Doyle's work actively encouraged.

Positivists and Pacifism

Another group of individuals loosely included under the umbrella of Secularism that took a slightly different attitude were the Positivist followers of Auguste Comte. Comte's system argued that humans were progressing through levels of evolution to an inspirational state where the "positive" was the dominant theory within society. Having utilized scientific knowledge to escape the restrictive and tyrannical stage of the metaphysical, Positivists hoped that this would, by definition, bring an end to philosophical and religious conflict. In his earlier years, J. S. Mill had found himself drawn to positivism, although ultimately he rejected its overarching explanations. Mill's criticisms, however, had left an impression, and the dogma moved away from its universalist origins to an admission that individual discretion and conscience had a role to play in public life and the conduct of society.[35] Many Positivists were themselves able to channel their beliefs into an ethic of humanitarian service that saw many of them enter the diplomatic service and colonial government as well as the teaching and medical professions. In the arena of imperial policy positivists were particularly strong advocates of decolonization and saw in the ongoing development of society a move from the "barbarism" associated with theism to the scientific Positivism of the final coming of age of civilization.

The work of Gilbert Murray and his associates at Cambridge has been well documented, although his attachment to Positivism was more tenuous than that of many other advocates.[36] Murray was a leading member of the South Africa Conciliation Committee and wrote—with the renowned labor historian John Hammond—a condemnation of Milner's helot dispatch. Murray and Hammond were two of the three essayists (the other being Francis Hirst) in *Liberalism and the Empire,* in which Murray's piece compared the conditions of slavery in the Greco-Roman world with those in Britain's colonies. He concluded that it was almost axiomatic that Britain's rule of indigenous peoples had singularly failed to advance their moral and material welfare. Murray's reaction was apposite, since his position as Regius Professor of Greek led him to compare British imperialism with Athenian imperialism, noting with singular foreboding that the corruption of Athens had followed the city-state's abandonment of democracy.[37] This was a fundamentally important aspect of the Positivist approach to reconstructing society. The blueprint for a mutually moral future lay in selectively compiling and publicizing the benefits and achievement of past societies. Thus, a Positivist pantheon of mankind contained scholars, missionaries, democrats, philosophers, scientists, and social reformers who could be invoked as representative of the true uplifting spirit of humanity. These individuals and the characteristics and virtues they represented could be contrasted with the destruction wrought by soldiers and imperialists.

Another luminary of the Positivist Movement was Frederic Harrison, a former professor of constitutional and international law as well as the leading proponent of Positivism in Britain. He was a founding member of the Conciliation Committee and was also the chief speaker at a meeting held in December 1899, attended by Emily Hobhouse.[38] Harrison had an impressive history, stretching back more than fifty years, of writing about imperial questions. He had opposed the Crimean War and the Indian Mutiny, and he now opposed the Boer War, which infuriated him because of what he saw as the apparent impotence of the Liberal party.[39] In particular, he noted that the wishes of the British government that a permanent English population be established as the dominant power in South Africa had effectively been shattered by the conflict.[40]

Harrison was joined in his Positivist criticism by the respected former Oriel College physician John Henry Bridges, who had been medical inspector to the Poor Law Board of London until his retirement in 1891. The outbreak of the South African War affected Bridges deeply and he described it as a "particularly strong shock to his faith in humanity."[41] While Gilbert Murray had held British imperialism up to the mirror of Athenian society, Bridges preferred the model of Roman imperialism, which he averred had done far more than the British in terms of extending citizenship to previously subject races.[42] Bridges also considered the British failure to offer positions of power to members of the native population in India a dangerous oversight. The centralization of the British Empire's armed forces and its ability to finance those of Britain's dominions, as far as Bridges was concerned, prevented the empire itself from developing into a true federation because devolved responsibility was sadly lacking. He saw this as a prerequisite for the dissolution of empire into something more acceptable, although he doubted how long such a structure would last in the face of modern warfare. Bridges also refuted the accusation that Positivists were unpatriotic by arguing that they ultimately aimed to save Britain from itself, in this case from "the imperialistic taint." This was why they had made common cause with the Boers, to prevent "the establishment of a new Ireland seven thousand miles away."[43]

Two of the most energetic of the second generation of Positivists were Malcolm Quin and Frederick James Gould. Quin was a vocal opponent of the war and linked Positivist reverence for the achievements of the Boer dead with a veneration of republican civic virtue.[44] Meanwhile, Frederick James Gould sought to promote Positivism through his actions in the local political and public life of England. After conversion to Positivism in London, he became "pastor" of the Secular Society in Leicester.[45] Gould's main concern was the search for a "governing theory" he could use to promote and establish the moral health of the nation. As well as journalistic work, Gould had already embarked on the construction of a curriculum of moral instruction that consciously avoided any connection between Christian belief and morality. Instead, it espoused an ethical position, informed by socialism as well as the radical rhetorics of anti-imperialism, antimilitarism, and anticompetitiveness. Serving on the school board in Leicester, he was the first to get this curriculum introduced in its schools and disseminated in socialist circles, thus achieving considerable recognition in the world of moral education. Gould's defense of the anti-imperialist cause also extended to defending the liberty of conscience of teachers who refused to be involved in victory parades or refused to distribute coronation medals.[46]

It is clear that some secular and anti-imperialist thought rubbed shoulders with republican critiques of monarchy. While anti-imperialists questioned the militarism of Queen Victoria's funeral, there was also criticism of the way the monarchy had endorsed militaristic and jingoistic ends in the last years of her reign. Moreover, this was a moral issue for some who believed that the legitimacy of monarchy was being undermined by its complicity in an escalating and vulgar imperialism.[47] *The Reformer,* edited by Charles Bradlaugh's daughter, Hypatia Bradlaugh-Bonner, was typical in its attacks on the militarism of the monarchy:

> The Queen is said to have loved peace, yet her whole reign from 1837 to 1901, is marked with bloodshed, and the expenditure on armaments has increased from thirteen millions of pounds to fifty millions.... A monarch's position is doubtless a very difficult one, and that is a very good reason for having no monarch.... No excuse of age, or sex, or health should be allowed to weigh against the welfare of the Empire. If we are told that the personality of the monarch has no real effect upon the welfare of the empire then of course the monarch is nothing but a cumbrous unnecessary burden.[48]

Robertson, as ever, saw the failure of morals as a consequence of the failure of civic society to outgrow the monarchy. He did not see, as some republicans argued, that individuals who accepted monarchy were, by definition, in a morally debased state. Rather, he argued that

> An instituted imbecility, a habitual irrationalism, is infectious; each civic state of mind reacts on the others; and the cultivation of a feudal mummery and a feudal abjectness infallibly fosters the temper and the unintelligence, the incivilisation and the forethoughtlessness of the feudal age.[49]

At times Bradlaugh-Bonner regarded the war and the concept of a "military regimen" in league with Christianity as a dangerous barrier to women's emancipation. She noted that the editor of the *Church Family Newspaper* had suggested that "the sex that risks its life in war will always insist on ruling" and replied that "women suffragists should bear the *Church Family Newspaper*'s dictum in mind and diligently inculcate a love of peace and hatred of war as a means of obtaining the franchise."[50]

Pacifism's Legacy

In the final analysis most (not all) Secularists, Freethinkers, and Positivists opposed the South African War for a number of reasons, some of which they shared with other members of the antiwar lobby. However, it should be remembered that these various stances were more heterogeneous than has perhaps been appreciated up to now. Not only was a variety of motives involved, but the attitudes of those opposed to the war also changed over time. Outright opposition to imperialism was important, as were more nuanced objections to its conduct or the wisdom of this kind of coercive foreign imperial policy, but antiwar sentiment was by no means universal, nor did it adopt uniform strategies.

Despite this, the Boer War brought all Secularists together in their condemnation of the role played by religion in the conflict. It was a singularly unpleasant reminder of how two Christian countries could marshal their respective conceptions of God to defend and justify their actions in battle. This epic and unsavory war is depicted most graphically in a cartoon that appeared in J. W. Gott's Secularist newspaper, the *Truthseeker,* which in its editorial style and content was often quite flippant. From the divine nature of the imperial mission to Kruger's brand of saddle-and-rifle bibliolatry the two forces were not simply introducing new tactics made necessary by the smokeless high-velocity rifle, the man-stopping revolver, or the expanding bullet; they were engaging in a more dangerous escalation of religio-moral

J. W. Gott's *Truthseeker* was uncompromising about the role of religion
in the South African conflict.

SOURCE: *Truthseeker,* various editions, 1900 onward

rearmament that from the perspective of 1902 had no end. Such moral rearmament could appear to be just as threatening as physical rearmament—
the escalation in arms expenditure that concerned observers were predicting
before the conflict. They worried about what would be left of civilization
after the devastation of war: "Lest any foe be left alive / Keep them from
Matthew chapter five."[51]

Not only did this appear to signal the end of reason or of compromise
as primary considerations in the relationship between the two nations; such
attitudes stoked the jingoism that had led to infringements of civil rights
that those opposed to the war had to endure. Arguably this view needed
to look no further than the excesses of the Khaki election of 1901, which
Robertson himself, perhaps wisely, boycotted. The escalation of religious
and moral rearmament must have felt to Secularists like the escalation of the
cold war when cruise missiles arrived in western Europe in the early 1980s.
Peace campaigners at Greenham Common and elsewhere felt not only that
they stood between civilization and barbarism, but also that the climate
of fear created a situation in which civil liberties could easily be compro-
mised. This atmosphere of gathering gloom is conveyed for the 1980s most
cogently in E. P. Thompson's *Writing by Candlelight* and *The Heavy Dancers*
in a way that the work of Hobson and Robertson does for the first years
of the twentieth century. For Secularists looking back in 1919, it would increasingly appear that the religio-moral rearmament instigated during the
Boer War had led inexorably to the wanton sacrifice of the First World War.[52]
Hypatia Bradlaugh-Bonner wrote of the feeling of desolation the South
African War engendered in those who feared that jingoism was the ideology
of the future, that moves toward meritocracy would be thwarted by the
resurgence of the "military regimen," and finally that war was an essential
part of imperialism:

> Where, then, is the gain from all this sickness and suffering, from all this
> death and despair? That is the question we must put to one another. The
> gain is not to be counted by earldoms and money grants to generals; by
> fortunes to army contractors; by 200 per cent dividends to Birmingham
> Small Arms shareholders; by the aggrandisement of a few capitalists. It is
> to be counted by the gain to us, the people's gain, the national gain, the
> imperial gain, the gain of which a true patriot may be proud. It is to be
> counted by the verdict which posterity will pass on this two years' history,
> which has been traced in indelible letters of blood.... In South Africa the
> seeds we have sown are the fruitful tares of iniquity, and the harvest we are
> leaving our children to reap is a harvest of hatred and sorrow.[53]

Indicative of how attitudes could change is the later verdict on the South African War of W. Stewart Ross, who initially believed the British cause to be just and the conflict unavoidable. The escalation of the war and the deployment of all its weapons meant that by the end of 1900 Ross was fearful of what religious moral rearmament could achieve:

> The hills of the Transvaal have been shaken by thunders more terrible than ever, in the barbaric imagination, roared and crashed over Sinai: and the veldt has been drenched with the gore of Christians in the death grapple with brother Christians. . . . To perdition with the religion that can sanction or stimulate havoc like this! Were it under the sanction of fifty Christs or Jehovahs I would hate it! I hate it in memory of the bones that bleach and rot on the banks of the Tugela and by the Modder's turbid tide. I hate it for the multitudinous graves of Briton and Boer who, under banners blest in the name of the same god, committed legalised and sanctified murder. I hate the accursed creed, if possible, still more bitterly when I think of the mothers in English homes, or in African Kraals, whose sons, who should have been their pride and joy, now lie in the unknown and bloody graves into which their butchered remains were thrown under the auspices of Cantuar's Intercession or Kruger's prayers.[54]

While this indictment of the war and religion's part in it was central to the views of some Secularists, others (such as Robertson, Bridges, and Gilbert Murray) found in it only a starting point. For them, war seemed a symptom of a wider and more dangerous malaise that afflicted imperial nations with their own rapidly growing spheres of popular discourse. From a moral condemnation that had successfully stepped outside the warring moral codes espoused by the two aggressor nations was born a radical critique of imperial policy and popular sentiment that drew strength from a series of closely related alternative moral codes. Elements of this wide critique were eventually to bear fruit in an altered attitude to empire among many mainstream liberals. Eventually the effectiveness of this can be seen in the adoption of its elements by individuals in the socialist and labor movements who argued that only an uplifting and morally just "labor-inspired" culture could rescue British civilization from the twin capitalist tyrannies of popular hedonistic indulgence and imperial jingoism.[55]

Ultimately, however, opposition to the Boer War bequeathed a more lasting legacy. Our perspective on the nature of war and how it is waged has undergone a complete transformation in the course of the twentieth century. It is now possible to say that the Boer War demonstrated simultaneously the changing nature of modern conflict, the problems faced by those who opposed such conflicts, and the range of legitimate responses and modes of protest that could be employed to oppose them.

The war in South Africa did much to discredit imperial adventures. Popular responses to incidents such as the relief of Mafeking may have depressed radicals, but imperialists were unable to make any lasting gain from these because postwar clamors for compulsory conscription went unheeded. In many respects this indicates the level of success enjoyed by the pacifist analysis, which saw a military complex as a danger to civilization. Likewise, Robertson's identification of the danger posed to civil society by total war became still more prescient in the First World War. Despite this, the campaigns of organizations such as the Union of Democratic Control and individuals like H. N. Brailsford to invite popular opinion to pronounce on foreign policy and take a more active interest in its formulation were the positive inheritance of the peace campaigners of the Boer War.[56] A closer look also suggests that other components of modern peace politics had their genesis in this conflict. Hypatia Bradlaugh-Bonner's conception of women's special role as peace brokers and guardians of civil liberties, personified by the women prepared to stand in the firing line between Briton and Boer, had their counterparts in the Hague Congress of 1915 and in the peace campaigns against cruise missiles in the 1980s.[57] Moreover, the peace campaigners of the Boer War for the first time focused on the sheer destructiveness of the weapons and tactics employed. This line of argument was to be used by peace campaigners and balance-of-power advocates alike in the Edwardian period who tried to persuade Western civilization that war was to be avoided. The South African War also gave birth to the genre of "military incompetence" literature that leads onward through Sassoon to "Oh What a Lovely War."[58]

In most respects the lasting legacy of the Boer War has been the absorption into Western democracy of Secularist and pacifist attitudes toward war during the course of the twentieth century. Conscientious objection became thoroughly viable by the Second World War and its acceptance was in part a recognition of the destructive power of war itself. Thus, as James Hinton puts it, what had begun as a movement for resistance to the new apparatus of militarism "became itself a tolerated part of that apparatus."[59] By the end of the twentieth century, war was no longer an adventure, an opportunity for commercial expansion, or indeed a conflict fought solely by members of the military. Nor could war be fought so ardently with the unequivocal support of religion. With the arrival of total war, the sanction of Christianity has been tentative or ambivalent. The Boer War gave us popular knowledge of concentration camps, scorched earth, and the dum-dum bullet, but it also gave us "a growth culture for the largest body of anti-war poetry that any war to date had produced."[60] Drummer Hodge's legacy to Western culture can be seen in the works of Sassoon and Owen and perhaps also in the genre of films critical of the Vietnam War in all its manifestations.

Notes

1. The Secular Movement can be investigated through S. Budd, *Varieties of Unbelief* (London, 1971); D. S. Nash, *Secularism, Art and Freedom* (London, 1992); three works by E. Royle: *Victorian Infidels* (Manchester, 1974), *The Infidel Tradition from Paine to Bradlaugh* (London, 1976), and *Radicals, Secularists and Republicans: Popular Freethought in Britain, 1866–1915* (Manchester, 1980); and two by D. Tribe: *One Hundred Years of Freethought* (London, 1967) and *President Charles Bradlaugh, M.P.* (London, 1971).

2. Arthur Davey's thorough and informative work, *The British Pro-Boers, 1877–1902* (Cape Town, 1978), missed Secularist and Freethinking objections to the war apart from scant coverage of some individual Positivists.

3. See J. Hinton, *Protests and Visions: Peace Politics in 20th Century Britain* (London, 1989), 2.

4. *Freethinker*, 25 September 1898, reprinted from the *Rochdale Observer*.

5. See O. Anderson, "The Growth of Christian Militarism in Mid-Victorian Britain," *English Historical Review* 86 (1971): 46–72. M. van Wyk Smith, in *Drummer Hodge: The Poetry of the Anglo-Boer War, 1899–1902* (Oxford, 1978), makes the point that throughout the Victorian period, the army in Britain was an expeditionary force to be sent abroad and that it was therefore able to retain a sense of gentility.

6. See Hinton, *Protests and Visions*, 21.

7. G. W. Foote, "Fighting Christians" (editorial), *Freethinker*, 8 October 1899.

8. See, for example, the *Freethinker*, 29 October, 5 November, and 12 November 1899.

9. *Freethinker*, 14 January and 25 February 1900.

10. Foote declared in one article in the *Freethinker*, 27 May 1900, that his support for the war could be justified on the grounds that "if your boy is in a race you naturally enough want him to win."

11. See the *Random Recollections of Sydney Ansell Gimson*, part 2, 1938, 10–11 (typescript in Leicestershire Record Office, Wigston Magna). See also Nash, *Secularism*, 137; R. van Reenen (ed.), *Emily Hobhouse: Boer War Letters* (Cape Town, 1984), 15.

12. *The Reformer*, April 1900.

13. *Agnostic Journal*, 30 September 1899, 228. It is worth noting that some other sections of Secularist opinion took a different line that might be construed as more conventionally "pro-Boer." *The Reformer*, in September and November 1901, suggested that accusations of Boer cruelty to Africans were a smokescreen that hid British brutality to the indigenous populations of Africa, particularly against the

Matabele and the Zulu, as well as throughout Australasia. It concluded that it was imperial situations that made the behavior of both Briton and Boer reprehensible. Nevertheless, another of its correspondents was anxious to indicate the inherent danger of arming "native tribes," which was seen as making a popular rising against "the white man" more likely.

14. *The Reformer,* April 1900.

15. Hinton (*Protests and Visions,* 21) suggests that a Eurocentric racism pervaded Edwardian pacifism in the guise of the distinction often made by the Quakers between the role of the soldier and that of the policeman. This sanctioned action against the "heathen" but warned of the dire consequences of war between Christian nations. This view tends to underestimate the sophistication of the views outlined above. Those who took a keen interest in Africans indicted Christians for their treatment of this group.

16. J. M. Robertson, *Toryism and Barbarism* (London, 1885).

17. See, for example, M. Freeden's introduction to *J. A. Hobson: A Reader* (London, 1988), 20.

18. Hinton, *Protests and Visions,* 20, 25–26.

19. J. M. Robertson, *Patriotism and Empire* (London, 1899). See especially Robertson's direct allusion to Hobson's "Under-Consumptionist Critique" on p. 178.

20. Ibid., 52.

21. Ibid., 52, 69.

22. Ibid., 59. Hobson similarly railed against this popular form's celebratory "glorification of brute force and an ignorant contempt for foreigners." Quoted in M. van Wyk Smith, *Drummer Hodge,* 77.

23. H. G. Jones (ed.), *Illustrations of Positivism: A Selection of Articles from the "Positivist Review" in Science, Philosophy, Religion and Politics* (London, 1907). Chapter titled "War and Peace," article titled "Democracy and War" (1898), 405.

24. *The Reformer,* 15 March 1897.

25. For an analysis of Cobden and the Manchester School's contribution to the development of peace politics see Hinton, *Protests and Visions,* and M. Howard, *War and the Liberal Conscience* (Oxford, 1981).

26. Robertson, *Patriotism and Empire,* 77–78, 83.

27. Anderson, "Growth of Christian Militarism," *passim.*

28. Hinton, *Protests and Visions,* 9. See also Howard, *War and the Liberal Conscience,* 59–60.

29. This worry about the growth of pro-war sentiment, which was linked to a vulgarization of contemporary culture, was noted also by Emily Hobhouse, as indeed it was by a number of prominent Anglican clergymen such as Canon S. A. Barnett, the Dean of Durham; Dr. G. W. Kitchin; and the Royal Chaplain, Charles Gore. See van Reenen, *Emily Hobhouse,* 16; Davey, *British Pro-Boers,* 145, 147–48.

30. Robertson, *Patriotism and Empire,* 145.

31. Ibid., 202.

32. Davey, *British Pro-Boers,* 57.

33. *The Reformer,* 15 December 1900, 49–50.

34. *Radical Review,* 15 April 1903.

35. T. R. Wright, *The Religion of Humanity: The Impact of Comtean Positivism on Victorian Britain* (New York, 1986).

36. See, for example, R. Symonds, *Oxford and Empire: The Last Lost Cause?* (Oxford, 1986), and Wright, *Religion of Humanity*, 271.

37. Wright, *Religion of Humanity*, 90–93.

38. Van Reenen, *Emily Hobhouse*, 15.

39. Davey, *British Pro-Boers*, 161.

40. Symonds, *Oxford and Empire*, 85–86.

41. Wright, *Religion of Humanity*, 115, 118.

42. Van Wyk Smith (*Drummer Hodge*, 103) notes that the use of imperial Rome as an analogy for the British Empire and its motives began to be contested in other spheres. Increasingly, the grandiose comparisons of Rosebery and Curzon could be contrasted with the ambivalent use of the comparison in Conrad's *Heart of Darkness* and Hardy's *Embarcation*.

43. Jones, *Illustrations of Positivism*, chapter titled "Politics," article titled "Roman and British Imperialism," 397–99.

44. Quin spoke in July 1902. Quoted in Davey, *British Pro-Boers*, 151.

45. For a deeper discussion of Gould's career see R. Berard, "Frederick James Gould and the Transformation of Moral Education," *British Journal of Educational Studies* 35, no. 3 (1987): 233–47; and D. S. Nash, "F. J. Gould and the Leicester Secular Society: A Positivist Commonwealth in Edwardian Politics," *Midland History* 16 (1991): 126–40.

46. See Nash, "F. J. Gould," *passim*.

47. R. Williams, *The Contentious Crown: Public Discussion of the British Monarchy in the Reign of Queen Victoria* (London, 1997), 175, 177, 254.

48. *The Reformer*, 15 February 1901, 66.

49. *The Reformer*, April 1902.

50. *The Reformer*, 15 March 1900, 130.

51. *The Academy*, 18 November 1899. Quoted in van Wyk Smith, *Drummer Hodge*, 32.

52. See van Wyk Smith, *Drummer Hodge*, 23, 136.

53. *The Reformer*, 15 February 1901.

54. *Truthseeker*, 3 November 1900.

55. C. Waters, *British Socialists and the Politics of Popular Culture, 1884–1914* (Manchester, 1990).

56. Hinton, *Protests and Visions*, 36, 45.

57. Ibid., 43–44.

58. Van Wyk Smith, *Drummer Hodge*, 196.

59. Hinton, *Protests and Visions*, 53.

60. Van Wyk Smith, *Drummer Hodge*, 33.

CHAPTER 14

The South African War and Imperial Britain

A Question of Significance?

ANDREW PORTER

BECAUSE "IN HISTORY, as in all serious matters, no achievement is final ... [so] every new generation must rewrite history in its own way; every new historian, not content with giving new answers to old questions, must revise the questions themselves; and—since historical thought is a river into which none can step twice—even a single historian, working at a single subject for a certain length of time, finds when he tries to reopen an old question that the question has changed."[1] The title of this collection, *Writing a Wider War: Rethinking Gender, Race, and Identity in the South African War, 1899–1902*, and the variety of its essays could hardly do more to illustrate the accuracy of R. G. Collingwood's reflections on the transitory nature of any historical writing, the shifting sands of scholarly investigation, and the constant flux of historiography. In very recent years there has been both a marked widening of range among scholars interested in the war and striking shifts in the particular subjects attracting their attention.

Not so long ago, it might have been said that the focal points were comparatively few, and in some respects, perhaps, that they were also narrowly defined. There were for instance—and perhaps always will be—the preoccupations of military historians, for whom the significance of the South African War lay in regimental histories, in the blood, smoke, and tactics of individual engagements, and, more broadly, in regional topography and the strategic planning of the conflict. Like the best art galleries, the war of 1899–1902 was sufficiently varied to sustain interest and not so large that energy gave out and one lost sight of the whole.[2]

However, there were other, larger canvases on which overarching issues of causation, dynamics, and consequences were mapped out. For some historians the war stood at the center of South Africa's century-long economic and social transformation: it was crucial to the local emergence of a modern industrialized state with both its own peculiar solution to the conflicts of capital and labor and its lopsided integration into a global capitalist system. Internally, for Briton and Afrikaner the Boer War or the Second War for Freedom was represented, like the Great Trek, as critical in defining the terms of a continuing communal conflict by political means. In the history of Britain's overseas expansion, it was widely seen as a prime example of the manner in which metropolitan imperialists were compelled—some less reluctantly than others—to respond to peripheral crises. Presented in general terms as a classic example of imperialism breeding its antithesis in uncompromising nationalism, the war also provided one of the last significant episodes in that globally significant transformation, the partition of Africa. In another arena, through the contemporary writings of J. A. Hobson, the war apparently provided the principal early source of theorizing about the links between capitalism and imperialism.

In their day these analyses represented attempts to answer what the historians involved regarded not simply as interesting questions but as "big" or "important" ones. Their view still seems reasonable: to ask of a war that strained the resources of one of the most powerful states in the world why it occurred and what were its main consequences can hardly be dismissed as an entirely trivial pursuit. But what has happened to these questions now? Have they lost their point, or have they been answered to general satisfaction? Have they simply become boring as a result of reiteration, or have they been exposed as unimportant after all?

Among the many subjects in this volume, such questions at first sight certainly seem conspicuous by their absence. This provokes the speculation that perhaps we have reached a point where rethinking the South African War can no longer be achieved by approaching the war head-on, by making it our starting point or principal focus of concern. This might be one implication of the fact that many of the topics for debate here appear to have been generated out of a prior interest in quite other issues, the questions for examination to have been stimulated in settings entirely different from the war or even South Africa. The war is being approached via new or reviving interests in the history of identity or of memory; in the dissection of representations; and in religion, medicine, or gender. In other words, the key to rethinking the war may depend, somewhat paradoxically, not simply on insights provided from elsewhere but on its having lost its centrality in our individual preoccupations.

If this is so, then further questions might follow. Is the South African War no longer a fit or serious subject in itself for scholarly examination, by reason of its having become a subject incapable of generating from within questions of the first magnitude? Is its future to be that of simply one among many other complex historical episodes fit for plunder by students of a thousand and one disciplines in search of evidence with which to flesh out their hypotheses? Indeed, perhaps we should envisage a world in which historians cease their attempts to study the war in the round, because of assumptions that all historical questions have equal status in terms of their capacity to illuminate the war's essential nature or significance and that all evidence, however partial or incomplete, is deemed to be representative of the whole.

These reflections are offered in part by way of introduction, in part in the hope of providing gentle provocation. They are given added point, however, by the main purpose of this chapter, which is to consider the significance of this South African War in the *fin-de-siècle* history of the metropolitan British politics of imperialism and anticolonialism. In what ways and to what degree did the war prompt the contemporary rethinking or even the redefinition of political principles, of party alignments, or of standpoints on major issues? How central or far-reaching a concern were South Africa and the war before 1914? The claim made by A. F. Madden in the *Cambridge History of the British Empire* may stand for those who have little doubt as to its fundamental importance.

> "Imperial policy," wrote Bernard Shaw in his Fabian apologia for Empire, "will mean South Africa." Throughout this period, from the unbelievable folly of the Raid of 1895 to the singular spectacle of Afrikaner suppression of anti-British rebellion in 1914, South Africa was the focus of the empire in British politics, and its challenge was concentrated, severe, and decisive.[3]

The onetime readiness of metropolitan or imperial historians to attach great significance to the war has been paralleled in the belief among South African-ists—albeit for quite different reasons—that the war was of metropolitan, even global importance quite apart from any local significance it possessed.[4] However, in the light of recent historiography, there appears to be good reason to consider the view that for all the passion it generated at the time, the impact of the war and South African matters on Britain and the wider empire before 1914 was less far-reaching or singular and far less direct than has often been imagined. This chapter looks in turn at imperial politics, economy, and defense and concludes with some reflections on the relation-ship of the war to Britain's *fin-de-siècle* political crisis.

The Metropole's Politics and the War

The Victorians are reputed to have been serious, but how far this extended in their politics has long been a matter of dispute. There would perhaps be widespread agreement that questions of taxation, education, religion, and Ireland raised passions and generated lasting political commitment both to principle and to party allegiance. But in other areas of political life things were different. The waywardness, deep ignorance, and general unhelpfulness of much public and electoral opinion on critical issues disturbed prominent figures at many different points on the political spectrum. For instance, Lord Salisbury's concern to keep foreign affairs out of the limelight and his notorious desire to keep even close colleagues in the dark as to his foreign policy are well known. J. A. Hobson despaired of the irrationality and aggressiveness he felt marked the dominant culture of the late 1890s. In part he attributed it to the machinations of press magnates; but, like many a radical, he was also inclined to see in the "psychology of jingoism" evidence that power would only be appropriately applied if placed in the hands of people like himself. Sir Alfred Milner deplored the fickleness especially of "high society" with its penchant for novelty and liability to boredom with serious issues. In such a setting, issues of foreign and imperial politics, defense, or trade rarely set the world of British politics alight. As Sir Edward Hamilton put it, "so long as John Bull is not called upon to pay, he does not interest himself much in 'oversea' affairs."[5] Not just South Africa, but even the war, did little if anything to alter this.

Let us consider in what sense this was so. If one examines the party politics of the metropole itself, then the lack of serious impact attributable to the war stems from a characteristic shared with South African questions more generally between 1880 and 1910. They were a source of such embarrassment that party leaders wished to be rid of them as quickly as possible. It was always incumbent upon a British ministry—however difficult it might be in practice—to create where possible the illusion of security and an impression that it was dealing deftly with British interests overseas. Inaction or the avoidance of issues through minimal responses were often means to that end.

For all his appearance of vigorous determination, Joseph Chamberlain was constantly wrong-footed on South African questions. Within weeks of his taking office in 1895, this Secretary of State with a Great Power's global empire to be reorganized was forced to lower his sights drastically. Aiming initially to make the Colonial Office "to be reckoned as highly as the Foreign Office" and to show the nation "what a part [the empire] might play in the world,"[6] he soon found himself offering the prime minister his resignation. He was compelled under a watchful public eye to bargain about borders with Tswana paramount chiefs, and he was caught up in the Drifts Crisis.[7] Behind the scenes, presented with the determination of Rhodes and his cronies to upset Kruger's government, Chamberlain had no alternative but to tread the finest of lines between "official" and "unofficial" knowledge in an effort to protect imperial influence in South Africa. The Jameson Raid, incriminating telegrams, and a Parliamentary investigation only exacerbated the complications of political life and multiplied diversions from his main concerns.

A pattern was thus established well ahead of the South African War itself. Subsequently, Chamberlain lost to Milner control of the handling of relations with the Transvaal, and as a result got the war neither he nor his colleagues desired or even seriously anticipated until late summer 1899. Government failings and military incompetence, although to some extent countered by conquest of the Republics in 1900 and shrouded in the faint satisfaction of military victory in 1902, turned the war into a chapter of accidents seen as best forgotten as soon as possible. Before October 1899, Chamberlain's skilled improvisation had turned the Uitlander question to the advantage of his wider promotion of empire,[8] but the early course of the war and still more its degeneration into an affair of concentration camps, guerrilla tactics, and private revenge drained it of any remaining moral and political capital. Chamberlain and the Unionists eventually dropped it altogether. There was widespread avoidance of war issues by Unionist candidates during the general election campaign in autumn 1900, and, with considerable relief, a steady turning of attention to the more traditional political battlegrounds of religion in education in 1902 and of protectionism in 1903. The Royal Commission on the War, by becoming mired in much detail, also served to divert attention elsewhere.

For the Liberals things were hardly better, despite their place in opposition. Just as the Liberal government of 1892–95 got rid of the High Commissioner, Sir Henry Loch, rather than facing up to the complexity of Cape-Transvaal relations or Uitlander affairs, and handed Swaziland over to the Republic, so the party's response to the Raid and the Unionist government's misfortunes was to take the line of "least said, soonest mended." Liberal representatives on the parliamentary committee of enquiry into the Raid, Sir William Harcourt and Henry Labouchere, avoided any serious pursuit of Chamberlain.

Liberals found the war itself, of course, still more embarrassing. It was long ago remarked of even the Liberal imperialists within the party that they were "involved in imperial affairs because such affairs were prominent, not because they were inherently interesting."[9] Conscious of a widespread general enthusiasm for empire, figures in the group such as Lord Rosebery and his chief acolytes, Asquith, Grey, and Haldane, hoped to use imperial issues as a way of bridging many of the party's internal splits, notably that between Gladstonians and radicals or social democrats divided over questions of financial economy, poverty, social reform, the role of the state, and national defense. This was a vain hope, for it was founded in Liberal imperialists' indifference to many aspects of empire, for instance expansion and development in Africa, and their peculiar ignorance of others, such as South Africa. If the war brought a measure of detailed enlightenment—not only to Liberal imperialists but also to pro-Boers—it also revealed the impossibility of uniting the party around things South African. The Liberals were split several ways by the war, their views shifting in different directions as they responded to military events or to government policy. The conflict generated personal bitterness and mutual incomprehension, a degree of division that undoubtedly contributed to their defeat in the election called by the Unionists in 1900. When campaigning, many Liberals followed the example of their Conservative rivals in trying where possible to avoid war issues.

For Liberals, therefore, as for Unionists, it was a profound relief to return to familiar domestic arguments with their main political opponents in the course of 1902–3. Smarting from their experience of the war, Liberals thereafter continued to retreat from the South African front. Self-government for the Transvaal and Orange River Colony offered an escape from the deplorable legacy of Chinese labor, the construction of the Union from uncomfortable reminders of the abandonment of African interests their policies entailed. Lord Selborne, a recent study has concluded, spent his career in South Africa rescuing the Rand from both a Liberal lack of understanding and Westminster's neglect.[10] For most Liberals the war faded into the past as an aberration. An event for which they had not been responsible, its spirits largely exorcised by the departure of Chamberlain and the Unionists in 1905, the war was not felt to require of them much rethinking of imperial issues.

If attention is turned to the wider politics of empire, a similar picture of halfhearted engagement and limited attention seems to emerge. At the colonial and imperial conferences of the period, after Sir Gordon Sprigg's offer in 1897 of a contribution to the empire's naval defenses, the Cape and Natal and eventually the Union governments made no distinct impact. In 1902, preoccupation with the details and aftermath of the war effectively neutralized their prime ministers. There was a common reluctance to dwell on the demonstrations of imperial weakness reemphasized by the war; and any indecent triumphalism in the presence of Cape and Natal delegates arising from other dominions' military contributions to the war was counterbalanced by

Canadian and Australian opposition to any form of common military reserve to cope with emergencies in the future. Both in 1902 and 1907, South African representatives did little more than reinforce the dominant concern of Canada and Australia to avoid any institutional centralization of empire and to keep any imperial intervention at a safe distance from their future proceedings.

The war certainly intensified the reluctance of South Africans to involve themselves in imperial affairs. This was given still clearer definition when, at the Imperial Conference of 1911, Prime Minister Botha spoke for the new Union government of the "policy of decentralization which has made the Empire."[11] But in this Botha did no more than reflect a majority view, one shared by the imperial government itself. Presiding over the conference, Asquith happily accepted the consensus. It only confirmed a course he had seen as inevitable and had supported for many years. This had been defined by Lord Rosebery in 1896. "I ... should not earnestly strive to bring the unity of the Empire very much nearer than it is at present, because it seems to me to rest ... on a liberal and affectionate comprehension—and what surer basis of an Empire is there than that?"[12] As prime minister, Asquith saw no reason to change his mind. As so many others, even Chamberlain, sooner or later recognized, a decentralized empire was not simply a realistic concession to the political forces of dominion nationalism; it was one that in practice recognized Britain's own nationality and particular interests, and it offered imperial governments a freedom of maneuver that they too valued. Making South African problems as far as possible a local responsibility was no less welcome to British policy makers than it had ever been, nor any less desirable than in the case of the other settlement colonies.

South Africa's Small Economy in the Big World of International Exchange

In recent years historians have paid increasing attention to the importance for Britain's economic strength in the nineteenth century of the "regions of recent settlement" or what are also called the "neo-Europes" of the world— areas, quite distinct from tropical regions, that included not only Britain's colonies of white settlement, but Argentina and other Latin American countries as well as the United States. "These areas came to prominence in the international economy after 1850 as colonization, fuelled by the demand requirements and supply capacities of industrial Europe, imposed an alien ecology and alien patterns of land use in a process of ecological imperialism." They steadily developed their own identifiable political economy in the form of what has been labeled "settler capitalism."[13]

Within this world of international exchange, South Africa gradually established herself as essentially one within a range of similar economies rather
than as one with an unusual or particularly dominant position. In the statistics of British trade there was little to distinguish the region from those
others just mentioned.

The movement of economic factors between one part of the settlement
empire and another, or between different regions of recent settlement, responded to common stimuli. Australasia's serious slump at the beginning of
the 1890s was succeeded by a fall in investment there and a subsequent rise
in the region's exports to pay off outstanding debts. Emigration and some
investment moved instead to South Africa, until rumors of war intervened.

When the South African War broke out, there were some who anticipated
further significant expansion once it was concluded, but they were mis-
taken.[14] Three years of conflict not only destroyed life and livelihood inside
the country, but had a seriously discouraging effect externally as well. It reduced the significance of the South African colonies for Britain and heightened that of other trading partners. The postwar recovery turned out to be
merely a flash in the pan, as Milner, for example, found to his chagrin. Emigration and Britain's flow of funds overseas were diverted to other arenas by
the war and by comparable expectations of profit or well-being.

TABLE 14.1 Exports of British Produce to the White-Settlement Empire

Source	1854–57		1909–13	
	£m	%	£m	%
Australasia	9.94	30.5	39.78	24.7
South Africa	1.23	3.8	19.56	12.1
Canada	4.33	13.3	21.23	13.2

Britain's Imports from the White-Settlement Empire

Source	1854–57		1909–13	
	£m	%	£m	%
Australasia	5.12	13.1	56.33	32.6
South Africa	1.23	3.1	10.68	6.2
Canada	6.29	16.0	27.26	15.8

SOURCE: Figures from Cain, "Economics and Empire: The Metropolitan Context," in A.
Porter (ed.), *The Oxford History of the British Empire*, vol. 3: *The Nineteenth Century*
(Oxford, 1999), Tables 2.2 and 2.4.

South Africa experienced a marked inflow of investment in 1902–3 to address the immediate needs of reconstruction, but levels then collapsed and, despite a brief optimistic flurry in 1908–10, remained poor in comparison with figures for the 1890s. Canada and Argentina were the favored outlets for overseas investment from 1900 on and forged ahead with their own expansion through to 1914. South Africa continued to lag in a world where between 1865 and 1914 it had attracted only five percent of the total capital calls on the London market. In the period from 1901 to 1914 almost 80 percent of an enormous surge of emigrants from Britain—5.4 million out of a total 6.76 million—crossed the Atlantic to Canada and the United States; even Australia and New Zealand once again attracted comfortably more than South Africa, as they had done in the 1880s. The dismal record of the official search for new British settlers for the Transvaal is well known. Only after 1908 did South Africa begin to recover its position, and even then it only did so in a setting marked by Britain's continued competitive expansion throughout the temperate white settler world.[15]

The economic picture is thus hardly one in which the war can be said to have established its importance by focusing British attention either on new opportunities to be opened up or on crucial resources waiting to be secured by conquest. Its impact involved quite as much if not more the diversion of economic interest to less disturbed and entrepreneurially more attractive parts of the globe.

The War and Imperial Military Reform

In the realm of imperial defense, the South African War has been portrayed as the great catalyst to thoroughgoing reform. The reconstruction of the Victorian army in the wake of the Queen's death was the work of those who concluded—like the young Leopold Amery did on the basis of his experience organizing war correspondents for *The Times*—that the Boer War revealed "how slight and uncertain was the reserve of military power of the British Empire."[16] There is much truth in his assessment. An army that revealed itself as wholly unable to anticipate the kind of war it was likely to have to fight; that was depleted by the malnourishment of volunteers from home and incapable of reinforcement from India not least because of the diseased state of its regular troops; and that was ill-trained and often incompetently supplied was under almost any circumstances going to find it hard to go on in its old ways after the Peace of Vereeniging. The British army was hardly even allowed to try.

However, perhaps the most important point to be made about the reform of Britain's armed forces between 1902 and 1910 was that changes were not directed to solving the kind of problems the South African War itself had raised. Not only was the prospect of war against the Transvaal hardly thought to require serious preparation in 1898–99;[17] well before it was even over, the war had begun to be seen as of little relevance to future military and naval planning.

Even in the budget of 1901 army estimates were less than naval; by 1914 while in monetary terms the navy's budget had increased by two-thirds, that of the army had declined by about 3 percent even from the reduced postwar levels of 1903–5.[18] The army reforms of St. John Brodrick, H. O. Arnold-Forster, and the long-serving Liberal Secretary of State for War, R. B. Haldane, culminated in a system that centered on a British Expeditionary Force of some 35,000 based in the United Kingdom and a new nonregular Territorial Force. Emerging in piecemeal fashion, reforms were aimed at fitting the army to fight not rebellious nationalists but quite other and more powerful enemies much closer to home. They reorganized the defense of the empire in ways that recognized that Britain was also inescapably a European power and were intended to reduce its dependence on imperial troops, whether based in Britain or in India.[19]

From a naval point of view, the South African War proved to be a still grander irrelevance. Arthur Balfour's claim that "Without the Navy we should never have been allowed to fight out the South African War to a successful conclusion; without the navy we should be incapable of fighting Russia in Central Asia" was evidence of the political weight of naval interests rather than an accurate commentary or guide to naval strategy.[20] As with the pattern of army reform, the remodeling of Britain's navy was equally dictated by quite other problems than fighting another distant war overseas. The steady shift toward constructing larger and more powerful warships for a battle fleet to be concentrated in home and Atlantic waters accentuated both the European dimensions of naval thinking and the Admiralty's refusal to be seen as little more than a glorified transport machine for an imperial army. Significant elements of Britain's performance in South Africa had in fact depended overwhelmingly on the successful mobilization of the mercantile marine to provide supplies and transports.[21] A far-reaching strategic reliance on private enterprise to provide the sinews of war, although it was finally to prove incapable of coping with the demands of the First World War, survived the South African War unmodified.

The reconstruction of British defenses was inseparably linked to the equally well-known "diplomatic revolution" of the early 1900s, that change of direction marked by stages in 1901, 1902, 1904, and 1907 of Britain's entry

into the alliance system of continental Europe. South Africanists have perhaps to resist a temptation to see in "their war" the critical agent of this
change. Rather than attribute it to the panicky reaction of a Britain seriously
disturbed by her isolation and threats of a Great Power counterstrike, there
is every reason to see in the shift the slow working out of a response to the
conditions of Europe and the policies of France, Germany, and Russia since
the early 1890s. South African complications counted for little alongside
Britain's mounting worries over the indefensibility of Indian frontiers, tensions in the Near East, and international competition for spheres of influence
and concessions in the Far East. These were challenges to British planning
and resources that many realized well before the War of 1899 had to be
addressed sooner rather than later, and they therefore saw South Africa as an
unwelcome if only temporary diversion of national attention from essentials.
By demonstrating in part the extent of imperial limitations and the empire's
vulnerability, South Africa was of less significance on its own account than
it was for opening more eyes to the wider problems and offering an additional spur to their solution.

It is intriguing to see how the capacity of the war to muddy the waters in
respect of the direction of British development and overseas connections
extended even to theoretical analyses of the imperialism of the period. J. A.
Hobson was long felt to be primarily concerned with Africa and the events
of the "Scramble," which he had approached via his well-known writings on
the South African War. Increasingly scholars have rejected such a view. First,
the role of South Africa as the principal source of Hobson's inspiration has
been called into question; in its place, much importance has been attributed
to the influence on him of American ideas, as well as to his understanding
of both the Egyptian crisis of the 1880s and Western expansion in the Far
East from 1895 onward. As the canvas was thus broadened, so the functional
emphasis placed on financial conspiracy has seemed to decline, both as an
element in Hobson's own thought and as a phenomenon given analytical
weight by historians. Peter Cain found himself concluding that Hobson's

> experiences as a journalist in South Africa were not helpful to the cause.
> The second Boer War inevitably focused his attention upon the machina-
> tions of a few financiers such as Rhodes and tempted him to overlay his
> emerging analysis of British financial capitalism with a conspiracy theory
> which was not easy to reconcile with it.[22]

Indeed, it has been argued that, despite the confusion induced by the circumstances of the South African War, Hobson was beginning to "develop

a picture of a finance capitalist Britain" and a "conceptual analysis which modern historians can use" akin to that which has informed Cain and Hopkins's own recent analysis of British global expansion and "gentlemanly capitalism."[23] This may, of course, only go to show that Hobson was not so much correct as simply no less partial and highly selective in other areas of his work as in that on South Africa, and that he therefore constitutes a most unreliable source of inspiration. Nevertheless his emancipation from a largely South African perspective and the minimizing of South African influences on his central thinking now seems to be complete.

Britain's More Pressing Crises

It is perhaps unsurprising that politicians, policy makers, and many others— investors, emigrants, journalists, churchgoers[24]—can be shown either to have had only a limited or passing interest in South Africa and the war or to have been preoccupied chiefly with other, often wider issues. More significant is the fact that the Boer War, while it heightened those wider concerns, seems simultaneously to have made it more difficult for politicians to tackle them in a concerted manner and to have diverted much attention from them into personal rivalries and political detail. It is worth considering briefly how this was so.

The South African War occurred in the midst of what is now generally regarded as a period of prolonged crisis for Britain's political parties, evident in the mid-1880s and persisting at least until the First World War. The mid-Victorian consensus based around a vision of a liberal, laissez-faire political economy was rapidly breaking down. Contemporaries of all political persuasions agreed that the country faced a worrying variety of major problems. These included challenges to Britain's international position, weaknesses in defense, disquiet about Britain's economic performance in both industry and agriculture, serious urban poverty, and unemployment. Liberals and Conservatives were divided not only on questions of the priority to be attached to particular issues, but on the means of recovery. These differences involved major principles touching the rights of citizens and property, the role of the state, the value of free trade, and above all, the financing of reforms.[25]

It is impossible here to illustrate the many ways in which the war had a bearing on all these matters of concern; a defense example will have to suffice. In the mid-1890s, recent confrontations with America and Germany prompted one commentator well ahead of the crisis in South Africa to voice the widely shared view that no-one can compare the growth ... of the Empire, and ... the growth of the army ... and say that one has kept pace with the other, or that in the light of our recent experiences, 300,000 men is a sufficient British regular force for the defence of an Empire comprising one fifth of the surface of the land portion of the globe and one quarter of its estimated population.[26]

For the editor of the same journal in 1900 the South African War served not to reveal but simply to reemphasize this "great and grave alternative which has been long approaching.... We must either contract the boundaries of our Empire or we must expand our military forces."[27] Since the former was generally felt to be if not undesirable then at least impracticable, means had to be found of achieving the latter. A resort to Parliament was therefore inescapable. The war thus served to push major issues firmly back into the party political arena, as the Edwardian obsession with military and naval reform clearly indicated. In a similar way, difficulties during the war of recruiting able volunteers for the army reinvigorated the debate about imperative social reforms at home.

In other words, the war redirected attention away from the immediate detail of South African events toward persistent underlying problems. Contemporaries then—rather like historians now—plundered the war in search of evidence that related to their existing preoccupations and supported their favorite panaceas. As they did so, they also returned inevitably to questions of resources. It has often been remarked how costly the war was in both men and finance, but, as many also recognized, it "was not in any sense the main cause of the fiscal crisis or controversies of the Edwardian age."[28] It brought home yet again the fundamental reality of rapidly rising ordinary expenditure that had so worried successive Chancellors of the Exchequer from 1886 onward, and it compelled parties to address the question of where additional finance was to be found.

The answers to this question inevitably raised fundamental issues of wealth, property, and taxation: who was to pay, how much they should pay, and by what means. These matters involved in turn the very nature and identity of Britain's political parties. Reactions in Britain to the South African War were added to the many other pressures already edging party leaders and the electorate toward a fresh analysis of Britain's place in the world and a redefinition of party goals and allegiances to match. South Africa was only briefly at the center of imperial policy, and imperial policy itself was only intermittently at the heart of government concerns. The most striking consequences of the war for Britain were to heighten further an existing sense of crisis in domestic politics and to increase the demands for its resolution.

The war diverted attention away from the empire and refocused it on the makeup and constitution of Britain itself. It exacerbated the internal difficulties of both main parties, not by increasing their preoccupation with imperial interests, but by stimulating dispute over domestic political concerns.

Looking back on the South African War after a few years, L. T. Hobhouse observed that it was without doubt "the test issue for this generation."[29] If, however, the significance of the war is open to deflation in the manner sketched out above, one may well ask what of substance really is left to support such a claim. Interpreted narrowly, Hobhouse was probably right. For progressive Liberal intellectuals like himself, the war certainly stimulated fears of the corrupting impact of imperialism on domestic life and politics; in doing so, it revived a tradition of criticism of empire inherited from the eighteenth century via Cobden and Bright. Those who shared those fears and were conscious of their line of descent passed Hobhouse's "test." They were, Hobhouse might have said, "one of us"; but they were also few in number, as was illustrated by the failure even of groups on the Left such as the Fabians to meet these criteria.

In a wider sense, however, Hobhouse was quite wrong. There were issues wholly unrelated to the war yet capable both of arousing passion and political commitment and of having greater electoral effect. This was demonstrated, for instance, by the debate and divisions over Free Trade and cheap food, especially when opened up by Chamberlain from 1903 onward. For most people in the metropole, neither the war nor other South African issues ever captured their attention in such a lasting way. Failures in the war began both to undermine the view that empire held the key to national greatness and to destroy the ability of empire presented in South African terms to provide a diversion from domestic troubles. Once that process had begun, only by exploiting an alternative vein of enthusiasm could any political party reclaim empire for itself. With a shift of focus, a new "test" was devised and widely applied. The rapid displacement of South African issues by others with far more domestic resonance revealed just how shallow had been the impact of the war and how limited had been its capacity to redefine the boundaries of political action.

Notes

1. R. G. Collingwood, *The Idea of History* (Oxford, 1946; repr. 1963), 248. And, of course, historians generally are no longer overwhelmingly "he."

2. For two studies that have appeared since this chapter was written, see K. T. Surridge, *Managing the South African War, 1899–1902: Politicians v. Generals*, Royal

Historical Society Studies in History (Woodbridge, 1998); S. M. Miller, *Lord Methuen and the British Army: Failure and Redemption in South Africa* (London, 1999).

3. *The Cambridge History of the British Empire*, vol. 3: *The Empire-Commonwealth, 1870–1919* (Cambridge, 1959), 354.

4. For contrasting approaches, see L. Thompson, *A History of South Africa*, rev. ed. (New Haven and London, 1995); and S. Marks and S. Trapido, "Lord Milner and the South African State Reconsidered," in M. Twaddle (ed.), *Imperialism, the State and the Third World* (London, 1992), 80–94.

5. Diary, 18 July 1890, British Library Add.MS. 48653, f. 81.

6. "Some Memories and Reflections in My Old Age," Selborne Papers 191, ff. 76–77.

7. N. Parsons, *King Khama, Emperor Joe, and the Great White Queen: Victorian Britain through African Eyes* (Chicago and London, 1998); K. E. Wilburn, "The Drifts Crisis, the 'Missing Telegrams' and the Jameson Raid," *Journal of Imperial and Commonwealth History* 25, no. 2 (1997): 219–39.

8. An argument developed in A. N. Porter, *The Origins of the South African War: Joseph Chamberlain and the Diplomacy of Imperialism, 1895–99* (Manchester, 1980).

9. H.C.G. Matthew, *The Liberal Imperialists: The Ideas and Politics of a Post-Gladstonian Elite* (Oxford, 1973), 151.

10. D. E. Torrance, *The Strange Death of the Liberal Empire: Lord Selborne in South Africa* (Liverpool, 1996).

11. Botha quoted in *Cambridge History*, 3.433.

12. Rosebery speaking in March 1896, quoted in Matthew, *Liberal Imperialists*, 163–64.

13. B. R. Tomlinson, "Economics and Empire: The Periphery and the Imperial Economy," in A. Porter (ed.), *The Oxford History of the British Empire*, vol. 3: *The Nineteenth Century* (Oxford, 1999), 55; D. Denoon, *Settler Capitalism: The Dynamics of Dependent Development in the Southern Hemisphere* (Oxford, 1983).

14. A. Porter, *Victorian Shipping, Business and Imperial Policy: Donald Currie, the Castle Line and Southern Africa* (Woodbridge, 1986), 243.

15. For these themes, see most recently D.C.M. Platt with A.J.H. Latham and R. Michie, *Decline and Recovery in Britain's Overseas Trade, 1873–1914* (London, 1993).

16. Quoted by E. M. Spiers, *The Army and Society, 1815–1914* (London, 1980), 236.

17. M. Yakutiel, "Treasury Control and the South African War 1899–1905" (D.Phil. thesis, Oxford University, 1989).

18. Figures were as follows: 1901: total government revenue £132.25 million; navy £30.87m; army £30.03m. 1914: total £209.45 million; navy £51.55m; army £28.84m. Source: R.C.K. Ensor, *England 1870–1914* (Oxford, 1936), 526.

19. For a recent account, R. Williams, *Defending the Empire: The Conservative Party and British Defence Policy, 1899–1915* (New Haven and London, 1991).

20. Cabinet memorandum, February 1904, quoted in M. Beloff, *Britain's Liberal Empire, 1897–1921*, 2d ed. (London, 1987), 86.

21. See Papers of the Admiralty Transport Department, Series M.T. 23, Public Record Office, Kew.

22. P. Cain, "J. A. Hobson, Financial Capitalism and Imperialism in Late Victorian

and Edwardian England," in A. N. Porter and R. F. Holland (eds.), *Money, Finance and Empire, 1790–1960* (London, 1985), 4.

23. Ibid., 20. See also P. J. Cain and A. G. Hopkins, *British Imperialism*, 2 vols. (London, 1993); for the editors' acknowledgment of their debt to Hobson, see 1.16–17.

24. For the war's place amidst the preoccupations of Nonconformist congregations, see e.g. D. W. Bebbington, *The Nonconformist Conscience: Chapel and Politics, 1870-1914* (London, 1982), especially chap. 6; and G. Cuthbertson, "The Nonconformist Conscience and the South Africa War, 1899–1902" (D. Litt. et Phil. thesis, University of South Africa, 1985).

25. See, most recently, E.H.H. Green, *The Crisis of Conservatism: The Politics, Economics and Ideology of the British Conservative Party, 1880–1914* (London, 1995); R. Shannon, *The Age of Salisbury, 1881–1902: Unionism and Empire* (London, 1996); A. Howe, *Free Trade and Liberal England, 1846–1946* (Oxford, 1997).

26. Quoted from *The Nineteenth Century*, June 1896, in A. L. Friedberg, *The Weary Titan: Britain and the Experience of Relative Decline, 1895–1905* (Princeton, N.J., 1988), 232.

27. Friedberg, *Weary Titan*, 233. For the longer period, A. N. Porter, "Lord Salisbury, Foreign Policy and Domestic Finance, 1860–1900," in R. Blake and H. Cecil (eds.), *Salisbury: The Man and His Policies* (London, 1987), 148–84.

28. Green, *Crisis of Conservatism*, 49.

29. *The Nation*, 30 March 1907, quoted in Clarke, *Liberals and Social Democrats* (Cambridge, 1978), 68.

CHAPTER 15

Imperial Propaganda during the South African War

ANDREW THOMPSON

WHILE BRITISH AND Boer troops were fighting in South Africa, a fiercely contested propaganda war raged in Britain. The vociferous and well-known critics of this conflict—the so-called pro-Boers—have long fascinated historians, and recent scholarship suggests that their allure has not diminished.[1] Yet however influential they may seem in retrospect, the pages of print devoted to the enemies of the imperial idea have tended not only to exaggerate their contemporary significance, but to divert attention away from antithetical attempts to mobilize public opinion in support of military intervention in the Transvaal. Weighted heavily toward the "official mind" of imperialism and the diplomatic road to war, the existing historical scholarship is largely silent about the grassroots imperial activism inspired by events in South Africa at the end of the nineteenth century.[2] Indeed, it is only during the last fifteen years or so that enthusiasm for empire—as opposed to resistance to it—has established itself as a fruitful field of enquiry. The work of historians of popular culture and of gender has alerted us to the fact that whereas anti-imperial feeling was mostly marginal to public life, the active propagation of imperial sentiment was undertaken by a wide range of British institutions over a very long period, dating back at least to the 1870s and continuing well beyond the First World War.[3]

Fought on the hustings as well as the veld, the South African War is central to the study of pro-imperial activity and its modes of organization, publicity, and propaganda. Not only did the war lead directly to the formation of a clutch of new nationalist and imperialist pressure groups, but it also gave a fresh lease of life to many existing extraparliamentary movements. The difficulty of containing imperial interests and enthusiasms within the structures of formal party politics has recently been explored by historians of popular Conservatism.[4] In seeking to explain why right-wing pressure groups proliferated, these historians point to the organizational weaknesses of the National Union of Conservative and Constitutional Associations. By the late 1890s, the Tory Party caucus had constructed a solid base of support among the propertied classes of suburban England—the "Villa Tories"—but its working-class membership was far less reliable, based on popular dislike of the moralizing crusades of the Liberal Party and religious hostilities toward the Irish.[5] The function of the extraparliamentary right, therefore, was to build a stronger relationship between the party and the urban working classes. Studies of the Primrose League,[6] Conservative working men's clubs,[7] and pressure groups like Ashmead Bartlett's Patriotic Association[8] all emphasize the importance of these groups in pioneering new styles of political organization, in marshaling patriotic and imperial sentiment behind the Tory Party, and in broadening the basis of the formal party machine.

The main propaganda body regarding South Africa—the Imperial South Africa Association (ISAA)—moved within this milieu, supplying speakers to constituency associations, communicating with the party's local agents, and organizing meetings in association with the "Patriotic," "Open-Air," and Primrose leagues. Though almost completely ignored by historians, the ISAA was galvanized by the same new imperial ideology of the 1880s and 1890s as other right-wing pressure groups. This ideology received its most powerful expression in Seeley's canonical text, *The Expansion of England,* which originated in a set of lectures delivered at Cambridge University in 1881–82. Seeley's positive concept of empire, based upon the uniqueness of the English-speaking peoples and their special aptitude for political organization, exerted a strong influence on a generation of later-Victorian and Edwardian imperialists. In the case of South Africa, it meant that British "supremacy" in the region was never felt to be an end in itself. Rather, control over the Dutch republics was consistently presented as part of a bigger political project aimed at transforming the English-speaking empire into a more consolidated and cohesive unit, a unit capable of holding its own in an age of intensifying military rivalry and cutthroat economic competition.

The pro-war activists who belonged to the Imperial South Africa Association were closely involved with the two ministries responsible for imperial policy making (the Foreign and Colonial Offices) and with the South African High Commissioner (Alfred Milner). The nature of the relationship between "private" propaganda—produced by groups that were not part of government—and "public" propaganda—produced by the state—has recently been raised by the influential Manchester University Press *Studies in Imperialism* series. The general editor of the series, John Mackenzie, suggests that although the British state did not become deeply involved in propaganda and publicity work until the First World War, it did cultivate relationships with various unofficial, extraparliamentary bodies that educated the public about the empire. This private-public partnership, it is claimed, was highly effective in propagating imperial values and ideals and rested on a "striking and unique convergence" between "Establishment" and "popular" interests in respect of the empire.[9] Yet recent studies of the South African War have not endorsed Mackenzie's thesis. To be sure, much is made of the importance of the triangular relationship between mining capitalists, the Uitlander press, and the High Commissioner, both in mobilizing loyalist sentiment in South Africa and in controlling the flow of news back home. But the possibility that the same degree of interdependence characterized relations between pro-war propagandists and the government in Britain is not seriously entertained. Even Andrew Porter's effort to put metropolitan politics at the center of the study of the causes of the war gives little credence to the idea that official diplomacy and private propaganda were closely entwined.[10] Porter maintains that the substance and style of British diplomacy after 1895 "owed much to the relationship between imperial policy-makers and metropolitan public opinion."[11] He is, however, remarkably reticent on the question of *how far* Chamberlain became involved in the task of drumming up popular support for the war. Despite the Colonial Secretary's commitment to educating the public on South African affairs, the active participation of ministers and officials in the extragovernmental promotion of policy is hardly discussed. In fact, Chamberlain's political activities beyond Whitehall and Westminster are said to have been severely circumscribed. Two explanations are offered. First, there was the question of electoral expediency, it being dangerous for the Colonial Secretary to align himself too closely with the Uitlander cause.[12] Second, the Colonial Office displayed a very cautious attitude toward the press. Under constant pressure from their proprietors, editors could not be relied upon and were in any event wary of interference from officialdom, while the department itself lacked the necessary administrative apparatus for "detailed" or "consistent" involvement with newspapers and periodicals.[13]

This argument that the British state fought shy of the more populist forms of propaganda activity from 1899 to 1902 needs to be scrutinized a lot more carefully and critically than it has been to date. The Imperial South Africa Association developed strong links with government, and Chamberlain, Milner, and Salisbury all made use of its propaganda machinery before, during, and after the war. That is not to argue that pro-war propaganda was orchestrated by government. Nor yet was it simply left to voluntary patriotic organizations. On the contrary, imperially oriented pressure groups, though independently organized and privately funded, were deliberately sought out by ministers at home and officials overseas. Part of their attraction as propaganda instruments lay in their freedom from the type of commercial considerations that weighed so heavily upon the minds of newspaper proprietors. Beyond that, the ISAA had the additional advantages of a secure funding base (including money from the South African mining magnates), strong support from Tory backbenchers, and a detailed knowledge of South African affairs.

Neither can the study of pro-war activism in Britain afford to ignore the internal politics of South Africa in the 1890s. As well as developing close links with the British government, pro-war propaganda received a strong stimulus from the mobilization of "loyalist" opinion in the Cape, Natal, and the Transvaal. For example, the major women's imperial movement in Britain—the Victoria League—was actually formed as a result of a South African delegation from a "Guild of Loyal Women" that came to Britain in 1900–1901 to raise money for the care of soldiers' graves.[14] In the case of the ISAA, support came from several pro-empire organizations, including the South African League and the South African Vigilance Committee. It seems likely that this type of grassroots political activism, which had one foot in the "metropole" and another in the "periphery," contributed significantly to a developing consciousness of empire at this time. Recent studies of the Victorians' sense of their own identity emphasize how that identity was forged in a context larger than the United Kingdom.[15] But if the empire did impinge powerfully upon the popular imagination, we remain remarkably ignorant of the political processes that drew it to the attention of a wider British public. In particular, we need to know more about the role played by imperially oriented, pan-British movements in raising awareness of what was happening in the colonies and bringing the colonial viewpoint to the center of domestic political debate. Like the ISAA, pro-imperial pressure groups in South Africa set great store by the state of political feeling in Britain. Their aim was to assemble a coalition of metropolitan support in favor of a military showdown with the Kruger (Afrikaner) government in the Transvaal. Thus in addition to a blurring of the boundaries between "private" and "public" propaganda, pro-imperial movements in Britain and South Africa ricocheted off each other, relaying information about their respective political situations, supplying propaganda literature to their "sister" movements, and exchanging personnel. Taken together, the active cooperation of pro-war activists with the British government and their close involvement with South African loyalists suggest a much more complex (and interesting) picture of imperialist propaganda activity at the turn of the century than that presently on offer.

Selling the War

The war in South Africa was not just another of the nineteenth century's small colonial wars. It was a prolonged and costly campaign, fought at a time when the nation's fiscal structure was already under great pressure.[16] No wonder, then, that Chamberlain was apprehensive about the reaction to intervention in the Transvaal from the electorate at home. In February 1901, he broached the issue directly with Milner:

> No one here dares any longer to fix a limit to the war and its expenditure, which is going on at the rate of at least a million a week.... But if some progress is not made before long, I think public dissatisfaction may become serious and threaten the existence of the Government in spite of its enormous majority.[17]

By the time this letter was written, early estimates of the cost of the war had been swept aside. Expenditure on the army rose from £20 million to £43.6 million in the first year of hostilities, producing a budget deficit of £14 million for the year 1899–1900.[18] By 1902, the British government was having to spend £1.5 million a week just to keep the war going.[19] It was imperative, therefore, that the British public be brought to an appreciation of the need for such an expensive military campaign.

The task of "selling the War" did not, however, fall directly to the government. The main sources of pro-war propaganda were extraparliamentary and included the press, pulpit, pamphleteers, and pressure groups. The *Daily Mail* and *The Times* set the standard for pro-war papers. The *Mail* insisted on firmness in the British government's dealings with the Boers, was unwavering in its admiration of Chamberlain, and brought pro-war propagandists into direct contact with a lower-middle-class audience.[20] *The Times* set the tone of much of the London press in emphasizing the warlike intentions and general backwardness of the Boers, in clamoring for the dispatch of troops to South Africa after the Jameson Raid, and in treating the war as a test case of British prestige and the cohesion of the empire.[21] In the religious sphere, the Anglican church defended the justice of the British cause,[22] and many Nonconformist ministers, too, played their part in sanctifying military conflict with the Boers.[23] Pamphleteering was another important form of propaganda.[24] A "Transvaal series" of pamphlets was issued by the National Union of Conservative and Constitutional Associations in 1899; the Conservative Central Office issued additional pamphlets in 1901[25]; and the Primrose

League distributed more than 100,000 leaflets on the situation in South
Africa during the war.[26]

Pro-war pressure groups included the Primrose League, the Patriotic
Association, the South African Colonisation Society, the Victoria League, the
British Women's Emigration Association, and the League of Empire. The
Primrose League was the first to enter the fray. As early as 1890 one of its
habitations (local branches) passed a resolution against further encroach-
ments by the Boers, and many of the pro-war resolutions that reached the
Colonial Office in the summer and autumn of 1899 were forwarded by the
League.[27] The most active organization to campaign on South Africa, however, was the Imperial South Africa Association.[28] Formed in April 1896 at a
time of heightened popular interest in the empire, the Association was ostensibly a nonpartisan organization that set out "to uphold British supremacy
and to promote the interests of British subjects" in South Africa.[29] Its nonpartisan credentials were not very convincing—four successive chairmen
(George Wyndham, Geoffrey Drage, Alfred Lyttelton, and Horatio Gilbert
Parker) were all Tory MPs or ministers, and of the fifty-seven MPs on its
general council only one (J. M. Paulton) was a Liberal—ten were Liberal
Unionist and forty-six were Conservatives.[30]

The ISAA was deeply involved in various forms of extraparliamentary
activism. In addition to producing and distributing pamphlets and leaflets, it
supplied speakers to working men's clubs; organized mass meetings; raised
a special fund for the "khaki" election in the autumn of 1900; and intervened
in by-elections to oppose pro-Boer candidates. What marks the association
out from other pro-war pressure groups is the scale of its activity, to be
accounted for in part by the money it received from the mining magnates
Alfred Beit and Cecil Rhodes.[31] An impression of its political achievement is
conveyed in Table 15.1.

TABLE 15.1 Summary of ISAA Activity from 1896 to 1899*

Year	Meetings	Total Attendance	Leaflets and pamphlets distributed (UK and colonies)
1896	130	50,000	150,000
1897	140	55,000	200,000
1898	146	65,000	250,000
1899	406	248,000	500,000

* Annual Report of the ISAA (1899–1900)

The Imperial South Africa Association

The ISAA actively sought advice from the South African High Commissioner on when and how to conduct its campaigns.[32] In August 1899, Geoffrey Drage asked how best the association could back the government and counteract its critics if peaceful negotiations failed.[33] The previous month Milner had already thanked the ISAA for its "extremely valuable support": "Indeed I don't know where we should have been without it."[34] Nearly nine years later, he was persuaded to speak at the association's annual dinner, and he chose the occasion to express his gratitude formally: "I owe a great deal to this Association. And what is of much greater importance, the country owes it a great deal for the excellent work it has done in more than one crisis of the Empire's fortunes in South Africa."[35] The ISAA's loyalty to Milner stemmed partly from the personal affection and admiration of four chairmen. George Wyndham, the first incumbent of the post, went so far as to assure the High Commissioner that the view he was trying to inculcate was "Milner, Milner, Milner" and that the ISAA would "wait and be patient, or charge home, just as you decide."[36] And shortly before the association was wound up in 1909, its last chairman, the popular novelist Horatio Gilbert Parker, declared that he had "known but three men" whom he could follow and that Milner was the only one of them left in public life.[37] The ISAA, moreover, continued to support Milner well beyond the Peace of Vereeniging. It argued forcefully for representative institutions to precede the grant of responsible self-government; it defended his reputation during the controversy surrounding Chinese labor; and it attached great significance to the issue of emigration, even hiring a lecturer to publicize its own land settlement schemes.

Yet in emphasizing its affinity with Milner, it is important not to overlook the ISAA's importance to the Colonial Secretary. As a recent study of the "Age of Salisbury" reminds us, the South African War could not have happened had the Conservative Party not been willing that it should happen.[38] From 1896 to 1899, the ISAA worked tirelessly to rally the party faithful behind the Uitlanders and against Kruger's administration. This aspect of its activities was highly valued by the Colonial Secretary. Well before the outbreak of war, Drage and Wyndham sprang to Chamberlain's defense in the press and on public platforms.[39] Subsequently, in December 1897, the association wrote to assure the Colonial Office that it would not press the issue of the treatment of the Transvaal's native population if either Selborne or Chamberlain thought the moment not right.[40] Moreover, there are numerous other references to other interviews and conversations with the Colonial Secretary. In the summer of 1899, the ISAA contacted local Conservative associations at Chamberlain's behest, "urging the immediate summoning of meetings to denounce the Transvaal Government and to demand action on the part of H. M. Govt."[41] There was also a request to Drage from Chamberlain for a mass meeting in Manchester.[42] Andrew Porter's claim that the Colonial Secretary never gave "any special encouragement" to the ISAA is therefore unjustified.[43] There existed a much more intimate relationship, as is shown by two further episodes.

The first of these involves one of the two Conservative MPs to dissent openly over the war—J. M. Maclean. Maclean was well known for his bitter parliamentary denunciations of Chamberlain following the Jameson Raid.[44] Although it beggars belief, he was asked to be the principal speaker at an ISAA meeting, held in his Cardiff constituency at the time of the Bloemfontein conference in May and June 1899. Maclean wrote to Windsor (then president of the ISAA) to express strong reservations about staging a demonstration in favor of the Uitlanders at a time when Milner was trying to reach an accommodation with Kruger. Windsor replied that meetings were not held by the association "in opposition to the wishes of the Government." He was to regret writing the letter, as this remark was seized upon as evidence that the negotiations with Kruger were being conducted in bad faith: while the Colonial Secretary publicly professed to be anxious for a settlement, he was privately inciting pro-war activists to keep up an anti-Kruger agitation.[45] As a result, Maclean refused to have anything to do with the proposed meeting, which was eventually abandoned.

The second episode concerns the ISAA's attempt to carve out a role for itself after the war. In June 1903, when Chamberlain was launching the movement for tariff reform, C. W. Boyd, previously Rhodes's political secretary,[46] wrote to the Colonial Secretary:

> As you are probably aware, a meeting has been called at Stafford House on Wednesday, of Liberal Imperialists devoted to your policy. Pending the institution of any proper organization, on the Tariff side, that of the Imperial South Africa Association will be at the service of the Cause. Amery[47] will explain this at Stafford House.... I shall keep Goulding & CO ... in touch with the I. S. Africa Association.[48]

A recent reconsideration of official policy in the 1890s, which advances a "metropolitan" and "political" interpretation of the causes of the war, plays down any such link between Chamberlain's diplomacy and the economic imperialism of tariff reform.[49] There was, however, a substantial overlap in membership between the ISAA and the Tariff Reform League, the two major propagandist bodies that campaigned on South Africa and the fiscal question; and it is also arguable that the "constructive" imperialist ideology that underpinned tariff reform was to some extent prefigured in the speeches of Chamberlain (and Milner) prior to and during the war.[50] Moreover, the above letter by Boyd is intriguing insofar as it shows that Chamberlain was not only able to rely upon the ISAA, but sufficiently familiar with its way of working to understand what it could contribute to a new movement against free trade. A further letter written by Boyd to Chamberlain at this time states explicitly that the ISAA was temporarily at the Colonial Secretary's disposal.[51]

What this evidence suggests is that Chamberlain was not only interested in pro-war propaganda activity, but actively involved in it. Publicity directed at his own party was of particular concern: leadership from the Cecil clan was decidedly deficient in the early months of the war, and by the beginning of 1900 the party whips were showing anxiety about backbench unrest.[52] Thus, the ISAA's lobbying and publicity effort was vitally important in ensuring that Chamberlain's policy was regarded as that of the party's rank and file, not simply of its leaders. To be sure, there were some signs of dissent in the parliamentary party, but it was either stamped out or it fizzled out. The memoirs of Percy Thornton MP,[53] for example, recall an anti-Chamberlain back-bench "cabal" approaching Tory backbenchers during a Lords cricket match and asking them to sign a round robin opposing a war with the Boers.[54] Thornton politely declined. More resolute resistance risked reprisals, as J. M. Maclean learned to his cost. Maclean's assertion in 1899 that the ISAA was simply an alias for Cecil Rhodes stung Lord Windsor into action.[55] A meeting was arranged of the joint councils of the Cardiff Conservative and Liberal Unionist associations at which a resolution was passed asking Maclean to step down as sitting member. He was replaced by the ardent imperialist, J. Lawrence, who lost the seat in the general election the following year.

Neither was the ISAA's involvement with the government limited to the Colonial Office. The association was also in close touch with T. H. Sanderson, permanent Under-Secretary at the Foreign Office, and a trusted adviser to Salisbury.[56] As Foreign Secretary and Prime Minister, Salisbury was naturally concerned with the possible repercussions on international opinion of a forward policy in South Africa, particularly in the case of the United States.[57] Anti-British elements of American opinion were powerfully represented in Congress,[58] and reports from British officials in Washington indicated considerable political sympathy among American citizens for the Boers.[59] Letters from Sanderson to Drage, written in 1900 on Foreign Office notepaper, discussed the possibility of sending an ISAA lecturer to America.

Acting on the advice of Lord Pauncefote, the British ambassador in Washington,[60] Sanderson rejected the idea for fear of provoking counterdemonstrations.[61] However, mindful of the impending visit of Transvaal delegates to the United States, Pauncefote suggested hiring a political agent to distribute ISAA literature, address public meetings, and write to the press. On Sanderson's invitation,[62] Drage visited the Foreign Office to discuss the proposal, and Salisbury instructed Sanderson to telegraph the association's reply to the Washington embassy.[63] It seems likely that the Foreign Office played a part in funding the venture.[64] Understandably reluctant to become further "mixed up in the matter,"[65] the embassy requested that the agent (Alleyne Ireland) be engaged directly by the ISAA, though it did invite Ireland to its Washington buildings "to settle terms and a plan of campaigns."[66]

In addition to its connections with the government, the ISAA was closely aligned with various loyalist organizations in South Africa, which were instrumental in drawing together South Africa's English-speaking communities and in fanning the flames of the heightened sense of British nationalism that emerged after the Jameson Raid. These organizations included the South African League (SAL), the South African Vigilance Committee (SAVC), and, to a lesser degree, the Uitlander Council (UC). The significance of their involvement with imperial movements in Britain did not escape Cape Afrikaners. J. X. Merriman, the Prime Minister of the Cape, was hostile to the interference of English "Imperial Leagues" in the Cape's internal affairs and opposed the formation of an Afrikaner Committee in England on the grounds that South Africans had to stop "looking across the water" for aid in their own political questions.[67]

Formed at the same time as the ISAA, the South African League emerged from a "loyal colonial league" that had spread rapidly among English colonists on the eastern frontier of the Cape.[68] It was an "ultra-imperialist" organization,[69] covertly financed by Rhodes and his colleagues,[70] that aimed to break the power of the Afrikaner Bond in the Cape and to build a solid working-class base of support for administrative reform in the Transvaal.[71] Initial contact between the SAL and pro-war activists in Britain was by necessity limited. From 1896 to 1899, the league was intent on establishing itself as a force in South African politics.[72] In particular, it had to contend with the restrictions on Uitlander political activity imposed by the Kruger government. These restrictions impeded the growth of membership and funds in the Transvaal, and only later did the league become "the organised vanguard of the determined Uitlander movement" on the Rand.[73] Thus before the outbreak of the war, the SAL's attempts to rally imperialist opinion within South

Africa did not preclude overseas work but they did constrain it. The SAL, however, was not the only loyalist pressure group active in British politics, even if the existing historiography suggests that this was so. Although our understanding of grassroots loyalist sentiment in South Africa is heavily skewed toward the Rand, and the years following the Jameson Raid, pro-war activists in Britain were just as closely linked to the South African Vigilance Committees (SAVC), based in the Cape and Natal, formed in 1900, and mainly concerned with the terms of a future peace settlement. The SAVC's chairman was the Cape Premier, Sir Gordon Sprigg, a strong supporter of the British connection.[74] Convinced of Milner's "self-sacrificing devotion" to the cause of a "Greater Britain," the organization's aim was to put an end to the independence of the republics and to incorporate them within the empire.[75] This was to be achieved by organizing public meetings in the Cape, by supplying literature to political organizations in the United Kingdom, and by raising a "South African Imperial Defence Fund."

The ISAA was to play a key role in ensuring that the views of South African loyalists were asserted and listened to in Britain. Working together, the association and the SAVC arranged for the circulation of various pamphlets and for the distribution of Percy Fitzpatrick's account of life under Kruger, *The Transvaal from Within*.[76] The ISAA also acted as host to several SAVC delegates who came to England in 1899–1900 and who spoke to a range of audiences in London and the provinces about the significance of the war from the perspective of South Africa's English-speaking communities.[77] The delegates included Theophilus Schreiner, teacher and temperance worker, brother of William and Olive, yet strongly pro-British in politics; Rev. J. S. Moffat, the assistant commissioner to northern Bechuanaland from 1892 to 1896, who retired to live and preach in the Cape; the Hon. A. Wilmot, Cape parliamentarian, prolific author, and admirer of Cecil Rhodes; and L. Zeitsman, a Progressive member of the Cape parliament from 1898. In December 1900, these four men formed part of a large deputation from the SAVC to the Colonial Office, which was introduced by Windsor and Drage and received by Chamberlain.[78] The deputation presented the Colonial Secretary with a twelve-point plan—the basis for a comprehensive peace settlement after the war—that proposed Milner's retention as High Commissioner; an intervening period of Crown Colony rule to follow military withdrawal; a war indemnity to be imposed on the Transvaal; and a scheme of state-aided colonization. The plan reflected the by then acute anxieties about what would happen to "British" South Africa after the withdrawal of imperial military forces.

Safeguarding British Supremacy

In trying to rally public opinion behind direct intervention in the affairs of the Transvaal, a key aspect of pro-war propaganda was its appeal to the "national interest." As recently recognized, the "national interest" was not a term with a fixed or transparent meaning: on the contrary, what was best for Britain was largely a matter of public perception.[79] In the case of South Africa, pro-war propagandists sought to show that "British supremacy" was in jeopardy; that it was vitally necessary for such supremacy to be upheld; and that for it to be upheld urgent action was required on the part of the government. Like other pro-war propagandists, the ISAA turned the position of the Uitlanders into something of an acid test of "British supremacy." Demanding "absolute political equality for all white men" in South Africa,[80] it made a tremendous effort to get the British public to understand and sympathize with Uitlander grievances and to persuade people that they were genuine and in need of redress.[81] This, in turn, led to a vilification of the Kruger regime: the government of the Transvaal was portrayed as backward, narrow-minded, and oppressive, and thus extremely unlikely to introduce reforms.

The "Britishness" of the Uitlanders was at least in part fabricated. Uitlanders were European immigrants (or non-Afrikaner whites) who had moved to the Rand in the years following the gold discoveries of the 1880s but had not been assimilated into Transvaal society. In 1896 Johannesburg's white population was approximately 50,000; about 45,000 were Uitlanders, and of these, just over 30,000 were British.[82] Yet pro-war propagandists consistently spoke of Uitlanders as a community of "British subjects," "fellow countrymen," and "our own people," placed by the Kruger government in a condition of total inferiority to the Transvaal Boers.[83] There was little recognition of the diverse nationalities that made up the Uitlander population—it was emphatically British rather than European. Similarly, although the Uitlanders had a very wide range of grievances, social and economic as well as political, the franchise requirement was elevated above all others.

For a society conditioned to think of its own recent political progress in terms of expanding enfranchisement and to regard Parliament as "the repository of the liberties of the people,"[84] the temptation to equate the political rights of Uitlanders with the vote must have been very strong. The advantage of the franchise as a campaigning issue was that it fixed in the public mind, in a way few other aspects of Uitlander life could have, the gravity of their grievances and the extent of Britain's responsibility to remedy them. There was, perhaps, a further reason for justifying military intervention in these terms. The political vocabulary used to describe the Uitlander population reflected and reinforced prevailing ideas about the national character of the British. By the end of the century a sense of British nationhood was becoming increasingly inseparable from Britain's imperial experience.[85] Various genres of literature, metropolitan and provincial exhibitions, colonial royal tours, and international religious gatherings all drew attention to the closeness of British society at home with the overseas British societies of the empire. The plight of Uitlanders, therefore, resonated with key aspects of contemporary language and culture.

The Uitlanders, however, were not the only topic of debate, and any meaningful assessment of the effectiveness of pro-war propaganda must take account of what was actually happening on the battlefield and its implications for public opinion in Britain. Pro-war activists played a conscious and creative role in the formation of domestic opinion until the general election of October 1900. Thereafter, the public mood began to change: there was growing impatience with a war that showed little prospect of ending, and there were signs of unease with the scorched-earth policy introduced by Kitchener in the spring of 1901. In the months immediately prior to the peace settlement in May 1902, public interest in South Africa appears to have abated, as reflected by diminishing newspaper coverage—both *The Times* and the *Daily Mail* lost interest in the war—and a lull in ISAA activity.[86] After the war, South Africa came back with a vengeance onto the British political agenda, partly as a result of a reemerging grassroots political concern with empire migration but mainly owing to the controversy surrounding the importation of indentured Chinese labor ignited by Campbell Bannerman's vote of censure in March 1904.

Even early on in the war, pro-war propagandists did not feel able to treat the British public as a blank page upon which they could write at will. Their appeals had to be adapted to fit perceptions of existing attitudes and perhaps prejudices. Jon Lawrence has described this process as the "mediatory aspect" of politics in a party democracy,[87] and it helps to explain why Uitlander grievances were taken up so enthusiastically. They were taken up in a positive sense because of the sympathy a fight for political rights was expected to evoke; and they were taken up in a negative sense because of the danger of the war being seen as a capitalists' war—a fight for the profits of mining magnates. In short, Uitlander grievances were assumed to have moral and popular appeal and to be the safest way of putting the question of British supremacy in South Africa onto the political agenda.

In his book, *The War in South Africa: Its Causes and Effects,* J. A. Hobson lamented that the "falsehood" propagated by pro-war propagandists about the Uitlanders had been driven into the "British mind."[88] Hobson may not have been a particularly dispassionate judge, but he was right to argue that alternative views were only rarely heard. While pro-Boer groups like the Transvaal Committee made it their business to remind British audiences that foreign workers on the Rand were only interested in "pushing their own fortunes and making money,"[89] the Uitlanders' grievances appear to have been accepted as real and in need of redress. Some may have reached this conclusion readily, others reluctantly. Either way, the concept of the "national interest" championed by pro-war propaganda had become deeply embedded in public discourse by the end of 1899. Clearly, this was not achieved single-handedly by the ISAA. Ashmead Bartlett had been campaigning on the issue on provincial platforms since 1894; *The Times* and the *Daily Mail* began "educating" their readers on the Uitlander question in the spring of 1899; and the "Transvaal series" of pamphlets produced by the National Union in 1899–1900 spelled out their grievances in great detail. Moreover, the success of pro-war activism in this regard must be set against a backdrop of a revitalized Tory party capable of mobilizing strong grassroots support in England's provincial towns and cities. Following the Liberal Party schism over Home Rule in 1886, Conservatives had made much political capital out of the charge that the opposition tended to place the interests of party above those of the nation in foreign and imperial policy.[90] In claiming to represent the "national" rather than the "party" interest during the South African War, Conservatives may have been making a "sweeping assertion,"[91] but it was an assertion working-class voters in many urban areas were probably predisposed to accept.

It is not until the summer of 1901 that the first sign of a falling away of public enthusiasm for the war can be identified. At the time of the "khaki election" in October 1900 it was widely thought that the war was near to being brought to successful conclusion. This assumption was shattered by a new guerrilla phase in the conflict, which gave rise to war-weariness and misgivings about the methods of making war. *Pari passu,* the center of gravity of criticism of the war shifted away from a weak and leaderless pro-Boer movement toward the official Liberal Party. From that point onward propagandists had a fight on their hands as they struggled to reinvigorate popular support for the war.

As already suggested, it was the expected cost of a war with the Transvaal that above all else conditioned attitudes toward military intervention. The public's initial acceptance of the need for intervention had rested on the belief that it would not be a big burden on the exchequer or involve many casualties. Recent experience had taught the British to think of colonial wars

as "small undertakings, in distant places, against exotic, non-European opponents who were poorly equipped and easily defeated"[92]: the possibility of a
prolonged conflict was never seriously considered. By the summer of 1901,
the atmosphere in the country was decidedly different. People had become
impatient with a war that showed no prospect of ending, that cost many
lives and much money, and that required the British to resort to harsh methods to crush Boer resistance. Something of the terrible devastation resulting
from Kitchener's scorched-earth policy—the razing of thousands of Boer
farms, the destruction of churches, and the laying of the land to waste—was
conveyed by Ramsay Macdonald in his travelogue, *What I Saw in South
Africa*.[93] But it was the crowding of the civilian population into guarded
camps, and their appalling death rates, that provoked the greatest concern.

News of the camps—the overcrowding, poor sanitation, malnutrition,
and rampant disease—filtered back to England through the reports of Emily
Hobhouse. An experienced philanthropist, Hobhouse had already been
invited by her uncle (the journalist, Leonard Courtney) to act as Secretary
to the women's branch of the South African Conciliation Committee. She
left for South Africa on behalf of the Women and Children Distress fund
in December 1900, and she visited camps around Bloemfontein and in the
Orange River and Cape colonies. At first her brother, L. T. Hobhouse, a journalist on the *Manchester Guardian,* held back from releasing the reports out
of fear for Emily's safety.[94] Not until June 1901 were her findings published
under the title *To the Committee of the Distress Fund, Report of a Visit to the
Camps of Women and Children in the Cape and Orange River Colonies.* The
significance of this pamphlet was threefold. First, it was based upon the
author's own experience of living in and observing the camps—this made
it harder for pro-war propagandists to discredit. Second, it was written as
an intimate diary rather than an official report, and as such it painted a vivid
picture of the human suffering the camps had caused. Third, it was publicized by a speaking tour during July and August 1901. At least ten meetings
were held, mainly in Lancashire and Yorkshire, at which Hobhouse defended
herself against the charges from her critics and emphasized her personal
knowledge of conditions in the camps. Full accounts of these meetings were
published in the *Manchester Guardian*.[95]

Hobhouse later attacked "the Authorities" for denying true expression to
the public feeling of moral indignation regarding the camps.[96] In particular,
she berated municipal councils for refusing her the use of town halls to hold
public meetings. While there may be some truth to these allegations,[97] it is
important to appreciate that the majority of Hobhouse's addresses were
given to groups—Radical and Nonconformist—*within* the Liberal Party.

In appealing directly to the Liberal conscience—rather than to the general public—her achievement was to prepare the way for Campbell-Bannerman's subsequent attacks upon Kitchener's conduct of the war. It is often forgotten that Campbell-Bannerman's famous "methods of barbarism" speech was far from favorably received in June 1901, even by elements of his own party. Indeed, in selecting the Lancashire-based National Reform Union rather than the NLF as his audience, the Liberal leader chose wisely. The NRU was one of the few pro-Boer Liberal pressure groups,[98] whereas successive meetings of the party caucus had recorded a wide diversity of opinion among Liberals in respect of the war.[99] The real significance of Emily Hobhouse's campaigning, therefore, was to rally moderate center opinion behind the Liberal party's leader.[100] Her success in doing so is attested to by a resolution passed at a special meeting of the NLF later that year. The resolution deplored "the terrible rate of mortality among the women and children in the concentration camps" and urged the government to take immediate steps to remedy their present condition.[101]

Yet disillusionment with the war did not spread from the precincts of the Liberal party to a wider public until after the peace settlement was signed. In 1904–5, the use of Chinese labor in the South African mines—sanctioned by the imperial government—reopened the debate on the justice of the conflict in a way few could have predicted. Pro-Boers likened the conditions of work for the Chinese to "slavery" and returned to their now familiar argument that the purpose of the war had not been to open up South Africa to British immigration (as was frequently claimed),[102] but to line the pockets of the Transvaal mine owners. The scandal surrounding Chinese labor reached its climax during the election campaign of 1906. As "pig-tailed coolies" were paraded in the streets[103] and a popular leaflet depicting a line of Chinese being shepherded along by a fat plutocrat posed the question "is THIS what we fought for?"[104] it became clear that the debate on the South African War was entering a very different phase.

The battle to secure a cheap and regular supply of Chinese labor—so central to Milner and the mining magnates' plans for the reform of the South African state—led to a second wave of pro-imperial propaganda. Not long after the NLF condemned any form of compulsory labor in South Africa, the ISAA began distributing pamphlets in support of a labor ordinance. In 1904, it set about forming a network of local committees to refute Liberal misrepresentations regarding importation and to extract pledges from parliamentary candidates to support the policy.[105] By the time of the general election campaign it had put together a team of twelve agents and thirty-four speakers. They visited 202 constituencies, addressed 505 meetings, and spoke on behalf of any candidate supporting the interests of labor in the Transvaal.[106] In addition, thirty special election pamphlets were produced, and four million copies of each were circulated. Even when measured against the activities of the Tariff Reform League and Free Trade Union, this was propaganda on a prodigious scale. On their own admission, however, pro-war activists were unable to overcome the strong domestic opposition to Chinese labor. According to the ISAA's chairman, Gilbert Parker, for example, the "sickly sentimentality" and "hysteria" of Radicals regarding the treatment of the Chinese was accepted all too readily by the British public, as was the idea that it was the government's policy to displace British labor.[107] Modern psephology has arrived at substantially similar conclusions. In the 1906 election campaign the issue was mentioned in 75 percent of Liberal and 67 percent of LRC election addresses. Unionist candidates, in contrast, fought shy of the issue of Chinese labor: only 19 percent dared to raise it, and some of those admitted the policy to have been wrong.[108] In Parliament, Milner's reputation suffered the same fate. In February 1906, forty-two of the ISAA's fifty MPs turned out to defend his conduct in sanctioning and supervising the Chinese Labour Ordinance, but they faced a huge Liberal majority and the vote was lost by a large margin.

The British Public and the War

Academic interest in imperial propaganda has risen rapidly in recent years. Yet when writing about popular attitudes to empire at the time of the South African War historians are still prone to the sweeping and all too often unsubstantiated statement.[109] They fail to recognize that the very question "did the British public support the War?" is in some sense delusive. Far from being constant, the factors that affected the political situation in Britain varied enormously from 1899 to 1902, so that the chronology of the conflict is central to our understanding of its domestic repercussions. For a while, pro-war activists succeeded in harnessing the imperial enthusiasms of the British public to their cause, and the war was widely, if passively, supported. Their repertoire included the familiar arguments of the racial superiority of South Africa's English-speaking loyalist population, the cultural and economic backwardness of the Transvaal Boers, and the suspect loyalties of Afrikaners in the Cape and Natal. No doubt the negative and at times blatantly racist side to this propaganda appealed to a strand of public opinion in Britain.

Yet pro-war activism took more subtle and sophisticated forms. Among the most important of the discursive processes that made it possible to justify and sustain the war was the link made between the Uitlanders and the "national good." Despite the pots of ink spilled on the Uitlander question, the reason it resonated with a domestic British audience has not been satisfactorily explored. By invoking the Uitlanders as "British" subjects and taking up the defense of their political liberties, pro-war propagandists were able to mine a deep seam of British public culture that put the parliamentary franchise on a pedestal, distinguishing it from all other forms of political representation. The Uitlander question also had political purchase as a result of the pan-British sense of national identity gaining ground at this time. Time and time again the Uitlanders were portrayed as an indispensable element of a wider and loyal British "diaspora," the consolidation of which was regarded as essential to the preservation of Britain's social structure and great power status.

Having captured the public imagination at the beginning of the conflict, Uitlander grievances were not nearly so salient in its final stages. By 1901–2, a combination of war-weariness, farm burnings, and the internment camps had recast the debate on the South African War. Some argue that the "imperial idea" suffered a "loss of moral content" at this moment.[110] This is misleading. While opinion within the Liberal Party certainly shifted toward the pro-Boers as a result of the suffering and devastation caused by Kitchener's military methods, there is little evidence to suggest a wider public disillusionment with the South African War when the Peace of Vereeniging was signed. Indeed, it was not until 1904–5, when the Chinese labor controversy erupted in British politics, that pro-war activists—rather than pro-Boers— were to be put on trial. Chinese labor aroused strong feelings because people felt misled about why the war had been fought and because the compounds in which the Chinese were forced to live, and the corporal punishment to which some of them were subjected, tarnished the imperial ideals trumpeted so loudly in 1899.

In the propagation of those imperial ideals, government had not taken a leading role: neither the Foreign Office nor the Colonial Office was directly involved in persuading the public of the need for military intervention in the Transvaal. But that is not to say that the British state fought shy of propaganda activity altogether. Thus it is clear that an imperially oriented pressure group like the Imperial South Africa Association was not only inspired by Milner's vision of a "united British South Africa," but prepared to go to great lengths to explain and defend the High Commissioner's actions to a domestic audience; that Chamberlain willingly exploited the association's usefulness as a propaganda body, both in stifling dissent within the Tory party and in rallying a wider public behind the war; and that, sensitive to

pro-Boer activity abroad, Salisbury and the Foreign Office actively collaborated with ISAA officials—especially Drage and Windsor—in organizing
publicity in the United States. Furthermore, unlike *The Times* and the *Daily
Mail*, the ISAA was never critical of the government. It was almost completely silent on Britain's unpreparedness for the war, as it was on questions
of military mismanagement.

This technique of delegating propaganda work to privately funded, extraparliamentary groups that had extensive campaigning experience continued
to characterize the government's handling of publicity and persuasion for
much of the First World War. From 1914 to 1917, propaganda was organized
in much the same way as in 1899–1902, with government working through
quasi-independent, patriotic organizations and refusing to extend its activity into the field of opinion-forming beyond the routine work of encouraging recruitment.[111] It was only when civilian morale began to weaken (a
result of war fatigue and uncertainty about the government's war aims) and
when Robert MacDonald's inquiry exposed a complete lack of coordina-
tion between government departments that a full-scale reorganization of
news management was finally undertaken.[112] With the encouragement of
Lloyd George, the secretive War Propaganda Bureau—known as Wellington
House—was upgraded into a Department of Information; the following
year it was raised to the status of a Ministry, with Lord Beaverbrook as its
head. Yet however slow it was to intervene after 1914,[113] there can be little
doubt that a new chapter in propaganda activity was opened by the British
government during the First World War. Although the Ministry of Information was rapidly dismantled after the Armistice, individual government
ministries were very active in "educating" public opinion on subjects like
industrial unrest, health and hygiene, and popular consumption during the
interwar years.[114] Among the best known of the state's publicity campaigns
was that run by the Empire Marketing Board (EMB) to promote the buying
and selling of empire goods. Though the EMB had only a brief life, from
1926 until 1933, and though it depended heavily upon expertise from outside
the government service, it marks a significant shift in official attitudes. Prior
to 1917, government had supported the propaganda work of a network of
voluntary organizations that sprang from, and were sustained by, the strong
associational culture of early-twentieth-century Britain. By the mid-1920s,
however, the propagation of imperial values and beliefs within British society was widely regarded as a legitimate sphere of the state.

Notes

1. For a sample of the most significant works see B. Porter, *Critics of Empire: British Radical Attitudes to Colonialism in Africa, 1895–1914* (London, 1968); A. Davey, *The British Pro-Boers 1877–1902* (Cape Town, 1978); S. Howe, *Anti-Colonialism in British Politics: The Left and the End of Empire* (Oxford, 1993), chap. 2; S. Koss (ed.), *The Anatomy of an Antiwar Movement: The Pro-Boers* (London, 1973).

2. For a welcome recognition of the need to locate Milner and Milnerism within the broader social and intellectual context of late-nineteenth- and early-twentieth-century imperialism, see the pathfinding essay by S. Marks and S. Trapido, "Lord Milner and the South African State," *History Workshop Journal* (1979): 52–55. On the general point of imperial history continuing to be written from the perspective of elites see S. Marks, "History, the Nation and the Empire: Sniping from the Periphery," *History Workshop Journal* (1990): 112.

3. It is impossible in a single footnote to do justice to this new historiography, which aims to inject imperial history back into Britain. In the sphere of popular culture, John Mackenzie has done pioneering work both alone, in *Propaganda and Empire: The Manipulation of British Public Opinion, 1880–1960* (Manchester, 1986), and in collaboration, by editing or commissioning various volumes of the Studies in Imperialism series, in particular *Imperialism and Popular Culture* (Manchester, 1986). Feminist historians have also opened up a long overdue gender perspective upon the empire's impact on metropolitan culture. Of particular interest here is the collection of essays edited by Claire Midgley, *Gender and Imperialism* (Manchester, 1998). But see also the seminal article by A. Davin, "Imperialism and Motherhood," *History Workshop Journal* (1978), and A. Burton's study of "imperial feminism," *Burdens of History: British Feminists, Indian Women and Imperial Culture, 1865–1914* (Chapel Hill, 1994). For the implications of Britain's long imperial involvement for its domestic political process see my own *Imperial Britain: The Empire in British Politics, c. 1880–1932* (Marlow, 2000).

4. F. Coetzee, *For Party or Country: Nationalism and the Dilemmas of Popular Conservatism in Edwardian England* (Oxford, 1990); M. Fforde, *Conservatism and Collectivism, 1886–1914* (Edinburgh, 1990); E.H.H. Green, *The Crisis of Conservatism: The Politics, Economics and Ideology of the British Conservative Party, 1880–1914* (London, 1995).

5. J. Cornford, "The Transformation of Conservatism in the Late-Nineteenth Century," *Victorian Studies* 3, no. 1 (1963): 66; J. A. Ramsden, *The Age of Balfour and Baldwin, 1902–40* (London, 1978), 48; J. Waller, *Democracy and Sectarianism: A Political and Social History of Liverpool, 1868–1939* (Liverpool, 1981), 48–52.

6. M. Pugh, *The Tories and the People, 1880–1935* (Oxford, 1985), chaps. 1–2.

7. J. Lawrence, "Class and Gender in the Making of Urban Toryism, 1880–1914," *English Historical Review* 108 (1993): 629–52.

8. H. Cunningham, "The Conservative Party and Patriotism," in R. Colls and P. Dodd (eds.), *Englishness: Politics and Culture 1880–1920* (London, 1986), 285–90.

9. MacKenzie, *Propaganda and Empire*, 2 and *Imperialism and Popular Culture*, 13.

10. A. N. Porter, *The Origins of the South African War: Joseph Chamberlain and the*

Diplomacy of Imperialism, 1895–99 (Manchester, 1980). Notwithstanding my criticism of Andrew Porter's argument, his book is extremely significant historiographically because it put the issue of propaganda and politics on the academic agenda in 1980.

11. Ibid., 271.

12. Ibid., 162.

13. Ibid., 62, 114–21.

14. E. Reidi, "Imperialist Women in Edwardian Britain: The Victoria League, 1899–1914" (Ph.D. thesis, University of St. Andrews, 1998).

15. C. A. Bayly, *Imperial Meridian: The British Empire and the World, 1780–1830* (Harlow, 1989); L. Colley, "Britishness and Otherness," *Journal of British Studies* (1992); J. M. Mackenzie, "Empire and National Identities: The Case of Scotland," *Transactions of the Royal Historical Society* (1998); A. S. Thompson, "The Language of Imperialism and the Meanings of Empire: Imperial Discourse in British Politics, 1895–1914," *Journal of British Studies* (1997).

16. A. L. Friedberg, "Britain Faces the Burdens of Empire: The Financial Crisis of 1901–05," *War and Society* 5 (1987): 15–18.

17. Extract from J. Chamberlain to Sir A. Milner quoted in C. Headlam (ed.), *The Milner Papers*, vol. 2: *South Africa 1899–1905* (London, 1931), 203.

18. Friedberg, "Britain Faces the Burdens of Empire," 22.

19. I. Smith, *The Origins of the South African War, 1899–1902* (London, 1996), 4.

20. M. Engel, *Tickle the Public: One Hundred Years of the Popular Press* (London: 1996), 64, 67, 76–78; F. A. McKenzie, *The Mystery of the* Daily Mail, *1896–1921* (London, 1921), 25–30.

21. J. Beaumont, "The *Times* at War 1899–1902," paper presented at "South Africa: Test of Empire" conference, St. Edmund Hall, Oxford, March 28–30, 1996.

22. M. Blunden, "The Anglican Church during the War," in P. Warwick (ed.), *The South African War: The Anglo-Boer War, 1899–1902* (Harlow, 1980), 280, 284–85, 290–91.

23. G. C. Cuthbertson, "The Nonconformist Conscience and the South African War 1899–1902" (D.Litt. et Phil. thesis, University of South Africa, 1986); S. Koss, "Wesleyanism and Empire," *Historical Journal* 24 (1952).

24. J. S. Galbraith, "The Pamphlet Campaign on the Boer War," *Journal of Military History* 24 (1952): 111–26.

25. "Boer Prisoners in Ahmednagar: Fact and Fiction," Conservative Central Office (CCO) pamphlet 15 (June 1901), and "The Road to Majuba," CCO pamphlet 16 (June 1901).

26. J. H. Robb, *The Primrose League 1883–1906* (New York, 1942), 214.

27. "Correspondence from the various public bodies respecting the relations of H.M.G. with the South African Republics," Public Record Office, Colonial Office (PROCO) 417/277 and 278.

28. It was initially named the South African Association. The designation "Imperial" was added in 1898.

29. "The South African Association," *The Times*, 1 May 1896, 10.

30. The association's parliamentary committee tells a similar story. Forty-eight MPs belonged to it; forty-two were Conservative, four were Liberal Unionist, and two were Liberal. See A. S. Thompson, "Thinking Imperially? Imperial Pressure

Groups and the Idea of Empire in Late-Victorian and Edwardian Britain" (D.Phil. thesis, Oxford University, 1994), 82.

31. For Rhodes's contact with the ISAA, see J. G. Lockhart and C. M. Woodhouse, *Rhodes* (London, 1963), 436–37. The conduit for the funding was the ISAA's treasurer, H. M. Bourke. A letter from Windsor to Drage, dated 8 February 1900, in the Geoffrey Drage papers, Christ Church Library, Oxford, refers to the "large financial support" the association received from Beit. Accounts of Beit and of Rhodes for the years 1896–97 reveal regular payments to Bourke. I am grateful to Mr. Anthony Bryan for drawing this to my attention: see "Wernher, Beit & Co: statement of Rhodes' Account," Cecil Rhodes papers, MSS Afr. s.228, C24 (50).

32. G. Wyndham to A. Milner, 13 July 1899, cited in Headlam (ed.), *Milner Papers,* 2.454.

33. Windsor to Drage, 18 August 1899, Drage Papers (hereafter DP), Box 4, File 2.

34. Milner to Drage, 26 July 1899, DP, Box 4, File 2.

35. "Imperial South Africa Association," 21 May 1908, in A. Milner, *The Nation and the Empire: Being a Collection of Speeches and Addresses* (London, 1913), 279.

36. G. Wyndham to A. Milner, 18 May 1899, Alfred Milner Papers (hereafter MP), Bodleian Library, Oxford, dep. 209, fos. 99–100.

37. G. Parker to A. Milner, 24 May 1908, MP, dep. 34, fos. 158–61.

38. R. Shannon, *The Age of Salisbury, 1881–1902: Unionism and Empire* (London, 1996), 497.

39. G. Drage, "Mr Chamberlain and His Allies," *The Times,* 8 April 1895, 10; speech delivered on behalf of the South African Association by Mr. George Wyndham MP, 9 March 1898, copy contained in MP, dep. 337, fo. 11.

40. H. M. Bourke to Selborne, 21 December 1897, PROCO 417/223, fos. 98–114.

41. McDonnell to Salisbury, 14 June 1899, Salisbury Papers, quoted in P. Marsh, *The Discipline of Popular Government: Lord Salisbury's Domestic Statescraft, 1881–1902* (Hassocks, 1978), 264.

42. Wyndham to Milner, 28 April 1899, MP, dep. 209, fos. 123–26; Windsor to Drage, 2 October 1899, DP, Box 4, File 2; H. Bourke to F. Wilson (private secretary to Chamberlain), 15 October 1896, J. Chamberlain Papers, Birmingham University Library, 10/5/1/29; C. W. Boyd to C. J. Rhodes, 22 July 1899 and 2 March 1901, Rhodes Papers MSS Afr. s.228, C16 and C27.

43. Porter, *Origins of the South African War,* 274.

44. "Mr Maclean and His Constituents," *The Times,* 9 December 1899, 10; H. W. Lucy, *A Diary of the Unionist Parliament, 1895–1900* (London, 1901), 123.

45. Windsor to Drage, 11 November 1899, DP, Box 4, File 6.

46. Boyd served as Rhodes's political secretary from 1898 to 1902. He was appointed vice chairman of the ISAA's literature committee in 1904–5, but he was actively involved in the association before that date.

47. Leo Amery joined the ISAA's general council in 1903.

48. C. Boyd to J. Chamberlain, 28 June 1903, quoted in J. Amery, *The Life of Joseph Chamberlain, Vol. 5, 1901–3: Joseph Chamberlain and the Tariff Reform Campaign* (London, 1969), 306.

49. A. Porter, "The South African War (1899–1902): Context and Motive Reconsidered," *Journal of African History* (1990): 49, 56.

50. Thompson, *Imperial Britain*, chs. 2, 4.

51. C. W. Boyd to J. Chamberlain, undated, J. Chamberlain Papers, 18/18/16.

52. Marsh, *Discipline of Popular Government*, 295–96; R. Shannon, *The Crisis of Imperialism, 1865–1915* (London, 1974), 294–95.

53. Thornton was a member of the ISAA's general committee.

54. M. Thornton, *Some Things We Have Remembered* (London, 1912), 270.

55. Lord Windsor was president of the Cardiff Conservative Association as well as the ISAA.

56. T. H. Sanderson to G. Drage, 5 March 1900, DP, Box 4, File 6.

57. For Salisbury's concern for the possible repercussions of a forward policy on foreign opinion, see A. Porter, "Lord Salisbury, Mr. Chamberlain and South Africa, 1895–99," *Journal of Imperial and Commonwealth History* (1972): 21.

58. J. H. Ferguson, *American Diplomacy and the Boer War* (Philadelphia, 1939).

59. C. Eliot (Secretary at the Washington embassy) to J. Bryce, 26 December 1899, Bryce Papers, 62. I am grateful to Jacky Beaumont for supplying this reference.

60. Sanderson to Drage, 8 March 1900, DP, Box 4, File 6.

61. Ibid.

62. Pauncefote to Sanderson, 4 May 1900, copy in DP, Box 4, File 5.

63. Sanderson to Drage, 5 March 1900, and Sanderson to Windsor, 6 May 1900, DP, Box 4, File 6.

64. C. Eliot to Drage, 12 February 1900, DP, Box 4, File 5. Eliot expressed the hope that the ISAA would come to a satisfactory arrangement—"pecuniary and otherwise"—with the Foreign Office.

65. Pauncefote to Sanderson, 9 March 1900, DP, Box 4, File 5.

66. Pauncefote to Sanderson, 4 May 1900, DP, Box 4, File 5.

67. J. X. Merriman to J. C. Smuts, 3 June 1903, quoted in J. van der Poel (ed.), *Selections from the Smuts Papers*, vol. 2 (Cambridge, 1966), 98.

68. J. L. McCracken, *The Cape Parliament 1854–1910* (Oxford, 1967), 117.

69. M. Tamarkin, *Cecil Rhodes and the Cape Afrikaners: The Imperial Colossus and the Colonial Parish Pump* (London, 1996), 258.

70. S. Marks, "Southern and Central Africa, 1886–1910," in R. Oliver and G. N. Sanderson (eds.), *The Cambridge History of Africa*, vol. 6: *From 1870 to 1905* (Cambridge, 1985), 476.

71. E. van Heyningen, "The Relations between Sir Alfred Milner and W. Schreiner's Ministry, 1898–1900," *Archives Yearbook for South African History* 39 (Pretoria, 1978), 204–5.

72. R. Ovendale, "Profit or Patriotism: Natal, the Transvaal and the Coming of the Second Anglo-Boer War," *Journal of Imperial and Commonwealth History* 8 (1980): 209–34.

73. M. F. Bitensky, "The South African League: British Imperialist Organisation in South Africa 1896–1899" (M.A. thesis, University of the Witwatersrand, 1950), 43.

74. The ISAA cabled Sprigg in 1900 to say that it would cooperate with the SAVC. See Windsor to Drage, 25 March 1900, DP, Box 4, File 2, and Minutes of the SAVC's Organising Committee, 20 and 26 March 1900, Cape Town Archives, South Africa, Acc 539.

75. *Sir Alfred Milner and his South African Policy, Vigilance Papers*, no. 5, published

by the ISAA (London, 1900); Minutes of the SAVC's Literary Committee, 21 March 1900, Cape Town Archives, South Africa, Acc 539.

76. Minutes of the SAVC's Literary Committee, 2 and 9 April 1900, and of the Executive Committee, 17 April 1900, Cape Town Archives, South Africa, Acc 539.

77. Minutes of the SAVC's Executive Committee, 10 and 27 July 1900, Cape Town Archives, South Africa, Acc 539; Drage to Handcock (secretary of the ISAA), 26 August 1900, DP, Box 4, File 6.

78. Handcock to Drage, 29 November 1900, DP, Box 4, File 6; "Deputation to Mr Chamberlain," *The Times,* 1 December 1900, 12.

79. Darwin, "Imperialism and the Victorians," 622, 628, 641; J. Cain and A. G. Hopkins, *British Imperialism: Innovation and Expansion 1688–1914* (Harlow, 1993), 381.

80. "The South African Association," *The Times,* 1 May 1896, 10; "Deputation to Mr Chamberlain," *The Times,* 1 December 1900, 12; and the resolutions listed in the Annual Report of the ISAA (1899–1900).

81. For ISAA pamphlets on the Uitlanders see *Story of the Outlanders Agitation* (London, 1898) and *The British Case against the Boer Republics* (London, 1900).

82. The "British" element of the Uitlander population included settlers from the United Kingdom (16,265), the Cape (15,162), Natal (1,242), and Australasia (992).

83. Thompson, "Language of Imperialism," 153–54; "Mr Wyndham and Mr Chamberlain on the War," *The Times,* 26 October 1899, 6.

84. R. McKibbin, *The Ideologies of Class: Social Relations in Britain 1880–1950* (Oxford, 1994), 20.

85. Marks, "History, the Nation and Empire," 113, 117; J. Marshall, "Imperial Britain," *Journal of Imperial and Commonwealth History* 23, no. 3 (1995): 384–85; Colley, "Britishness and Otherness," 325–29.

86. For the ISAA, compare the number of meetings and their aggregate attendance, as recorded in the association's annual reports: in 1899–1900, 406 meetings were held with an aggregate attendance of 248,000; in 1901–2, 145 meetings had an attendance of 66,000 and in 1902–3, 115 meetings had 40,000 attending.

87. Lawrence, "Class and Gender," 631.

88. Hobson, *The War in South Africa: Its Causes and Effects* (London, 1900), 205, 228, and *The Psychology of Jingoism* (London, 1901), 20.

89. "The Transvaal Committee: Report of a Public Meeting in London at St. Martin's Town Hall, 10 July 1899," quoted in Koss, *Anatomy of an Antiwar Movement,* 7.

90. Lawrence, "Class and Gender," 635, 637–38.

91. P. Clarke, *Lancashire and the New Liberalism* (Cambridge, 1971), 343–44.

92. Smith, *Origins of the South African War,* 3.

93. R. MacDonald, *What I Saw in South Africa* (London, 1902).

94. R. van Reenen (ed.), *Emily Hobhouse: Boer War Letters* (Cape Town, 1984), 121.

95. For a full list of venues and dates see Manchester Guardian Index (City of Manchester Cultural Services, 1988), 372.

96. Van Reenen (ed.), *Emily Hobhouse,* 122–23.

97. Five such instances are referred to in the *Manchester Guardian,* 3 July 1901, 5. The Northampton municipal authorities granted use of the town hall on the

condition that no resolution except a vote of thanks be passed. *Manchester Guardian*, 18 July 1901, 10.

98. A. H. Crosfield, *The True Causes of and the False Excuses for the War in South Africa*, NRU Pamphlets (undated), Box 4, The South African War, John Johnson Collection.

99. R. Spence Watson, *The National Liberal Federation: From its Commencement to the General Election* (London, 1907), 242, 254, 261.

100. Koss, *Anatomy of an Antiwar Movement*, xxxvi–xxxvii.

101. Spence Watson, *National Liberal Federation*, 262.

102. Speech delivered on behalf of the ISAA by Mr George Wyndham, Edinburgh, March 9, 1898, copy contained in the Milner Papers, dep. 337, fo. 11.

103. Pugh, *Tories and the People*, 161.

104. A. K. Russell, *Liberal Landslide: The General Election of 1906* (London, 1973), 69.

105. Annual Report of the ISAA (1904–5).

106. Annual Report of the ISAA (1905–6).

107. For these admissions see Gilbert Parker, *Report of an Address Entitled "Our Imperial Responsibilities in the Transvaal,"* ISAA pamphlet no. 11.

108. Russell, *Liberal Landslide*, 83.

109. See, for example, M. Beloff, *Imperial Sunset: Britain's Liberal Empire, 1897–1921* (Lonson, 1969), 78: "Whatever the historian may now see as being the primary cause of the conflict, to many people at the time the case against Britain seemed overwhelming"; Marsh, *Discipline of Popular Government*, 298: "The Boer War did not breed disenchantment with imperialism, it bred impatience with the traditional practices and civilian restraints of British military administration"; Pugh, *The Tories and the People*, 161: "the fillip that the Boer war gave to Conservative morale petered out in the face of ... popular discontent"; and Price, *An Imperial War*, 241: "it is evident that the ethos of imperialism which surrounded the Boer war had little impact on the working class."

110. A. Thornton, *The Imperial Idea and Its Enemies* (London, 1959), 109.

111. C. Haste, *Keep the Home Fires Burning: Propaganda in the First World War* (London, 1977), 2.

112. M. L. Sanders, "Wellington House and British Propaganda during the First World War," *Historical Journal* 18 (1975): 122–24.

113. G. S. Messinger, "An Inheritance Worth Remembering: The British Approach to Official Propaganda during the First World War," *Historical Journal of Film, Radio and Television* 13 (1993), and *British Propaganda and the State in the First World War* (Manchester, 1992), 4, 22–23.

114. M. Grant, *Propaganda and the Role of the State in Inter-War Britain* (Oxford, 1994).

Contributors

Helen Bradford was formerly Associate Professor of History at the University of Cape Town. She is author of *A Taste of Freedom: The ICU in Rural South Africa* (1988) and *"You Call that Democratic?" Struggles over Abortion in South Africa* (1994). She has also challenged the androcentric canon of South African historical writing in a range of chapters and journal articles.

Greg Cuthbertson is chair of the Department of History at the University of South Africa and coordinating editor of the *South African Historical Journal.*

Manelisi Genge obtained his Ph.D. in history at Michigan State University. His dissertation is titled "Power and Gender in Southern African History: Power Relations in the Era of Queen Labotsibeni Gwamile Mdluli of Swaziland, ca. 1875–1921." He currently holds a director position in the Policy, Research, and Analysis unit in the Department of Foreign Affairs of the South African government. He is also affiliated with the University of South Africa as a Research Fellow of the Department of History.

Albert Grundlingh is Professor of History at Stellenbosch University and has published widely on the South African War and Afrikaner nationalism and historiography.

Alan Jeeves is a research associate at the University of South Africa and Professor of History at Queen's University, Canada. At Queen's, he has developed an undergraduate course focused on South Africa's Truth and Reconciliation Commission and the history of apartheid. His current research examines the history of public health in South Africa, 1920–60. He has written on the histories of farm and mine labor in the region and is co-editor of *White*

Farms, Black Labor: The State and Agrarian Change in Southern Africa (1997) and co-author of *South Africa's Labor Empire: A History of Black Migrancy to the Gold Mines* (1991).

John Lambert is Associate Professor of History at the University of South Africa. He is editor of the *South African Historical Journal* and his research interests center on colonial Natal and the identity of English-speaking South Africans.

Shula Marks was formerly Director of the Institute of Commonwealth Studies, London (1982–92) and Professor of Southern African History at the School of Oriental and African Studies, London. She retired as an Emeritus Professor in September 2001. She is a Fellow of the British Academy and holds honorary degrees from the Universities of Cape Town and Natal. She has lectured and written widely on South African history.

Bernard Mbenga is Senior Lecturer in History at the University of the North-West. Research interests and publications include the role of black people in the South African War, chiefly authorities and missionaries, and land acquisition by blacks in the Transvaal. He is a member of the editorial boards of the *Journal of African History* and the *South African Historical Journal.*

Richard Mendelsohn is Associate Professor and chair of the Department of Historical Studies at the University of Cape Town. He is author of *Sammy Marks: "The Uncrowned King of the Transvaal"* (1990) and is presently completing a book on Jews and the South African War.

David Nash is Senior Lecturer in Historical Studies at Oxford Brookes University and author of *Secularism, Art and Freedom* (1992) and *Blasphemy in Modern Britain, 1789–Present* (1999). He is currently researching British public opinion and the construction of national identity.

Bill Nasson is Professor of History at the University of Cape Town. He was born in Cape Town and educated at the Universities of Hull, York, and Cambridge. His publications include *Abraham Esau's War: A Black South African War at the Cape, 1899–1902* (1991, reissued 2003), *The South African War, 1899–1902* (1999), and *Uyadela Wen'Osulapho: Black Participation in the Anglo-Boer War, 1899–1902* (1999). He is an editor of the *Journal of African History* and is also writing a concise history of British imperialism.

Andrew Porter is Rhodes Professor of Imperial History in the University of London and teaches at King's College. His books include *The Origins of the South African War* (1980); *Victorian Shipping, Business and Imperial Policy* (1986); *European Imperialism, 1860–1914* (1994); and, as editor and contributor, *The Oxford History of the British Empire, Volume 3: The Nineteenth Century* (1999). He has also published extensively on religion, empire, and Protestant missions, for instance, in the *Journal of Imperial and Commonwealth History*, and is currently writing a book on British Protestant missions and imperial expansion, 1700–1914.

Fransjohan Pretorius is Professor of History at the University of Pretoria. He has received several awards for his publications on the South African War, his most recent books being *Life on Commando during the Anglo-Boer War* (1999), *Scorched Earth* (2001), and *The Great Escape of the Boer Pimpernel, Christiaan de Wet* (2001).

Keith Surridge gained his Ph.D. at King's College, University of London, in 1994 and is currently a part-time lecturer at the University of Notre Dame, London program, the University of Delaware, London Centre, and Queen Mary College, University of London. He is the author of *Managing the South African War, 1899–1902: Soldiers vs Politicians* (1998) and, with Denis Judd, *The Boer War* (2002). He has also written several articles on aspects of the South African War.

Mary-Lynn Suttie is a senior research librarian for history and politics at the University of South Africa.

Andrew Thompson is Senior Lecturer in modern British history at the University of Leeds. He is author of *Imperial Britain* (2000) and co-editor of *The Impact of the South African War* (2002). He is presently researching the impact of imperialism on Britain from the mid-nineteenth century to the present day.

Elizabeth van Heyningen is Research Associate in the Department of Historical Studies at the University of Cape Town. She has published widely on the South African War and is co-author of *The Making of a City: Cape Town in the Twentieth Century* (2000).

Index